European Revolutions and the Ottoman Balkans

European Revolutions and the Ottoman Balkans

Nationalism, Violence and Empire in the Long Nineteenth Century

Edited by

Dimitris Stamatopoulos

I.B. TAURIS
LONDON • NEW YORK • OXFORD • NEW DELHI • SYDNEY

Published in association with the
British Institute of Archaeology at Ankara (BIAA)

I.B. TAURIS
Bloomsbury Publishing Plc
50 Bedford Square, London, WC1B 3DP, UK
1385 Broadway, New York, NY 10018, USA
29 Earlsfort Terrace, Dublin 2, Ireland

BLOOMSBURY, I.B. TAURIS and the I.B. Tauris logo are trademarks
of Bloomsbury Publishing Plc

First published in Great Britain 2019
This paperback edition published in 2021

Copyright © Dimitris Stamatopoulos and Contributors 2019

Dimitris Stamatopoulos has asserted his right under the Copyright, Designs and Patents Act, 1988, to be identified as the Editor of this work.

Cover image: 'Turquie d'Europe', map of Greece and the Balkans as part of the great Ottoman Empire, by Delamarch, 1832. (© Geographicus)

All rights reserved. No part of this publication may be reproduced or transmitted in any form or by any means, electronic or mechanical, including photocopying, recording, or any information storage or retrieval system, without prior permission in writing from the publishers.

Bloomsbury Publishing Plc does not have any control over, or responsibility for, any third-party websites referred to or in this book. All internet addresses given in this book were correct at the time of going to press. The author and publisher regret any inconvenience caused if addresses have changed or sites have ceased to exist, but can accept no responsibility for any such changes.

A catalogue record for this book is available from the British Library.

A catalog record for this book is available from the Library of Congress

ISBN: HB: 978-1-7883-1104-5
PB: 978-0-7556-4623-4
ePDF: 978-0-7556-0327-5
eBook: 978-0-7556-0328-2

Typeset by RefineCatch Limited, Bungay, Suffolk

To find out more about our authors and books visit www.bloomsbury.com and sign up for our newsletters.

Contents

List of Illustrations   vi
List of Contributors   viii

1 War and Revolution: A Balkan Perspective – An Introduction
    Dimitris Stamatopoulos   1

2 Emulating Petrine Russia: Thick Mechanicism and the *Foundations of Government* in Istanbul after the Rebellion of 1730   *B. Harun Küçük*   19

3 New Horizons of Political Possibility: Greek Political Imagination after the Russo-Ottoman War of 1768–1774   *Vasilis Molos*   37

4 Military Reforms as a Diplomatic Bargaining Chip: French-Ottoman Relations at the End of the Eighteenth Century   *Antoaneta Atanasova*   65

5 Echoes of Tumultuous Wars: Prosperity and Poverty of the Balkan Entrepreneurial Strata (1800s–1880s)   *Evguenia Davidova*   93

6 The Final Phase of the Greek Revolution: Delimitation, Determination and Demarcation of the First Greek Borders in Ottoman Sources   *Dilek Özkan*   111

7 Petko Voivoda: A Re-evaluation of Nineteenth-Century Bulgarian Military History   *Assia Nakova*   139

8 Uprisings, Revolutions and Wars: Visual Representations in the Bulgarian Illustrated Press at the End of the Nineteenth and Early Twentieth Century   *Dobrinka Parusheva*   149

9 *Under a Gun*: Eugen Kumičić on the Austria-Hungarian Occupation of Bosnia and Herzegovina   *Klara Volarić*   183

10 War, Intellectuals and the Balkan States: French Intellectuals' Perception of Serbia and Serbs in the Great War   *Aleksandra Kolaković*   199

11 The New Ottoman Conception of War, State and Society in the Prelude to the First World War   *Banu Turnaoğlu*   219

12 War, Revolution and Diplomacy: The October Revolution of 1917 and the Turkish Anatolian Resistance Movement, 1919–1922   *Nikos Christofis*   243

Index   263

Illustrations

1. 1907, no. 11–12, pp. 20–21 – *Bulgarian forces chase the enemy behind Pirot. The November victory over the Serbs*, painting by Antoni Piotrowski. — 151
2. 1896, no. 1, p. 5 – *Massacres in Trebizund.* — 152
3. 1903, no. 3, p. 13 – *Heroes and trophies. Macedonian events.* — 153
4. 1913, no. 3, p. 28 – *Before the siege of Odrin (Edirne)*, photo by Ivan Mihaylov. — 157
5. 1913, no. 1–2, p. 33 – *Heroes fallen in the Great War.* — 158
6. 1913, no. 1–2, p. 53 – *The Heroes: Treatment at the Red Cross Hospital – Sofia.* — 160
7. 1912, no. 8–10, p. 4 – *Turkish defeat at Lozengrad.* — 160
8. 1913, no. 11–12, p. 4 – *Photos of refugees.* — 161
9. 1913, no. 1, p. 60 – *The force of the Balkan states is in the agreement* (portraits of the four heads of the allied states). — 162
10. 1913, no. 7–8, p. 1 – *Bulgaria fights heroically her perfidious allies. Bulgarian artillery sowing death in the Serbian positions at Kotchani* — 162
11. 1913, no. 7–8, p. 29 – *The Greek massacres upon Bulgarian people in Kukush. Devious lies of the Greek King.* — 163
12. 1916, no. 3, p. 8 – *The actions of our artillery.* — 165
13. 1916, no. 9–10, p. 5 – *The tandem of pilots Captain Ivanov and Lieutenant Vakafchiev.* — 166
14. 1916, no. 2, p. 12 – *The Central Union.* — 167
15. 1916, no. 11–12, p. 13 – *General August von Mackensen at the Dobrudzha front.* — 168
16. 1916, no. 1, p. 12 – *Field Marshal Paul von Hindenburg in front of his headquarters at the Eastern front.* — 169
17. 1915, no. 9–12, p. 21 – *French 'culture' at the Macedonian front.* — 170

18	1916, no. 1, p. 8 – *Russian captives at the time of their capture vs. Cleaned by the Germans after capture.*	171
19	1916, no. 9–10, p. 1 – *The Wallachian massacres in Dobrudzha.*	172
20	1916, no. 4, p. 12 – *Theatre at the front.*	173

Contributors

Antoaneta Atanasova recently obtained a PhD in Modern Balkan History from the University of Sofia 'St. Kliment Ohridski'. Her research was conducted in the framework of a co-directorship between Sofia University and the National Institute of Oriental Languages and Civilizations (INALCO) in Paris. The title of her dissertation is 'Army Advisors and Diplomacy: France and the Military Reforms in the Ottoman Empire in the 18th Century'. She is also a member of the Regional Studies Programme at the Centre of Excellence in the Humanities 'Alma Mater', University of Sofia 'St. Kliment Ohridski' (programme director Associate Professor Dr. Habil Ivan Parvev). Antoaneta's interests revolve around the history of Franco-Ottoman relations during the eighteenth century and the development of the Eastern Question during that period.

Nikos Christofis is a Teaching Fellow at the Department of Balkan, Slavic and Anatolian Studies at the University of Macedonia in Greece. He has taught also in the Department of History and Archaeology at the University of Crete, Greece; Turkish and Middle Eastern Studies at the University of Cyprus; and at Fatih University in Istanbul, Turkey. He is currently a post-doctoral researcher in the Research Centre for the Humanities (RCH) in Athens, Greece. He holds a PhD from the Institute for Area Studies (LIAS) in Leiden, the Netherlands. His work focuses on comparative historical analysis in the Eastern Mediterranean, specifically Greece, Turkey and Cyprus. He is currently working on turning his doctoral thesis into a monograph (with I.B. Tauris). He has published articles in Greek, Turkish, English and Spanish, and is the chief editor of the academic website Ottoman and Turkish Studies, Dissertation Reviews.

Evguenia Davidova is Professor of International and Global Studies at Portland State University, Portland, Oregon in the USA. Her research interests focus on the late Ottoman and post-Ottoman Balkans: commerce, nationalism, travel and medical practices. Evguenia is the author of *Balkan Transitions to Modernity and Nation-States: Through the Eyes of Three Generations of Merchants (1780s–1890s)* (2013) and the editor of *Wealth in the Ottoman and post-Ottoman Balkans: A Socio-Economic History* (I.B. Tauris, 2016).

Aleksandra Kolaković is a historian and Research Fellow at the Institute for Political Studies, Belgrade, Serbia. Her main areas of academic interest include the intellectual history, history of ideas, the cultural history of the Balkans, identities, cultural diplomacy, culture of remembrance, protection of cultural heritage and methodology of history teaching. Aleksandra is author of the book *U službi otadžbine: saradnja* *francuskih i srpskih intelektualaca 1894–1914* [For the Homeland: Cooperation of French and Serbian Intellectuals 1894–1914], two history textbooks, one lexicon (*Lexicon of Multiculturalism*) and several scholarly papers.

B. Harun Küçük is Assistant Professor of History and Sociology of Science at the University of Pennsylvania, USA. He has previously published on science and religion, and on the history of science, medicine and technology in the early modern Ottoman Empire. His work focuses on science and intercommunal sociability, on the practice of astronomy and medicine and on the relationship between technology and early modern state-building. He is currently completing a monograph that explores science during one of the most tumultuous periods in Ottoman history titled, *Early Modern Ottoman Science, 1650–1750: Commerce, State-Building and the Question of Enlightenment*. Harun has a PhD in History and Science Studies from the University of California, San Diego. Before joining the University of Pennsylvania, he was a pre- and post-doctoral fellow at the Max Planck Institute for the History of Science.

Vasilis Molos is an Assistant Professor of History at NYU Abu Dhabi. His research focuses on political imagination, notions of belonging and intellectual production in the Ottoman Balkans. Vasilis is currently working on a book entitled *The Russian Mediterranean: Shaping Sovereignty and Selfhood on the Island of Paros*. His work has been supported by the Marie Curie Actions Research Fellowship Programme, and generous fellowships from NYU Abu Dhabi, New York University and York University.

Assia Nakova is a History doctoral candidate at Princeton University with a particular interest in nineteenth-century Balkans nationalism. Her dissertation examines the emergence in the Bulgarian lands of the so-called gymnastic societies in the immediate aftermath of the Russo-Turkish War of 1877–1878 and the Berlin Treaty, and examines the interplay between Russian tutelage and influence and Bulgarian initiatives. A symbol of spiritual and physical reawakening of the Bulgarian people after a long period of oppression, the gymnastic societies in effect an army in training, are often mentioned but have until now not been studied in detail.

Dilek Özkan is currently affiliated with the Faculty of Oriental Studies, University of Oxford, as an academic visitor. Dilek graduated from Istanbul's Bilgi University in 2005 and obtained a master's degree in History from Boğaziçi University in 2010, with her thesis focusing on the role of philanthropy in the Greek Orthodox Community of Istanbul. She received her PhD in History in 2016 from the University of Athens. In her dissertation, she examined the first Ottoman-Greek borders and borderland in Thessaly. During her studies in Athens, she was granted scholarships from the Greek State Scholarship Foundation (IKY) and the Alexander Onassis Public Foundation. Her research interests include the socio-economic and political history of non-Muslim communities of the Ottoman Empire, imperial borders, borderlands and migration and population movements in the Eastern Mediterranean and the Black Sea regions.

Dobrinka Parusheva is Associate Professor of Theory and History of Culture in the Department of Ethnology, Faculty of Philosophy and History, University of Plovdiv and Senior Research Fellow at the Institute of Balkan Studies, Bulgarian Academy of Sciences, Sofia. She has published widely on Balkan history in the late nineteenth and early twentieth century. Her academic interests are in the areas of social history (including the social history of politics), political elites and political culture, culture and caricature, visual representations and history and anthropology of everyday life.

Dimitris Stamatopoulos is Professor in Balkan and Late Ottoman History in the Department of Balkan, Slavic and Oriental Studies at the University of Macedonia, Thessaloniki. A member of the School of Historical Studies at the Institute for Advanced Study, Princeton, New Jersey, he is the author of numerous articles and monographs on the history of the Œcumenical Patriarchate as well as of the Christian Orthodox populations in the Late Ottoman Empire. He is also the editor of the collection entitled *Balkan Nationalism(s) and the Ottoman Empire*, vol. 3 (2015), while his book entitled *Byzantium After the Nation: The Problem of the National Continuity in the Balkan Historiographies* (2009) will be published in English by the Central European University Press.

Banu Turnaoğlu is a Leverhulme Early Career Fellow at the Department of Politics and International Studies, University of Cambridge. She is the author of *The Formation of Turkish Republicanism* published in 2017. She received a PhD from Cambridge for her work on the development of Turkish republicanism, and was awarded the Political Studies Association's 2015 Sir Ernest Barker Prize for Best Dissertation in Political Theory for her doctoral thesis. She earned a BA in International Relations and History from Koç University, Turkey and an MSc in Political Theory from the University of Oxford. Her research interests include republicanism, late Ottoman political thought, anti-imperialism and theories of war and peace.

Klara Volarić graduated from the Central European University. Her main research interest is the late Ottoman Balkans. Klara has published several articles on the Serbian propaganda campaign in Ottoman Macedonia and inauguration celebrations of Abdulhamid II. She was also part of the 'Istanbul Memories' research project; her book chapter on the 'Diplomatic Memories of Alka Mažuranić Nestoroff' appeared in the first volume to be published in the project's series.

1

War and Revolution: A Balkan Perspective – An Introduction

Dimitris Stamatopoulos
University of Macedonia

The War as Revolution

The Balkans emerged as an historical entity in modern times through a dual process, first with the Ottoman Empire's gradual loss of control over its European provinces – a loss associated with the rise of nationalist movements in the area, especially in the early nineteenth century. The 'morphogenesis' of this geographic space as a peculiar geopolitical entity will take place with the complete substitution of the imperial space by new national states in the region.[1] But the loss of this imperial control was not solely the result of successive nationalist revolts; it was also due to the Ottoman Empire's continuous clashes with other continental empires, that is, the Austrian and Russian empires. In reality, the Balkans were not a mere western border for the Ottomans but a perennial field of military clashes, against both the Austrians and the Russians in the northern provinces above the Danube as well as the Venetians (and French) in the Mediterranean.[2]

This drawn-out process of military clashes from the end of the seventeenth to the beginning of the twentieth century includes three wars against the Habsburg Monarchy, seven wars against the Russian Empire, and, of course, the Napoleonic Wars and the Great War where the Ottoman Empire faced strategic dilemmas of far more complex alliances and confrontation than those it faced in a one-on-one competition with the other continental partners.[3]

The wars in which the Ottoman Empire engaged are usually examined from the perspective of the effectiveness of the Ottoman arms and the impact of the military conflicts on attempts to modernize the State and military mechanisms,[4] while the beginning of nationalist uprisings is linked to the Napoleonic Wars and the dissemination of the ideas of the European Enlightenment. Nonetheless, such a correlation between revolutionary events and armed clashes could be made over a far longer period than the early nineteenth century, where the Serbian and Greek revolts are usually compared to the upheaval wrought by Napoleon's invasion of Egypt in 1798 and to the multi-faceted economic and social crises triggered by the end of the Napoleonic Wars, especially in the Greek islands after 1814.[5]

The relationship between the armed clashes and the restructuring of the Ottoman Empire can already be detected in the Austro-Turkish wars of the late seventeenth and early eighteenth century, which, along with the war against Peter the Great's Russia, are linked to the first reformist efforts during the rule of Ahmed III (B. Harun Küçük). But even after the French Revolution, the particular relationship developed between Revolutionary France and Selim III's Ottoman Empire[6] raised the issue of the military's modernization (Antoaneta Atanasova). The long period of the Tanzimat and its final collapse leads to new forms of imperial nationalism that peak with the Young Turk Revolution. The Balkan Wars that follow and the great losses suffered by the Empire in its European territories will lead to new ideological processes that lay the groundwork for the establishment of the Kemalist regime (Banu Turnaoğlu).

But the armed clashes did not impact only the Ottomans – they also affected the revolutionary movements that emerged in Ottoman territory: the Russo-Turkish War of 1768–1774 is directly linked to the failed Orlov Revolt in the Peloponnese (Bill Molos); the 1806–1812 Russo-Turkish War shaped the uprising of the Serbian knezes; and the recognition of an independent Greek State (Dilek Özkan) and an autonomous Serbian State stem from the 1828–1829 Russo-Turkish War.

Yet, the Empire's breakdown as a result of Russian pressure and the growth of nationalist movements did not only result in geopolitical changes and international political upheavals. It was directly linked to the social and economic repercussions of the wars on the affected populations (Evguenia Davidova) and the different cultural perceptions of those wars, especially when followed in its wake by national liberation characteristics as in the case of the Eastern Crisis and the Russo-Turkish War of 1877–1878 on the Bulgarian Question (Dobrinka Parusheva) or the Croatian national movement (Klara Volarić).

The Revolution as War

However, the paradox of the uprisings within the Ottoman Empire was that they were completed with a 'regime' revolution, that of the Young Turks; the collapse of various versions of Ottoman imperial nationalism in the nineteenth century will lead one segment of the Empire's military elite to end reformist experiments while meantime implementing what appeared to be the demand of the times – the fall of Sultan Abdul Hamid and the reinstatement of the 1876 Constitution. The Empire's transformation by the Young Turk Revolution, but mainly its entry into the First World War, paralleled the transformation of its biggest rival. The Russian Empire, which was responsible for the large wave of (usually victorious) armed clashes with the Ottoman State will be wracked by two great revolts. The first, in 1905, should be viewed and linked to events in Istanbul in the summer of 1908 although, in Russia's case, its defeat in the Russo-Japanese War and social inequality issues were primary factors. Nonetheless, the common denominator in both revolts was the transformation of Russian absolutism and Ottoman despotism to constitutionally controlled monarchies.

Both Russia and the Ottoman Empire were on the losing side of the First World War: Russia was defeated by the war's losers, the Ottoman Empire by its victors. In the aftermath of the Great War, both were forced to wage long and tough battles against foreign invaders. From 1917 to 1921, the Bolsheviks managed to stabilize their control over Soviet territory, thus legitimizing their struggle (and the October Revolution) through clashes with the Whites and their foreign allies. From 1919 to 1922, Kemal will do the same: he will start a liberation war against many foreign occupation forces by deploying alternately military and diplomatic means. The convergence of these two forces came sooner rather than later, not only in the military sphere – and this is what's interesting – but also, to a degree, in the ideological realm (Nikos Christofis). But in contrast to Russia, where the October Revolution and the ensuing civil war led to Russia's transformation to the Soviet Empire, what Kemal's movement managed under the circumstances was to transform the Ottoman Empire to a national state. In a way, the First World War completed the process of the Ottoman elite's adaptation of the Western ideology that led to the Empire's dissolution: nationalism. Meantime, the national groups in the Balkans that had already adopted it had now moved into its irredentist phase. But the big issue for both the Ottoman Empire and the national states was their relationship with the West. If adopting nationalism was a first step towards the Balkans' Westernization, this did not mean that negotiating the position of either the Empire or each national state in relation to the West was not continual, frequently dissolving old hierarchies. Serbia offers a typical example. When the war began, it was a Russian protégé and seen as an extension of the old pan-Slavism. But its alignment with the Entente reinforced its Western orientation and made possible the establishment of the first Yugoslav State in the twentieth century under its control (Aleksandra Kolaković).

The interactive relationship between the wars waged by the Ottoman Empire against the continental (such as Russia and Austria) and the colonial empires (such as France) and the growth of national movements is not only evident, but also occurs on multiple levels. It is, of course, linked to the regime changes and the appearance of new state entities – that is, with the unravelling of the social and economic fabric of entire regions and subsequent reconstruction. Along with weapons, ideas were also spread by other social groups specializing in military and ideological wars – from the hajduk and klephts to the merchants and travellers. But the armed clashes, especially those extending over a long period, were indicators of gaps in the strategies of the Great Powers and often, as least in the case of the western Great Powers and especially France, linked to the great revolutionary events that marked the history of Western Europe. Earlier, we mentioned the relationship between the Serbian and Greek revolutions with the French Revolution of 1789 and the Napoleonic Wars. But the 1848 Revolution is also directly linked to the changes in strategic competition in the Balkans which will be expressed with the outbreak of the Crimean War. The parallel dominance of the ideas of Romantic Nationalism will have an important impact on the development of the nationalist movements such as those in Bulgaria, Romania and Croatia.

The Revolution as Civil War

The February Revolution is warmly accepted by the Romantic Nationalists in the Balkans. Their enthusiasm is spurred less by the dethroning of Louis Philippe in Paris and more by the prospect of German, but especially Italian, unification that would strike deeply against the Austrian Empire. Indeed, the prospect of the House of Hapsburg granting a constitution was, in turn, linked to state experimentation in Greece, Serbia, as well as the Ottoman Empire with the start of the Tanzimat reforms roughly a decade earlier. During this period, Greek commentators especially find an opportunity to emphasize that the revolt against the Hapsburg royal house is a type of historical revenge for the death of Rhigas Feraios and Alexander Ypsilantis.[7] To be precise, the 1848 Revolution is translated in terms of the 'Eastern Question'. Most analysts from this period will refer to the onset of 'balance', a prevalent principle in the West since the beginning of the nineteenth century. The policy of the Great Powers, mainly Austria, 'as shameless defenders of Turkism', is seen as a 'slap' based on the new situation triggered by 1848. The Western policy that preserved the Ottoman Empire's position cancelled the hopes of not only the Greeks but of all Balkan nations. Support for the peoples of the Austrian Empire, Germany and Italy was a subsequent vindication of the emergence of national movements in the provinces.

Of course, the Balkans' Russophile nationalists, especially the Greeks and Bulgarians, found it quite difficult to deal with Russia's active participation in putting down the revolts in Austria-Hungary and Moldavia-Wallachia; naturally, there was no such dilemma for the Romanian revolutionaries.

For example, an extensive review of Greek foreign policy in the pro-Russian newspaper *Aeon* by one commentator focuses on the 'bias' spread by the English and French party as well as in the Western countries at the time about Russia that shaped Greece's anti-Russian stance even though Greeks were 'Russia-leaning'. He describes this animosity towards Russia as 'unfair':

> We accuse the nation of being pro-Russian as if accusing the light of being white or water of being liquid. We accuse the Russians of being Scythians and barbarians, of being heinous despots, of being treacherous foxes of the freedom of nations. [We accuse] pan-Slavism of tending to absorb the Turkish Empire and Greece, and the Russians of being new Goths and Vandals who intended to destroy and barbarize Europe.[8]

The author cites every characterization of Russia made at the time in order to highlight the exaggerated and excessive effort made by the government domestically and the Western powers abroad to foment an anti-Russian sentiment that he doesn't appear to share.

But while it was easy for a Russophile to defend Russia in 1848 or even more in 1849, it was hard to do the same after the end of the Crimean War. Supporters of the February Revolution would face even greater difficulties after its radicalization in June. The expectation that constitutionalism would prevail fostered by the February Revolution was overshadowed by the fear and reservations generated by its radical evolution in June 1848:

> This Revolution, which in a different era could have assumed a character that was revolutionary and effective against the Monarchy, could not prevail against the

principle of national sovereignty. This, which it seems, had as leaders the fans of communalism and the various supporters of those who continued to have claims against the former French crown were moving in the darkness, without meaning or purpose.[9]

The de-legitimization of the Revolution and the 'horrible dogma of communalism and cooperativism' that loomed as Democracy's great enemy and threat to the class of 'owners and merchants',[10] paved the way not just for viewpoints that identified the radicals with the pro-monarchists' intentions of returning to power, but also the legitimization of the New Bonaparte, which would mean a new French foreign policy in the Balkans even though Cavaignac had seemed the most likely solution right up to the elections.[11]

In 1848, one of the most interesting issues raised by the concerns of the Balkan revolutionaries was the stance of the military, both in France and Austria as well as in Bavaria and the other German states, at least in the early phases of the Revolution when, instead of moving against the rebelling peoples, it aligned itself with them. Primarily, 1848 returned the Revolution's shadow to the Balkans with uprisings in Moldavia-Wallachia that appeared to extend the uprisings of the Greeks and Serbs: 'The glorious nations of the Danubian Principalities, Christian nations, or in any case Greek', as one Athenian newspaper commentator typically described them.[12] The Romanians also perceived the uprisings in a similar vein, that is, as the 'national struggle of the Romanians who, for three centuries, with the sword defended Christianity against all the forces of Islam'.[13] The Russian army's participation in putting down the uprising was seen as a paradox: the Treaty of Adrianople provided for Russian intervention in the event that the Ottomans violated the Danubian Principalities' rights of autonomy, yet in 1848 the Russians intervened alongside the Ottomans to put down a revolutionary movement. The Principalities' union in 1859, against the wishes of the Ottomans and Russians, had been heralded a decade earlier.

Of course, there was another paradox in the Ottoman Balkans, that the 1848 Revolution did not affect either Greece or the Ottoman Empire where the 'vision' of constitutional reform had begun a few years earlier – in Greece with the 1843 uprising that ended with the Bavarian ruler Othon conceding to the drafting of a constitution, and in the Ottoman Empire with the start of the Tanzimat reforms in 1839. The latter, while not especially radical in their first phase, in reality activated the constitutional change in Greece. As one commentator noted at the time, 'Greece ... made the transition via the regime change of 3 September 1844 to the full acquisition of constitutional freedoms ... France acquired these only after the Republic (of 1848).'[14] But just as the rise of Napoleon III and the onset of the Second Empire placed a tombstone over the revolutionary dreams of 1848, Othon in Greece would undermine the functioning of the constitution's principles by continuing to appoint governments that were initially oriented towards the Western powers but later turned towards Russia: 'If, then the [Greek] constitutional system did not progress like the French one, in whose heart one can find the most brilliant politicians and orators ... how could it prosper in Greece which is rife with poverty and lacking in education ... having all the faults and none of the virtues.'[15]

In the Greek case, of course, it wasn't just the feeling of disappointment triggered by the cancellation of the revolutionary visions but also a fundamental change in the country's political orientation expressed in the *Megali Idea*. If in its cultural version this meant a pro-Western foreign policy and a shared Greek-Ottoman vision based on constitutional change, in its irredentist form it led to a convergence with Russia at the time of the Crimean War, which carried a high cost for the country (a two-year blockade of the port at Piraeus) and the Bavarian dynasty (the ousting of the royal couple in 1862). The expression of a corresponding *Megali Idea* by the Serbs, the *Nacertaniye*, would also face great difficulties in its implementation as it clashed with the Austrian Empire's interests.

Thus the 1840s would, in reality, fix three different zones in the Ottoman Balkans: a synchronization of political developments in the Greek Kingdom and the Ottoman Empire with the common concern of countering the 'pan-Slavism' threat; a movement of the peninsula's Slavic peoples (the Bulgarians in the Ottoman Empire and the Croats in the Austrian Empire) to follow the example of the Greeks and Serbs, respectively; and the zone of Moldavia-Wallachia, which was the only one directly affected by the revolutionary wave of 1848 but also the only one subjected to the joint suppression of the Russian and Ottoman armies.

Thus the link between 1848 and the Crimean War should not be limited to the issue of the change in relationships between the Great Powers but also to the direct impact on the geopolitical shaping of the Balkan peninsula. In contrast with the 1848 Revolution, which was met with ambivalence in the Balkans, the 1871 Revolution prompted a generalized rejection across the spectrum of the political world. The Revolution was perceived as a civil war, while measures taken by the Commune, such as abolishing the courts and expropriating church property, sent shivers through conservative circles.[16] Nonetheless, just as events of 1848 led to the eruption of the Crimean War, we could say that the Franco-Prussian War of 1870 and the Paris Commune shaped a new power relationship in Europe and triggered the developments that eventually led to the Great Eastern Crisis of 1875–1878.

The Revolution as Imperial Nationalism

If the rise of the Bonapartist regime in France meant a new strategic defeat of the Russian Empire, its defeat by the Prussians in 1870 marked the dynamic return in the next few years of Russia, not only in Europe's affairs but in the Balkans too with the creation of the Bulgarian State and the emergence of new nationalist movements such as the Albanian and Slav-Macedonian. In post-revolutionary France itself, the model of a Russian-style governance aimed at 'reforms' – as represented by Peter the Great or even viewing Alexander I as a liberator rather than conqueror – began to gain ground in 1815, albeit with the Prussians as the rebels' suppressors.

The Eastern Crisis marked, in a way, the peak of the 'Eastern Question', precisely because it was the culmination of the Ottoman Empire's clash with the other two continental empires, Austria and Russia. All the actors' movements in this confrontation are seemingly made out of fear. Feeling the threat of the establishment of a 'federal alliance of Serbs and Romanians', Austria will invade and annex Bosnia-Herzegovina. To save the Bulgarians from massacre, Russia will send its army to impose the creation of a Bulgarian State. Faced with external threats, the Ottoman Sultan will rescind the Constitution. In Greece, of course, the unanticipated questioning of the dogma of the Ottoman Empire's integrity even by Gladstone's England will rekindle the fading dream of the *Megali Idea*. As one commentator noted in Alitheia, 'the map of Turkish integrity will burn inside Haghia Sophia and the Barbarians' minaret will be razed and the bell tower of Constantine the Great erected'.[17] But this was not the only option available for Hellenism: Constantinople's elites had a different perspective on what should happen regarding the Slavic threat, and that wasn't to dissolve the Ottoman Empire – on the contrary. Amid the Great Eastern Crisis, the prominent Greek banker Georgios Zarifis will approach the English embassy with a plan for uniting the Greek Kingdom and Ottoman Empire modelled on the Austro-Hungarian *Ausgleich*. The convergence of kingdom and empire in the 1840s with the prospect of adopting constitutional reforms before the 1848 revolution forced the issue, and seemed to be taking a more organic shape under the pressure of the Slavic zone, which was taking the form of a State with Russia's assistance.[18]

Once more, a revolution provoked a war. Although its ending seemed to resolve many issues pending from the previous period (Serbian, Romanian and Bulgarian independence), it opened new ones. The occupation of Bosnia-Herzegovina by Austria, the occupation of Cyprus by Great Britain, and the successive annexations of Thessaly and parts of Epirus by Greece and Eastern Rumelia by Bulgaria showed that the Berlin Conference was a turning point but not a final resolution. This will set off 'internal' clashes in two of the zones described earlier: the 'Slavic' and 'Greco-Ottoman'. These were clashes between supposed partners.

Eastern Rumelia's annexation would result in an armed clash between Serbs and Bulgarians (1885), while Greece's attempted annexation of Crete would lead to a clash between Greeks and Ottomans (1897). Although the victors' military victory appeared to reaffirm their geopolitical advantage, in reality it was defeat that gave the losers a good excuse to move forward to a new phase of economic, social and military restructuring. Their initial response, however, was ideopolitical: the Serbs replied by promoting the ideology of Macedonism aimed at wrenching the Slavophone populations of mainly central Macedonia from Bulgarian influence (a tactic that would be embraced, to some extent, by the Greek nationalists who considered these Slavs to be Grecomans); the Greek response was to amend their irredentist orientation, from the nineteenth-century *Megali Idea*, which died in the 1897 war (that is, the desire to reach the Balkan mountains and Constantinople) to a more realistic version in which the desire to annex Ottoman territories was linked to a demand for political and social modernization (in other words, what the first Venizelos government did), with support for indirect military action (guerrilla war) against the Bulgarians in Macedonia.

This protracted silent war triggered by the two defeats at the end of the nineteenth century led, in reverse order, to a revolution in the twentieth century: the Young Turks in 1908. This return to the fount of modernization and its ideals once again touched Greece. The 1909 Goudi coup in Athens seemed to be a direct echo of what was happening at the time in Constantinople. Nonetheless, and not so unexpectedly, this return to the principles of constitutionalism did not lead to a new period of 'Greek-Ottoman' rapprochement – or at least geopolitical synchronization – but conversely to the adoption of an aggressive policy against the Great Patient. Venizelos will openly promote this policy in 1911 and afterwards in concert with other Balkan Slavs and in the wake of the Ottomans' defeat in the war with the Italians. But this direction had been given by a new generation of nationalists in Athens like Vlassis Gavriilidis, publisher of the newspaper *Akropolis*.

After the Young Turk Revolution, the newspaper published an article that was the product of interviews with Greeks of all classes by the paper's correspondent in Thessaloniki aimed at gauging their views on Macedonia's Hellenism and, by extension, throughout the Ottoman Empire ahead of the 1908 November elections. The article notes the following:

> Now we will have justice, freedom and all the other benefits that the European peoples have enjoyed for years, but these have a general character and their advantage must be considered to regard [the Ottoman subjects] at the personal level. However, from the perspective of racial progress, that is, the whole, the national whole, the Constitution gives rise to doubts and troublesome points that must be diligently studied by the Greek government ... On what basis do we declare that the constitutional rule renders Hellenism's place in Turkey better than that which prevailed for some many centuries? ... Thus the danger to our entities in Macedonia and Thrace grows rather than shrinks ... we have before us a Turkey inspired militarily and bureaucratically by the idea of pan-Slavism ... The Young Turks program is conservative with regards to the various peoples of the Empire or pan-Slavic, not recognizing the existence of Greeks, Serbs, Albanians, Armenians, Bulgarians, etc., but only a total of Ottoman citizens ... To which citizens ... it will ban the use of their ethnic language ... the maintenance of Turkish dominance in Europe seems somewhat problematic ... given that all those in the Young Turk Committee are Albanians ... they will comprise an self-contained Albanian State whose highest authority will be based in Thessaloniki.[19]

The identification of Ottomans and Albanians is not random for Greek irredentism's ambitions at the time. Despite the criticism of the Young Turk movement, Athens had an admiration for how the movement derived its power from the army as well as for its insistence on bringing back into effect the 1876 Constitution. Moreover, everyone understood that a revolution in Constantinople itself, even if based mainly on the army's mobilization rather than the people's, could not be compared to other national revolutions in the Balkans but to the great revolutions that had shaken the West until then – even if the comparison was not in its favour.

Gavriilidis himself notes in an article published after the March 1909 coup and shortly before Abdul Hamid is dethroned:

> The Young Turk Committee, which is nothing but a pale copy of the Jacobin Club ... because the Christian şeriat and the French Revolution could not come to terms with each other, the [monarch's] head had to be cut ... Will this also be the first of

the Turkish Louis XVI? ... The Young Turks think they serve freedom. And not only do they think that, but they believe it ... Those who have conquered it thus far are officers of the Young Turk army, but no one is conquering anything for someone else ... What did the Turkish Revolution bring? ... Is it a political revolution like that of the English, social like the French, religious like the German? They did not even succeed in creating a chaos but perhaps creativity will come from that.[20]

The fact that this was a revolution from above rendered the Young Turk revolt as problematic in contrast with the Western revolutions: 'In today's revolution, the aristocracy and the army, which in Turkey's case are one and the same, and the clergy – that is, all the forces – joined in a final reform effort in the face not of an internal danger but the ultimate external danger of losing national independence.'[21]

This goal would not be achieved. The Young Turk Revolution was not a bloody revolution precisely because it was a movement by the empire's leadership classes to save it. At the same time, what loomed as a positive element became its disadvantage. The Ottoman-Italian War, the Balkan Wars that followed, and the engagement in the First World War would show how limited the possibility was for saving the empire by preserving its multi-ethnic character. And when this mobilization from 'below' finally took place, it resulted in ethnic cleansing and genocide.[22]

This volume is an attempt to delve deeper into the mass emergence of revolutionary uprisings in the heart of continental Europe – even though this process was touched off by the Anglo-Saxon world and culminated with the Communist revolts in Eurasia – as this occurred in the Balkan states, which, at the time, were in the embrace of the Ottoman and Austrian empires.

More specifically, B. Harun Küçük deals with geographer İbrahim Müteferrika's *Foundations of Government in Various Social Orders* (1732), one of the key Ottoman political texts of the eighteenth century, written exactly after the rebellion of 1730 in Istanbul. 'We are like ants on a watermelon', Müteferrika said, highlighting the contingent, local and voluntarist basis of politics. Not only did this text represent a clean break with seventeenth-century Ottoman political literature, but it also included a call to emulate Petrine Russia. The chapter highlights the Russian use of machines, printing presses, and mechanicist military practices (ranks, drilling) in the Russo-Ottoman proxy war in the wake of the Safavid collapse, and the use of machines by the Ottoman central administration. His goal is to reconcile Müteferrika's reformism with his sympathy for Cartesian philosophy.

Vasilis (Bill) Molos reassesses the influence of the Orlov Revolt on Modern Greek Enlightenment Thought. A new era was proclaimed in France with the passing of the 'Declaration of the Rights of Man and of the Citizen' by the National Constituent Assembly in August 1789. Drawing upon the political philosophy of the Enlightenment, the revolutionary ideals contained within this statement quickly reverberated way beyond France, as the revolution took on a global dimension. Within the Ottoman Balkans, the French Revolution opened new horizons of political possibility, polarizing Greek intellectuals, and inspiring many to advocate for the establishment of a sovereign Greek polity. The undeniable influence of the French example on Greek authors in the

1790s makes it very appealing to identify 1789 as the dawn of a new era in Greek political thought, and the stories of Rigas Velestinlis, the 'Friendly Society' and the War of Independence are easily situated within such a history. While this narrative is appealing, it overlooks the significant impact of the Orlov Revolt (1770) on Greek political thought. Through an examination of the writings of Iosipos Moisiodax and Dimitrios Katartzis, two prominent intellectual voices of the 1770s and 1780s, Molos outlines the range of novel political ideas circulating in the Greek-speaking world from the Treaty of Küçük Kaynarca (1774) to the outbreak of the French Revolution. In so doing he recasts these figures, heretofore portrayed as unsophisticated voices in an intellectual backwater, as contributors to a broader conversation about sovereignty during the transformative age of revolutions.

Like B. Harun Küçük, Antoaneta Atanasova also concentrates on the eighteenth-century Ottoman Empire though not on relations with Russia but instead those with France. The chapter is based on French archival materials and its aim is to reveal the diplomatic efforts of the French government to urge the Ottomans to implement army reforms during the rule of Selim III (1789–1807). This research question has two sides. The first is purely technical – the Sublime Porte hires foreign military specialists, whose job is to instruct the army, as well as to persuade it to use the new European technology. This is needed to bolster the resilience of the Ottoman Empire, so that other powers could be prevented from increasing their influence in southeast Europe. On the other hand, it is believed that military advisors are a strong diplomatic weapon, a weapon very well used by the French throughout the eighteenth century. A range of political goals are achieved by the French ambassadors due to the army advisors' influence over the Sultan. Atanasova explains in detail the role of the French military experts in the Ottoman Empire for bilateral relations as well as for the development of the Eastern Question during the period. The analysis compares these issues before and after the political changes of the French Revolution and also evaluates the new French attitude towards the Ottomans and vice versa.

In her chapter, Evguenia Davidova explores the social and ethnic reshuffling that various economic groups in the Balkans experienced as a result of war. Wars offered opportunities for accumulating wealth, social mobility and the building of ethno-economic networks. However, wars also brought impoverishment to some crafts and agricultural producers and their communities declined. Thus, this chapter not only traces changes that happened during wartime but also the complex ramifications that ensued in peacetime, including nationalist aspirations. The chapter is grounded in archival materials, travelogues, newspapers and memoirs and tries to add a neglected dimension to the issue of the socio-economic impact of cataclysmic events such as wars on society in the Ottoman and post-Ottoman Balkans.

Dilek Özkan, in her chapter on the Greek boundary in the final phase of the Greek Revolution, examines the impact of the Greek Revolution on the Ottoman language of diplomacy, by focusing on discussions between the European Powers and the Ottoman Porte that determined the first Ottoman–Greek border. She first discusses how a theoretically determined border (a product of lengthy meetings spanning almost six years [1826–1832], existing only on maps) was realized on the ground. The chapter demonstrates that the Sublime Porte had reluctantly accepted negotiations with the

European Powers on determination of the boundary and had in such regard, moreover, postponed its ratification to the greatest possible extent. In contributing to earlier works on the subject, Özkan provides an analysis of Ottoman terminology used during negotiations on delimiting the boundary. Overall, this chapter contributes to the discussion that the Greek Revolution and the establishment of the Greek State as an independent entity precipitated a major change in the Ottoman Empire.

Assia Nakova, in her re-evaluation of Bulgarian military history of the second part of the nineteenth century, deals with the *haiduks*, or the Balkans' nineteenth-century version of modern guerrilla fighters, who have been a mainstay of many national founding legends throughout the area. Bulgarian historiography of this period in particular may be said to reinforce the attractiveness of these legends. Usually they depict an ordinary Bulgarian man struggling under the burden of Ottoman rule, who finally, and in exasperation, finds himself no longer able to tolerate his oppressive circumstances and takes not to the hills but to the mountains. In fact, the very elevation of the terrain in which he now comes to reside seems to mirror the 'elevation' of his new moral and fighting spirit. In the mountains, and for the first time, he becomes a free man and, joined by other like-minded men, is able to fight for the freedom of his people, his nation, and his country. Romantic though such a story may sound, and providing as it does rich material for historians as well as for traditional and tradition-based Bulgarian poems, songs and films, the reality behind it has proved to be quite different, if not unpleasant and murderous. An important case in point is that of the widely celebrated guerrilla fighter Petko Voivoda. Operating in the key Rhodope region, he is purported to have fought to preserve its 'Bulgarian character' in the aftermath of the Berlin Congress (1878), which split an initially Greater Bulgaria into Bulgaria itself, Eastern Rumelia and Macedonia. Bulgarian historiography consistently, and to this day, flatters and celebrates his exploits. The chapter proposes a revision of his influential reputation, and indeed of the type of legend which he exemplifies, through an examination of English and French primary documents. Of particular interest is an event rarely touched on: the burning to the ground of two villages by Petko and his men in retribution for the villagers' supposed betrayal of the *haiduks*. The contradiction between a romanticized falsehood and the horrifying reality that Nakova demonstrates, highlights the need for a more balanced and detailed view of traditional Bulgarian national heroes in general and Petko Voivoda in particular. The author hopes there will be a large-scale revision of conventional nation-centred and nationalistic interpretations of Bulgarian military and social history.

Dobrinka Parusheva analyses the role of images in the coverage of uprisings and wars in the Bulgarian illustrated press, exemplified by *Ilyustratsiya Svetlina* (Illustration Light), from its inception in 1891 to the end of the First World War. The discussion is presented in three main sections following the chronology: first, Parusheva addresses the visual representation of uprisings and wars on the *Light*'s pages in the 1890s and 1900s; then she analyses the coverage of the Balkan Wars of 1912–1913; finally, she scrutinizes the visual presence of the Great War. One focus of attention, especially when it comes to coverage of events in which Bulgarians are directly involved, are the different ways in which allies and enemies (or self and the other) are depicted. The question of the (in)visibility of women is also addressed. The dominant types of image and the role of images in the coverage receive special attention. According to the author, the uprisings and wars were characterized by a mix of 'traditional' (e.g. paintings, lithographs) and 'modern' (press photography) representations. As for the role of images, the visual material was used by the editor of *Light* in two main ways: first, as a tool of maintaining collective memory and, second, as a means of communicating news about contemporary events. Parusheva is aware of the importance of the audience, since the meaning of all images depends on what their public constructs with them. She claims, however, that during time of war visual materials were used extensively for massive national and military mobilization and propaganda and, bearing in mind the existence of censorship, assumes that what the editor of the journal *Light* made its Bulgarian readership take notice of was exactly what the Bulgarian government wanted its citizens to pay attention to.

Klara Volarić, in her contribution, addresses one of the outcomes of the Great Eastern Crisis brought on by the Berlin Congress in 1878 – the Austria-Hungarian occupation of Bosnia and Herzegovina. While this occupation did not fit into the Serbian nationalist and expansionist programme which was now redirected to the south, Croatia, at that time part of Austria-Hungary, saw in this occupation the possibility to resolve its own territorial and governmental issues known as the Croatian Question. Volarić investigates the stance of the Croatian public towards this occupation and how the occupation could, in their opinion, resolve the Croatian Question. Moreover, she also explores why the two leading figures of Croatian politics and intelligentsia, J.J. Strossmayer and Ante Starčević, although having completely opposite political views, shared the belief that the occupation meant nothing for the Croatian Question. In addition, Volarić analyses *Under a Gun*, a novel by Croatian writer and politician Eugen Kumičić, who unlike the previously mentioned armchair thinkers, participated directly in the process of occupation and described it in his novel. Volarić examines how Kumičić's experiences in the war shaped his later political and writing career, traces of which can be seen in this novel.

Aleksandra Kolaković examines the perception of French intellectuals regarding Serbia and Serbs during the years of the Great War. From the Franco-Russian alliance (1894) to the Annexation Crisis (1908–1909), the Balkan Wars (1912–1913) and the Great War (1914–1918), the interest of French intellectuals in Serbia and Serbs increased and was intertwined with issues of relations among the Great Powers, the end of Ottoman power on European territories and the German *Drang nach Osten*. The reputation of Serbia among the French public during the First World War was very high owing to the activities of a number of French intellectuals: Ernest Denis, Emile Haumant, Charles Loiseau, Auguste Gauvain, Albert Malet, Victor Bérard, André Chéradame, Henry Barby, Auguste Boppe and Pierre Lanux. On the basis of an image of the 'other', Kolaković attempts to highlight the awareness of French intellectuals for Serbia and Serbs in the period before and during the Great War (1914–1918).

The development of international relations after the Annexation Crisis, which highlighted the path of the German breakthrough in the East, as well as a new political map of the Balkans established in the Balkan Wars, fostered closer and more vigorous cooperation between French (Ernest Denis, Emile Haumant, Charles Loiseau, Auguste Gauvain, Albert Malet, Victor Bérard, André Chéradame, Henry Barby, Auguste Boppe,

Pierre Lanux) and Serbian intellectuals (Milovan Milovanović, Jovan Žujović, Bogdan Popović, Jovan Skerlić, Milenko Vesnić, Grgur Jakšić). At the turn of the twentieth century, besides analysis of Serbia's foreign policy, the political, economic and cultural development of Serbia featured in the writings of French intellectuals. French intellectuals noticed that Serbia was going through tumultuous changes and challenges. Focusing on the specifics of the development of both Serbian society and state, between 1894 and 1914 there was a significant change in the image of Serbia in France. The Balkan Wars showed that the Serbs had gained political maturity and enough economic and social progress to take responsibility for the fate of their nation and state. Reporters from the Balkan battlefields (1912–1913) wrote that 'the Serbian race [was] amazingly resistant' and brisk at crucial moments. When Serbia was caught by an epidemic of typhus fever after the first victories in the First World War, humanitarian organizations in France, backed by the support of French intellectuals and indirectly supported by the French State, played an important role. At the same time, Serbian intellectuals established a centre of Serbian academic propaganda in Paris. A group of eminent French scholars (Denis, Bérard, Haumant, Loiseau, Gauvain) contributed to the affirmation of Serbian victories and engendering sympathy for the Serbs among international public opinion. Auguste Gauvain saw the Serbs as warriors and Serbia as a country 'with a mission which had to fight, to strive for the national liberation and to unite with liberated brothers into one community'. Exploring the history of small nations became important for French science and politics. In his book *Yugoslavia: France and the Serbs*, Pierre Lanux wrote that French policy towards the Serbs and the Slavs in the Balkans (until the First World War) was formed based on the 'fantasies' of famous French authors, including Pierre Loti and his glorification of the Turks. Lanux pointed out that it was necessary to visit Belgrade and create an objective image. French intellectuals admired greatly the patriotism of the Serbs and the 'completely justifiable pride of a nation, a nation who was shedding blood for the cause of its own independence throughout the centuries'. French intellectuals observed the role played by folk heroic songs, memories of the glorious mediaeval Serbian State, and the Kosovo legend on the formation of Serbian identity and patriotism ('The memory of Kosovo has perhaps further impassioned their patriotic belief because the glory of the victims was more noble than the celebration of triumph'). The starting point of French intellectuals educated in a patriotic spirit was a revision of the position of France in international relations, and Serbia and the Serbs became the subject of their considerable interest and served during the Great War as a pretext for refreshing the spirit of French patriotism. Owing to the significant role of scholars in the Great War, as well as the importance of the struggle in the area of propaganda, the image of Serbia and the Serbs created by French intellectuals shaped Franco-Serbian relations.

Banu Turnaoğlu's chapter on Ottoman political thought in the prelude to the First World War examines how the Balkan Wars influenced the articulation of Ottoman ideas of war and the image of an ideal state and society. The Balkan Wars revealed that modern warfare was not merely driven by the desire for economic expansion in the matters of trade and territory, but by a combination of psychological, sociological, national, political, military and religious factors. The Triumvirate of Enver, Cemal and

Talat Paşa, whose collective decisions dominated Ottoman politics from 1913 to 1918, blended German militarist, nationalist and Darwinist elements. Their ideology was constructed through an intense dialogue with public opinion and leading intellectuals like Ziya Gökalp and Ahmed Ağaoğlu, the ideological founders of the Republic. This new ideology overturned the universalist commitments of the Revolution of 1908 and prepared the ground for the outbreak of the First World War.

The final chapter by Nikos Christofis focuses on the October Revolution of 1917 and the Anatolian Resistance Movement. The French Revolution and the Russian Revolution of 1917 were transitional paradigms that effected radical ruptures in global history. Their actors stepped into unknown and unknowable futures. This uncertainty was lost to later emulators who read results back into beginnings, and attributed them to the earliest intentions of real or imaginary actors. Within this context, the revolution in the Ottoman Empire by the Young Turks and, later, the Anatolian Resistance Movement led by the founder of Turkey, Mustafa Kemal (Atatürk) in 1919–1922, was continuous with the short-term wave of democratic movements that swept across the world (Russia in 1905, Mexico in 1910, China in 1911 and Russia again in February 1917). The historical development of Russia and the Ottoman Empire provides a good example to test the reciprocity between the two. In order to better understand both the influence and the relations – political and diplomatic, friendly and hostile to one another – between Russia and the Ottoman Empire, and specifically with the Anatolian Resistance Movement, the chapter attempts to draw parallels with the 1905 revolution in Russia and the 1908 revolution of the Young Turks. Drawing examples from the past, the author attempts to trace how the October Revolution influenced the Anatolian Resistance Movement and in what respect. The initial hypothesis of the chapter is that there is an implicit or explicit link between the Young Turk Revolution and the Anatolian Resistance Movement, as there is between the 1905 Revolution and the October Revolution of 1917 in Russia. Finally, the chapter aims to evaluate relations between Bolshevik Russia and the Ottoman Empire during the Turkish War of Independence of 1919–1922, through three concepts directly intertwined with each other: war, revolution and diplomacy.

The nationalist movements in eastern and southeastern Europe, an area that extended from Poland to Greece, continuously negotiated their identities according to the West's internal fragmentations. We could describe here the Balkan national movements from their inception as a ripple effect from the revolutions in the West, especially that in France.

Approaching Balkan revolutionary movements as the result of ruptures sustained by the Great Powers, either internally (revolutions) or externally (wars), would allow us to take the long view of this process so that the inversion of events from the start of the nineteenth century at its end do not seem coincidental.

Notes

1   Leften Stavros Stavrianos, *The Balkans Since 1453*. New York: Rinehart, 1958; Barbara Jelavich, *History of the Balkans*, vol. 2. Cambridge: Cambridge University Press, 1983.

2   Dimitris Stamatopoulos, *The Eastern Question or Balkan Nationalism(s): Balkan History Reconsidered*. Vienna: Vienna University Press, 2018, p. 20.
3   Gábor Ágoston, 'Military Transformation in the Ottoman Empire and Russia, 1500–1800', *Kritika: Explorations in Russian and Eurasian History*, 12, no. 2 (2011), pp. 281–319; Ágoston, 'Information, Ideology, and Limits of Imperial Policy: Ottoman Grand Strategy in the Context of Ottoman–Habsburg Rivalry', in Virginia H. Aksan and Daniel Goffman (eds.), *Early Modern Ottomans: Remapping the Empire*. Cambridge: Cambridge University Press, 2007, pp. 75–103; Virginia H. Aksan, *Ottoman Wars, 1700–1807: An Empire Besieged*. London: Routledge, 2007.
4   Virginia H. Aksan, 'Mobilization of Warrior Populations in the Ottoman Context, 1750–1850', in Erik-Jan Zürcher, *Fighting for a Living: A Comparative Study of Military Labour 1500–2000*. Amsterdam: Amsterdam University Press, 2013, pp. 331–351.
5   See the relevant discussion in Dimitris Stamatopoulos, *The Eastern Question*, 23–24. The connection of the 1789 revolutionary events and the rise of the Serbian and Greek revolts was fundamental for the construction of the nation-building historiographical paradigm in the Balkans. See, for example, respectively: Dušan T. Bataković, 'Balkan-Style French Revolution? The 1804 Serbian Revolution in European Perspective', *Balkanica*, XXXVI (2005), pp. 113–128; Paschalis Kitromilidis, *Η Γαλλική Επανάσταση και η Νοτιοανατολική Ευρώπη* [*The French Revolution and Southeastern Europe*]. Athens: Diatton Publishing House, 1990.
6   Anne Mézin (ed.), *Français et ottomans en Illyrie et dans l'Adriatique au temps de Napoléon: inventaire des papiers du général Donzelot (1764–1843)*. Beylerbeyi, İstanbul: Les Editions Isis/Centre d'histoire diplomatique ottomane, 2009; Luca Zuccolo, *La presse francophone ottomane et le discours patriotique ottoman*. Istanbul: Les Éditions Isis, 2017.
7   *Aeon* newspaper, 15 September 1848.
8   *Aeon* newspaper, 28 August 1848.
9   *Aeon* newspaper, 10 November 1848.
10 *Aeon* newspaper, 10 November 1848.
11 One of the most widely disseminated articles during this period was the proclamation issued in March 1848 by Lamartine, the Revolution's foreign minister, that distinguished between events in Paris in 1848 and what happened in 1789 and 1792. Lamartine's main goal was to reassure the rest of Europe that the Revolution did not mean war, as had been the case during the reign of the first Napoleon. But his crucial point was that in 1792 the nation had not been uniform, that there had been 'two peoples residing in the same place', and that in 1792 power was not taken by all the people but only the middle class, with the working class as its tool. Whereas 1792 was the triumph of the middle class and the war was an attempt by the pro-monarchists and Girondists to override it, 1848 involved the masses whose demand was for the complete liberation of French society. Such a theoretical process that sought to negate the revolutionary radicalism and obvious class nature of the Revolution was particularly attractive for Balkan scholars and intellectuals (and, in general, revolutionaries in Central and Eastern Europe) as it allowed them to present the Revolution as having broad acceptance among the population. It also allowed them to link it to the demand for a constitutional monarchy and national unification rather than with Jacobin-inspired communal ownership. Or, as Lamartine put it, democracy indisputably wants glory but for itself, not for Caesars or Napoleons.
12 *Efimeris ton Sizitiseon* newspaper, 26 September 1848.

13 Mihail Kogălniceanu, Inaugural speech for the course of the National History in *Academia Mihăileană*, 24 November 1843, in *1848 La Români o Istorie în Date și Mărturii* [*1848 in Romanians or History in Documents and Testimonies*], vol. I. Bucharest: Editura Științifică și Enciclopedică, 1982, p. 216.
14 *Ethniki* newspaper, 14 October 1848.
15 *Anexartitos* newspaper, 25 December 1848.
16 In an article dated 14 May 1871, the commentator of the newspaper *Alitheia* calls the Commune revolutionaries 'Parisian Arvanites'. Using as pretext the torching of some of France's historical and notable buildings, he argues that the Arvanites from the periphery of Athens are far less monstrous and crude than the Commune members.
17 It's impressive but long before the issue of Macedonia's autonomy as a principality was raised by VMRO's two factions – the Bulgarian and Slav-Macedonian; after 1893, it was raised by Greek nationalists during the years of the Great Eastern Crisis, precisely in order to avoid its incorporation into the Greater Bulgaria of San Stefano and which Russia would have to accept 'in order to show the world that it spilled Russian blood to truly liberate Christians and not for one group to enslave another'. See *Alitheia of Athens*, 23 February 1878. Nonetheless, the Greek nationalists of Constantinople, as expressed in the pages of the *Neologos* newspaper, were far more reserved regarding the 'principality' solution proposed by the Great Powers for Bosnia-Herzegovina, believing that this promoted Russian and Austrian interests and as such entities could easily be annexed by them or become protectorates in the future. See *Neologos* newspaper, 28–29 September 1875.
18 A typical example of this stance is a circular issued by Patriarch Joacheim II, a cleric who was dependent on the bankers' circle and Georgios Zarifis, inviting the Ottoman Empire's Christian citizens to close their ears to the siren calls of the Slavic people's uprisings. The circular asked recipients to affirm their dedication and subjugation to the Sultan and his efforts to suppress the uprisings, noting that they were obligated to support this effort morally but also materially by offering the Empire financial assistance to relieve it from the huge expenditures it was being forced to make in order to restore peace. Christians' financial contribution was a sacred duty that showed their gratitude for the Sultan's benevolence in tending to their security, life, wealth, peaceful coexistence and prosperity. See the article in the newspaper *Avgi* that describes the circular as 'satanic' from its pro-Russian interpretation (17 July 1876, 'The Patriarch's Satanic Document').
19 'The Program of the Greeks of Macedonia: Macedonia-Constitutional Organization', *Akropolis* newspaper, 23 August 1908.
20 'The Activities of the Young Turks', *Akropolis* newspaper, 15 April 1909. Gavriilidis will continue in a separate article: 'From Young Turkism's proclamations on freedom, equality, and fraternity, for the peoples in Turkey these have remained but words ... The great revolution for Turkey will not be the Constitution or the monarchy, but the transformation of the spirit and soul of Islamism' ('The New Turkey and the Old Turkey', 1909).
21 *Alitheia* newspaper, 10 August 1908.
22 Richard C. Hall, *Balkan Wars 1912–1913: Prelude to the First World War*. London: Routledge, 2000; M. Hakan Yavuz and Isa Blumi (eds.), *War and Nationalism: The Balkan Wars, 1912–1913, and Their Sociopolitical Implications*. Salt Lake City, UT: The University of Utah Press 2013; Dimitris Stamatopoulos (ed.), *Balkan Nationalism(s) and the Ottoman Empire*, vol. II: *Political Violence and the Balkan Wars*. Istanbul: Isis Press, 2015.

Bibliography

Ágoston, Gábor, 'Information, Ideology, and Limits of Imperial Policy: Ottoman Grand Strategy in the Context of Ottoman–Habsburg Rivalry', in Virginia Aksan and Daniel Goffman (eds.), *Early Modern Ottomans: Remapping the Empire*. Cambridge: Cambridge University Press, 2007, pp. 75–103.

Ágoston, Gábor, 'Military Transformation in the Ottoman Empire and Russia, 1500–1800', *Kritika: Explorations in Russian and Eurasian History*, 12, no. 2 (2011), pp. 281–319.

Aksan, Virginia H., *Ottoman Wars, 1700–1807: An Empire Besieged*. London: Routledge, 2007.

Aksan, Virginia H., 'Mobilization of Warrior Populations in the Ottoman Context, 1750–1850', in Erik-Jan Zürcher (ed.), *Fighting for a Living: A Comparative Study of Military Labour 1500–2000*. Amsterdam: Amsterdam University Press, 2013, pp. 331–351.

Anscombe, Frederick F., 'The Balkan Revolutionary Age', *Journal of Modern History*, 84, no. 3 (2012), pp. 572–606.

Armour, Ian, *A History of Eastern Europe, 1740–1918: Empires, Nations and Modernization*. New York: Bloomsbury Academic, 2012.

Bataković, Dušan T., 'Balkan-Style French Revolution? The 1804 Serbian Revolution in European Perspective', *Balkanica*, XXXVI (2005), pp. 113–128.

Davies, Brian L., *The Russo-Turkish War, 1768–1774: Catherine II and the Ottoman Empire*. London: Bloomsbury, 2016

Hall, Richard C., *Balkan Wars 1912–1913: Prelude to the First World War*. London: Routledge, 2000.

Hobsbawm, Eric J., *The Age of Revolution: 1789–1848*. Toronto: New American Library, 1962.

Jelavich, Barbara, *History of the Balkans*, vol. 2. Cambridge: Cambridge University Press, 1983.

Kitromilidis, Paschalis, *Η Γαλλική Επανάσταση και η Νοτιοανατολική Ευρώπη* [*The French Revolution and Southeastern Europe*]. Athens: Diatton Publishing House, 1990.

Kogălniceanu, Mihail, Inaugural speech for the course of the National History in *Academia Mihăileană*, 24 November 1843, in *1848 La Români o Istorie in Date și Mărturii* [*1848 in Romanians or History in Documents and Testimonies*], vol. I. Bucharest: Editura Științifică și Enciclopedică, 1982, p. 216.

Lieven, Dominic, 'Dilemmas of Empire 1850–1918. Power, Territory, Identity', *Journal of Contemporary History*, 34, no. 2 (1999), pp. 163–200.

Mazower, Mark, *The Balkans: A Short History*. New York: The New Library, 2000.

Mézin, Anne (ed.), *Français et ottomans en Illyrie et dans l'Adriatique au temps de Napoléon: inventaire des papiers du général Donzelot (1764–1843)*. Beylerbeyi, İstanbul: Les Editions Isis/Centre d'histoire diplomatique ottomane, 2009.

Miller, William, *The Balkans. Roumania, Bulgaria, Servia, and Montenegro*. New York: G.P. Putnam's Sons, 1896.

Stamatopoulos, Dimitris (ed.), *Balkan Nationalism(s) and the Ottoman Empire*, vol. II: *Political Violence and the Balkan Wars*. Istanbul: Isis Press, 2015.

Stamatopoulos, Dimitris, *The Eastern Question or Balkan Nationalism(s): Balkan History Reconsidered*. Vienna: Vienna University Press, 2018.

Stamatopoulos, Dimitris, *Byzantium after the Nation: The Problem of the National Continuity in the Balkan Historiographies*. Budapest: CEU Press, 2019 (forthcoming).

Stavrianos, Leften Stavros, *The Balkans Since 1453*. New York: Rinehart, 1958.

Tilly, Charles, *European Revolutions, 1492–1992*. Oxford: Blackwell, 1993.
Walt, Stephen M., *Revolution and War*. Ithaca, NY: Cornell University Press, 1996.
Yavuz, M. Hakan and Isa Blumi (eds.), *War and Nationalism: The Balkan Wars, 1912–1913, and Their Sociopolitical Implications*. Salt Lake City, UT: The University of Utah Press, 2013.
Zuccolo, Luca, *La presse francophone ottomane et le discours patriotique ottoman*. Istanbul: Les Éditions ISIS, 2017.
Zürcher, Erik-Jan, *The Young Turk Legacy and Nation Building: From the Ottoman Empire to Atatürk's Turkey*. London: I.B. Tauris, 2010.
Zürcher, Erik-Jan (ed.), *Fighting for a Living: A Comparative Study of Military Labour 1500–2000*. Amsterdam: Amsterdam University Press, 2013.

2

Emulating Petrine Russia: Thick Mechanicism and the *Foundations of Government* in Istanbul after the Rebellion of 1730[1]

B. Harun Küçük
University of Pennsylvania

On 13 February 1732, İbrahim Müteferrika, now printer to Sultan Mahmud I (r. 1732-1754), concluded his *Foundations of Government in Various Social Orders* with the following words:

> Take, for example, the Russians. The infidels of this completely Christian nation used to be held in the lowest esteem, nay, they were positively despised. They were a group of men deserving the worst insults and the most unpleasant titles. They did not even have the power to make real enemies. Because of this, they had to retreat from those places civilized by other nations and live in a dark land, where they were content with making do with the meager resources at their disposal. Yet, a reasonable Tsar appeared twenty or thirty years ago, and brought, from many other countries, men who were competent in the military arts and in the other sciences. He listened to their advice and admonitions and thus, rapidly brought order to his army ... Not only that, he hired English and Dutch artisans who were excellent at shipbuilding and built for himself a magnificent navy – a navy that could withstand the storms and other rigors of the Baltic Sea, a navy the likes of which you have never seen. And, he brought engineers from neighboring countries to map each and every part of the Baltic Sea, and later, to learn about and then to conquer many parts of Iran and of Dagestan. He added Azov first to his title, then to his possessions.[2]

Hungarian-born Müteferrika's understanding of the Petrine project was not about Westernization, still the standard interpretation of his role in the Ottoman context, but about good governance. It was about order, about reason, about the mechanical arts, and about the organization of labour. Russia – not France, the Low Countries, or England – was his model for government reform. Here, I would like to focus on 'thick mechanicism', on how Müteferrika, as a person who spent the majority of his career as a printer and a geographer, might have come to appreciate mathematics and the mechanical arts as important tools for solving social problems.[3] Müteferrika harboured Cartesian sympathies and there is a discernible Cartesian vector in the three publications that came off his press in 1732.[4] However, the key element in understanding his predilection for Cartesian philosophy had little to do with philosophy as such – he never touched Cartesian metaphysics or epistemology – but with the practical implications of a mechanistic understanding of the world. What I also propose to do in this chapter is to situate myself in the material crises and expediencies in Istanbul in 1732.[5]

The contexts most relevant to Müteferrika's text were the collapse of the Safavid Empire and the rebellion of 1730, which raged for two years in Istanbul. His intended audience were in the highest ranks of government, especially Sultan Mahmud I (r. 1730–1754) and Grand Vizier Topal Osman Paşa (in office 1731–1732). The most visible results of his efforts were the establishment of a school for artillery corps and the appointment of Alexander Comte de Bonneval (1675–1747), who converted to become Humbaracı Ahmed Paşa, to lead the artillery corps.

Limits of Competitive Emulation

The key advantages that Müteferrika attributed to Russian reforms were employing competent men regardless of nationality and patronizing the sciences with special emphasis on the military arts. He is clear that these changes took place under the leadership of Peter the Great, a 'reasonable tsar'. The result was an orderly army and a formidable navy. The take-away lesson was, if Peter could make an empire from what Müteferrika so emphatically described as a miserable nation, imagine what the Ottomans could do by following the same route. The proposal to emulate Russia in matters of mechanical arts and warfare may seem obvious and unproblematic to a pragmatic modern reader, while others might take issue with the implications for the Ottoman populace. Following the Petrine strategy required considerable negotiation with the Empire's political stakeholders and would be possible only if it was coupled with a social agenda, what we today call enlightened absolutism.[6]

By enlightened absolutism, I mean the consolidation of the state as a regulatory entity in the lives of its subjects based on secular ideas and ideals. Historians of the Ottoman Empire are increasingly interested in speaking about enlightenment(s) in the Ottoman context.[7] I believe many of the ideas that we encounter in the writings of not only İbrahim Müteferrika, but also many other early eighteenth-century Ottoman authors, make the discussion unavoidable.[8] The issues that we generally find in the eighteenth-century Ottoman Empire range from the authority of empirical knowledge to separation of secular and religious learning, from cosmopolitanism to the discomfort with the rapprochement between capital and political power. We also find that Ottoman-Greek, Ottoman-Jewish and Ottoman-Armenian authors contemporaneously articulated the need to educate the masses in the early eighteenth century.[9] And, public education and public order mutually supported one another.

The rise of merchants and artisans to a position of political power, and the political recognition of the values and worldviews of these individuals, were important developments in the eighteenth century.¹⁰ However, trade by itself could not explain the convictions and values we find in the literature. Since the Empire's Islamic feudal system did not readily allow for converting cash capital into political or social capital, most traditionalist authors read the rise of the merchants and artisans as a corruption of the old ways. Some wealthy individuals paid their way to the top, while the less wealthy tried to join the ranks of the janissary corps, which, by the eighteenth century, counted many of the Empire's artisans among their ranks.¹¹ Also in tow were religious movements that catered to the sensibilities of the merchants, the chief among which was the famous Kadızadeli movement.¹² In other words, the corruption of the old feudal order was key to the formulation of a commercial capitalist order – bribery and tax-funnelling were important sources of wealth.¹³ As far as the creeping influence of commerce on religious communities and offices was concerned, the Greek Orthodox and the Jews were hardly different from their Muslim counterparts.¹⁴ Over the seventeenth century, many Ottoman political thinkers tried to address the 'corruption' problem from the standpoint of balance (*mizan*). The society lacked the balance between the men of the sword, the men of the pen, the peasants and the merchants.¹⁵ Following their Perso-Islamic predecessors, many opted for a four-part model of society. Some, like Katip Çelebi (1618–1657), even considered the merchants to be equal and opposite to the feudal men of the sword.¹⁶

The organicism of seventeenth-century Ottoman political thought ended in the eighteenth century – no one after Müteferrika invoked the idiom of balance when addressing social problems. In the eighteenth century, mechanistic understanding favouring order (*nizam*) as the foundation of a good society was on the rise. To the best of my knowledge, Müteferrika's *Foundations of Government* is where we first see order as an explicit ideal, something he calls *nizam-ı cedid*. It is quite likely that he had his fair share of *nizam* discussions at other venues as new rules of trade regulating the hierarchical relationships within a guild were part of the daily fare of eighteenth-century Ottoman administrators. Given the strained relationship between the merchants and the men of the sword for much of the seventeenth and eighteenth centuries, it is noteworthy that Müteferrika suggested to deploy an artisanal model – that of guild hierarchy – to give new direction to the military.¹⁷

Just as emulating Russia implicated the entire body politic, a military reform, the so-called *nizam-ı cedid* or new order, also required a host of social changes. Müteferrika argued for a clear chain of command not unlike Peter's Table of Ranks, with educated officers and drills, an army that amply used standardization and military science, an army comfortable with the use of firearms as opposed to swords – the whole bevy of disciplinary factors we associate with the so-called military revolution.¹⁸ However, even something as simple as drilling and rule-following required a host of social changes. These meant that soldiers should be able to follow orders as if they were machines. And, machine-like rule following was not an Ottoman military virtue in the eighteenth century, valour was.¹⁹ Yet, it was nothing but lack of social and military discipline that had caused a dead-end war and a two-year rebellion in the imperial capital.²⁰ Müteferrika made the difference clear: rationality was the missing element, and it was key to the transformation of the Ottoman military.²¹ And, it was the spiritual practice of comprehending orderliness in the world through mathematics and geography that was the pivotal change. It is, therefore, not 'Westernization' but a particular way of emulating Russia that gave rise to the first military academy in the Ottoman Empire, which was a school that placed its sole emphasis on mathematics and geography.[22]

The Rebellion of 1730

What made orderliness the most urgent requirement was, without doubt, the rebellion of 1730.[23] Müteferrika had begun *The Foundations of Government in Various Social Orders* by stressing his desire to prevent another event like the 1730 rebellion, which Mahmud I had quelled merely months before the book came out in 1732.[24] The two-year-long uprising had been far more disruptive than any in recent history. While the rebellion of 1703 had given rise to an interim Janissary government in Istanbul, the turmoil then had been short-lived.[25] The rebellion of 1730 cast a long shadow of disorder and led to recurrent riots and instability. This is why some sources reported the events between 1730 and 1732 as not one but two rebellions. Quelling the unrest thirty years previously was merely a matter of changing one set of elites with another set of elites. In 1730, there was not a single elite household that was powerful enough – or willing – to put an end to the atrocities.[26] The rebels appointed whoever they pleased, irrespective of rank or loyalty, to whatever appointment they wanted. A Greek butcher from Istanbul became the Prince of Moldavia, while a rebellious commander on his way back from Tabriz became the governor of Karaman.[27]

In 1737, five years after order had been restored, the events were greeted in England and the Netherlands – the only two nations Müteferrika recognized as democracies – as a warning to all monarchs:

> These Murmurs at last broke into a Rebellion: But, long before this, a general Discontent to the Government was observed as well among the Troops as the People and it was publicly said, that it was most plain to see a Rebellion come on. The Scarcity of the Provisions which had been felt a while; the raising the Price upon every Thing; the Misery of the whole Country, reduced for want of Commerce; the great number of Taxes, and the Vexations on account of the Troops sent to the Frontiers of Persia, where it was said they had already made a sort of Revolt, had caused a general disgust among the Populace. The Instruments for this Sedition were most miserable ones. Patrona Kalil of Albania, who sold old Cloths about the Streets, Muslah a Fruit-Seller and Emir Hali, not of much superior Rank with the former, were the Agents which Providence had singled out for producing this great Event, so singular it its circumstances that it deserves to be transmitted to Posterity, as a proper Example to Persons in high Trust, who, however distinguished, ought never to forget their mean Extraction, but endeavour to merit a general Approbation, as always surrounded with proper Persons to punish their evil Administration; like Patrona and his Companions, who however incapable they appeared for so great an Enterprize, did nevertheless oblige the Sultan Achmed III to renounce the Throne of his Ancestors.[28]

Unlike the 1703 rebellion, this one was defined by thoroughgoing insubordination. No man would take up arms against the rebels for almost a year. Ahmed III and Grand Vizier Damad İbrahim had managed to build such a strong web of family ties and patronage relationship between 1718 and 1730 that anyone who had any connection to the central government was deemed the cause of widespread disenfranchisement by the rebels.[29] Moreover, as eighteenth-century historian Şemdanizade related, Ahmed III's rule had been so disruptive to the 'Ottoman way' that the very fabric of society was now destroyed. Husband and wife, father and son, patron and client, commander and soldier no longer had the hierarchical relationship that once defined Ottoman society.[30] In this setting, one could hardly find anyone who would take up the cause of the Sultan as his own.

One salient feature of the Ahmedian regime was the consolidation of the elite. This was in no small measure due to the creation of a court where the rich and the powerful, even those who would never enter an administrative or a business transaction with one another under normal circumstances, came together. It was perhaps this type of solidarity at the very top that gave rise to its antithesis, namely, an equal but opposite solidarity at the bottom. In short, the rebellion of 1730 was a crisis of the regime.

The New Order in 1732

Since Mahmud I was finally able to re-establish order in 1732, it is worthwhile to ask whether the political rule under the new Sultan was a return to 'business as usual'. Was the Ottoman world in 1732 fundamentally similar to what it was in 1729, or in 1702 for that matter? According to Baki Tezcan, there was something qualitatively different about Mahmud's regime: the new administrators came from a civilian, as opposed to military background, and most of them also had little or no pedigree.[31]

One intellectual product of this revolution was *nizam-ı cedid* or new order, which Müteferrika articulated for the first time in his *Foundations of Government*. In the early eighteenth century, in this context, when the new order first emerged, it was a political project that took Russian progress, with good reason, as its role model. It was also a project that had its sights not on territorial expansion, but on maintaining order at home. Military reform always was part of the new order, but, in the early eighteenth century, the idea was to civilize the officers within a broad mechanistic re-conception of Ottoman rule – establishing a chain of command, using geometry to discipline the minds of officers, and so forth.

The new order was also a description of the political plurality of the world – in this sense, Cartesian philosophy worked as well for politics as it did for astronomy by establishing some meta-level parameters. There was no single regime or social structure that worked everywhere. In Europe alone, one could see at least three incompatible ways to govern flourish equally well: monarchies, aristocracies, as well as democracies. This variety, Müteferrika argued, arose from the quest for a just government: while sharia could prove to be the best route to justice for the Ottoman Empire, the European nations could build just orders by appealing to reason and self-interest.[32] And, one of the strongest monarchies, that of Peter the Great, did not really have much of a social structure except that which was dictated by the monarch himself.[33]

Both *nizam-ı cedid* (new order) and *nizamü'l-ümem* (various social orders) were subversions of the classic Ottoman concept of *nizam-ı alem* or world order. When Hasan Kafi el-Akhisari spoke of 'world order' in the sixteenth century and Katip Çelebi spoke of the Ottoman body politic in the seventeenth, they were projecting the idealized political configuration of the Ottoman Empire as a normative model for the entire world: a just empire under a strong Sultan and composed of four balanced parts of society (the peasants, the merchants, the clergy and the soldiers) was the best way to govern everywhere and at all times.[34] In 1732, the unflinching confidence in this order had been irretrievably lost.

Also included in Müteferrika's new order was a mechanistic understanding of the body politic.[35] He pithily summarized this view when he said, 'Earth is like a watermelon suspended in a vacuum and covered in ants, where all corners thereof are home to generations of mankind and filled with edifices of men.' According to Müteferrika, we were individuals, with no particular qualities and no connections with one another, who happened to be feeding on one corner of the world rather than another. States, in turn, were nothing more than their geographic extensions, not unlike Cartesian bodies. This was, of course, quite at odds with the organicist view – one that associated the parts of society with Galenic *humors* – of the Ottoman polity that had dominated Turkish political thought from the sixteenth century onwards. According to Müteferrika, there no longer were any natural divisions within society and no part of society was different from any other – a claim borne out by Ottoman realities.

Mechanical Arts and the Russian Precedent

So, if we were like ants on a watermelon and if there was no particular order that emerged from a polity, how could a monarch establish his authority? For Müteferrika, it was nothing other than orderliness (*intizam*) itself – an intellectual virtue similar to rule-following – that made societies orderly. This was only possible if people were trained into order. For example, another book that Müteferrika published the same year, Katip Çelebi's geographical masterpiece *Cihannüma*, espoused the virtues of geography as a gateway to the study of geometry, which, in turn, helped individuals to cultivate orderly minds and to follow rules.[36] This was a mechanistic view that sought to turn the state from an organism into an automaton.

Russia was the paradigmatic example of this kind of absolutist order that reproduced itself mechanically. By using the mechanical arts – geography, engineering and the printing press – the Russians had established a strong monarchy.[37] The Ottomans, alongside Sweden and Safavid Persia, were the first to get a (bitter) taste of Russia's recent progress. From 1722 onwards, Sultan Ahmed III was fighting against the crumbling Safavids on the one hand, and trying to prevent Russia from getting a piece of the old Safavid territories on the other. And, the mechanical arts were at the front lines of this conflict.

In 1722, when the Safavid Empire was collapsing under Afghan pressure, both the Ottomans and the Russians had their eyes set on Revan (Erivan) and their strategies for establishing order could not have been more different. The Ottomans sent a pretender to the Khanate of Shirvan, Davud, over to the region and declared him the *de facto* ruler of what is now Armenia and Azerbaijan. As part of his tactics, Davud looted most of the region, including the seaports in 1722. During the same year, Peter the Great put a ship on the Black Sea and distributed pamphlets printed on the ship that sailed from port to port. The pamphlet was penned in broken, or possibly Çağatay, Turkish and its alleged author was Dimitrie Cantemir. On this pamphlet, Peter the Great claimed that he was a friend of the Safavid Shah, that he would send an army to help establish order in the region, that he had heard about just how much harm the 'usurper' Davud had caused to the people of the region, and that he intended to punish the brigands and brigands only. Surprisingly enough, the flyer was addressed to the general population — each profession and all parts of society, regardless of rank — and promised them safety. This in itself defied any existing hierarchy.

Peter said that the army had express orders not to touch the civilian population, but only to punish those who had engaged in criminal looting. Cantemir addressed the last part of the pamphlet to the Ottoman merchants. While that rascal (*yaramaz*) Davud had killed and robbed the Russian merchants, Peter would not harm the Ottoman merchants at all and they could go on doing business as usual, provided they did not take up arms against Russia.[38] This pamphlet revealed a different approach to conquest: while the Ottomans dealt with leaders, Peter addressed the people. While the Ottomans used looting as a tool of conquest, Peter adopted a more diplomatic, legalistic and surgical approach – and produced consent by mechanical means in many senses of the word.

Pamphleteering also revealed the ambiguities involved in fighting for territory in the early eighteenth century, when land was no longer the primary source of income for many of the monarchies across Europe – it was, rather, cash revenue drawn from commerce. We know that, through the early 1720s, Peter attempted to get Greek merchants on his side against the Ottomans – an attempt that failed. And, one could say, that one of the main objectives of getting Revan was to control the important and lucrative Armenian silk trade between India and the Mediterranean. The former is borne out in the documentary record. And the latter is clear in Rudolph Matthee's work and in Armenian chronicles from the 1720s.[39]

Secondly, in the opening quotation, Müteferrika said that the Russians had managed to create a certain synergy between geography and conquest: geographical knowledge *led to* conquest. The Ottoman state deployed map-making as a political tool for the first time in 1729, just as the Ottomans were losing on the Eastern front. The first item that came off the Sultanic press was not, as is sometimes assumed, a Turkish–Arabic dictionary, but a printed map of Iran that celebrated the recent diplomatic victory of the Ottomans against the new Afghan rulers of Safavid Persia. Ottomans enjoyed at best a precarious and at worst a nominal control over western parts of Iran. And, the 1730 rebellion was a reaction to the Sultan's failure to hold onto these lands – the merchants and artisans had already been heavily and happily taxed for a war that barely happened and for a conquest that was only on papers signed by the not-yet-legitimate Afghan regime in Safavid lands. The map advertised a certain political vision where such propaganda would have an effect – those who were paying for the war.

A third element connecting Russia with the new order, which was also evident in Müteferrika's testimony I quoted above, was the orderly army – one that had a strict chain of command, one that the Ottomans had never seen on the Western front except in French ceremonial settings – that was also fluent in the mechanical arts. This was perhaps the only part of the original sense of the 'new order' that survived until the late eighteenth century. Of course, by 1774, when there was no rebellion at home and no shortage of well-trained officers and schools of engineering in the Empire, some of the original elements of the *nizam-ı cedid* disappeared into the background.[40] And, long gone was Müteferrika's press, which printed its last book in 1742.

It is noteworthy that Müteferrika, the veteran printer who had been more or less quiet as an author, revealing himself only in prefaces to other people's works, concluded his only monograph with an encomium to Russia. While he is best known as one of the *ur*-Westernizers in Ottoman historiography, the passage that I have tried to explain points to how a particular set of ideas clustered around machines and mechanicism appealed to this ex-Socinian convert to Islam. The 'West' was there as important background, but it was the Petrine precedent above anything else that proved how deploying certain social and physical technologies yielded immediate results and quickly translated into power. Peter, so to speak, was the object of competitive emulation in Istanbul.[41] This was not merely how Russia looked from Istanbul. Practical mechanicism was integral to the stated intentions of the Petrine project itself.[42] Finally, there were important connections between Ottoman and Russian reform programmes, connections that go back to the Petrine era and that predate the crux of *nizam-ı cedid* thinking in the 1780s and 1790s by more than half a century.

Appendix: İbrahim Müteferrika, *Usülü'l-Hikem fi Nizamü'l-Ümem* [Foundations of Government in Various Social Orders], Istanbul: Sultanic Press, 1732

Book 1

Part 1: On the Necessity of a Sovereign and of Magistrates[43] Whose Actions are Guided by Natural Philosophy[44]

Pillars of the science of cosmography and those who have pulled open the drapes of philosophy have discovered and confirmed with geometrical evidence, and the travellers returning from the East to the West have provided additional observational evidence to the effect that the Earth has the shape of a round ball that turns slowly and has a circumference of 1080 *konaks*[45] and that, in fact, the top and the bottom of this ball are not perfectly even. They have established that the Earth is like a watermelon suspended in a vacuum and covered in ants, where all corners thereof are home to generations of mankind and filled with edifices of men. In some books on morals and philosophy, it is written that the Omnipotent God has wished to show his omnipotence with this beautiful form.

God, in his infinite wisdom, has made man the target for the arrow of necessity and the mark for the shots trouble and suffering, where they lead a mortal life in malady and sadness. He has also impressed civility into the nature of each person, where they desire to get together. Every man needs another in some way and, no one is strong enough to subsist and perpetuate his kind without reciprocal effort and exchange. Thus, men seek to organize themselves in societies and look for ways to enter all manners of transactions with one another. However, since their institutions, constitutions, their communities of ritual and their sects were opposed to one another, some have subjugated others either by force or by a combination of wealth and power. The strongest and the mightiest have overwhelmed the weak, placed a yoke on the vanquished and seized their property. Not knowing the principles that were truly proper for them and following their passions, aspirations and love of strife, the strong became obstinate.

Rulers and judges who are knowledgeable and wise, who are learned and talented and who have mastered practical philosophy have commended justice and the rule of law. It was they who kept the hand of man short of the property of another, and separated the goods of men from public property; thus making each feel content with what he has. The finest philosophers called him who had articulated this law and originated such caution Gabriel, and theologians called him the Prophet of God. His commendations and prohibitions are truly like a soap that washes away filth. And it is thus that the world has found peace from the passions of the sons of Adam. And when that prophet, that preacher of the law, passed away, he required a just and judicious judge for the application of the laws of religion and the peaceful execution of the orders given to the Muslims, a judge who would sustain the precepts of the Prophet, conduct politics according to his laws and set a fair limit that separates the rights of man from the authority of government and who would attach himself to religion, as faith and government are twins.

Since human life is limited and men are destined for an afterlife, and since there is an inherent weakness in their mortal condition, human beings have sought a mutually agreeable way to get together according to their natural inclination to civility. Since men were unable to achieve this on their own, they had been sent prophets and messengers. And, after these prophets, men have tried to uphold the laws and guard the weak by appointing wise and just judges, and have organized around various societies and polities, following their natural inclination to follow these wise laws. Thus, each polity elected someone who would govern them and have submitted to his decisions in civil matters. As a consequence of the religious and rational principles that brought together such polities, organized by location and common interest. And, the countless judges they appointed became caliphs, kings, emperors, monarchs and caesars, each bearing a different title and different authorities.

Part 2: On the Opinions of Philosophers Regarding the Foundations of the Laws of Countries

It is an undisputed truth, clear in all histories and current affairs that there has always been a great variety of princes, sovereigns and judges of the Son of Adam. Because of sect and religion, because of laws and constitutions, there is always a conflict regarding their authority, and, as a consequence, regarding the ways of settling human affairs and, regarding styles and manners of government. Each state, polity and republic has been established on a different set of foundations.

And, on this matter, the majority of the philosophers follow the opinions and judgments of three celebrated ancient philosophers.

The party of Plato: He has said that the people need a rational and just king and, they must collectively submit to his opinions and judgments. This manner of government, in the philosophical language of the Greek lands is *monarchia*. Most existing rulers have come into existence in this manner. And, it is a prestigious thing to have become a dynasty through *monarchia*.

The party of Aristotle: He said that the authority of the sovereign should be in the hands of the noblemen of state. According to this opinion, the ministers decide on a leader, and each individually retains an equal portion of power and authority in order to prevent the aberration of the laws as a consequence of one among them becoming too great and independent. Such a government, in the language of the philosophers, is called an *aristocratia*. Cratia means government, and the phrase means the government of noblemen. Venice is governed according to these principles.

The party of Democritus: He has claimed that government belongs to the common people to the extent that they can dispel their own tyranny. This is the desirable manner of their organization: For example, each village selects one or two individuals they deem rational and able, vest it with authority and government and send the man to the place where the council convenes. The council elected in this manner from ten villages are thus governed by a council of ten and the total population agrees to follow their decisions. The following year, they once again elect ten men, who inspect the budgets of the past government. Any person who has betrayed such trust is punished. Such a government is called *democratia*. It means governing according to the principles set out by Democritus or government of the consenting.

Notes

1 I would like to thank Simon Werrett and Claire Sabel for their valuable comments on an earlier draft of the manuscript.
2 İbrahim Müteferrika, *Usülü'l-Hikem fi Nizamü'l-Ümem*. Istanbul: Sultanic Press, 1732, pp. 98a–b. For a detailed analysis and transliteration, see Adil Şen, *İbrahim Müteferrika ve Usülü'l-Hikem Fi Nizami'l-Ümem*. Ankara: Diyanet Vakfı, 1995. On an exceptionally well-documented biography of Müteferrika, see Orlin Sabev, *İbrahim Müteferrika ya da ilk Osmanlı matbaa serüveni, 1726–1746: yeniden değerlendirme*. Istanbul: Yeditepe, 2006. On the transformation of the Russian army and navy, see James Cracraft, *The Petrine Revolution in Russian Culture*. Cambridge, MA: Belknap Press, 2004, pp. 55–58. The adoption of new technologies and new military discipline took place side by side. Cracraft, ibid., p. 105, also notes that the very idea of military drills was of Dutch origin.
3 The idea that Cartesian philosophy was the mechanics' philosophy was already raised by Jim Bennett in his 'The Mechanics' Philosophy and the Mechanical Philosophy', *History of Science*, 24 (1986), pp. 1–28. For a further elaboration of the relationship between mechanicism and military drills, see Harald Kleinschmidt, 'Mechanismus und

Biologismus im Militärwesen des 17. Und 18. Jahrhunderts: Bewegungen – Ordnungen – Wahrnehmungen', *Aufklärung*, 11, no. 2 (1999), pp. 51–73 at p. 56.
4   For a detailed treatment of Müteferrika's Cartesianism, see B. Harun Küçük, 'İbrahim Müteferrika's Copernican Rhetoric', in *Translating Early Modern Science*, ed. Karl A.E. Enenkel, Sietske Fransen and Niall Hodson. Leiden: Brill, 2017, pp. 258–285. Russian Cartesianism, on the other hand, followed a completely different route. Christiaan Huygens's *Kosmotheoros* was the immediate source. Valentin Boss, *Newton and Russia: Early Influence, 1698-1796*. Cambridge, MA: Harvard University Press, 1972, p. 50. On the primacy of military power in Peter's reform projects, see Jonathan I. Israel, *Enlightenment Contested: Philosophy, Modernity, and the Emancipation of Man, 1670-1752*. Oxford: Oxford University, 2006, p. 297.
5   For the methodological background for mixing the natural sciences and the humanities in this chapter, see Carlo Ginzburg, 'Morelli, Freud and Sherlock Holmes: Cludes and Scientific Method', *History Workshop Journal*, 9, no. 1 (1980), pp. 5–36.
6   On enlightened absolutism, see Franco Venturi, *Utopia and Reform in the Enlightenment*. Cambridge: Cambridge University Press, 1971, pp. 18–46.
7   Most recently, see Molly Greene, *The Edinburgh History of the Greeks, 1453 to 1768*. Edinburgh: Edinburgh University Press, 2015, pp. 192–215. For a recent reopening of the question on the Muslim front, see Christoph Herzog, 'Aufklärung und Osmanisches Reich: Annäherung an ein historiographisches Problem', *Geschichte und Gesellschaft*, 23 (2010), pp. 291–321.
8   The classic articulation of the modernism of eighteenth-century Ottoman Empire is Niyazi Berkes, *Development of Secularism in Turkey*. Montreal: McGill University Press, 1964. Most recently, Sebastian Conrad has redefined the Enlightenment as 'globality' and has included the Ottoman Empire in the mix, albeit by reference to the *Tanzimat*. Sebastian Conrad, 'Enlightenment in Global History: A Historiographical Critique', *The American Historical Review*, 117, no. 4 (2012), pp. 999–1027.
9   The parallel rise of secular learning dates to the mid-seventeenth century in all cases. On the Ottoman Greeks, see especially the works of G.P. Henderson and Paschalis Kitromilides. On modern science in seventeenth- and eighteenth-century Greece, see Manolis Patiniotis, 'Eclecticism and Appropriation of the New Scientific Methods by the Greek-Speaking Scholars in the Ottoman Empire', in *Science between Europe and Asia: Historical Studies on the Transmission, Adoption and Adaptation of Knowledge*, ed. Feza Günergun and Dhruv Raina. New York: Springer, 2011, pp. 193–206; for a recent and very accessible overview, see Efthymios Nicolaidis, *Science and Eastern Orthodoxy: From the Greek Fathers to the Age of Globalization*. Baltimore, MD: Johns Hopkins University Press, 2011. While the Armenian engagement with secularism remains unexplored, at least in the Western languages. See, for example, Aṛak'el of Tabriz, *Book of History*, trans. George A Bournoutian. Costa Mesa, CA: Mazda Publishers, 2010, pp. 302–321. İbrahim Müteferrika's printing press clearly illustrates that public education was on the palace's agenda. The Jewish case is best exemplified by Abraham Asa's Ladino translations of the Bible and rabbinic literature. Matthias Lehmann, *Ladino Rabbinic Literature & Ottoman Sephardic Culture*. Bloomington, IN: Indiana University Press, 2005, pp. 34–38. The establishment of Greek academies in the Western half of the Empire is also noteworthy in this regard. Ariadna Camariano-Cioran, *Les Academies princières de Bucarest et de Jassy et leurs professeurs*. Thessaloniki : Institute for Balkan Studies, 1974.
10 For a discussion of artisans in Ottoman politics, see Suraiya Faroqhi, 'Guildsmen and Handicraft Producers', in *Cambridge History of Turkey*, vol. 3: *The Later Ottoman*

Empire, 1603–1839, ed. Suraiya Faroqhi. Cambridge: Cambridge University Press, 2006, pp. 336–355.
11. Christoph K. Neumann, 'Political and Diplomatic Developments', in *Cambridge History of Turkey*, vol. 3: *The Later Ottoman Empire, 1603–1839*, ed. Suraiya Faroqhi. Cambridge: Cambridge University Press, 2006, p. 55.
12. Marinos Sariyannis, 'The Kadızadeli Movement as a Social and Political Phenomenon: The Rise of a Mercantile Ethic?', *Political Initiatives from the Bottom-Up in the Ottoman Empire: Halcyon Days in Crete VII*, a symposium held in Rethymno, 9–11 January 2009, ed. A. Anastasopoulos. Rethymno: Crete University Press, 2012, pp. 263–289.
13. This stands in stark contrast to Max Weber's account and approaches what Werner Sombart has described in his *Moderne Kapitalismus: historish-systematische Darstellung des gesamteuropäischen Wirtschaftslebens von seinen Anfängen bis zur Gegenwart*. Commercial capitalism in the Ottoman Empire is a hotly debated topic. The work of Mehmet Genç remains one of the best sources for the development of capitalism in the Ottoman Empire. *Osmanlı İmparatorluğunda Devlet ve Ekonomi*. İstanbul: Ötüken, 2000. On foreign trade, see Edhem Eldem's authoritative account, *French Trade in Istanbul in the Eighteenth Century*. Leiden: Brill, 1999. For a remarkable study showing how trade and credit – and not industry – were key to wealth accumulation in the eighteenth-century Ottoman Empire, see Phokion Kotzageorgis and Demetrios Papastamatiou, 'Wealth Accumulation in an Urban Context: The Profile of the Muslim Rich of Thessaloniki in the Eighteenth Century on the Basis of Probate Inventories', *Turkish Historical Review*, 5 (2014), pp. 165–199.
14. Dimitris Stamatopoulos, 'The Poor Men of Christ and Their Leaders: Wealth and Poverty within the Christian Orthodox Clergy of the Ottoman Empire (Eighteenth–Nineteenth Century)', in *Wealth in the Ottoman and Post-Ottoman Balkans: A Socio-Economic History*, ed. Evguenia Davidova. London: I.B. Tauris, 2016, pp. 85–101; Jacob Barnai, *The Jews in Palestine in the Eighteenth Century: Under the Patronage of the Istanbul Committee of Officials for Palestine*, trans. Naomi Goldblum. Tuscaloosa, AL: University of Alabama Press, 1992, pp. 83–90.
15. Marinos Sariyannis and Ekin Tuşalp Atiyas, *Ottoman Political Thought up to the Tanzimat: A Concise History*. Rethymno: Foundation for Research and Technology-Hellas, 2015, pp. 80–97, 123–136.
16. Vasileios Syros, 'Galenic Medicine and Social Stability in Early Modern Florence and Islamic Empires', *Journal of Early Modern History*, 17 (2013), pp. 161–213.
17. Suraiya Faroqhi, *Travel and Artisans in the Ottoman Empire: Employment and Mobility in the Early Modern Era*. London: I.B. Tauris, 2014, p. 187.
18. Müteferrika, *Foundations of Government*, pp. 19–30; Simon Werrett, 'An Odd Sort of Exhibition: The St. Petersburg Academy of Sciences in Enlightened Russia', unpublished PhD dissertation, University of Cambridge, 2000, p. 32.
19. On the rifle as a symbol of the Sultan's civilizing efforts and the army's resistance to the technology, see Tim Stanley and Ünver Rüstem, 'Armed and Splendorous: The Jeweled Gun of Sultan Mahmud I', in *Pearls on a String – Artists, Patrons and Poets at the Great Islamic Courts* [exhibition catalogue], ed. Amy Landau. Baltimore, MD: Walters Art Museum, 2015, pp. 205–241.
20. Münir Aktepe, *Patrona İsyanı (1730)*. Istanbul: Edebiyat Fakültesi, 1958, pp. 135–168.
21. Müteferrika, *Foundations of Government*, p. 13v: 'For the want of ranks, soldiers are dispersed as individuals and stay in a state of confusion and haste. This foolishness gives ample opportunity to the enemy soldiers, who are rational and judicious, patient

and silent, each of whom stands in ranks organized according to the rules of geometry and march in perfect order.'

22 Fatih Yeşil, 'Bir Fransız maceraperestin savaş ve diplomasiye dair görüşleri: Humbaracı Ahmed Paşa'nın layihaları', *Hacettepe Üniversitesi Türkiyat Araştırmaları Dergisi*, 15 (2011), pp. 205–228.

23 For an excellent overview of historiography, see Selim Karahasanoğlu, *Politics and Governance in the Ottoman Empire: The Rebellion of 1730*. Cambridge, MA: Department of Near Eastern Languages and Civilizations, Harvard University, 2009.

24 Müteferrika, *Foundations of Government*, 2a–b.

25 For a brief discussion, see Cemal Kafadar, 'Janissaries and Other Riffraff of Ottoman Istanbul: Rebels without a Cause?', in *Identity and Identity Formation in the Ottoman Empire: A Volume of Essays in Honor of Norman Itzkowitz*. Madison, WI: University of Wisconsin, Center for Turkish Studies, 2007, pp. 113–134.

26 Aktepe, *Patrona*, pp. 138, 146.

27 Faik Reşit Unat, *1730 Patrona İhtilali Hakkında Bir Eser: Abdi Tarihi*. Ankara: TTK, 1943, p. 52.

28 *A particular account of the two rebellions, which happen'd at Constantinople, in the years MDCCXXX, and MDCCXXXI, at the deposition of Achmet the Third, and the elevation of Mahomet the Fifth: composed from the original memorials drawn up in Constantinople: . . . publish'd in French . . . translated into English*. London: G. Smith, 1737, p. 6. On the genealogy of this book, see Selim Karahasanoğlu, 'Osmanlı İmparatorluğu'nda 1730 İsyanı Üzerine Yeni Bir Eser: Vâkıa Takrîri Bin Yüz Kırk Üç'de Terkîb Olunmuşdur', *Tarih Araştırmaları*, 28/46 (2009), pp. 179–187.

29 Tülay Artan, '18. Yüzyıl Başlarında Yönetici Elitin Saltanatın Meşruiyet Arayışına Katılımı', *Toplum ve Bilim*, 83 (1999/2000), pp. 292–322.

30 Şemdanizade Fındıklılı Süleyman, *Şem'dânî-zâde Fındıklılı Süleyman Efendi Târihi Mür'i't- Tevârih*, ed. Münir Aktepe, 3 vols. Istanbul: Edebiyat Fakültesi Matbaası, 1976–1981, vol. 1, p. 5.

31 Baki Tezcan, *The Second Ottoman Empire: Political and Social Transformation in the Early Modern World*. Cambridge: Cambridge University Press, 2010, pp. 195–196.

32 See Appendix.

33 Werrett, p. 27.

34 Gottfried Hagen, 'World Order and Legitimacy', in *Legitimizing the Order: The Ottoman Rhetoric of State Power*, ed. Hakan Karateke and Maurus Reinkowski. Leiden: Brill, 2005, pp. 55–84.

35 See Appendix.

36 İbrahim Müteferrika, 'Printer's Preface', in Katip Çelebi, *Cihannüma*. Istanbul: Sultanic Press, 1732, p. 17. On mathematics as spiritual exercise, see Matthew Jones, *The Good Life in the Scientific Revolution: Descartes, Pascal, Leibniz, and the Cultivation of Virtue*. Chicago, IL: University of Chicago Press, 2006, p. 17.

37 İbrahim Müteferrika, *Usülü'l-Hikem fi Nizamü'l-Ümem*. Istanbul: Sultanic Press, 1732, p. 97.

38 *Manifestul lui Petru cel Mare*, *Integrala Manuscriselor Cantemir*, XXV, ed. Constantin Barbu. Bucharest: Revers, 2012.

39 Rudolph Matthee, *Politics of Trade in Safavid Iran: Silk for Silver, 1600–1730*. Cambridge: Cambridge University Press, 1999. For a contemporary account of the Armenian silk trade, see Voltaire, *The History of Peter the Great, Emperor of Russia*, trans. Tobias George Smolett. Leavitt: Trow, 1818, pp. 340–341. For the active involvement of Armenian merchants and craftsmen on both the Safavid and the

Ottoman sides, see Abraham of Crete, *The History of the Wars: 1721–1738*, trans. George Bournoutian. Costa Mesa, CA: Mazda Publishers, 1999, pp. 22, 42, 43. On Armenian loyalty to the Ottomans, see especially the case of Petros Abro of Smyrna, *Armenians and Russia, 1626–1796: A Documentary Record*, trans. George Bournoutian. Costa Mesa, CA: Mazda Publishers, 2001, pp. 86, 93, 110. On the rise of the Armenians in eighteenth-century Ottoman society, see Marlene Kurz, *Ways to Heaven, Gates to Hell: Fazlizade Ali's Struggle with the Diversity of Ottoman Islam*. Bonn: EB-Verlag, 2011. Idris Bostan, 'Rusya'nın Karadeniz'de Ticarete Başlaması ve Osmanlı İmparatorluğu (1700–1787)', *Belleten*, CLIX (1995), pp. 353–394.
40 For a good summary treatment of *nizam-ı cedid*, see Kahraman Şakul, 'Nizam-ı Cedid Düşüncesinde Batılılaşma ve İslami Modernleşme', *Divan İlmi Araştırmalar*, 19 (2005), pp. 117–150.
41 While there had been some debate about whether Müteferrika was Calvinist or Socinian, Sabev clearly shows that there is an overwhelming amount of evidence that suggests he was indeed a Socinian prisoner of war whom no European monarch would ransom. Orlin Sabev, 'Portrait and Self-Portrait: İbrahim Müteferrika's Mind Games', *Osmanlı Araştırmaları*, XLIV (2014), pp. 99–121. On competitive emulation in early modern Europe, see Sophus A. Reinert, *Translating Empire Emulation and the Origins of Political Economy*. Cambridge, MA: Harvard University Press, 2011.
42 Werrett, pp. 20–22.
43 Both wisdom and rulership derive from the same root in Arabic. It is not clear whether he is referring to judges or administrators.
44 Ḥikmet-i ṭabiʿiyye: This phrase, which I often take to mean natural philosophy or wisdom pertaining to nature, has been translated as 'loi naturelle' by Jean Thomas de Trattern in 1767. The ambiguity is inherent in the phrase and it is possible to variously translate it as natural philosophy, wisdom pertaining to nature, natural wisdom, government according to nature or natural government.
45 The distance that can be traversed in a day.

Bibliography

A particular account of the two rebellions, which happen'd at Constantinople, in the years MDCCXXX, and MDCCXXXI, at the deposition of Achmet the Third, and the elevation of Mahomet the Fifth: composed from the original memorials drawn up in Constantinople: ... publish'd in French ... translated into English. London: G. Smith, 1737.

Abraham of Crete, *The History of the Wars: 1721–1738*, trans. George Bournoutian. Costa Mesa, CA: Mazda Publishers, 1999.

Aktepe, Münir, *Patrona İsyanı (1730)*. Istanbul: Edebiyat Fakültesi, 1958.

Ařak'el of Tabriz, *Book of History*, trans. George A Bournoutian. Costa Mesa, CA: Mazda Publishers, 2010.

Artan, Tülay, '18. Yüzyıl Başlarında Yönetici Elitin Saltanatın Meşruiyet Arayışına Katılımı', *Toplum ve Bilim*, 83 (1999/2000), pp. 292–322.

Barnai, Jacob, *The Jews in Palestine in the Eighteenth Century: Under the Patronage of the Istanbul Committee of Officials for Palestine*, trans. Naomi Goldblum. Tuscaloosa, AL: University of Alabama Press, 1992.

Bennett, Jim, 'The Mechanics' Philosophy and the Mechanical Philosophy', *History of Science*, 24 (1986), pp. 1–28.

Berkes, Niyazi, *Development of Secularism in Turkey*. Montreal: McGill University Press, 1964.
Boss, Valentin, *Newton and Russia: Early Influence, 1698–1796*. Cambridge, MA: Harvard University Press, 1972.
Bostan, İdris, *Osmanlı Bahriye Teşkilatı: XVII. Yüzyılda Tersane-i Amire*. Ankara: TTK, 1992.
Bostan, İdris, 'Rusya'nın Karadeniz'de Ticarete Başlaması ve Osmanlı İmparatorluğu (1700–1787)', *Belleten,* CLIX (1995), pp. 353–394.
Camariano-Cioran, Ariadna, *Les Academies princières de Bucarest et de Jassy et leurs professeurs*. Thessaloniki: Institute for Balkan Studies, 1974.
Conrad, Sebastian, 'Enlightenment in Global History: A Historiographical Critique', *The American Historical Review*, 117, no. 4 (2012), pp. 999–1027.
Cracraft, James, *The Petrine Revolution in Russian Culture*. Cambridge, MA: Belknap Press, 2004.
Eldem, Edhem, *French Trade in Istanbul in the Eighteenth Century*. Leiden: Brill, 1999.
Eldem, Edhem, *Travel and Artisans in the Ottoman Empire: Employment and Mobility in the Early Modern Era*. London: I.B. Tauris, 2014.
Faroqhi, Suraiya, 'Guildsmen and Handicraft Producers', in *Cambridge History of Turkey*, vol. 3: *The Later Ottoman Empire, 1603–1839*, ed. Suraiya Faroqhi. Cambridge: Cambridge University Press, 2006, pp. 336–355.
Faroqhi, Suraiya, *Travel and Artisans in the Ottoman Empire: Employment and Mobility in the Early Modern Era*. London: I.B. Tauris, 2014.
Genç, Mehmet, *Osmanlı İmparatorluğunda Devlet ve Ekonomi*. İstanbul: Ötüken, 2000.
Ginzburg, Carlo, 'Morelli, Freud and Sherlock Holmes: Cludes and Scientific Method', *History Workshop Journal*, 9, no. 1 (1980), pp. 5–36.
Greene, Molly, *The Edinburgh History of the Greeks, 1453 to 1768*. Edinburgh: Edinburgh University Press, 2015.
Hagen, Gottfried, 'World Order and Legitimacy', in *Legitimizing the Order: The Ottoman Rhetoric of State Power*, ed. Hakan Karateke and Maurus Reinkowski. Leiden: Brill, 2005.
Herzog, Christoph, 'Aufklärung und Osmanisches Reich: Annäherung an ein historiographisches Problem', *Geschichte und Gesellschaft*, 23 (2010), 291–321.
Israel, Jonathan I., *Enlightenment Contested: Philosophy, Modernity, and the Emancipation of Man, 1670–1752*. Oxford: Oxford University, 2006.
Jones, Matthew, *The Good Life in the Scientific Revolution: Descartes, Pascal, Leibniz, and the Cultivation of Virtue*. Chicago, IL: University of Chicago Press, 2006.
Kafadar, Cemal, 'Janissaries and Other Riffraff of Ottoman Istanbul: Rebels without a Cause?', in *Identity and Identity Formation in the Ottoman Empire: A Volume of Essays in Honor of Norman Itzkowitz*. Madison, WI: University of Wisconsin, Center for Turkish Studies, 2007, pp. 113–134.
Karahasanoğlu, Selim, 'Osmanlı İmparatorluğu'nda 1730 İsyanı Üzerine Yeni Bir Eser: Vakıa Takrîri Bin Yüz Kırk Üç'de Terkib Olunmuşdur', *Tarih Araştırmaları*, 28/46 (2009), pp. 179–187.
Karahasanoğlu, Selim, *Politics and Governance in the Ottoman Empire: The Rebellion of 1730*. Cambridge, MA: Department of Near Eastern Languages and Civilizations, Harvard University, 2009.
Kleinschmidt, Harald, 'Mechanismus und Biologismus im Militärwesen des 17. Und 18. Jahrhunderts: Bewegungen – Ordnungen – Wahrnehmungen', *Aufklärung*, 11, no. 2 (1999), pp. 51–73.

Kotzageorgis, Phokion and Demetrios Papastamatiou, 'Wealth Accumulation in an Urban Context: The Profile of the Muslim Rich of Thessaloniki in the Eighteenth Century on the Basis of Probate Inventories', *Turkish Historical Review*, 5 (2014), pp. 165-199.

Küçük, B. Harun, 'Ibrahim Müteferrika's Copernican Rhetoric', in *Translating Early Modern Science*, ed. Karl A.E. Enenkel, Sietske Fransen and Niall Hodson. Leiden: Brill, 2017, pp. 258-285.

Kurz, Marlene, *Ways to Heaven, Gates to Hell: Fazlizade Ali's Struggle with the Diversity of Ottoman Islam*. Bonn: EB-Verlag, 2011.

Lehmann, Matthias, *Ladino Rabbinic Literature & Ottoman Sephardic Culture*. Bloomington, IN: Indiana University Press, 2005.

Manifestul lui Petru cel Mare, *Integrala Manuscriselor Cantemir*, XXV, ed. Constantin Barbu. Bucharest: Revers, 2012.

Matthee, Rudolph, *Politics of Trade in Safavid Iran: Silk for Silver, 1600-1730*. Cambridge: Cambridge University Press, 1999.

Mehmed b. Mustafa el-Vani, *Terceme-i Sıhahü'l-Cevheri*. Istanbul: Sultanic Press, 1729.

Müteferrika, İbrahim, 'Printer's Preface', in Katip Çelebi, *Cihannüma*. Istanbul: Sultanic Press, 1732.

Müteferrika, İbrahim, *Usülü'l-Hikem fi Nizamü'l-Ümem*. Istanbul: Sultanic Press, 1732.

Neumann, Christoph K., 'Political and Diplomatic Developments', in *Cambridge History of Turkey*, vol. 3: *The Later Ottoman Empire, 1603-1839*, ed. Suraiya Faroqhi. Cambridge: Cambridge University Press, 2006.

Nicolaidis, Efthymios, *Science and Eastern Orthodoxy: From the Greek Fathers to the Age of Globalization*. Baltimore, MD: Johns Hopkins University Press, 2011.

Patiniotis, Manolis, 'Eclecticism and Appropriation of the New Scientific Methods by the Greek-Speaking Scholars in the Ottoman Empire', in *Science between Europe and Asia: Historical Studies on the Transmission, Adoption and Adaptation of Knowledge*, ed. Feza Günergun and Dhruv Raina. New York: Springer, 2011, pp. 193-206.

Petros Abro of Smyrna, *Armenians and Russia, 1626-1796: A Documentary Record*, trans. George Bournoutian. Costa Mesa, CA: Mazda Publishers, 2001.

Reinert, Spohus A., *Translating Empire Emulation and the Origins of Political Economy*. Cambridge, MA: Harvard University Press, 2011.

Sabev, Orlin, *İbrahim Müteferrika ya da ilk Osmanlı matbaa serüveni, 1726-1746: yeniden değerlendirme*. Istanbul: Yeditepe, 2006.

Sabev, Orlin, 'Portrait and Self-Portrait: İbrahim Müteferrika's Mind Games', *Osmanlı Araştırmaları*, XLIV (2014), pp. 99-121.

Şakul, Kahraman, 'Nizam-ı Cedid Düşüncesinde Batılılaşma ve İslami Modernleşme', *Divan İlmi Araştırmalar*, 19 (2005), pp. 117-150.

Sariyannis, Marinos, 'The Kadızadeli Movement as a Social and Political Phenomenon: The Rise of a Mercantile Ethic?', in *Political Initiatives from the Bottom-Up in the Ottoman Empire: Halcyon Days in Crete VII*, a symposium held in Rethymno, 9-11 January 2009, ed. A. Anastasopoulos. Rethymno: Crete University Press, 2012, pp. 263-289.

Sariyannis, Marinos and Ekin Tuşalp Atiyas, *Ottoman Political Thought up to the Tanzimat: A Concise History*. Rethymno: Foundation for Research and Technology-Hellas, 2015.

Şemdanizade Fındıklılı Süleyman, *Şem'dânî-zâde Fındıklılı Süleyman Efendi Târihi Mür'î't- Tevârih*, ed. Münir Aktepe, 3 vols. Istanbul: Edebiyat Fakültesi Matbaası, 1976-1981.

Şen, Adil, *İbrahim Müteferrika ve Usülü'l-Hikem Fi Nizami'l-Ümem*. Ankara: Diyanet Vakfı, 1995.

Stamatopoulos, Dimitris, 'The Poor Men of Christ and Their Leaders: Wealth and Poverty within the Christian Orthodox Clergy of the Ottoman Empire (Eighteenth–Nineteenth Century)', in *Wealth in the Ottoman and Post-Ottoman Balkans: A Socio-Economic History*, ed. Evguenia Davidova. London: I.B. Tauris, 2016, pp. 85–101.

Stanley, Tim and Ünver Rüstem, 'Armed and Splendorous: The Jeweled Gun of Sultan Mahmud I', in *Pearls on a String – Artists, Patrons and Poets at the Great Islamic Courts* [exhibition catalogue], ed. Amy Landau. Baltimore, MD: Walters Art Museum, 2015, pp. 205–241.

Syros, Vasileios, 'Galenic Medicine and Social Stability in Early Modern Florence and Islamic Empires', *Journal of Early Modern History*, 17 (2013), 161–213.

Tezcan, Baki, *The Second Ottoman Empire: Political and Social Transformation in the Early Modern World*. Cambridge: Cambridge University Press, 2010.

Unat, Faik Reşit, *1730 Patrona İhtilali Hakkında Bir Eser: Abdi Tarihi*. Ankara: TTK, 1943.

Venturi, Franco, *Utopia and Reform in the Enlightenment*. Cambridge: Cambridge University Press, 1971.

Voltaire, *The History of Peter the Great, Emperor of Russia*, trans. Tobias George Smoletts. Leavitt: Trow, 1818.

Werrett, Simon, 'An Odd Sort of Exhibition: The St. Petersburg Academy of Sciences in Enlightened Russia', unpublished PhD dissertation, University of Cambridge, 2000.

Yeşil, Fatih, 'Bir Fransız maceraperestin savaş ve diplomasiye dair görüşleri: Humbaracı Ahmed Paşa'nın layihaları', *Hacettepe Üniversitesi Türkiyat Araştırmaları Dergisi*, 15 (2011), pp. 205–228.

3

New Horizons of Political Possibility: Greek[1] Political Imagination after the Russo-Ottoman War of 1768–1774

Vasilis Molos
NYU Abu Dhabi

[...] and I tell you, dear heart! it will be quite a fire. Ha! may it reach to the tower's top and melt its vane and rage and swirl about it until it bursts and falls! – and you must not take offense at our allies. I know that the good Russians would like to use us as firearms. But let that pass! when our strong Spartans have once learned in the field who they are and of what they are capable, when once we have conquered the Peloponnesus with them, then we will laugh in the North Pole's face and make a life of our own.

Alabanda to Hyperion[2]

Introduction

In 1797, Friedrich Hölderlin published the first part of an epistolary novel titled *Hyperion oder Der Eremit in Griechenland* (Hyperion or The Hermit in Greece). Set around the time of the failed Orlov Revolt, which took place in the Ottoman Balkans in early 1770, the work is comprised of letters between the novel's namesake, his friends and his love, Diotima. In the passage above, a youthful Hyperion recounts the cries and promises of freedom made by his dear friend, Alabanda, in the lead-up to the revolt. Hyperion, too, expresses his enthusiasm within the same letter to Diotima, sharing his delight in participating in the revolutionary struggle to resurrect Greece from its deplorable state.[3]

Here and elsewhere, authors animated by Enlightenment principles and revolutionary sentiments began reshaping the historical memory of the Orlov Revolt. Informed by the shifting sensibilities of their times, commentators cast the episode as a heroic and tragic effort by the Greeks to reclaim their national sovereignty and restore their ancient grandeur. Indeed, from the 1790s, Philhellenic Europeans like Friedrich Hölderlin, Richard Polwhele, Sydney Owenson, Lord Byron, Thomas Hope and Percy Shelley began reshaping the memory of this event.[4] Following the successes of the

American and French Revolutions, the Orlov Revolt begins to be represented as a failed revolution for national liberation, and is wedded to the struggle of the European Philhellenes to liberate the oppressed Greeks.

Greek contemporaries, who shared this vision of a pending revolutionary struggle, were quick to incorporate the Philhellenic interpretation of 1770 into their collective memory. Most notable among them was Emmanuel Xanthos – one of the three creators of the Φιλική Εταιρεία – who attributed the founding of the revolutionary organization, in part, to the Orlov Revolt.[5] The view that the uprisings were a first attempt at a war of national liberation is perpetuated after the War of Independence as well. Deploying the language of German romanticism, nineteenth- and twentieth-century historians further coloured the collective memory of the Orlov Revolt by portraying the rebels as members of a primordial nation.[6] Specifically, six studies published between 1869 and 1967 discussed the episode in some detail.[7] All six offered a narrow portrayal of the event, depicting it as a precursor to the successful war for national independence in 1821, and largely detaching it from the broader crisis of imperial sovereignty that began in the 1760s. Reshaping the memory of the Orlov Revolt was part of a larger effort to narrate the history of the Greeks over the early modern period as a redemption story; as an account of a nation's occupation in 1453 and the struggle for liberation that followed.[8]

Recently, historians have challenged the view that the events of 1770 were part of a war for national liberation, suggesting that this period is in dire need of re-examination.[9] Nevertheless, within modern Greek studies, the dominant narration of the age of revolutions remains a teleological account of how a 'stateless nation' evolved into a 'nation-state'. While this account emphasizes the novelty of the nation-state as a political form, it tends to miss the political possibilities and imaginaries opened up within Greek culture during the 'Orlov moment' – the period between 1762 and 1774, when the Russian Empire called upon their co-religionists in the Balkans to rise up, assert their right to self-rule, and challenge the Ottoman system of sovereignty. This chapter broadly considers how Greek political imagination was influenced by the Orlov moment. It describes how the conclusion of the Russo-Ottoman War of 1768–1774 was greeted by shock and disappointment by Greek commentators who believed that the Russian victory would lead to the supplanting of Ottoman rule in the Balkans and/or parts of the Aegean. Outlining the landscape of Greek political thought at this time, it contrasts the liberal views of Iosipos Moisiodax, who developed a model of popular sovereignty that empowered subjects to enforce limits on imperial authority, with the communitarian views of Dimitrios Katartzis, who promoted a novel image of the Romioi as a distinctive and self-determining political society. Through the examination of these two prominent intellectual voices of the second generation of the Greek Enlightenment,[10] the chapter reveals the range of new political visions circulating in the Greek-speaking world from the Treaty of Küçük Kaynarca (1774) to the outbreak of the French Revolution. In so doing, it is suggested that these figures, heretofore portrayed as unsophisticated voices in an intellectual backwater, were the first Greek contributors to a broader conversation over sovereignty during the transformative age of revolutions.[11]

The Shock of 1774: The Treaty of Küçük Kaynarca and Greek Political Imagination

In late June 1774, the Russian army soundly defeated their Ottoman counterparts at the Battle of Kozludzha in modern Bulgaria. Within a month, the Russo-Ottoman conflict was decided in Catherine II's favour, and the Treaty of Küçük Kaynarca was signed. While a decisive diplomatic victory for the Russian Empire, the treaty failed to improve the political status of the Romioi. Article III affirmed the sovereignty of the Tartar peoples; however, no such affirmation of the 'independent sovereignty' of the Greek peoples was included. Quite the contrary, Article XVII restored the semi-autonomous principality established in the Aegean in 1770 to its status as an Ottoman dependency. Under section 5 of the latter article, the Russian navy also agreed to leave the Mediterranean within three months.[12] With a few pen strokes, the great hope of a '(restoration) of the Greek empire', proclaimed by Edmund Burke in the *Annual Register* years earlier, had turned to ashes.[13]

The Russian Empire had emerged as the great victor of Catherine's first war with the Ottomans, having greatly expanded its influence in the Crimea and the Danubian Principalities. From the Greek perspective, the political status quo remained largely unaltered by the peace of 1774. For observers like Eugenios Voulgaris, all that was left was to congratulate his patron, Catherine, for her victory, and so the famed scholar took to this task in his 'Ἐπί τῇ Πανενδόξῳ Εἰρήνῃ' (On the All-Glorious Peace).[14] Laden with effusive praise for the Russian Empress' triumph, the epistle neglects to reiterate any of the arguments for establishing a Greek 'buffer state' that he proffered in his appeals from the 1771–1772 period.[15] The war had concluded, the possibility for a Greek liberation had come and gone, and the Orlov Revolt had failed to effect any meaningful change to the political status of the Romioi. Voulgaris acknowledged these realities, and turned the page on this unfortunate chapter in the history of the Greeks.

Far from wishing to rejoice in the Russians' great victory, Kaisarios Dapontes lamented the failure of his people to liberate themselves:

> the empire of the Romans does not want to be resurrected, as prophesied in the oracles, and as the poor Romioi gladly believed; [...] since the oracles were not proven true in the years that they predicted the (empire) would be resurrected, the empire does not want to be resurrected; the time appointed by the oracles for the resurrection was three hundred and twenty years after the fall.[16]

Like many Greeks, the great poet's political outlook had been informed by a tradition of prophetic literature and folk prophecies, which portrayed the fall of the Byzantine Empire as divinely ordained, and anticipated a forthcoming 'resurrection of the race', 320 years after the fall of Constantinople.[17] As a young man, Dapontes had internalized these ideas to such an extent that visions of the great city's liberation began to creep into his dreams.[18] Over the years, though, he began to favour a particular strand of millenarianism. Proponents of what has come to be known as the 'Russian expectation' anticipated that a race of northerners – specifically a 'blond race' – would play a role in bringing about the divinely ordained liberation of the Romioi.[19] By the time of the

Orlov Revolt, Dapontes was heavily invested in the Russian cause – so much so that he dedicated his *Χρηστοήθεια* (Goodness of Heart) to Panos Maroutsis, a key cog in the conspiracy to foment revolution in the Balkans.

Following the peace of 1774, the poet's disappointment was captured in an excerpt from his *Γεωγραφική Ιστορία* (Geographic History), titled 'Έκστηθι φρίττων, ουρανέ' (Stand aside and Sudder, heavens). Unpublished during his lifetime, this short reflection on the period was highly critical of the Russians, exclaiming, 'It is for the Russians to lament now for the wretched Romioi, their brothers, who remain slaves and again ruined!' The work also pointed blame inward, within Greek culture, singling out 'false prophets' in particular. More broadly, Dapontes attributed responsibility for this wretchedness to all the members of his race. Dapontes' poem suggested that his culture might benefit from a period of critical self-reflection, claiming that the Romioi should mourn their 'vileness' because it was principally responsible for them losing their 'illustriousness'.[20]

The dissatisfaction felt with the outcome of the Russians' intervention in the Mediterranean was also documented by the renowned merchant, Ioannis Prigkos, in a note written on 3 September 1774. Free of the constraints imposed on scholars like Voulgaris and Dapontes, who often self-censored so as not to offend their respective patrons, Prigkos was more at liberty to record his impressions of the settlement. The merchant was quick to contrast the grand promises made by Catherine and her emissaries in the lead-up to the Orlov Revolt with the failure of the diplomatic settlement to change the political status of the Romioi:

> Encouraged by the Russians, the Romioi had fought to be free and did whatever they could, aiding the Russians by any means, however their freedom did not arrive. Perhaps they failed because they placed their hopes for freedom in the Russians rather than God. Russia concerns herself with her own interests. She provided the Romioi with a free trip, in order to bring them to her parts, to settle people in her wilderness. This is the freedom that it suits her interests to provide, one that leads the Romioi to leave their vineyards, fields and homes, to go and make others, to leave their fine climate to live in a cold land. Russia should have designated part of the Dodecanese as a refuge for the Romioi. However, she only concerned herself with her own interests.[21]

Prigkos was unambiguous in portraying the Russians as selfishly pursuing their own interests, and of misleading their co-religionists with false promises of freedom. His words capture the sense of disenchantment with the Russians that was felt acutely by many in the aftermath of the war, but which was conspicuously absent from the writings of more prominent intellectual figures of this period.

His suggestion that the failure of the revolt may have stemmed from the Romioi placing their faith in their co-religionists, rather than in God, is perhaps the most interesting comment in this passage, as it is unclear if Prigkos was being facetious here. There is ample proof to suggest that he was being genuine, as many of his writings document his faith that God would help to liberate the Romioi;[22] however, a shift in his thinking was evident after the Treaty of Küçük Kaynarca. While remaining firm in his belief in Divine Providence, he began to question the nature of God's intervention in the world. Writing from London on 12 October 1774, the merchant questioned why the Russians were blessed with all of these victories, but were not endowed with the vision to keep a small piece of land or an island like Paros[23] for the Greeks. Prigkos seemed to be especially frustrated that the diplomatic settlement did not establish a space over which the Romioi could exercise their autonomy, noting that the Russians could have easily established a princely state or a toparchy for their Orthodox brethren.[24] The document is highly critical of the Russians, suggesting that they should have been more generous to the Romioi, who sacrificed so much for this victory. Prigkos portrayed the Russians as ungrateful for the victory that God provided them, and then implored the refugees who were resettled in the Crimea to leave and join him in Amsterdam.[25]

The peace of 1774 seemed to provoke a period of philosophical introspection in the merchant, who suddenly seemed troubled by the problem of evil. He began to question why an omniscient, omnipotent and omnibenevolent God would not save the Romioi from the Ottomans – a people that Prigkos portrayed as 'the biggest sinners in the world' and described as being animated by genocidal desires.[26] Prigkos questioned Divine Providence explicitly, writing that God could easily have enlightened the Russians to provide the Romioi with the free island that they had hoped to obtain in exchange for their contributions to the war effort.[27] By the latter stages of the war, he firmly believed that a national liberation would only be achieved by God's hand; so, when the political status of the Romioi remained unaltered after the diplomatic settlement, Prigkos wondered why it was that his people were to remain enslaved. Specifically, he began to question what horrible sins the Romioi had committed in order to merit such a fate.

Prigkos was not alone in raising these questions in the aftermath of the war. In fact, this questioning seemed to mark a watershed moment within Greek culture. The narrative to which he and most Romioi had subscribed, which had been promulgated by Gemistos Plethon, Theoklitos Polyeidis, Voulgaris and countless others, began to be openly questioned. It was no longer obvious that the Romioi were paying for the sins of the Byzantines, as it had been for most Greeks at the dawn of the Orlov Revolt. Three hundred and twenty-two years[28] of suffering seemed like adequate penance for Prigkos and, like Dapontes, he began to look more closely at his people, wondering why they had been left in this deplorable condition.[29]

Yet, the Romioi had not been left in the same condition that they had been prior to the outbreak of the Orlov Revolt. The world had changed, and Greek commentators had taken notice. The almighty Porte now appeared frail and decaying, as multiple sovereignties appeared throughout the empire.[30] Moreover, the 'Eastern Question' became an open topic of conversation among European powers with competing visions of how to handle the Ottoman Empire's 'imminent' dissolution. At the same time, the failure of the Russian intervention in the Mediterranean challenged the veracity of the prophecies that foresaw the resurrection of the race, while also leading many to abandon their faith in the Russian expectation.[31] In the aftermath of the settlement of 1774, Greek authors set about trying to determine how the Romioi fit into this new world, if not as subjects of the Ottomans or clients of the Russians.

Unsurprisingly, Greek intellectual culture witnessed several shifts over the last quarter of the eighteenth century. The Quarrel of the Ancients and Moderns accelerated, as proponents of Enlightenment views became increasingly vocal in their support of modern philosophy.[32] Within the field of historiography – where, up to mid-century, all but one work had taken the Christian past as its subject of analysis – the Byzantine heritage was increasingly supplanted in favour of discussions of the Hellenic past.[33] At the same time, the secularization of Greek literary production increased its pace over the last quarter of the century.[34]

1774 provoked a shift in Greek intellectual culture. The Treaty of Küçük Kaynarca signalled the end of the Orlov moment and any expectation that the Russian Empire would supplant Ottoman rule in the Balkans, while also introducing the Eastern Question as a thorny diplomatic problem. As it became increasingly apparent that neither the Russian nor the Ottoman Empire could assert political control over the Balkans, Greek commentators entered an ever-growing – and increasingly global – conversation over sovereignty. Over the course of the decade and a half that followed, figures like Moisiodax and Katartzis began to openly reflect upon the political relationship between the Ottoman Empire and the Romioi within discussions of government, epistemology, language, history and geography.

Iosipos Moisiodax's 'Liberal'[35] Sensibilities

During the latter part of the eighteenth century, Moisiodax's influence on Greek intellectual culture is paralleled by few. A lone, marginal voice for much of his career, the great scholar seemed ahead of his time in endorsing empiricism, in espousing a liberal political outlook, and in advocating for secular solutions to the problem of the Greeks' 'belatedness'.[36] While many contemporaries failed to appreciate the sophistication of his thought, his students and intellectual heirs would embrace and extend his vision during the 1790s.[37]

Moisiodax's biographer marks out the two decades between 1761 and 1781 as his creative period. This stage in his intellectual life began with his translation of Ludovico Muratori's *Filosofia Morale* (Moral Philosophy).[38] The prologue to this translation revealed Moisiodax's openness to European intellectual currents and alternative epistemologies. At the same time, it also betrayed his secular worldview, his faith in progress, and his hostility to the view that Greek scholarship could do no better than to imitate ancient philosophy. The work established Moisiodax as a vocal proponent of modern philosophy, while also secularizing the 'improving text'.[39] Moisiodax's arguments for educational renewal found an advocate in the Prince of Moldavia, Grigorios Alexandros Ghikas III, and in 1765 he was invited to teach at the Princely Academy of Jassy. He would quickly come to regret the decision after falling into ideological disputes with more conservative colleagues. The personal toll these disputes took on Moisiodax is revealed within his *Απολογία* (Apology), where the great scholar described how the slander disturbed him and motivated him to defend his views in writing.[40] Soon after the confrontations began, Moisiodax would resign from his position at the Princely Academy. Vanishing for the following decade, one of the last records from the pre-war period locates him in Bucharest in September 1767, where he set about composing a preliminary draft of his *Θεωρία της Γεωγραφίας* (Theory of Geography).[41]

When he resurfaced after the war, he did so with a handful of manuscripts that were ready for publication. A different, more sophisticated Moisiodax announced himself in these later works, which are among his most well-known. Indeed, his influence on Greek intellectual culture is gauged largely through three books published in the 1779–1781 period.[42] The tendency to interpret Moisiodax through these later works has spawned an image of the scholar that assumes a rather rigid ideological outlook from 1761 to 1781. The conventional view has been that he identified the problems plaguing his people within the prologue to his translation of Muratori's work, before proposing solutions in these later works.[43]

The younger Moisiodax exhibited a distinct ideological orientation in his early work. In 1761, he was clearly motivated by the need to elevate his race, which he perceived as a cultural endeavour rather than a political one. While his argument explicitly stated that the freedom and political autonomy of the ancient Hellenes helped to foster their cultural achievements, he did not attribute the belatedness of the race to its subjugation. Rather, he identified an ignorant clerical class and teachers who cut themselves off from European intellectual developments as responsible for stifling the development of Greek culture. Prior to the outbreak of the Russo-Ottoman War, Moisiodax's hope was that the educated and clerical classes would avail themselves of foreign ideas and begin to nurture reform. Very much advocating for *cultural* renewal rather than an explicitly *political* solution, he saw these classes playing a role like Peter I, 'refining' and 'regenerating' the Greeks so that they resembled their glorious ancestors once more.[44] While the great scholar's views differed from those of contemporaries, the views that he espoused in 1761 were considerably more modest than those he endorsed after the resolution of the war, when he appears more attuned to European discussions of sovereignty.

Lost to the public eye during the war, Moisiodax reappeared in 1776, when he was once more appointed to the position of scholarch of the Princely Academy. He would resign this post in a matter of months. Fleeing to Brașov, before travelling to Trieste, Venice and then Vienna in the 1777–1781 period, Moisiodax set about his most fruitful period of publication, all the while lamenting his plight as a vagabond.[45] Nevertheless, his work during this time demonstrated how significantly his political views had matured since his translation of *Moral Philosophy* was published. The contrast was perhaps most evident within the Παραλλαγή του προς Νικοκλέα (Paraphrase to Nicocles).

On its surface, this work was part of the established 'mirrors for princes' literary tradition, and as such has been interpreted as providing a criticism of the Phanariots' shortcomings.[46] However, while fitting his argument into this traditional form, there was something novel in the content of this pamphlet. For one, Moisiodax directed it towards a larger audience, translating the work into French, and publishing it under the title *Chapitres Politiques*.[47] Despite the influence of Machiavelli and Montesquieu,[48] the *Paraphrase to Nicocles* communicates liberal ideas about sovereignty and governance.[49] Echoes of Hobbes' core arguments in *Leviathan* (1651) find their way into the first chapter of the work, where Moisiodax contended that a ruler's primary obligation is to maintain social order. Highly informed by the emergence of multiple sovereignties within the Ottoman Empire, Moisiodax portrayed the popular masses as oppressed by regional elites. Moreover, he asserted that the role of a ruler was to protect the majority from the influence of local strongmen and self-seeking officials.[50] In this way, the pamphlet begins by acknowledging that, in the post-war world, sovereignty must be absolute and vested in the monarch.

The *Paraphrase to Nicocles* does not, however, endorse absolutism. Far from it, Moisiodax was advancing a case for popular sovereignty. A ruler's policies must ensure stability and promote social utility, and, if not, 'there should be no hesitation in changing them'. Critical of appeals to tradition, the scholar wrote that 'it is an act of excessive piety, which indeed is frequently harmful, to maintain old traditions simply because they happen to be old traditions'.[51] Consistently advocating for reform from 1761, one can detect a continuity in spirit within Moisiodax's work; however, after the war, he was doing more than identifying the causes of the Greeks' ignorance – he was endorsing liberal principles of governance. For instance, he presumed that a ruler's actions must conform to 'rational thought' and the needs of the subjects.[52] Far less explicit than Rousseau in his espousal of popular sovereignty, Moisiodax's argument that a ruler must act in the common good seems more in line with Locke's views – as communicated in the ninth chapter of the *Second Treatise of Government*.[53]

In many ways, the *Paraphrase to Nicocles* worked as a companion piece to the prologue of *Moral Philosophy*, supplementing the earlier work with political content, and adapting it in response to the crisis of Ottoman sovereignty exposed in 1774. Whereas the former work identified the problem of ignorance within Greek culture, the latter provided a road to renewal: rulers amenable to liberal reform. From Moisiodax's perspective, the regeneration of the race would be enabled from the bottom up, so long as rulers maintained order, and submitted to the will of the people to enable this progress.

The works also paralleled each other in another sense: much as he had before the war, Moisiodax co-opted an established literary tradition, and set it to work towards new ends. Whereas in 1761 he cleverly recast the role of the improving text, he now employed the mirror for princes tradition as a way of introducing liberal notions of governance into Greek political thought. While it is unclear whether Moisiodax was consciously using established literary forms to make his ideas more palatable, it is clear that he succeeded in informing the views of the next generation of political thinkers, while avoiding the unfortunate fate of more strident reformers, like Kosmas of Aetolia.

While the *Paraphrase to Nicocles* contains a handful of arguments that clarify Moisiodax's political views, the *Apology* stands out as the great scholar's masterwork. Written over the course of twelve years, between 1765 and 1777, the *Apology* is also his most revealing work. Moisiodax was open in acknowledging how the work was intended to redeem his reputation, which had been sullied by attacks from personal and ideological opponents;[54] however, while he was motivated to proffer a public defence of his views, his desire to improve the condition of his race was always his overriding concern.[55]

Clear continuities exist between the *Apology* and his writings before the war. In particular, one recognizes continuity in terms of the problem identified, 'I am not a bit shy to say that Hellas has a need, it has a need for Europe, for while Hellas goes without everything, Europe abounds with everything. Given the dearth of works that circulate among us, philosophy, history, theology and others, how can we not need Europe?'[56]

For Moisiodax, 'Greekness' continued to be defined in opposition to 'Europeanness'; Europe functioned as Hellas' 'constituting other', and where the former had progressed, the latter had regressed.[57] By extension, Europeans were correct to portray the Greeks as the depraved progeny of the glorious Hellenes, as a clear intellectual imbalance existed between the two groups. Accordingly, it was incumbent upon the purveyors of knowledge to transmit Europe's wealth of knowledge into the amorphous cultural space that Moisiodax referred to by the toponym 'Hellas'.[58]

Moisiodax took the argument in the *Apology* a step further than he did before the war though, providing a template for how this change could be achieved. In praising the patriotism of those merchants who had helped to finance the publication of his book, he acknowledged the critical role the merchant classes were to play in the Greeks' cultural renewal.[59] In fact, the *Apology* provides a clearer picture of the roles that various classes were to play in this process. While the *Paraphrase to Nicocles* limits the role of rulers to maintaining order and introducing legislation that reflects the popular will of the people, the *Apology* clarifies Moisiodax's opposition to Voltaire's view that the Greeks could be reinvigorated by the introduction of new laws.[60] The impetus for cultural renewal was to come from changes within the public sphere; specifically, the distinct cultural group of intellectual figures, publishers, Phanariots and merchants brought together in the middle part of the eighteenth century through the introduction of a subscription-based method of funding new publications.[61] By 1780, a fuller image of Moisiodax's project emerged: rulers were to maintain order and provide intellectual figures with the freedom to introduce foreign ideas into Hellas, while patriotic merchants with modernist sensibilities were to provide funds to facilitate this process.

The idealism of the vision is captured well in the following passage: 'I recommend nothing more than sound Philosophy, which, in addition to other things, is rich in its power to win over all the nations, bringing them to the knowledge that human beings, as human beings, are all brethren, *all deserving mutual love*.'[62] Inspired by the humanism of the Enlightenment, Moisiodax exhibited an unequivocal faith that the transmission of Europe's knowledge into Hellas would engender toleration. The language that he used in this passage and elsewhere is telling, as Moisiodax uses the language of moral philosophy to advance a political argument about an individual's right to tolerance and equality. While it is unclear whether this was Moisiodax's intent, it would be consistent with the liberal sensibilities that he seems to have developed over the course of the Russo-Ottoman War.

The liberal elements of Moisiodax's thought have been overlooked to now, in large part because he couches many of his claims in the language of moral philosophy, rather than advancing more familiar statements about individual liberties and the rights of citizenship. One can assume that he neglected to articulate his argument in this language because he was not concerned with the abuses of the Sultan; rather, he sought to address the issue of Hellas' cultural and intellectual parochialism. By 1780, Moisiodax exhibited an overwhelming faith in the power of ideas to address this problem, and to ensure the prosperity of his people *within* the Ottoman Empire:

> If we devote ourselves wholeheartedly to mathematics and to physics, it is possible that not only will learning find some recognition with the powerbrokers, but also

that our Race will find through it some calm with them. [...] I believe that (the Ottomans) too are human beings, by nature longing to know, and that since they are born in Hellas and breathe hellenic air, that they too have the same intelligence as other Hellenes.[63]

Moisiodax neglected to speak of rights at any point in this passage because his utopianism led him to believe that rulers, informed by sound philosophy, would inevitably create sensible laws that conformed to the rational will of the people. Therefore, any discussion of rights was superfluous, as there would be no need to defend one's self from the will of an enlightened ruler who respected the limits of their authority.

Moisiodax's political outlook had changed significantly between 1761 and 1779, as he began to embrace liberal conceptions of sovereignty, governance and, to some extent, individual rights. Predictably, descriptions of the benefits that could be yielded under the rule of an enlightened absolutist like Peter I gave way to more contemporary examples. The success of the Dutch Republic was held up as a model of what could be accomplished by a people open to new ideas and free from imperial constraints.[64] Moisiodax reserved more glowing praise for the Swiss and their system of governance. Citing another example of the success that a people could achieve after liberating themselves from imperial rule, he presented Swiss republicanism as an ideal towards which the Greeks could aspire: 'Frugal and freedom loving, they never desired to expand, nor did they ever suffer to be ruled by a king, but *all of them submit to the authority of their laws, which protect the weak against the oppression of the powerful*, and they all enjoy an equality unparalleled in the other aristocracies of Europe.'[65] While Moisiodax seemed to work hard to keep his politics somewhat opaque, a distinctly republican tinge colours some passages from the *Apology*.[66] Despite Moisiodax extolling the virtues of these republics, there is little in his work to suggest that he would have endorsed a republican revolution. Rather, his overriding concern with the cultural renewal of his race merely led him to identify the problem of competing sovereignties in the empire, and to suggest a model of liberal reform for the Ottoman Empire.

Following the peace of 1774, Moisiodax's project became one of liberal reform, and he seemed to feel that it could be achieved within the Ottoman Empire. His criticisms were never directed at the Sultan, and where he was critical of the Phanariot Princes of Moldavia and Wallachia, his criticism only extended to suggesting that they should better understand their *duty* to their subjects, and that they should rebuke self-serving officials more forcefully.[67] Moisiodax was not seeking to overthrow the Ottoman Empire, nor was he seeking to establish a republic; he was merely declaring that the Phanariot Princes should be judged by secular, liberal standards of rule. He cited the examples of the Dutch and the Swiss, simply to provide models of government that encourage intellectual development. In his *Apology*, Moisiodax adapted his project of cultural renewal to conform to his emerging liberal sensibilities, and redefined the ideal roles of rulers, merchants and intellectual figures in the process.

The idea that Moisiodax embraced a liberal outlook during the Russo-Ottoman war is reinforced in his *Theory of Geography*. Published in 1781, the work was dedicated to the reigning Princes of Moldavia and Wallachia. The dedication has been interpreted as an olive branch to the Phanariots, who may have taken some of his comments in the *Apology* as personal criticisms of their rule.[68] While there may be some truth to the suggestion that Moisiodax was trying to smooth over ill will that had arisen after the publication of his *Apology*, in order to facilitate his return to the Danubian Principalities, the dedication seems consistent with the *reformist* character of his project. Moisiodax consistently portrayed his ideal of a liberal ruler as one who *facilitates* the transmission of knowledge from scholars to the general population. Beyond praising the Princes Constantinos Mourouzis and Ioannis Ypsilantis, he applauded the example of the seventeenth-century Holy Roman Emperor, Rudolf II, whose positive legacy he attributed to the Emperor's patronage of the renowned astronomers of that era, Johannes Kepler and Tycho Brahe.[69]

Despite the numerous comments of this sort that were hidden in its extensive footnotes, the *Theory of Geography* was not intended to be a political work. It was in fact a revised version of a manuscript that had originally been written thirteen years before it was published. More so than anything else, the published version of this work signalled Moisiodax's wholesale embrace of empiricism, European philosophy and the philosophy of the moderns.

That said, the monograph does provide a number of examples of how Moisiodax's ideological outlook had shifted during the war, and specifically how his political views had evolved. It was in this work where the Hellenized Vlach made explicit reference to his admiration for the English, and how their great example could be emulated. Moreover, Moisiodax added that the Philhellenism of the English made them a potential ally in the cause of transmitting European knowledge into the Greek-speaking world. Portraying them as conscientious and honest, he suggested that their status as the 'first among the European races' derived from the attention that they paid to new scientific discoveries. Reading these comments next to those in the *Apology*, one may surmise that Moisiodax felt that liberal rule had enabled English thinkers to make use of scientific discoveries and uplift the people.[70]

Beyond providing further evidence of Moisiodax's liberal outlook in the post-war period, the *Theory of Geography* also contains subtle claims about Greekness. These ideas were communicated through the scholar's contributions to the language question, a debate that emerged in Greek intellectual circles during the latter half of the eighteenth century. The language and syntax employed when writing became politicized, as authors questioned whether it was appropriate to write in the common vernacular spoken by most Greek-speakers, or in a 'purer' form, more akin to the Attic Greek used by the ancient Hellenes. Voulgaris initiated the language question in his 1766 monograph, Λογική (Logic), by arguing that understanding philosophy required a knowledge of ancient Greek.[71] He felt that the language had grown corrupted because of the admixture of foreign and barbarous words, and that Greek must be cleansed of words that were unable to adequately represent meaning.[72]

Moisiodax took issue with these arguments, vocalizing his support for the common style. In the prologue to his *Theory of Geography*, he argued for the importance of clarity in writing. Moisiodax felt that authors should write in a manner that was accessible to the greatest number of Greek speakers.[73] Deriding the tortuous prose of

Atticists who tried to incorporate ancient words and syntax into their writing, he asserted that the clarity of the common tongue was equal to any benefit that could be conferred by using the ancient dialect.[74] He attacked Voulgaris' claims directly, pointing, once more, to the accomplishments of the Europeans in the recent past, and arguing that it demonstrated that truth was accessible in all languages, not just ancient Greek.[75] For good measure, Moisiodax added one more not-so-veiled jab at Voulgaris and the Russians: 'The Great Man, instead of degrading our simple style, ought to have endorsed it, defining the terms according to which it should be regulated, and ought not to have degraded it in a manner that not even the language of the *Scythians*, which he now knows well, should be degraded.'[76] His association of the Russians with the Scythians here is especially interesting, as he identified the latter within a list of barbarian tribes within *Moral Philosophy*.[77]

Moisiodax's opinions on the Russians had clearly evolved over the course of the Russo-Ottoman War, and this derisive comment about the Russian language had a larger significance. Debates over language became intertwined with the discourse on Greekness in the latter part of the eighteenth century, as figures like Voulgaris and Moisiodax engaged in veiled debates over whether the cultural renewal of the race would be achieved by emulating their glorious ancestors or Europeans. Moisiodax's ideological outlook had evolved considerably between the publication of *Moral Philosophy* and *Paraphrase to Nicocles*. While he did not perceive the Orlov moment as a shock and betrayal, as Prigkos and Dapontes had, his project of cultural renewal was reshaped by the delegitimization of the Russian expectation and the emergence of the Eastern Question. As such, the works that he published between 1779 and 1781 revealed a new, liberal sensibility.

Moisiodax who resurfaced in 1776 had been markedly transformed by the Orlov moment. His project of cultural renewal evolved as he grew keenly aware of how the emergence of multiple sovereignties within the Ottoman Empire created obstacles, while also presenting opportunities. By 1779, he had grown convinced that imperial subjects could make demands upon their rulers to maintain order and ensure toleration and equality within their realms. He became committed to the belief that rulers must be accountable to their subjects' will. The Moisiodax of the post-war period firmly believed that governance occurs within certain prescribed limits and that rulers should not intrude upon the actions of intellectual figures operating within the public sphere. From his perspective, the regeneration of the race would begin within that space, but only after the threats to Ottoman sovereignty were addressed.

Dimitrios Katartzis' Communitarianism

After publishing his *Theory of Geography*, Moisiodax returned to Bucharest in 1781, where he would assume the role of tutor to the Prince's sons. At that point in time, the city had emerged as an important centre of Enlightenment learning within southeastern Europe, as a group of young scholars had gathered around another intellectual giant of the era, Dimitrios Katartzis. Both Moisiodax and Katartzis would become important teachers in the city in the subsequent decade, and would prove hugely influential in informing the views of more familiar figures of the Balkan Enlightenment, such as Adamantios Korais and Rigas Velestinlis.[78]

While the two scholars travelled in the same circles in Bucharest, they were products of vastly different contexts. Where Moisiodax was always an outsider, due to his Vlach ethnicity and his militant espousal of modernist philosophy, Katartzis was born into the Phanariot class. Educated in Constantinople, he held important judicial and administrative posts in Wallachia over the course of his career. In 1779, Katartzis was appointed to the Presidency of the High Court in Bucharest, and years later he would be assigned to the office of Μέγας Λογοθέτης (Head of the Princely Chancellery), the uppermost lay administrative post within the Patriarchate of Constantinople.[79]

By the 1780s, the influence of the Enlightenment on Katartzis' thought became evident. Like Moisiodax, he adopted a favourable view of European culture, while also lamenting the sorry state of his own. Accepting the view of many European commentators that the Romioi were the depraved progeny of the glorious Hellenes,[80] Katartzis would comment on the desperate need to transmit European knowledge to the Greek nation: 'There is no need here to say again any more about our ills, and in what ocean of absurdity we sail, but to consider well how to undo them and how to bring about to our nation the education and learning of Europe.'[81] Fluent in French, Katartzis' views were highly influenced by the ideas of Bacon, D'Alambert, Rousseau, Voltaire and other French philosophers. Captivated by the *Encyclopédistes* in particular, he hoped to oversee the writing and publication of a series of encyclopaedic works in vernacular Greek.[82]

Like Moisiodax, he wanted to contribute to a project of cultural renewal. He did not, however, subscribe to Moisiodax's liberal vision, which drew clear boundaries between the political and the public spheres. On the contrary, Katartzis espoused a more communitarian outlook. He saw the Romioi forming a distinctive and self-determining political society, albeit one that was belated in its development. Regarding it as such, he wished to develop the intellectual faculties of his people, while protecting them from the corrupting influences of foreign ideas. This vision was captured in a series of manuscripts authored between 1783 and 1791, which remained unpublished until the twentieth century.

Katartzis' sense of what distinguished the Romioi as a distinct nation derived from his views on language, which he outlined in a piece titled 'Γνῶθι Σαυτόν' (Know Thyself). When discussing the relationship between the common dialect of the Romioi and Attic Greek, he portrayed the former as being descended from the latter, in the same sense that Romance languages descended from Latin.[83] Beyond language, he identified a host of criteria that differentiated the Romioi from the Hellenes, including historical destiny, political status, religion, customs, as well as dress and household utensils.[84] By Katartzis' estimation, these differences signified that the two groups constituted distinct nations.

The Phanariot drew a distinction between these two nations, which he outlined in some detail in the 'Συμβουλή στους Νέους' (Advice to the Youth). Influenced by the scholarship of seventeenth-century historian Dorotheos and the secular methodology of Alexandros Kagkellarios, Katartzis advanced a secular theory of historical continuity:

> Initially, we were called Graikoi [...] and then we took the name Hellenes [...] When Constantine the Great moved the capital to Constantinople, we called ourselves Romioi, and that is how all of the nations of the world referred to us, and we referred to pagans as 'Hellenes.' [...] Only when we have enriched and cultivated our Romaic language [...] will it not be shameful for us to say we have the Hellenes as our ancestors, surely a great honor, (but one that we can accept) without claiming their name.[85]

In the aftermath of 1774, Katartzis tried to reconcile the seemingly incongruous demands of crafting a distinct national identity and situating the Romioi within an Ottoman legal system organized on the basis of religious adherence. In arguing that the Romioi had evolved in meaningful ways from their pagan ancestors, he prioritized the latter demand.

Elsewhere in this piece, Katartzis associated the Hellenes with paganism once again, working to distance the Romioi from that tradition. Arguing against Romioi using the demonym 'Hellenes', he added:

> That name, which, from the birth of Christ up until our captivity, was used for so many centuries and its meaning was confirmed with the passing of time to mean pagan, how can certain personages, going against the very rules of grammar, dare to change the meaning of a word and call themselves Hellenes, and not deem it a disgrace since they are Christians and an infamy since they are Romans, when our Roman progenitors did not accept it, save for one, Julian the Apostate, who delighted in calling himself a Hellene?[86]

Katartzis saw himself as a 'Romio Christian', and as a 'citizen of a nation'. In presenting himself in this manner, he introduced a novel image of the Greeks as a 'political society' with defined political laws and ecclesiastical regulations; a notable departure from the non-political representations of the Greeks that preceded the Orlov moment.[87]

While his insights on Greekness are interesting, his contribution to the language question stands out as his most significant contribution to Greek thought. Within the 'Σχέδιο ότ,η Ρωμαίκια Γλώσσα' (Grammar of the Romaic Language), he argued that language miscomprehension was the biggest contributor to the ignorance of the Romioi. In his view, his people's problems stemmed from the lack of a universal and standardized medium of expression. As various dialects were often combined in conversation and writing, numerous meanings could be interpreted from any phrase.[88] By his estimation, the Greek language should be adapted to mirror the Romaic spoken by the women of Constantinople, who did not mix the vernacular with the 'school idiom'.[89]

Katartzis claimed that the Greek spoken in antiquity by the Hellenes was altogether different from the language spoken by the Romioi. While the latter was more deficient, he declared that he 'loved and cherished and delighted' in his native tongue nonetheless.[90] The Phanariot argued that his people should develop their vernacular language, as the European nations had done. He felt that such an effort would contribute decisively to their cultural renewal.[91]

Much as Moisiodax had in 1761, Katartzis advocated for a proactive solution to the problems plaguing the Romioi, suggesting that solutions to the problem of belatedness did not have to come from God or a foreign patron, but from *within* the culture itself.[92] Echoing Moisiodax's view that the race had a need for European knowledge, Katartzis invited those with knowledge of foreign languages to produce translations of important foreign works.[93] For the Phanariot, the transmission of knowledge from elites to the masses would assure the development and future prosperity of the Romioi.[94]

On this point, his vision was more expansive than Moisiodax's. In many ways, Katartzis' concern with nurturing the bonds that united his people recalls Benedict Anderson's insights into the connection between the cultivation of vernacular languages and nation-building. Revealing the importance of situating the Romioi in time and space to his project, Katartzis would note that 'One must study before anything else the two eyes of history, chronology and geography, *sciences that we chiefly need*.'[95] Where Moisiodax's support for writing in the vernacular language was premised on his desire to make *sound* philosophy available to the greatest number of Greeks, Katartzis regarded authors producing works in the vernacular as a method of nation-building. In the aftermath of a conflict that established that the Romioi were not destined to be either Russian clients or Ottoman subjects, the Phanariot's views on language came to be subsumed within a larger project of preserving the cultural distinctiveness of his nation. Unlike Moisiodax, nurturing the bonds that united the Romioi took precedence over the transmission of knowledge for Katartzis.

Influenced by Aristotle's *Politics*, Katartzis strongly believed that the interests of the community should be prioritized over those of the individual.[96] Accordingly, unlike Moisiodax, whose liberal sensibilities inspired him to clarify the limits of a ruler's jurisdiction over her subjects, Katartzis' communitarian outlook led him to focus on the need to foster patriotism among the Romioi. He wrote specifically of the patriotic zeal that could be realized by the comprehension of their proud heritage, and cited the heroes of classical Greece and the champions of the Orthodox Christian faith in the Byzantine Empire.[97]

Like Burke, Katartzis felt that each people had a distinctive ethos, a unique history, and specific customs and conventions that unified them.[98] The great teacher feared that the bonds that gave the Romioi their distinctive ethos were growing lax, owing to the influence of enlightened Europe. Within the 'Advice to the Youth', he advised parents to expose their children to new ideas, but cautioned them about the corrupting influences of foreign languages, which undermine 'our principles, which are healthy and salvational'. He added,

> Our nation begins to be filled with that which it shouldn't, with foreign ideas, young people do not have (ideas) that are fitting to us, (and) they eliminate from the Greek texts even the Christian ideas included in them, they love other nations, hating our own, they are indifferent to our religion; and if a reasonable course of action is not adopted, the natural consequence will be that the youth of the next generation will not even study their primary courses in Greek, and the absurdity in this is obvious.

The Romioi suffered from a lack of quality texts written in their vernacular, and so Katartzis wished to 'cultivate' the language by encouraging the production of intellectual works that were accessible to his people. He saw these works as serving as a foundation upon which Greek learning could develop.[99]

While Moisiodax's embrace of certain liberal ideas seems to have been inspired by challenges to Ottoman sovereignty, Katartzis' communitarianism was also a self-conscious response to the negative European representations of the Greeks that followed the failure of the Orlov Revolt. The 'Advice to the Youth' was also highly critical of Voltaire in particular, and, specifically, of his view that the Greeks did not meet Aristotle's definition of nationhood. Irritated by this allegation, Katartzis countered,

> At this time, we are not a nation that in truth forms a state, but we are subject to a greater one. For this, and viewing it through the definition of the citizen given by Aristotle, certain Franks accuse of us not having a homeland. But this is not so; for the aforementioned writer thus distinguishes the citizen from the enslaved nations, who were called helots and outsiders, and who worked for the Spartans and Cretans as their actual farmers. But we are not such, with the help of God, and if perhaps we do not take part in the administration of all aspects of our polity together with those in power, nevertheless we are not entirely uninvolved in it. Whence we constitute a nation in which our ecclesiastical rulers bind us to the supreme administration and among ourselves. In many respects, our ecclesiastical rulers are also our political rulers; many of our political laws, which are named âdet (customs), and all our ecclesiastical laws which are named ayin (religion), draw validity from their self-governing power.[100]

Far from being slaves of the Ottomans, the Romioi who comprised the *millet-i Rûm* formed a *self-determining* nation – albeit not a *sovereign* nation. Where Voulgaris and Prigkos had aspired to see the establishment of an autonomous Greek polity during the war, Katartzis argued that the Romioi already enjoyed a great deal of autonomy.

The response to Voltaire also highlights how, after 1774, Greek intellectual culture increasingly began reorienting itself away from the Orthodox Christian east and towards the enlightened west. Whereas, prior to the Orlov Revolt, Greek self-representations did not seem to be significantly informed by the views of Europeans, a marked shift occurred after the diplomatic settlement of 1774. The Russian expectation had been delegitimized, and enlightened Europe now seemed to be the template for progress; however, as Greek intellectual figures looked to Europe for inspiration in the aftermath of the war, they saw European commentators gazing back upon them with harsh judgement for the failure of the Orlov Revolt. A figure like Katartzis was both sufficiently aware and sensitive to these negative representations to formulate a response.

Additionally, Katartzis' comments in this piece underscore how the reorientation from the Orthodox east towards the enlightened west also entailed a shift away from Greeks portraying themselves as supplicants. The Phanariot's response to Voltaire not only assumed that the Romioi possessed a right to self-government, but that this right had been realized within the *millet-i Rûm*. It seemed that in the post-war era, self-government – limited or not – was an ideal to be pursued and celebrated.

It would be misleading to portray Katartzis as a wholesale supporter of modernist philosophy, as he truly struggled with the problem of how to introduce Enlightenment thought into the Greek-speaking world in a manner that did not break the unity of the Romioi or disrupt the political status quo. Unfortunately, this left much of his political project seeming confused. For instance, while in his response to Voltaire he celebrated self-government, elsewhere he seemed to endorse enlightened absolutism – particularly when discussing Frederick the Great.[101] He expanded upon these views in another writing, titled 'Εγκώμιο του Φιλόσοφου' (In Praise of the Philosopher), within which he outlined the various qualities possessed by a 'good ruler'.[102] Elsewhere still, he intertwined his project of cultural renewal with a divine-right theory of kingship, portraying any ruler who neglected to educate her subjects as an 'enemy of almighty God'.[103]

In the aftermath of the Russo-Ottoman War, the great teacher's writings highlight his personal struggle to reconcile conflicting loyalties.[104] While the war inspired commentators to reflect on the political status of the Romioi in new ways, informed by the idea that they formed a self-determining nation, the persistence of Ottoman political institutions prevented them from advancing more radical claims. Whereas Moisiodax's dependence on the patronage of the Princes of Moldavia and Wallachia led him towards more veiled political criticisms and the development of a tempered liberalism, Katartzis seemed to struggle to foster a coherent political project that squared his patriotism and his faith with his loyalties to the Ottoman Empire and his Phanariot class. Nevertheless, within the writings of Moisiodax and Katartzis, one can detect the influence of the abrupt conclusion of the Orlov moment in 1774, and how it compelled Greek intellectual figures to enter a broader conversation over sovereignty during the transformative age of revolutions.

Conclusion

The historical memory of the 'Orlov moment' has been shaped by Philhellenes, opportunistic revolutionaries, and historians of modern Greece. Eager to establish a record of nationalist struggle, each of these groups reduced the history of this period to a few months of violent uprisings in 1770, thereby diminishing the Russian role, and misrepresenting the cause for widespread enthusiasm in the Morea in early 1770. The excitement that greeted the first appearance of the Russian fleet followed a nearly eight-year-long conspiracy to foment revolution among the Romioi – one that involved networks that extended from St. Petersburg west to Tuscany and south to Girīt (Crete). More immediately, it was accompanied by public pronouncements of the Greeks' right to self-rule by Empress Catherine II and, later, General Alexei Orlov, as well as odes anticipating an Athenian renaissance by Voltaire.[105] Seen from this perspective, the arrival of the Russian fleet raised the realistic possibility that Ottoman sovereignty would be supplanted.

Unfortunately for those eager to see Russian words translated into deeds, the arrival of the first naval squadron was followed by a series of disappointments, as the uprisings of 1770 were quickly suppressed. Nevertheless, hope persisted in pockets of the Greek-speaking world, as high-ranking officials from the Russian Empire continued open discussions with local allies over how sovereignty would be redefined in the eastern Mediterranean after the conclusion of the Russo-Ottoman War. The two sides spent years in deliberations over the future of the Archipelagic Principality, the federation of Aegean islands which had existed as a Russian protectorate since the summer of 1770.[106] In spite of the failure of the uprisings in the Morea and Rumelia, so long as the war persisted, and the Russian fleet remained in the Mediterranean, many held out hope that a forthcoming Russian victory would improve the political status of the Greeks. These hopes were dashed by the Treaty of Küçük Kaynarca, which failed to establish the legal autonomy of the Aegean principality or change the political status of the Greeks within the Ottoman Empire.

While this elicited shock from Prigkos and Dapontes, it also engendered a period of critical self-reflection within Greek intellectual circles. The delegitimization of the Russian expectation and the emergence of the Eastern Question produced a radical rupture in Greek intellectual thought. As a result, a range of new political possibilities emerged for figures like Moisiodax and Katartzis, who felt compelled to determine how the Greeks fit into this world, if not as Ottoman subjects or Russian clients.

For Moisiodax, the Russo-Ottoman War inspired a new liberal outlook. The Orlov moment had convinced him that governance occurs within prescribed limits and that rulers should not intrude upon the actions of intellectual figures operating within the public sphere. The war endowed his project of cultural renewal with political content. It led him to carve out a space within which the cultural renewal of his people could occur. The Russo-Ottoman War not only affirmed Moisiodax's faith that the Greeks should become more European, but it also inspired him to think about the political preconditions necessary for the fulfilment of this vision.

For Katartzis, on the other hand, the reorientation of Greek intellectual culture that followed the peace of 1774 presented new dangers. Greek authors had been provoked to determine where the Romioi fit into the post-1774 world, but now the increasing embrace of foreign, secular ideas threatened to corrupt a culture united around ecclesiastical customs and laws. The Phanariot's communitarian sensibilities led him to argue that the development – and indeed the preservation – of his people's culture was dependent upon nurturing the religious bonds that united the Romioi. A degree of self-government had already been realized within the *millet-i Rûm*, but the preservation of Katartzis' culture required the production of books in the vernacular dialect that reinforced the core principles of the Romioi.

Over the decade and a half that followed the diplomatic settlement of 1774, figures like Moisiodax and Katartzis developed their ideas on cultural renewal in a manner that revealed an appreciation for the challenges facing Ottoman sovereignty. Careful to avoid making explicit statements that could be perceived as treasonous, or torn between conflicting loyalties, the tensions in the thought of intellectual figures of this generation would not be resolved until the 1790s. After the French Revolution, a younger group of authors began to advance more radical political ideas, and the compromise positions of Moisiodax and Katartzis no longer seemed tenable.

That said, the significance of Moisiodax's and Katartzis' political thought should not be understated. For one, their works highlight the range of ideas that were circulating in the Greek-speaking world in the late eighteenth century, and the ways in which Greek authors were reimagining empire. Their works also challenge the linearity of the narrative of a stateless nation turning into a nation-state. More significantly, their writings highlight the diversity of voices that were contributing to a broad conversation about sovereignty during the age of revolutions. In doing so, Moisiodax's and Katartzis' work suggests a need to re-evaluate intellectual proposals and institutional practices in other imperial peripheries, so as to gauge whether the age of revolutions was truly a *global* crisis in sovereignty.

Notes

1 The paper uses a variety of demonyms (Greeks, Romioi) and toponyms (Balkans, Hellas) in an effort to accurately reflect the meaning intended by the figures discussed. Where the term 'Greek' is used, it is employed in the broadest sense to refer to all who participated in Hellenic culture, self-identified as members of an amorphous Greek community (τὸ γένος τῶν Ῥωμαίων), as well as those who exhibited a sense of belonging to a people unified by a broad sense of kinship, shared interests and conventions. In no way does this suggest that a Greek community, united by language, location, ethnicity and/or religious affiliation, can be identified at this time. Where the term 'Romioi' is used, the term is employed in a much narrower sense, to refer to Orthodox Christians primarily residing within the Ottoman Empire.

2 Friedrich Hölderlin, *Hyperion and Selected Poems*, ed. Eric L. Santner, vol. 22. New York: Continuum, 1990.

3 'A life of our own, a new and honorable life. Were we born of the swamp, like a will-o'-the-wisp, or are we descended from the victors at Salamis? How is this? how, O free nature of the Greeks, have you become a maidservant? how have you declined, ancestral race, of which the divine images of Jupiter and Apollo were once only the copy? – But hear me, sky of Ionia! hear me, my native soil, you that, half naked, dress yourself like a beggarwoman in the rags of your ancient glory; I will bear it no longer.' Ibid., p. 88.

4 For specific references to these authors, consult David E. Roessel, *In Byron's Shadow: Modern Greece in the English and American Imagination*. New York: Oxford University Press, 2002.

5 Emmanouel Xanthos, *Απομνημονεύματα περί της Φιλικής Εταιρείας* [Memoirs on the Filiki Etaireia], ed. E.G. Prōtopsaltēs, vol. 9. Athens: Tsoukalas, 1956.

6 Nikos Rotzokos, *Εθναφύπνιση και Εθνογένεση: Ορλωφικά και Ελληνική Ιστοριογραφία* [Nation-awaking and Ethogenesis: The Orlov Events and Greek Historiography], Athens: Βιβλιοράμα, 2007, p. 35, 39–40.

7 Konstantinos Paparrigopoulos, *Ιστορία του Ελληνικού Έθνους* [History of the Greek Nation], Athens: S. Paulidou, 1860–1874; Konstantinos Sathas, *Τουρκοκρατούμενη Ελλάδα: Ιστορία των Ελλήνων από την Άλωση ως το '21* [Turk-Dominated Greece: History of the Greeks since the Fall of Constantinople to 1821]. Athens: Andreou Koromela, 1869. Pantelis Kontogiannis, *Οι Έλληνες κατα τον Πρώτον επί Αικατερίνης Β' Ρωσσοτουρκικόν Πόλεμον* [The Greeks During the First Russo-Turkish War of Catherine the Great]. Athens: I.D. Sakellariou, 1903. Michael B. Sakellariou,

Η Πελοπόννησος κατά την Δευτέραν Τουρκοκρατίαν [Peloponnese during the Second Turkish Domination]. Athens: Verlag der 'Byzantinisch-Neugriechischen Jahrbücher', 1939. Apostolos E. Vacalopoulos, *Ιστορία του Νέου Ελληνισμού*, vol. 4. Thessalonika, 1961. Tasos Gritsopoulos, 'Τα Ορλωφικά. Η εν Πελοποννήσω Επανάστασις του 1770 και τα Επακόλουθα Αυτής' [The Orlov Events: The Revolution of 1770 in the Peloponnese and its Consequences], PhD dissertation, University of Athens, 1967.

8   Antonis Liakos 'Hellenism and the Making of Modern Greece: Time, Language, Space', in *Hellenisms: Culture, Identity, and Ethnicity from Antiquity to Modernity*, ed. Katerina Zacharia. Aldershot: Ashgate, 2008, pp. 201–236.
9   Rotzokos, pp. 30, 220–222.
10 Paschalis Kitromilides, *Enlightenment as Revolution*. Cambridge, MA: Harvard University Press, 2013, p. 57.
11 For more detailed discussions of the model of 'world crisis', consult David Armitage and Sanjay Subrahmanyam, eds., *The Age of Revolutions in Global Context, c. 1760–1840*. New York: Palgrave Macmillan, 2010.
12 J.C. Hurewitz, ed., *The Middle East and North Africa in World Politics: A Documentary Record*, vol. 1. New Haven, CT: Yale University Press, 1975, pp. 94, 97–98.
13 Edmund Burke, 'The History of Europe', *The Annual Register*, 12 (1769), pp. 4–5.
14 Émile Legrand, ed., *Bibliographie Hellénique du Dix-Huitième Siècle*, vol. 2. Paris: Société d'édition Les Belles Lettres, 1928, pp. 204–205.
15 Vasilis Molos, 'Nationness in the Absence of a Nation: Narrating the Prehistory of the Greek National Movement', PhD dissertation, New York University, 2014, pp. 114–121.
16 Konstantinos Sathas, ed., *Μεσαιωνική Βιβλιοθήκη* [Medieval Library], vol. 3. Venice: Typois tou Chronou, 1872, p. 119.
17 As part of this literary tradition proclaiming the 'resurrection of the race', consider: Gemistos Plethon, 'Address to the Emperor Manuel' (1416) and Theoklytos Polyeidis, *Προφητεία του μακαρίου Ιερομονάχου Αγαθάγγελου* [Prophesy of the blessed Monk Agathaggelos] (1751). For more information about the resurrection theme, consult: Molos, pp. 98–110; Marios Hatzopoulos, 'Oracular Prophecy and the Politics of Toppling Ottoman Rule in South-East Europe', *The Historical Review*, 8 (2011), pp. 95–116; Asterios Argyriou, *Les Exégèses Grecques de l'apocalypse à l'époque Turque, 1453–1821*. Thessalonika: Etairia Makedonikon Spoudon, 1982; Rotzokos, pp. 252–253; D. Kostantaras, *Infamy and Revolt: the Rise of the National Problem in Early Modern Greek Thought*. Boulder, CO: Eastern European Monographs, 2006, p. 201.
18 In 1738, he would describe one of these dreams in the following terms, 'I saw [...] a two-headed eagle high in the heavens, shining like the sun [...] with a kingly crown upon its head, with a cross, as customary, on its peak. Eagle, crown, cross, all with innumerable shining stars forming all around. Nearby the eagle, Constantine the Great, together with his mother, and he too with a cross.' K. Dapontes, 'Όνειρον', in *Οι Πρόδρομοι*, ed. L. Vranouses. Athens: Ζαχαρόπουλος, 1955, p. 20.
19 For more on the Russian expectation, consult Molos, pp. 100–102. Rotzokos, pp. 171–174, 219–221.
20 Sathas, *Μεσαιωνική Βιβλιοθήκη*, p. μς.
21 Nikolaos Andriotis, 'Το Χρωνικό του Άμστερνταμ' [The Chronicle of Amsterdam], *Nea Estia*, 10 (1931), p. 920.
22 For instance, in one document from 1755, he would claim that 'as the wind lifts the grasshopper, that is how [this tyranny] will be lifted from us'. Quoted in translation from Vangeles Skouvaras, *Ιωάννης Πρίγκος: η Ελληνική Παροικία του Άμστερνταμ, η*

Σχολή και η Βιβλιοθήκη Ζαγοράς [Ioannis Prigkos: The Greek Colony of Amsterdam, the School and the Library of Zagora]. Athens: Έκδοση της Ιστορικής και Λαογραφικής Εταιρείας των Θεσσαλών, 1964, p. 208.
23 From 1770 to 1774, Paros was part of the semi-autonomous Archipelagic Principality that the Russians had helped to administer. For more information, consult: Elena Smilyanskaya, '"Protection" or "Possession": How Russians Created a Greek Principality in 1770–1775', in *Power and Influence in South-Eastern Europe, 16th–19th Century*, ed. Maria Baramova, Plamen Mitev, Ivan Parvev and Vania Racheva. Zurich: Lit, 2013, pp. 209–217.
24 Skouvaras, p. 208.
25 Ibid., p. 209.
26 Ibid.
27 Ibid., p. 208.
28 Prigkos dated the fall of the Byzantine Empire to 1452 in this document: Skouvaras, p. 209.
29 Ibid., p. 208.
30 Birol Gundoglu, 'Ottoman Constructions of the Morea Rebellion, 1770s: A Comprehensive Study of Ottoman Attitudes to the Greek Uprising', PhD dissertation, University of Toronto, 2012, pp. 30–89.
31 Paschalis Kitromilides, 'War and Political Consciousness: Theoretical Implications of Eighteenth-Century Greek Historiography', in *East Central European Society and War in the Pre-Revolutionary Eighteenth Century*, ed. Gunther E. Rothenburg, Béla K. Király and Peter F. Sugar. New York: Columbia University Press, 1982, p. 357.
32 See Paschalis Kitromilides, 'The Last Battle of the Ancients and Moderns', *Modern Greek Studies Yearbook*, 1 (1985), pp. 79–91.
33 Alexis Politis, 'From Christian Roman Emperors to the Glorious Greek Ancestors', in *Byzantium and the Modern Greek Identity*, ed. David Ricks and Paul Magdalino. Brookfield, VT: Ashgate, 1998, pp. 4–5.
34 From 25% of the total in the 1700–1725 period to 47% in the 1775–1800 period: Konstantinos Dimaras, 'L'apport de l'Auflärung au Développement de la Conscience Néo-hellénique', in *Les Lumières et la Formation de la Conscience Nationale chez les Peoples du Sud-est Européen*, ed. C. Grecescu and S. Râpeanu eds. Bucharest: Association internationale d'études du sud-est européen, 1970, p. 54.
35 While Moisiodax's thought in the post-1774 period departs significantly from that of Hobbes, Locke or John Stuart Mill, there is ample evidence to suggest that he had developed liberal sensibilities over the war. Consider, for instance, his concern with intellectual freedom, his endorsement of popular sovereignty and his desire to secure individuals' rights to tolerance and equality.
36 For a discussion of the importance of the idea of 'belatedness' within Greek intellectual culture, consult: Gregory Jusdanis, *The Necessary Nation*. Princeton, NJ: Princeton University Press, 2001, p. 102.
37 Moisiodax's biographer writes, 'On October 16, 1790, a small group of Greek radicals in Vienna issued a proclamation announcing their intention to publish the first Greek gazette to bring news of current affairs and enlightenment to their countrymen. The opening paragraphs of the *Announcement*, which refer to the cultural achievements of ancient Greece to illustrate the pressing needs of Modern Greek society, are taken verbatim from Moisiodax's prolegomena to his edition of Muratori's *Moral Philosophy*.' Paschalis Kitromilides, *The Enlightenment as Social Criticism: Iosipos Moisiodax and Greek Culture in the Eighteenth Century*. Princeton, NJ: Princeton University Press, 1992, p. 182.

38 Ibid., p. 135.
39 The 'improving text' was a standard literary form, within which the author presented their work as an instrument of progress and renewal. Take Fragkiskos Skouphos' 1681 work, *Τέχνη Ρητορικής* [The Art of Rhetoric], as a typical example. See also, Kostantaras, p. 75.
40 Alkis Aggelou, ed., *Απολογία*. Athens: Hermes, 1976, p. 126.
41 Kitromilides, *The Enlightenment as Social Criticism*, pp. 63–66.
42 *Πραγματεία περί Παίδων Αγωγή* [Treatise on the Education of the Youth] (1779), *Apology* (1780) and *Theory of Geography* (1781).
43 Kitromilides, *The Enlightenment as Social Criticism*, pp. 135–142.
44 Paschalis Kitromilides, *Ιώσηπος Μοισιόδαξ: Οι Συντεταγμένες της Βαλκανικής Σκέωης τον 18° Αιώνα*. Athens: ΜΙΕΤ, 1985, pp. 323, 325–326, 331, 339. See also: Molos, pp. 130–132.
45 Ibid., p. 81.
46 Kitromilides, *The Enlightenment as Social Criticism*, p. 97.
47 Kitromilides, *Enlightenment and Revolution*, p. 140.
48 Paschalis Kitromilides, *Νεοελληνικός Διαφωτισμός* [Modern Greek Enlightenment]. Athens: ΜΙΕΤ, 1996, p. 201.
49 It is unclear whether Locke's work influenced Moisiodax's political thought. Also, there is no evidence to suggest that Moisiodax knew English. G.P. Henderson, *The Revival of Greek Thought, 1620-1830*. Albany, NY: State University of New York Press, 1970, p. 90. Kitromilides suggests that it is unlikely that Locke influenced Moisiodax or any other intellectual figures during this period, writing: 'What is strikingly absent from this story of intellectual transmission, despite Mavrocordatos' original interest in the *Treatise of Civil Government*, is Locke's political thought. Up to the Greek War of Independence contact with Locke's ideas remained limited to his theories of knowledge and language and to his views on education. The political thought of the Greek Enlightenment remains stubbornly silent as far as Locke is concerned. Whereas the ideas of Montesquieu and Rousseau played a noteworthy role in the development of Greek and more generally Balkan political radicalism at the time of the French Revolution, Locke's views on legitimate authority and his theory of resistance remained foreign to Greek political thought.' Paschalis Kitromilides, 'John Locke and the Greek Intellectual Tradition: An Episode in Locke's Reception in South-East Europe', in *Locke's Philosophy: Content and Context*, ed. G.A.J. Rogers. Oxford: Oxford University Press, 1994, p. 229.
50 Iosipos Moisiodax, 'Παραλλαγή του προς Νικοκλέα λόγου περί Βασιλέας του Ισοκράτους η Κεφάλαια Πολιτικά', in *Ιώσηπος Μοισιοδάξ*, ed. Paschalis Kitromilides. Athens: ΜΕΙΤ, 1985, pp. 345–346.
51 Ibid., p. 346.
52 Ibid., p. 349.
53 See section 131 in particular.
54 Aggelou, p. 46.
55 Consider, for example, the description he provides of the first part of the text: 'A somewhat exhaustive discourse [...] in which are included various notes, some on philosophy, some on ethics, all of them relating in one way or another to the subject of the tract or to *the present condition of our race*.' Translated from: Ibid., p. 174. My Italics.
56 Ibid., p. 153.
57 The concept of the 'constituting other' is borrowed from Maria Todorova, who uses it in *Imagining the Balkans*. New York: Oxford University Press, 1997 on pages 147 and 156.

58 In describing 'Hellas' in 1761, Moisiodax would note that it included 'all the diasporas of the Hellenes.' Translated from Iosipos Moisiodax, 'Ηθική Φιλοσοφία', in Ιώσηπος Μοισιοδάξ, ed. Paschalis Kitromilides. Athens: MEIT, 1985, p. 325.
59 Aggelou, op. cit., p. 10.
60 Letter from Voltaire to Catherine, dated 9 February 1771, in William Fiddian Reddaway, ed., *Documents of Catherine the Great: The Correspondence with Voltaire and the Instruction of 1767.* New York: Russell & Russell, 1971, p. 96.
61 Molos, pp. 121–125.
62 Aggelou, p. 40. My italics.
63 Ibid., p. 36. For an additional discussion of this passage, consult: Kitromilides, *The Enlightenment as Social Criticism*, p. 172.
64 Aggelou, p. 167, ff. 1.
65 Ibid., p. 166, ff. 1.
66 Paschalis Kitromilides suggests that the work of Rousseau may have come to influence Moisiodax's thought by this time. Kitromilides, *The Enlightenment as Social Criticism*, p. 176.
67 Aggelou, p. 80, ff. 1.
68 Kitromilides, *The Enlightenment as Social Criticism*, p. 108.
69 Ibid., pp. 168–169.
70 I. Moisiodax, Θεωρία της Γεωγραφίας. Vienna: Johann Thomas Trattner, 1781, pp. 162–163, ff. 2.
71 Not one to mince words, Voulgaris proclaimed that 'the worthless books that profess to philosophize in the vulgar tongue should be hissed off the stage'. Translated from: Eugenios Voulgaris, *Η Λογική εκ Παλαιώντε και Νεωτέρων Συνερανισθείσα*. Leipzig: Vreitkopf, 1766, p. 49. For a more detailed discussion of Voulgaris' views, consult: Peter Mackridge, *Language and National Identity in Greece, 1766-1796*. Oxford: Oxford University Press, 2009, pp. 83–87.
72 Eugenios Voulgaris, *Εισήγησις της Αυτοκρατορικής Μεγαλειότητος Αικατερίνας Β'*. St. Petersburg, 1771, pp. 42–43.
73 Moisiodax, Θεωρία της Γεωγραφίας, pp. x–xi.
74 Ibid., p. xii.
75 Ibid., pp. x–xi.
76 Ibid., p. xii.
77 Kitromilides, Ιώσηπος Μοισιόδαξ, p. 324.
78 Consider also his influence upon geographers Grigorios Constantas and Daniel Philippides, the poet and linguist Ioannis Vilaras, the conservative linguist Panayiotes Kodrikas, and the Cephalonian doctor and mathematician Spyridon Asanis. Kitromilides, *The Enlightenment as Social Criticism*, pp. 115–116, 180, 182. Kostantaras, p. 186.
79 Balázs Trencsényi and Michal Kopeček, eds., *Discourses on Collective Identity in Central and Southeastern Europe*. Budapest: Central European University Press, 2006, p. 210.
80 This view was circulated in the writings of Burke, Charles Emmanuel de Warnery, Francesco Griselini and Giacamo Casanova after the failure of the Orlov Revolt. Molos, pp. 267–328.
81 Konstantinos Dimaras, ed., *Τα Ευρισκόμενα*, 2nd edn. Athens: Hermes, 1999, p. 206.
82 Mackridge, p. 92.
83 Dimaras, *Τα Ευρισκόμενα*, p. 104.
84 Ibid., pp. 104–105.

85 Ibid., pp. 49-50. On the significance of Katartzis advancing one of the first theories of the historical continuity of the Greek nation, consult: Kitromilides, Νεοελληνικός Διαφωτισμός, p. 215.
86 Dimaras, Τα Ευρισκόμενα, pp. 49-50.
87 Ibid., pp. 43-44.
88 Ibid., pp. 12-13.
89 Ibid., p. 12.
90 Ibid., p. 14.
91 Ibid., p. 22.
92 For a discussions of the importance of the idea of 'belatedness' within Greek intellectual culture, consult: Jusdanis, p. 102.
93 Dimaras, Τα Ευρισκόμενα, p. 9.
94 Ibid.
95 Ibid., p. 188.
96 Ibid., p. 68.
97 Ibid., pp. 44-45.
98 Edmund Burke, *Reflections on the French Revolution*. London: J.M. Dent & Sons, 1791, pp. 31, 58, 93.
99 Dimaras, Τα Ευρισκόμενα, pp. 56-57.
100 Ibid., p. 44.
101 Ibid., pp. 55, 65 and 70.
102 Ibid., pp. 91-92.
103 Ibid., p. 87.
104 Kostantaras, pp. 71-72.
105 Konstantinos Palaiologos, 'Ρωσικά περί Ελλάδος έγγραφα' [Russian Documents on Greece], Παρνασσός, 1881, pp. 147-148. Horace Mann included an Italian version of Catherine's proclamation in a diplomatic dispatch, which can be found in the National Archives in London, within the 'State Papers Foreign 1509-1782' collection: SP 98/75: p. 27. Orlov's proclamation can be found transcribed in: Kontogiannis, pp. 461-464. An original copy of the proclamation can be found in the Εθνικό Ιστορικό Μουσείο (National Historical Museum) in Athens. Voltaire, 'Ode Pindarique à Propos la Guerre Présente en Grèce', in *Oeuvres Complètes de Voltaire: avec des Notes et une Notice sur la Vie de Voltaire*, vol. 2, ed. Jean-Antoine-Nicolas de Caritat de Condorcet. Paris: Chez Firmin-Didot Frères, 1843, p. 572.
106 Smilyanskaya, pp. 213-217.

Bibliography

Aggelou, Alkis, ed., *Απολογία*. Athens: Hermes, 1976.
Andriotis, Nikolaos, 'Το Χρωνικό του Άμστερνταμ', *Nea Estia*, 10 (1931), pp. 914-920.
Argyriou, Asterios, *Les Exégèses Grecques de l'apocalypse à l'époque Turque, 1453-1821*. Thessalonika: Etairia Makedonikon Spoudon, 1982.
Armitage, David and Sanjay Subrahmanyam, eds., *The Age of Revolutions in Global Context, c. 1760-1840*. New York: Palgrave Macmillan, 2010.
Burke, Edmund, *Reflections on the French Revolution*. London: J.M. Dent & Sons, 1791.
Burke, Edmund, 'The History of Europe', *The Annual Register*, 12 (1769), pp. 1-73.
Dapontes, K., 'Όνειρον', in *Οι Πρόδρομοι*, ed. L. Vranouses. Athens: Ζαχαρόπουλος, 1955.

Dimaras, Konstantinos, 'L'apport de l'Auflärung au Développement de la Conscience Néo-hellénique', in *Les Lumières et la Formation de la Conscience Nationale chez les Peoples du Sud-est Européen*, ed. C. Grecescu and S. Râpeanu eds. Bucharest: Association internationale d'études du sud-est européen, 1970.

Dimaras, Konstantinos, ed., *Τα Ευρισκόμενα*, 2nd edn. Athens: Hermes, 1999.

Glykis, Nikolaos, *Ερμηνεία της κραταιοτάτης και σεβαστής Αικατερίνης Β'*. Venice: Nikolaos Glykis, 1770.

Gritsopoulos, Tasos, *Τα Ορλωφικά. Η εν Πελοποννήσω Επανάστασις του 1770 και τα Επακόλουθα Αυτής*. Athens: Etairia Historikon Spoudon, 1967.

Gundoglu, Birol, 'Ottoman Constructions of the Morea Rebellion, 1770s: A Comprehensive Study of Ottoman Attitudes to the Greek Uprising', PhD dissertation, University of Toronto, 2012.

Hatzopoulos, Marios, 'Oracular Prophecy and the Politics of Toppling Ottoman Rule in South-East Europe', *The Historical Review*, 8 (2011), pp. 95–116.

Henderson, G.P., *The Revival of Greek Thought, 1620–1830*. Albany, NY: State University of New York Press, 1970.

Hölderlin, Friedrich, *Hyperion and Selected Poems*, ed. Eric L. Santner, vol. 22. New York: Continuum, 1990.

Hurewitz, J.C., ed., *The Middle East and North Africa in World Politics: A Documentary Record*. New Haven, CT: Yale University Press, 1975.

Jusdanis, Gregory, *The Necessary Nation*. Princeton, NJ: Princeton University Press, 2001.

Kitromilides, Paschalis, 'War and Political Consciousness: Theoretical Implications of Eighteenth-Century Greek Historiography', in *East Central European Society and War in the Pre-Revolutionary Eighteenth Century*, ed. Gunther E. Rothenburg, Béla K. Király and Peter F. Sugar. New York: Columbia University Press, 1982, pp. 351–370.

Kitromilides, Paschalis, 'The Enlightenment East and West: A Comparative Perspective on the Ideological Origins of the Balkan Political Traditions', *Canadian Review of Studies in Nationalism*, 10, no. 1 (1983), pp. 51–70.

Kitromilides, Paschalis, 'The Last Battle of the Ancients and Moderns', *Modern Greek Studies Yearbook*, 1 (1985), pp. 79–91.

Kitromilides, Paschalis, *Ιώσηπος Μοισιόδαξ: Οι Συντεταγμένες της Βαλκανικής Σκέψης τον 18ο Αιώνα*. Athens: MIET, 1985.

Kitromilides, Paschalis, *The Enlightenment as Social Criticism: Iosipos Moisiodax and Greek Culture in the Eighteenth Century*. Princeton, NJ: Princeton University Press, 1992.

Kitromilides, Paschalis, 'John Locke and the Greek Intellectual Tradition: An Episode in Locke's Reception in South-East Europe', in *Locke's Philosophy: Content and Context*, ed. G.A.J. Rogers. Oxford: Oxford University Press, 1994, pp. 217–235.

Kitromilides, Paschalis, *Νεοελληνικός Διαφωτισμός: Οι Πολιτικές και Κοινωνικές Ιδέες*. Athens: MIET, 1996.

Kitromilides, Paschalis, *Enlightenment and Revolution: The Making of Modern Greece*. Cambridge, MA: Harvard University Press, 2013.

Kontogiannis, Pantelis, *Οι Έλληνες κατα τον Πρώτον επί Αικατερίνης Β΄ Ρωσσοτουρκικόν Πόλεμον*. Athens: I.D. Sakellariou, 1903.

Kostantaras, D., *Infamy and Revolt: the Rise of the National Problem in Early Modern Greek Thought*. Boulder, CO: Eastern European Monographs, 2006.

Legrand, Émile, ed., *Bibliographie Hellénique du Dix-Huitième Siècle*, vol. 2. Paris: Société d'édition Les Belles Lettres, 1928.

Liakos, Antonis, 'Hellenism and the Making of Modern Greece: Time, Language, Space', in *Hellenisms: Culture, Identity, and Ethnicity from Antiquity to Modernity*, ed. Katerina Zacharia. Aldershot: Ashgate, 2008, pp. 201-236.
Mackridge, Peter, *Language and National Identity in Greece, 1766-1796*. Oxford: Oxford University Press, 2009.
Moisiodax, Iosipos, Θεωρία της Γεωγραφίας. Vienna: Johann Thomas Trattner, 1781.
Moisiodax, Iosipos, 'Ηθική Φιλοσοφία', in *Ιώσηπος Μοισιοδάξ*, ed. Paschalis Kitromilides. Athens: ΜΕΙΤ, 1985, pp. 323-341.
Moisiodax, Iosipos, 'Παραλλαγή του προς Νικοκλέα λόγου περί Βασιλέας του Ισοκράτους η Κεφάλαια Πολιτικά', in *Ιώσηπος Μοισιοδάξ*, ed. Paschalis Kitromilides. Athens: ΜΕΙΤ, 1985, pp. 345-355.
Molos, Vasilis, 'Nationness in the Absence of a Nation: Narrating the Prehistory of the Greek National Movement', PhD dissertation, New York University, 2014.
Palaiologos, Konstantinos, 'Ρωσικά περί Ελλάδος έγγραφα νυν το πρώτον εις την Ελληνικήν Μεθερμηνευόμενα', *Παρνασσός*, 1881, pp. 143-152.
Paparrigopoulos, Konstantinos, *Ιστορία του Ελληνικού Έθνους από των Αρχαιότατων Χρώνων μέχρι της Βασιλείας Γεωργίου του Α*, vols. 1-4. Athens: S. Paulidou, 1860-1874.
Politis, Alexis, 'From Christian Roman Emperors to the Glorious Greek Ancestors', in *Byzantium and the Modern Greek Identity*, ed. David Ricks and Paul Magdalino. Brookfield, VT: Ashgate, 1998, pp. 1-14.
Reddaway, William Fiddian, ed., *Documents of Catherine the Great: The Correspondence with Voltaire and the Instruction of 1767*. New York: Russell & Russell, 1971.
Roessel, David E., *In Byron's Shadow: Modern Greece in the English and American Imagination*. New York: Oxford University Press, 2002.
Rotzokos, Nikos, *Εθναφύπνιση και Εθνογένεση: Ορλωφικά και Ελληνική Ιστοριογραφία*. Athens: Βιβλιοράμα, 2007.
Sakellariou, Michael B., *Η Πελοπόννησος κατά την Δευτέραν Τουρκοκρατίαν (1715-1821)*. Athens: Verlag der 'Byzantinisch-Neugriechischen Jahrbücher', 1939.
Sathas, Konstantinos, *Τουρκοκρατουμένη Ελλάδα: Ιστορικόν Δοκίμιον Περί προς Αποτίναξιν του Οθωμανικού Ζυγού Επαναστάσεων του Ελληνικού Έθνους*. Athens: Andreou Koromela, 1869.
Sathas, Konstantinos, ed., *Μεσαιωνική Βιβλιοθήκη*, vol. 3. Venice: Typois tou Chronou, 1872.
Skouvaras, Vangeles, *Ιωάννης Πρίγκος: η Ελληνική Παροικία του Άμστερνταμ, η Σχολή και η Βιβλιοθήκη Ζαγοράς*. Athens: Ekdosi tis Istorikis kai Laografikis Etarias ton Thessalon, 1964.
Smilyanskaya, Elena, '"Protection' or 'Possession': How Russians Created a Greek Principality in 1770-1775', in *Power and Influence in South-Eastern Europe, 16th-19th Century*, ed. Maria Baramova, Plamen Mitev, Ivan Parvev and Vania Racheva. Zurich: Lit, 2013, pp. 209-217.
Todorova, Maria, *Imagining the Balkans*. New York: Oxford University Press, 1997.
Trencsényi, Balázs and Michal Kopeček, eds., *Discourses on Collective Identity in Central and Southeastern Europe*. Budapest: Central European University Press, 2006.
Vacalopoulos, Apostolos E., *Ιστορία του Νέου Ελληνισμού*, vol. 4. Thessaloniki, 1961.
Voltaire, 'Ode Pindarique à Propos la Guerre Présente en Grèce', in *Oeuvres Complètes de Voltaire: avec des Notes et une Notice sur la Vie de Voltaire*, vol. 2, ed. Jean-Antoine-Nicolas de Caritat de Condorcet. Paris: Chez Firmin-Didot Frères, 1843, pp. 571-572.
Voulgaris, Eugenios, *Η Λογική εκ Παλαιώντε και Νεωτέρων Συνερανισθείσα*. Leipzig: Vreitkopf, 1766.

Voulgaris, Eugenios, *Εισήγησις της Αυτοκρατορικής Μεγαλειότητος Αικατερίνας Β'*. St. Petersburg, 1771.

Vranouses, Leandros, *Οι Πρόδρομοι*. Athens: I.N. Zacharopoulou, 1955.

Xanthos, Emmanuel, *Απομνημονεύματα περί της Φιλικής Εταιρίας*, vol. 9. Athens: Vivliothiki, 1956.

4

Military Reforms as a Diplomatic Bargaining Chip: French-Ottoman Relations at the End of the Eighteenth Century

Antoaneta Atanasova
Sofia University

Introduction

The tangibility of the Ottoman crisis in the eighteenth century forced a number of sultans to focus their attention on the development of European military technologies and practices, which soon grew into real attempts at reform. Encouraged by French ministers, this aspiration was also a constituent part of the Eastern Question, as it coincided with the interests of France to preserve the integrity of the Ottoman Empire without engaging in a French-Ottoman coalition against other Christian states. These were not the only factors that led France to develop a practice of providing military support to the Sublime Porte in the form of military experts. That way the French maintained their policy of neutrality, which was favourable to the Ottomans. It also helped the French to maintain their presence in the Ottoman Empire and to pursue their interests in the southeast without violating any principles or signing a political alliance.

These introductory sentences help to show the aims of this chapter go beyond cannon casting, fortress construction and engineering, but also beyond the strategy and tactics of war. The study of military reforms as a diplomatic bargaining chip involves several different fields – diplomatic and military history and the related intelligence history, as well as technology history and knowledge sharing. Without overlooking these aspects, emphasis is placed on the French political decisions which turned the Ottoman military developments into a diplomatic bargaining chip.

Aside from international relations, the conduct of the Ottoman military reforms and hence French influence depended to a great extent on internal processes. Innovation had its opponents in the parties of the Janissaries and the Ulema, who were constantly pushing for the end to European influence and for the abolition of the newly created corps. Additional difficulties in the late eighteenth century were caused by the Ayans, who challenged the power of the central Ottoman state and diverted the attention of French diplomats.

These obstacles compelled France to consider a 'back-up plan' for its Ottoman policy, in the hope of concluding a union treaty with the Sublime Porte, but stubbornness prevailed and no alliance was signed. Of course, Capitulations, or trade agreements between the two countries, existed, but they never led to a political alliance. Another reason for change in the political course is the possibility for France to invade the Ottoman territories. Its military experts carried out intelligence missions and drew up plans for military action when deemed prudent.

The successes of the French military missions mainly involved technical improvements to the Ottoman army. France received a strong diplomatic weapon because the experts were trusted by the Ottoman statesmen, which gave the French influence in Constantinople. The interest of the sultan and other statesmen in European practices and political processes increased thanks to the French experts. This led to the integration of the Ottoman Empire into the European system of states by the end of the eighteenth century.

French Military Experts in the Ottoman Army: A General Overview

Innovations to the Ottoman army based on the European model began in earnest in the eighteenth and nineteenth centuries when the Ottoman Empire began to concede defeats to its rivals. On the other hand, bringing military technologies to the Oriental capital became a means of helping to realize political interests. In this game, France played an important role, although this was not without effort. To induce an Ottoman intervention in international affairs, the French diplomats used a range of methods, including proposals to send military missions to the sultan.

Among the diplomatic actions used by the French, the aid received for Selim III's (1789–1807) reforms was used by the diplomats as a bargaining chip to fulfil French political interests. The strategy of sending military advisors to the sultan was not a new French policy. A retrospective overview of eighteenth-century Franco-Ottoman relations reveals several military missions closely connected to diplomatic ones. Furthermore, between 1784 and 1788 there was a merging of military and diplomatic missions as the French ambassador to the Porte, Choiseul-Gouffier (1752–1817), was also in charge of the military mission of more than three hundred French officers in Ottoman service. Although this case is very significant, it is not an exception. The success of the mission of the famous baron François de Tott (1733–1793), who was simultaneously a military advisor and diplomat to the sultan, would bring similar results.

In addition, the aforementioned missions were sent to the Porte during a period of intensive and dynamic changes to the political map of Europe. They were meant to counterbalance Russia's ambitions to rule politically as well as economically the Black Sea region. Despite their efforts, the French military advisors were not especially successful. This provoked King Louis XVI to look for a new policy in southeast Europe. In 1787 he signed a trade agreement with Russia that regulated the rights of both states in the Black Sea as well as in the eastern Mediterranean.[1] The intention of the French government was to turn the trade agreement into a political one. Eventually, France was tempted by the idea of partaking in a Christian alliance that would include France, Russia, the Habsburg monarchy and possibly Spain, the aim of which first and foremost was to push the Muslims out of Europe,[2] as well as acquire Ottoman territories. As compensation, France would acquire Syria and Egypt.[3] However, these plans were never realized because of the French Revolution. The new French regime had now to develop a different policy towards the Ottoman Empire.

Although after 1789 the Ottoman factor in European-Ottoman relations became less significant,[4] the new French policy-makers were trying to persuade Selim III to enter a formal Franco-Ottoman alliance[5] against the anti-French coalitions in Europe. This measure was far from being realized, especially after King Louis XVI was executed on 6 April 1793, when the sultan decided to end any political contacts with France. Diplomatic relations were not restored until 1795 when a new political alliance was offered to the Porte by the French Republic and French military experts were requested by the Porte.[6]

When negotiations got underway in 1795, the Porte sent to France an Ottoman representative – the French diplomat Jean-Baptiste Barthélemy de Lesseps (1766–1834). His mission was to arrange for an engineer to be sent to the Ottoman capital to build a dry dock for the sultan's navy. The dry dock would allow repairs to be made to naval ships and for soldiers to receive training.[7]

The main obstacle during the negotiations was the Ottoman requirement that the basin be built by the creator of its prototype in Toulon, Antoine Groignard. According to French analysts, who included the Minister of the Navy and Colonies, it was unnecessary for the Ottomans to have such a dry dock built, since they had so few vessels.[8] Thus the French government refused to send Groignard, offering instead the services of another specialist. France's excuse for not sending Groignard was his age – he was now seventy years old.[9] On 26 September 1795, the French Republic informed the Kapudan-Paşa that another engineer, Pierre Fergo, would instead be sent. Fergo, who had led the construction of the Port of Cherbourg in Lower Normandy, had the experience necessary to serve the Porte. In Constantinople, he was appointed head of the mission for hydro construction and was allowed to choose the specialists necessary for the realization of his task. These specialists included a draftsman-geographer, master stonemason, master carpenter, apprentice stonemason and a ship modeller. The costs of the tools, patterns and books were met by the French. The Republic granted the experts some transportation and other expenses, but expected to be reimbursed by the Ottomans.[10] Although Pierre Fergo designed the basin and docks to be similar to those in Toulon in 1797, their construction was entrusted by the Porte to the Swede Rodé, and the work was carried out between 1797 and 1800.[11]

After all these intense negotiations, Franco-Ottoman relations were more of a beneficiary than the Ottoman army. After several years of interrupted diplomatic contacts, relations were restored with new political opportunities for both governments.

When the Porte decided in 1796 to receive a new French diplomatic representative in Constantinople, France chose Jean-Baptiste Annibal Aubert-Dubayet (1757–1797), who took up his post saying: 'I am appointed to the most interesting embassy in Europe.'[12] One of the ambassador's tasks was to draw up and offer to the Ottomans the draft of a new treaty. The draft included clauses for the recovery of the Capitulations, and freedom of navigation for French commercial and military vessels in all Ottoman seas. It developed also the idea of mutual actions in war and a promise that neither side would sign a separate peace. Dubayet ended his report to the French Ministry of Foreign Affairs with the words: 'Finally, I said that the Republic, considering all Europe as enemy, appreciates the loyalty of his devoted ally, the Sultan; that I was sent to His Highness to strengthen, if possible, the ties that unite both nations to which the Fate gave common enemies.'[13]

Soon after, political events in Europe led the French government to abandon its explicit promise for a Franco-Ottoman alliance for fear of a new diplomatic crisis and submitted a new proposal to the sultan. Aware that the sultan was eager to reform his army, Dubayet had to organize military aid to the Ottoman capital. In March 1797, Dubayet presented to the sultan an entire artillery unit, composed of French officers. The Padişah approved their incorporation into the Ottoman army and agreed to pay their salaries direct from the Ottoman treasury.[14]

The French artillery assisted the ambassador in several ways. First, it reduced the influence of other European military specialists such as the English and Swedish, as well as some renegades from the French army. Furthermore, it was hoped the new artillery would convince the sultan to participate in the war against the anti-French coalitions in Europe. For a short period of time, France regained its dominant position in the Ottoman capital but could not persuade the sultan to start a war with any of the European powers.

Although the efforts of Aubert-Dubayet could have had far-reaching effects for French policy in the Orient, they were abandoned in 1798 when Napoleon began his campaign in Egypt (1798–1801). In response, Selim III declared war with France in September 1798, a few months after the Egyptian campaign commenced. It is well known that when the Porte was in a state of war, the diplomatic representatives of its enemies were imprisoned in the so-called prison of the Seven Towers. Between 1798 and 1801, almost all of the French military specialists were imprisoned there together with the ambassador. It is unclear whether the sultan was aware of the political influence of the military advisors or he considered them also to be diplomatic representatives. Whatever the reason for their imprisonment, two advisors continued their work with the Ottoman army – Jacques-Balthazard le Brun and Honoré Benoît.

Jacques-Balthazard le Brun (1759–1820) was the most influential French military advisor during the reign of Selim III. Under his supervision, new shipyards were built at Hasköy and Ayvansaray. He introduced new technology into the shipyards, including gantry cranes and the method of building ships on the coast before finishing them at sea. New building materials were also adopted by Le Brun. As the Ottoman territories were rich in copper deposits and the metal could easily be transported by sea from Trabzon to Constantinople, it was used instead of iron for the needs of the artillery and the navy, including nails and the hulls of ships.[15]

Between 1796 and 1797, Le Brun was also instructor at the school of geometry Hendesehâne, where he taught several disciplines, including mathematics and geometry (*ilm-i rakam u ilm-i hendese*), ship design (*resim ve gemilerin tasvîrât*) and practical education. Moreover, he insisted that the Ottoman government build a new academic field for training (*talimhâne*) in Constantinople. These educational undertakings were of great importance for the Ottoman navy, which improved beyond all recognition. Last but not least, Le Brun had an important role in attracting new French military specialists to the Ottoman army. Among them was his brother Polide le Brun, who arrived in Constantinople in 1796 and was assigned to the maritime arsenal.[16]

Recognizing Jacques-Balthazard le Brun's influence over the sultan's ministers, France recruited him as a diplomat, especially since the other French diplomatic representatives had been imprisoned. The diplomatic mission of Le Brun consisted of preparing the way for peace negotiations as well as persuading the sultan to recognize Napoleon as emperor. Unfortunately, little information is available on what Le Brun was actually able to do.

The presence of French military specialists was greatly reduced after 1800. After the peace treaty of 1801, France needed to focus its efforts on reducing Russian and British influence over the Ottomans. As a step towards improving bilateral relations, Napoleon sent two specialists to the Porte but they were not warmly welcomed and so had little impact on the development of the Ottoman army.

A French military engineer, Antoine de Juchereau de St. Denys, was tasked by the Ottoman government to report on the state of the fortifications of the Dardanelles at a time when threatened by an English fleet (1807). Upon concluding that the fortifications were not strong enough to repel an enemy fleet, he proposed strengthening Karaburnu with a fleet of twelve vessels.[17]

This last episode in Franco-Ottoman relations during the rule of Sultan Selim III shows that nothing had changed in France's Oriental policy even after the end of the Ancien régime. Throughout the entire eighteenth century, France sent military specialists to the Ottoman Empire as a means of diplomacy. Most often, the military advisors had more of an influence on Ottoman political decisions than they did improving the Ottoman army.

The Ottoman Empire under Sultan Selim III as a Part of the International Political System

The rule of Sultan Selim III (r. 1789–1807)[18] began during the Ottoman war against Russia and the Habsburg monarchy (1787–1791/92). Only a few months after taking the throne in Constantinople, in October 1789, the sultan saw the Habsburgs occupy Belgrade, while at the same time the Russians occupied Bucharest. If this course of action were to continue, during any further military campaign the Ottoman capital would find itself threatened by the European forces. Although the Ottomans signed a political contract with Sweden on 11 July 1789, and Sweden itself was engaged in the Russo-Swedish War of 1788–1790, the situation for the Ottomans did not improve. For this reason the sultan considered the option of signing a peace treaty with Russia and the Habsburg monarchy, which was realized in the autumn of 1789.[19] However, to avert such a treaty, in November 1789 the Prussian ambassador proposed an Ottoman-Prussian Union, according to which Prussia would have declared war on Russia and the Habsburgs. The Ottomans would have received help for the Crimea and the Caucasus, while in return the sultan would assist the acquisition of Danzig and Thorn from Russia and Galicia from Poland. On 31 January 1790, the alliance was formally signed but it was never ratified.

In addition to military conflict in Europe, the new Ottoman ruler had internal enemies to deal with. Among them were the so-called *derebeys* or *ayans*, who included Vidin Osman Pazvantoglu (1758–1807) and Janina Ali Tepedelenli (1741–1822). Although revolutionary France did not offer political support to the Ottoman war and insisted that peace should be concluded, the government in Paris played a game of double-cross by sponsoring both the central Ottoman government and the *derebeys*. This was one of the reasons why relations between Constantinople and France cooled.[20] France's relations with the secessionists was also among the reasons why the Ottomans did not accept France as a mediator of the peace with Russia and the Habsburgs. France's offer of mediation during the peace negotiations was aimed at strengthening her position in Europe and of declaring her commitment to the events in southeast Europe. Peace between the Habsburgs and Ottomans was ratified by the Treaty of Svishtov on 4 August 1791, which was followed by the Russian-Ottoman Iasi peace agreement of 9 January 1792.

Meanwhile, France had to deal with internal and external enemies of the Revolution of 1789.[21] Differences between the revolutionists and royalists in France culminated in civil war. In 1792, Charles-Louis de Huge Semonvil (1759–1839) was appointed French ambassador to Constantinople. He was forced to remain in the city on the Bosphorus without any accreditation from the sultan. This was not without good reason. The last representative of the old regime, Count Marie-Gabriel-Florent-Auguste de Choiseul-Gouffier (1752–1817), conducted an intensive campaign against the new regime in France and all of its representatives in the Ottoman Empire. His efforts were in support of the brothers of the last French king who were members of the Habsburg monarchy.[22]

In fact, the external enemies of the Revolution were united around the Habsburgs in seven military coalitions between 1792 and 1815. This was resistance against the 'dynamic force of French imperialism' according to Paul Kennedy.[23] Since 1792, the French had been trying to recruit the Porte to their side and the French Foreign Ministry saw the opportunity to conclude a defensive and offensive pact with the Porte.[24] The signing of such a document, according to some observers in Constantinople, was the only way to overcome the neutrality proclaimed by Selim III, and for the Porte to go to war.[25] In 1793, the proposal for a military alliance became a bargaining chip for the recognition of the French Republic by the Ottoman state. Its ambassador was the envoy extraordinary Marie-Louis Saint-Croix (1749–1830).[26] The sultan's response was that 'the Ottoman government will be not the last, but certainly not the first, which would recognize the French Republic'.[27] Thus Franco-Ottoman relations were interrupted between 1793 and 1795.[28] The reason for Selim III's decision was the execution of King Louis XVI, and the dominant influence of representatives of the royalist camp in the Ottoman capital.

France's international standing was threatened when Russia, taking advantage of the contradictions that existed between the other European powers, took part in the second and third partition of Poland in 1793 and 1795. While expanding Russian territory, it deprived France of an old ally – Poland – and thus of the opportunity to consolidate cooperation with the Habsburg monarchy and Prussia.[29] The reaction of France was delayed because of the war against the Allies from the First Coalition. Only in 1795, when France declared peace with Prussia and Spain, on the occasion of the second partition of Poland, did messages such as the following appear in French military reports:

> Day after day Russia becomes more and more dangerous and threatening. (…) If Europe remains blind, the greatness of France, and the interests of the French nation, ought to pull Europe out of delusion and put an end to the expansion of Russia (…).[30]

In order to keep its promise to 'put an end to the expansion of Russia', France decided to strengthen its diplomatic presence in the Danubian principalities, relying on its close ties with the Moldovan prince Michael Sutsu (r. 1792–1795), who, in 1794, was instrumental in supporting the Polish-Lithuanian uprising led by Tadeusz Kosciuszko (1746–1817). This support was assured by a well-organized network of informants and messengers established by the former French diplomatic representative in Poland, Marie Descorche-Ste-Croix (1791–1792), but also the granting of asylum to Polish refugees in the Danubian principalities.[31] Part of the strategy of the French government was to convince potential allies against Russia, including the Ottoman Empire, to reform their armies.[32]

At this strategic moment, in 1795, France was able to restore diplomatic relations with the Porte. Sultan Selim III recognized the French Republic and its new envoy extraordinary in Constantinople, Raymond de Verninac Saint-Maur (1762–1822). The same year that peace in Europe was restored, the representative of the Habsburg allies in Constantinople was forced to postpone all attempts to involve the Ottoman government in war against France. The French envoy offered the Porte a proposal for union that contained sixteen paragraphs, including the regulation of the passage of French vessels in the Straits of the Bosphorus and the Dardanelles.[33] The Ottomans responded with a counter-proposal requiring the French to send them a military mission and three ship designs that the Ottomans could use to build their own vessels.[34] To these negotiations, France sent Verninak, their envoy to Constantinople, and Truget-Delacroix, the French Minister of Foreign Affairs and Minister of the Fleet. As the Ottomans were uneasy with their contacts with the new French government, they appointed the Frenchman Jean-Baptiste Barthelemy Lesseps (1766–1834) to negotiate on their behalf.[35]

Given that the Ottoman Empire had restored its upstanding with France, the envoy extraordinary was quickly replaced by an ambassador, General Jean-Baptiste Anibal Aubert Dubayet or Du Bayet (1757–1797),[36] who stated: 'I have been appointed to the most interesting embassy in Europe.'[37] Dubayet was familiar with the task he faced in the Ottoman capital because he set off for the Bosphorus after having been Minister of War.[38] In his efforts to strengthen the Porte's resistance to Russian ambitions, Dubayet was instrumental in implementing military reforms in the Ottoman Empire during this time along the lines of the European model.

In the summer of 1796, Dubayet brought with him a small entourage to the Ottoman Empire – his friend Cara-Saint-Cyr, who became the embassy secretary, and generals Menan and Colencour. Dubayet was instructed to follow the diplomatic line of Franco-Ottoman relations inherited from the old regime. He was to restore the trading privileges of the Capitulations, but also to restore French patronage over the Catholics in the Ottoman Empire.[39] It was considered that this would give the French ambassador priority over the representatives of the other Great Powers in Constantinople by restoring the French to their position from a bygone age. Unlike the French kings, however, the new government was ready to sign a formal alliance with the Ottomans – a move that must have signalled friendly relations between the French Republic and the government of Sultan Selim III. Dubayet was advised that the:

> Turks are our oldest, most natural, most loyal and most indispensable allies (…) The French listened to the sound of reason and wisdom and they finally want to open their arms for old friends of theirs and to divert them from the storm that mad ambition would bring to their heads.[40]

The ambassador was tasked with drafting the terms of the future defensive and offensive treaty between France and the Ottomans. The text of the proposal drawn up by ambassador Dubayet[41] contained provisions for the recovery of the Capitulations, freedom of navigation for both French commercial and naval vessels in all Ottoman seas, the promise of mutual assistance in the case of war between either of the two of them and Russia, the Habsburg monarchy or England, the settling of payment for any land or naval support provided by France, and that neither party would sign a separate peace.[42] It seemed this time that France had gone too far in its relations with the Porte.[43] However, the granting of permission for French commercial and naval ships to sail through the Straits would give France a huge advantage and the Republic would strengthen its presence in the Mediterranean through three means: friendship with the Ottoman Empire, an alliance with Spain and Napoleon's influence in Italy.[44] Dubayet concluded his report on the results of his work in Constantinople with the following words:

> Finally I said that the Republic, having enemies all across the Europe, appreciates the loyalty of its dedicated ally, the Sultan; I am sent to His Highness to strengthen, if possible, even further the links that unite the two nations which have the same enemies.[45]

It is clear that this contract was aimed against a range of forces. If by the end of the eighteenth century France wished to encourage the Ottoman Empire to act against the Habsburg monarchy or Russia, Britain was now explicitly named as a common enemy of the potential alliance. So, permission to navigate in all Ottoman seas could be considered preparation for a Franco-British confrontation in the Mediterranean and in particular in Egypt. And Egypt was an integral part of French interests.

Above all, before the conclusion of any alliance, the contradictions between royalists and republicans in Constantinople, which occurred in the 1790s, had to be sorted out.[46]

Although Dubayet proceeded according to the requirements of the French government, the Republic renounced the union as a diplomatic move, the reason being that on 17 November 1796 Catherine II died, and French expectations were that her heir Pavel I (r. 1796–1801) would be more favourable to French interests. Unexpectedly for the French, however, the Russia of Pavel I was closer to the Sublime Porte, and so the five-member governing Directory – or Directorate – began to develop a new strategy towards southeast Europe. They first tried to increase France's influence over the sultan by sending French military specialists to the Ottoman Empire. They then decided to focus on the anti-Ottoman sentiments of the subordinate population.

For the purposes of the new military mission, the French Ministry of Foreign Affairs avidly began looking at the old practices of French military missions to the sultan, which had been popular among the politicians of the Ancien régime.[47] Meanwhile, the French had already begun recruiting specialists to be sent to the Ottoman Empire. For some French officers, the Ottoman state offered an ideal opportunity for career development.[48] Thus the military aid to the Ottomans was considered by senior French officers to be more of a business than a charitable act. Even Napoleon Bonaparte himself sent a request to the French government to be assigned to Dubayet's artillery in Constantinople. The Republic rejected his request, though it would be a mere two years before Napoleon led the army that invaded the Ottoman Empire.[49]

The artillery the French Republic provided as a gift to the sultan arrived in Constantinople in January 1797. Although the artillery had been ready to depart Toulon in 1796, obstacles that arose from the war with England in the Mediterranean prevented the artillery departing by sea. It was necessary for some units to travel the land route, which delayed their arrival in the Ottoman capital.[50] In March 1797, the artillery was presented to the sultan who immediately approved its incorporation into the Ottoman army and, as noted previously, agreed to pay their salaries direct from the Ottoman treasury.[51] Despite the ambassador's diplomatic efforts to engage the Porte in the French political game, he did not succeed, and the Ottoman Empire did not take part in any European conflicts.

Upon his failure, Aubert Dubayet had to find a means of compensating French interests. So, he analysed the geography of Moldavia with the intention of sending a French military specialist there, assisted by the French government. The military specialist in Moldavia was to organize an army composed of different nationalities and religions and financed by the Ottoman Empire. This second 'Ottoman army' was expected to be more disciplined and motivated in opposition to Russia because it would be composed of Ottoman subjects who were both Christian and Muslim refugees from the conquered Polish state, and refugees from Russia and the Habsburg army.[52] Dubayet discussed implementing this plan with Prince Alexander Callimachi (r. 1795–1799), and together they decided to encourage Poland to start a new rebellion that would coincide with the French campaign in Italy in 1797.[53]

By 1797, France undertook an intensive propaganda campaign aimed at the subordinate population, especially the Greeks in the Ottoman Empire. This French propaganda has been analysed in detail by Plamen Mitev, who stated that its objective was to incite 'patriotism and revolutionary spirit of the Greek population of the

Archipelago'.[54] Their methods included spreading rumours about requests by the French ambassador for the independence of Morea, Crete and Cyprus.

After the Treaty of Campo-Formio (October 1797) between France and the Habsburg monarchy, the French Republic acquired the Ionian Islands (Corfu, Cephalonia, Zakynthos, Ithaca, etc.) and Ancona and became a neighbour of the Ottoman Empire. The issue of these territories became a stumbling block in Franco-Russian relations, because the Russian tsar Pavel I intervened with his fleet in defence of the Ottomans and Russian interests in the Ionian Islands and Malta.[55] There is a curious fact about the French propaganda in Bucharest and Iasi, where demonstrations were organized on the occasion of the accession of the Ionian Islands from France.[56]

These events were part of the Directory's new policy of focusing attention on potential internal opponents of the Porte. During the previous decades, France had developed such a strategy in relation to the Habsburg monarchy and the Hungarian insurgents, and so after 1798 tried to apply the same model to the Ottoman Empire. This time French interests included the acquisition of some Ottoman territories, in particular Egypt.[57]

The Directory decided to apply this policy not only to the Greek population of the Ottoman Empire but also to the *derebeys*, or *ayans*, such as Osman Pazvantoglou of Vidin, who received French help against the Central Ottoman government during the siege of the city in 1798.[58] A French diplomat, Pierre Ruffin (1742–1824), proposed that policy-makers in Paris should support the *derebey* as a possible contender for the Ottoman throne and that France should receive certain territories – Egypt, Cyprus and Rhodes – in return. After the declaration of war, Ruffin insisted that the Directory should send financial aid to the *derebey* of Vidin. A sum of 30 million francs, offered by France, was to be used by Pazvantoglou to pay an army recruited against the Porte.[59] Unlike Pazvantoglou, Ali Tepedelenli felt threatened by the war between France and Russia in the Adriatic Sea and preferred a middle way between the two forces.[60] However, unlike Pierre Ruffin, the French ambassador in Constantinople, Auber Dubayet, was disturbed by the *derebeys*' actions and believed that if they united, the ambitions of Napoleon to conquer Egypt and revolutionize the Greeks would be facilitated. All that could destroy the Ottoman Empire.[61]

Against the arguments of Dubayet, the French government decided to go ahead at least with its policy towards the subordinate Greek population, and so all the consuls in their cities were instructed to encourage the Greek desire for freedom. The intentions of the Directory did not go unnoticed by the Ottoman government, and Dubayet had to give a pledge to the Ottomans that their territory would be respected. On 28 August 1797, the ambassador sent a communication to the Reis-Effendi,[62] in which he explained that these 'rumours' were made up by French and Ottoman enemies who wanted to create a rift between the two old allies.[63] The ambassador's assertions of a 'constant peace' were proved false at the beginning of the Egyptian campaign.[64]

After Aubert Dubayet's death, General Claude Cara-Saint-Cyr (1760–1834) took the role of ambassador before a new French representative could be sent to the Ottoman capital. Upon Dubayet's death, France's vigorous attempts to draw the Ottomans onto their side were interrupted. When Napoleon's Egyptian expedition began in May 1798, Sultan Selim III reacted only after several months and didn't declare war until

September of the same year. One reason for this delay was the 'civil war' between the central Ottoman government and the *derebey* of Vidin, Pazvantoglou.[65] Marie Descorche-Ste-Croix was sent to the Ottoman Empire for the second time in the hope of convincing the sultan that the actions undertaken by France in Egypt were directed against the Mamelukes and British, and were not a direct threat to the sultan. It would appear that the diplomat succeeded in his task as the Ottoman response to the expedition was softened.[66] In contrast, the threat hanging over the Ottomans attracted the attention of the other Great Powers and so the Ottoman Empire signed a treaty with Russia and Britain against Napoleon. This treaty provided for the first European-Ottoman alliance.[67]

This contract redirected Russian policy regarding the Eastern Question towards preserving the integrity of the Ottoman Empire. Clearly, this contrasted with previous Russian foreign policy, but in this case the sultan's help against France was needed.[68] Over the following years, Russia's influence at the Ottoman court increased significantly, to the point whereby the Russian ambassador began attending the Divan.[69] Meanwhile, in 1801, in an attempt to gain the patronage of France, Pazvantoglou sent two agents to Paris – Nedialko Popovich and Polisoy Condotti. Despite an attractive offer on the part of the *derebey*,[70] France chose to restore peace with Selim III. In September 1801, General Horace François Bastien Sebastiani de la Porta (1771–1851) was sent to Constantinople on a diplomatic mission to prepare peace with the Porte, and in June 1802 a treaty was signed. France gave up Egypt and the Ionian Islands, which became the Republic of the Seven United Islands. Russia acted as mediator for the treaty.

The peace treaty favoured a diplomatic rapprochement between Napoleon and Pavel I, and both rulers considered a future French attack on India in Georgia. Among their joint plans was a project to partition the Ottoman territories: the Straits to Russia, Egypt to France.[71] These plans were shelved, however, when on 8 March 1801 British shells landed in Egypt and soon after that, on 23 March, Pavel I was killed. Napoleon, however, did not give up on the idea of an alliance with Russia and made the same proposal to Alexander I (1801–1825) as soon as he succeeded the Russian throne on 24 March 1801. On 8 August 1802, Napoleon asked a Russian minister: 'Is there no one in the empire of Alexander who could succeed the throne of Constantinople?'[72]

In parallel with these 'negotiations' between France and Russia, Napoleon's anti-Russian feelings were also apparent. For example, he promised the Ottoman government he would help them regain the Crimean peninsula and other territories acquired by Russia. Sultan Selim III was supposed to close the Straits to Russian ships and to transfer the same privilege to Napoleon's navy.

Once again, however, the interests of France and Russia collided in southeast Europe. In early 1804, France began a propaganda campaign among the Greeks using manifestos in which the Greeks were called to freedom.[73] It was widely known that Alexander I had interests in the western part of the peninsula and expected cooperation from the subordinate Serbian population there.[74] All this contributed to Russia joining the Third Coalition against Napoleon, immediately after he was proclaimed emperor on 18 May 1804. This time, although Napoleon made the diplomatic effort to ensure the sultan of French loyalty and to put the Ottomans off an alliance with Britain and Russia,[75] the Ottoman Empire became part of the union against France together with

Russia, the Habsburg monarchy, Sweden, Britain, Prussia and the Kingdom of Naples. On 2 December 1805, the European coalition was defeated at Austerlitz, after which only Russia and Britain continued the war against Napoleon. At that time in Paris, two projects were developed for the future of the Ottoman territories. The author of the first of these was the Foreign Minister, Charles Maurice de Talleyrand-Périgord (1754–1838), and the author of the second – Napoleon himself.

According to Talleyrand's draft, France might offer the Habsburg ruler a defensive alliance against Russia, but the efforts of Vienna should be directed to Wallachia, Moldavia, including Bessarabia up to the shores of the Black Sea, and the territory between the Danube and the Stara Planina Mountains to act as an obstacle to Russian ambitions to the south. Moreover, in this way the Russians might need to meet the Habsburgs on the political field: 'When [the Habsburgs] acquire Wallachia and Moldavia Russians, who are now their allies, will become their rivals and natural enemies.'[76]

Napoleon continued his quest for an alliance with Russia and so weaken the Habsburgs. However, France was still in a state of war with Russia, so Napoleon tried once more to push the Ottoman Empire into a war with France's rival. On 27 December 1806, a few months after the signing in July of a Franco-Russian agreement to preserve the integrity of the Ottoman Empire, Napoleon began to fabricate anti-Russian propaganda during the Serbian rebellion in order to arouse fear and to counteract the eventual unification of the rebel forces with those of the Russian army.[77] However, Russian support for the rebels was used largely by Horace Sebastiani to convince the Turks to declare war on Russia.

The first job of Sebastiani in the Ottoman capital was to convince the sultan that the princes of Wallachia and Moldavia – Alexander Ypsilantis and Alexander Moruzi respectively – were not loyal to the Ottoman government.[78] He proposed replacing them[79] with others loyal to France, such as Alexander Sutso and Scarlat Callimachi.[80] This part of the French ambassador's strategy broke the political alliance between the Porte and Russia and provoked a war between the two powers.

Sebastiani assured the Ottoman government that France's aim was to affirm the power of the Ottoman Empire, which on this occasion was not simply a diplomatic move. At this time, Napoleon himself wished neither to destroy the Ottoman Empire nor to acquire parts of its territory. He wanted the Ottoman state to be in a position to oppose Russia, thus with Persia facilitating Napoleon's eastern campaign.[81] Such diplomacy was successful. In the autumn of 1806, the Ottoman government closed the Straits to Russian ships, and after the French victory at Jena in 1806 and the subsequent letter of Napoleon to Sultan Selim III, the Ottoman Empire declared war on Russia.

Britain took the side of Russia and in January 1807 sent an ultimatum to the Porte to restore its pact with Britain, recall its ambassador from Paris, break off relations with France, convey to England the forts on the Dardanelles and all the cannons stationed there, as well for Russia to take control of the Danubian Principalities. The Porte rejected these requests, upon which Anglo-Ottoman relations were shattered. In February 1807, British naval ships entered the Marmara Sea and threatened the Ottoman capital. New ultimatums were made: the Ottoman fleet was to surrender to the British and Britain take the control of all traffic through the Straits. Once again, French military experts led by the French ambassador were appointed to strengthen the Black Sea fortresses, and when Constantinople was threatened by the British fleet in February 1807, Sebastiani personally helped defend the Ottoman capital.[82]

The ensuing events in large part achieved the alliance desired by Napoleon. Moreover, on 21 June 1807, France and Russia reached a truce, complemented by a personal meeting between the two emperors on the River Neman on 25 June. The representative of Prussia offered Russia the Danubian principalities, the Bulgarian territories, Rumelia and the Straits; the Habsburgs were to acquire Dalmatia, Bosnia and Serbia; France the continental Greek territories and islands; while Poland was reborn under the sceptre of the King of Saxony, who acquired territories from Prussia.[83]

Apart from the Treaty of Tilsit on 7 July 1807, two other documents were created and signed, for an offensive and defensive alliance between France and Russia, according to which both sides agreed to act jointly both on land and at sea. The Russian ruler was obliged to conclude a truce with the Porte and pull his troops from the Danubian principalities and to conclude a peace mediated by France. Moreover, Russia had to abandon her desire to acquire Corfu and the Ionian Islands, as well as agree to joint Russian-French action against the Ottoman Empire, if it did not accept French mediation.

In the negotiations at Tilsit, the main discussions were about Constantinople - the city that every ruler wished for himself. On 7 September 1807, Sebastiani received a telegram from the French Minister of Foreign Affairs, which stated:

> However, if the Porte signs a peace with England, and if somehow broke relations with France, consider it lost. The Emperor will now adopt the draft presented after Tilsit for separation of its provinces and its political existence will be completed by the end of the year.[84]

Thus the attempts of Sultan Selim III to integrate the Ottoman Empire into the European system of international relations did not succeed because of internal difficulties, which contributed to the Ottoman state becoming a mere object of European diplomacy[85] and a bargaining chip in international negotiations. It would appear that the Ottoman state was saved from destruction, only because neither Napoleon nor Alexander I wished to engage in a serious war in the Balkans.[86]

The French policy of sending military missions to the sultan followed the general guidelines of international relations, and showed that military professionals took missions near the Bosphorus only when France needed to motivate the Ottoman Empire to become actively involved on the European stage. This practice was completely forgotten after 1800, except for the rescue of Constantinople in 1807, in which case the military experts did not undertake any practical activities to reform the Ottoman army. Thus, even the sultan, who wanted to introduce European practices at different levels of the Ottoman Empire (including the creation of permanent diplomatic missions in European capitals to aid internal reform efforts) failed to overcome the internal and external obstacles to achieve his aims.

French Military Specialists and the Nizam-i Cedid

The era of Selim III was not so unique as to be different from the attempts at the Europeanization of the Ottoman Empire earlier in the eighteenth century, and Selim III's policy was part of the same reform process initiated by his predecessors.[87] The main characteristic of this process was reforms mainly in the military sphere, aimed at improving the efficiency of the army, based on the experience and advice of European experts. The nationality of the invited foreign experts seemed predetermined, given Sultan Selim III's 'Francophily'[88] and the important role of Ottoman ministers trained by Frenchmen in the Empire or even in France. The inconsistency of Franco-Ottoman relations, however, made the incorporation of Frenchmen into the Ottoman artillery and fleet risky.

In 1787, Selim, not yet sultan, was already very interested in the politics of the French state, and he wrote a letter to Louis XVI. Selim asked the king if France would agree to an Ottoman war against Russia. The response of the French monarch was that any conflict should be postponed, as the Ottoman army needed to be reformed first and Louis promised to send fifteen officers as instructors to the army. The reason why France did not want a new Russian-Ottoman War at that time was because of new trade relations between Versailles and St. Petersburg, which would be threatened by a conflict. However, Louis did not want to destroy the impact of France's Ottoman policy, executed by the French military missions in Constantinople. Although there were already more than 300 French specialists in the Ottoman Empire under the command of ambassador Choiseul-Gouffier (1752–1812), France decided to strengthen French-Ottoman relations by offering further experts to the Sultan's army.

Selim was aware of the instruction conducted by the French advisers training the Ottoman army during the reign of Mustafa III (r. 1757–1774) and Abdul Hamid I (r. 1774–1789). Selim witnessed almost the entire process of Europeanization of the Ottoman army in the eighteenth century starting with the first artillery exercises conducted by Baron Francois de Tott (1733–1793).[89] Even more important for Selim's outlook towards France was the role played by French ambassadors Saint-Prix and Choiseul-Gouffier, who requested the French Foreign Minister Charles Gravier de Vergennes (1717–1787) allow a number of Ottomans to study in Paris.[90]

From the very beginning of his rule, Selim III had the idea of reforming the Ottoman army and had wanted to invite for this purpose French military advisers following the model of Europeanization inherited from his predecessors. This desire can be noted as early as the birth of the idea of a 'New Order' (Nizam-i Cedid)[91] for military reforms at the end of the eighteenth century, which quickly became a label for Selim III's entire internal policy.

In his desire to base his reforms on French developments, Selim III consulted the court advisory council (*Meclis-i Meşveret*) made up of statesmen, military men and ulema. It seems that this political decision mimicked the General States in France, given by Louis XVI on 24 January 1789 in order to achieve a solution to the financial crisis. As representatives of all estates took part in the meetings of 5 May 1789 in Versailles, Selim III also consulted the different sections of the Ottoman elite to express an opinion on future reforms. However, most projects, received in the Divan, were conservative and did not offer substantive changes.

Soon after the Revolution, it became clear that the diplomacy of the New regime, 'which characterized French society before the revolution,'[92] supported the Ottoman Nizam-i Cedid, keeping the practices of the Ancien régime. One example of French influence in the Ottoman capital was the court physician, Lorenzo, used by the politicians of both French regimes.[93] An even better illustration of the continuity of French policy in relation to the Ottoman Empire was the question of military reforms and the sending of military experts to the sultan.

In 1792, the Ottomans did not accept the French proposal for a political and military alliance between the two countries. The sultan at that time had no choice but to reject the proposal, highlighting the need for recovery from the war of 1787–1791/2, which had just ended. Selim III asked Versailles for thirteen military specialists: two engineers, two gunners, a cavalry officer, an infantry officer, a civil engineer and naval experts.[94] Although the Porte missed the chance for its first de facto alliance with a European force, it did hire the military experts Brune (naval engineer), Monnier (head of engineering battalion), Mazurie (captain same campus), Auber and Clugny (heads of artillery), all of whom supported restoration of the Ottoman army.

France hoped that this military mission would preserve the Ottoman hostility towards the Russians and Austrians, as in the recent war.[95] These hidden intentions created a foe in Marie-Gabriel-Florent-Auguste de Choiseul-Gouffier, a supporter of the old regime, who would have preferred the sultan to break diplomatic relations with the new French government rather than to accept military experts sent by it. The conflict between monarchists and republicans and its manifestation in the Ottoman capital, seen in the confrontation between the diplomats of the old and new regime, seems to have been the reason why Selim III considered borrowing European technology from another European country, not France. Former French ambassador Choiseul-Gouffier suggested that the sultan seek technology from Vienna – the court which gave refuge to Louis XVI's brothers after the French Revolution. Thus in 1792 the Ottomans sent their esteemed diplomat and scholar Ebubekir Ratab Effendi to the Habsburg court for six months. He described the organization of the Habsburg state and its army in his *Sefaratname*.[96] Meanwhile, Selim III broke off diplomatic relations with Revolutionary France, which was a result of anti-revolutionary propaganda by the former ambassador who made cooperation with Vienna more attractive to the Ottomans. However, an official Habsburg military mission was not sent to the Orient.

Although there was a period after the French Revolution when the French did not have a military mission in the Ottoman Empire, the manner in which training of the artillery and navy was conducted remained the same. Although the instructors and officers were now of Ottoman origin, they themselves had been trained by French instructors. Moreover, in 1795, Choiseul-Gouffier initiated the creation of a new school for military-technical staff, the Mühendishane-i Berri Hümayun (Imperial Military Engineering School). The man responsible for this project was the interpreter at the Swedish Embassy, Muradgea d'Osson (1740–1807),[97] who was of Armenian origin and who insisted that the school would also train non-Muslims as officers. Despite the ambitious intentions, up to 1830 the number of students enrolled was not significant, as was the role of the school in the reforms of the late eighteenth century.[98]

French influence over the Ottoman army continued for another reason: the large number of renegades in the Orient, both supporters of the French monarchy and fugitives from the Republic. Many of these renegades were involved in various military undertakings related to the defence of the Black Sea fortresses. The number of these renegades increased significantly after the Revolution of 1789, having been persecuted because of their ties to the Ancien regime; however, other officers simply did not wish to align themselves with the new political system. Of course, the new French government could not have these officers represent their interests in the Ottoman Empire; Paris was concerned about the loyalty of these men. Furthermore, a British officer became the leader of this group of fugitives, resulting in British influence over the sultan. With Britain managing to take advantage of the break in Franco-Ottoman relations, France was temporarily displaced by Britain in conducting the Ottoman military reforms. However, the Committee of Public Safety was looking for any opportunity to attract back these renegades to the French side, in an effort to protect French political interests in the southeast.[99] The reason why France failed in this regard was that the renegades had the diplomatic support of the British minister in Constantinople, Spencer Smith. One project completed by French renegades under the command of English officers was the construction of new fortifications at Anapa in 1793. These fortifications were built under the guidance of an English officer named Cook, whose team consisted of French fugitives and the Ottoman engineer Ibrahim, who had been trained by Lafite-Clave in the schools and barracks of Keui on the outskirts of Constantinople. At that time, Ibrahim was already a professor at the engineering school, founded by the French.[100]

Although British help in reforming the Ottoman military was limited in scope, it was one reason why Selim III categorically rejected a group of French military specialists sent by France in 1795: Turski, Lazovsi, Legou, Ranshu, Bond, Leons Trule and Timotee Trule never took up appointment in the Ottoman Empire. The execution of the king in 1793 made military cooperation between the Ottomans and the French impossible and was why the restoration of diplomatic relations with the Porte was so important to Paris. Ambassador Aubert Dubayet, the first French representative in the Ottoman capital after the renewal of political contact between the two governments, was able to convince the sultan to place the reconstruction of the fortresses on the Black Sea once more in French hands, those of Monnier and Mazurie. Because of Mazurie's death, however, Monnier undertook this obligation alone. He was an experienced member of the military mission of Choiseul-Gouffer from 1784 to 1788, and so was well acquainted with the state of the coastal forts. His appointment was to last three years, during which time he restored many forts based on the drawings of Lafite-Clave and even built five new ones, as well as drawing up plans for other new forts and buildings with a military purpose. Monier also measured the seabed 30 leagues offshore, probably the most impressive of all his undertakings.[101] Monier was dedicated to his mission in the Orient, and had hoped to be given new tasks by the Porte, but because of opponents to reform among the ministers in the Divan, this was not to happen.

Jean-Baptiste Barthelemy Lesseps and Pierre Fergo

Frenchman Jean-Baptiste Barthelemy Lesseps (1766–1834) was a diplomat who arrived in Constantinople at the same time as Pierre Ruffin (1742–1824), in 1794. Lesseps had contributed to the warming of Franco-Ottoman relations in 1795, when he delivered a telegram from Kapudan-pasha, the Grand Admiral of the Ottoman navy, to the Committee of Public Safety in Paris. With this document the sultan asked for French military help, especially engineers and architects, for the construction of a dry dock similar to that in Toulon that was to be used for the Bosphorus fleet.[102]

The idea for this dry dock was that of a friend and adviser of Kapudan-pasha, Ishak Bey, who had been sent by Choiseul-Gouffier to France for training during the reign of Louis XVI. Ishak Bey saw the facility in Toulon with his own eyes where it had been built between 1774 and 1778.[103] A dry dock would be invaluable for shipbuilding and ship repairs.[104] Although Ishak Bey convinced the Ottoman admiral that the construction of a dry dock was essential for maintenance of the fleet, he also had a personal interest in the matter: when he was in Toulon he became friends with the engineer of the dry dock there, Antoine Groignard.[105]

It seems that Ishak Bey had been very convincing, as the Porte gave Lesseps a messenger ship and an escort.[106] The Ottoman government was willing to invest a very large sum in this project. Two important French policy-makers were involved in negotiations for the dry dock, the Minister of Foreign Affairs and Minister of the Navy and Colonies.[107] Members of Choiseul-Gouffier's military mission were invited to act as advisors on how to undertake the project.[108]

The main obstacle to the project was Ishak Bey's insistence that the dry dock in Constantinople be built by Groignard. The French Minister of the Navy and Colonies deemed the venture questionable, believing instead the Ottomans should focus their efforts on increasing the size of their fleet.[109] In the end, the ministers in Paris did agree to send a specialist to Constantinople, though not Groignard. As noted previously, he was already seventy years old, but the French had another reason not to send Groignard – he held a high administrative post and was head of the port of Toulon.[110]

The architect offered to the Ottomans was Pierre Fergo, an engineer experienced in marine construction in the port of Cherbourg in Lower Normandy. After being appointed head of the mission for hydro construction, he had to choose the specialists necessary for realization of his task. They included a draftsman-geographer, master stonemason, master carpenter, apprentice stonemason and a ship modeller. The Republic granted the experts some transportation and other expenses, but expected to be reimbursed by the Ottomans.[111]

On 26 September 1795, French policy-makers in Paris informed the Kapudan-pasha that specialists other than Groignard were to be sent to the Orient.[112] Truget, a member of a previous French military mission to Constantinople and now Minister of the Navy and Colonies, was responsible for choosing the specialists to be sent to the Ottoman capital.[113]

At the end of 1797, Pierre Fergo's plans for the construction of the dry dock were entrusted to another specialist, a Swede named Rodé.[114] In 1798, Fergo returned home and France proposed replacing him with Groignard's son – Dushan Dumat. Another French military specialist already in the service of the sultan informed him that Groignard's son was even more capable than his father, and so Selim III took up the offer from Paris.[115]

Negotiations on sending these military specialists were intense, but they did achieve their goal since Franco-Ottoman relations were restored, Lesseps' diplomatic mission was considered in Paris to have been a success.[116]

Military Experts at the End of The Eighteenth Century

When relations between France and the Ottoman Empire were restored, there was no reason not to assign the experts who had arrived in 1795. Lazovski and Clugny were tasked with strengthening the borders of Moldavia, while Lusin and Ranshu were to train the infantry. However, Lusin and Ranshu experienced difficulties replacing already established Prussian officers and Habsburg refugees who instructed the infantry.[117] Two French officers, Turski and Legou, were not assigned to train the cavalry, either because the Ottomans did not allow foreigners to train cavalry, or, more likely, because the French themselves were not that enthusiastic about the task. All of the French officers sent reports to Paris in which they stated the poor financial state of the Ottoman Empire: 'Seeing that Turks reject almost all who want to teach them or to improve their defence, and accept only some of decency, we convinced ourselves in the poverty of their government.'[118]

Although as part of his reforms Selim III established a separate treasury for funding Nizam-i Cedid, the financial situation bothered the Ottomans and discouraged them from hiring too many foreign specialists. Moreover, the sultan invested heavily in ships, guns and equipment and paid much less attention to the human potential. In addition, the conservative Ottoman ministers remained a serious obstacle to reform. Combined with poor discipline in the Ottoman army, this was the view of the French in 1796:

> Fortresses in self-destruction before they were built; none of the gunners knows how to put cannonball in mortar; most officers do not train; guns in Tophane are similar to the Europeans but they are useless due to lack of cars and other machinery essential for artillery, etc.[119]

The French noted also that although the condition of the Ottoman army was deplorable, that of the maritime forces was even more woeful. It was believed that after all the efforts of the Kapudan-pashas and European specialists, the Ottoman fleet would not function like a real fleet because although ships were being built, the sailors were not up to scratch.[120]

The French military experts were unable to complete their mission because of the start of the French-Ottoman war in 1798. Only Francois Koffer (1751–1801) continued his work on mapping the Bosphorus, although he did not report to the central government but to Choiseul-Gouffier instead, an opponent of the Republicans. Other professionals, with the exception of Jacques-Balthazard Le Brun and Honore Benoit, were confined to the Seven Towers as a result of the Egyptian campaign of Napoleon Bonaparte, and in their place the Ottomans appointed Englishmen and Swedes.[121]

Jacques-Balthazard le Brun

Jacques-Balthazard le Brun (1759–1820) was the most influential of the French specialists to serve the Ottoman Empire under the rule of Sultan Selim III. He gained his influence at a time of broken diplomatic relations and managed to maintain it even during the Franco-Ottoman War (1798-1802). He was appointed as a shipbuilder for the Maritime Arsenal, or Tersana-i amire, created in June 1793 by the sultan. Under his management, not only did the number of naval vessels increase, he also updated the Ottoman shipbuilding technology and was successful in instructing new officers.

Under the direction of Le Brun in 1795, two new shipyards at Köy and Ayvansaray were built using a new method of shipbuilding that saw the vessels finished at sea. Also, copper, which was abundant, was used for the hulls of ships.[122] Le Brun was also able to attract other prominent French officers to the Porte to work for the Europeanization of the Ottoman army, including in 1796 his brother Polid Le Brun.[123]

In 1799, Le Brun left Constantinople and passed on Russian service. Upon his departure he recommended his place be taken by Honore Benoit.[124] This episode raised questions about the role of Russian diplomacy in Constantinople, which at the end of the eighteenth century included trying to 'steal' foreign specialists.

The first real test of Selim III's efforts to Europeanize the Ottoman army came against the French army in 1798. On 2 July 1798, Napoleon's squadron conquered Alexandria, and on 21 July the same year local Ottoman rulers fought alongside the Mamelukes against the French at the Pyramids near Cairo, the government in Constantinople having not yet been informed of events in Egypt. Its response was slowed further by the search for support from Britain and Russia. The two powers assigned command in the conflict to Admiral Nelson and Admiral Ushakov respectively. The Ottoman fleet was led by the Kapudan-pasha Abdulkadir Bey. The theatre of hostilities involved mainly sea battles. The strategy devised in London was not to enter into direct confrontation with the French fleet, and possibly for its actions to be restricted, and the Mediterranean Sea was to be partitioned – the western Mediterranean to the British and the eastern Mediterranean to the Russians and Ottomans.[125] In August 1798, Admiral Nelson destroyed 11 of the 15 French vessels, a retrograde step for Napoleon's search for a route to India. In September and October 1798, the united Ottoman-Russian armada led by Abdulkadir Bey conquered the Ionian Islands (acquired by France in June 1797). Ushakov led the siege of Corfu, which capitulated on 1 March 1799. In January 1799, the Ottoman-Russian and Ottoman-British treaties of alliance were signed, which included the guarantee of military assistance in case of attack. As a result, for the first time the Black Sea and the Straits were open to Russian warships, and the Republic of the Seven United Islands became a Russian naval base for continuing the war in the Mediterranean.

Since the summer of 1799, the Ottoman navy had acted together with the British, among their successes being the return of Naples on 10 July 1799. The French lost their position of strength to such an extent that the defeat of the Anglo-Ottoman armada in the port of Abukir on 25 July 1799 did not alter the outcome of the war. In searching for a way out of their ordeal, in January 1800 the French signed a truce, but renewed hostilities in March the same year.

This time the Ottoman forces were limited and Sultan Selim III desperately tried to recruit soldiers for the campaign against France. The Janissaries tried everything possible not to fulfil their obligations, and those who still entered into battle performed poorly. The only military unit to stand out was the Nizam-i Cedid artillery, which distinguished itself in the defence of Acre, where the Ottomans joined the British combat units under Sidney Smith.[126]

The French did not benefit from the poor Ottoman morale, as Napoleon renewed his interests in Central Europe, making the Egyptian front secondary. As a result, at the Battle of Alexandria on 8 March 1801, the Ottomans joined the English fleet with six battleships, eight frigates and 6,000 soldiers and, after several months, the city capitulated on 30 August. The war ended, a peace treaty was signed on 9 October 1801, the French restored Egypt and recognized the suzerainty of the Sultan over the Republic of the Seven United Islands.

The French diplomatic mission in Constantinople now faced the challenge of restoring its position in both the political and military sphere. Furthermore, France had to overcome the influence of the new Ottoman allies, Russia and Britain. Seeing the Ottoman government faced new challenges reforming the army, the Ministry of Foreign Affairs took the opportunity to send to Constantinople two military experts, Rica and Petro; however, whether because of deteriorating relations between the two governments, or internal Ottoman difficulties, the two Frenchmen had little impact on military developments of the Ottoman Empire.

Conclusion

Up until 1789, France used military missions sent to the sultan mainly as a counterbalance to the increasing Russian influence in central and southeast Europe. However, during the period prior to 1789, the policy-makers in Versailles did not wish to confront Russia directly in order to preserve the territorial integrity of the Ottoman Empire.

This policy changed during the reign of Sultan Selim III when the French Revolution created opponents in most European courts. At this time, Paris was looking to all possible allies, and used military missions to improve relations with the Ottomans, in the hope of securing the sultan's military intervention against the anti-French coalitions of the late eighteenth and early nineteenth century.

Irrespective of the political goals of the French military missions, they gave an important advantage to Paris – a constant French presence in the Ottoman Empire, and important key positions in the military and state government. Unlike the other European powers that could rely only on their diplomats in the Ottoman capital, the French government could also use their military experts as a means of influence. It was often the case that once an official French mission ended, some of its members remained in the Ottoman Empire to continue their work. These individuals continued to teach Ottoman officers and reported to the French government about the changes they witnessed in the Orient. In addition, they often recommended new specialists to the Ottomans, again French, thus securing a French monopoly in this area throughout the eighteenth century.

Without the French commitment to modernizing the Ottoman army, even when the effectiveness of the reforms and their durability were questioned, the forces of the Sublime Porte in the eighteenth century would have been much weaker. France's policy, however, led to unsuccessful armed conflicts with Russia or the Habsburg monarchy, and is one of the factors that likely speeded up the political demise of the Ottoman Empire. This, however, does not diminish the fact that only France had the ability to use 'military advisors' to influence the Ottomans at the Sublime Porte.

Abbreviations

AAE	Archives du Ministère des affaires étrangères (Archives of the French Ministry of Foreign Affairs)
AN	Archives nationales (French National Archives)
CCC	Correspondance consulaire – Constantinople
MC	Série Maréchaux de Camps
MDT	Mémoires et documents, Turquie
SHD	Service historiques de la Défense (French Military Archives)

Notes

1 J. L. van Regemorter, 'Commerce et politique: préparation et négociation du traité franco-russe de 1787', *Cahiers du monde russe et soviétique*, 4 (1963), pp. 232–233.
2 E. Driault, *La question d'Orient depuis ses origines jusqu'à la paix de Sèvres*. Paris: Félix Alcan, 1921, p. 56.
3 M. S. Anderson, *The Eastern Question, 1774–1923: A Study in International Relations*. London: Macmillan, 1966, p. 11.
4 I. Parvev, *Balkanite mezhdu dve imperii. Habsburgskata monarhiya i Osmanskata darzhava (1683–1739)* [The Balkans Between Two Empires: Habsburg Monarchy and Ottoman State (1683–1739)]. Sofia: Universitetsko izdatelstvo 'Sv. Kliment Ohridski', 1997, pp. 269–270.
5 A. F. d'Allonville, A. de Beauchamp and A. Schubart, *Mémoires tirés des papiers d'un homme d'état sur les causes secrètes qui ont déterminé la politique des cabinets dans la guerre de la révolution; depuis 1792 jusqu'en 1815*. Paris: Ponthieu, 1832, p. 247.
6 Extrait d'une dépeche du Cit. Verninac, envoyé à Constantinople, 22 Nivôse, An 4 (f. 18), 1795–1802, CCC, vol. 74, AAE.
7 D. Panzak, *La marine ottomane, De l'appogée à la chute de l'Empire (1572–1923)*. Paris: CNRS Editions, 2009, p. 226.
8 Extrait des régistres des délibérations du Directoire exécutif du 28 Prairial an 4e/16 Juin 1795 (f. 82-3), 1795–1802, CCC, vol. 74, AAE.
9 Ibid.

10 Ibid.
11 T. Zorlu, *Innovation and Empire in Turkey: Sultan Selim III and the Modernization of the Ottoman Navy*. London: I.B. Tauris, 2008, p.87.
12 Fazi du Bayet, *Les généraux Aubert du Bayet, Carra Saint-Cyr et Charpentier. Correspondances et notices biographiques 1757–1834*. Paris: Librairie Honoré Champion, 1902, p.13.
13 'Aubert du Bayet au citoyen ministre des relations extérieures de la République française, 12 Fructidor an IV (29 août 1796)', in Fazi du Bayet, *Les généraux Aubert du Bayet*, p. 13.
14 Essai sur les relations de la République Française et de l'Empire ottoman par le citoyen Jean Joseph Pain (1796), Précis historique des progrès des turcs dans les arts modernes de la guerre et course aperçu de l'état actuel de leurs forces de terre et mer (f. 12), MDT, vol. 111, AAE.
15 A. de Juchereau de St. Denys, *Histoire de l'Empire ottoman depuis 1792 jusqu'en 1844*, vol. 1. Paris: Guiraudet et Jouaust, 1844, p. 368.
16 Zorlu, *Innovation and Empire in Turkey*, p. 85.
17 Ibid., p. 90.
18 For further information about the era of Sultan Selim III, see E. Z. Karal (ed.), *Selim III'ün Hatt-ı Hümayunları* [Imperial Edicts of Selim III]. Ankara, 1942; Karal (ed.), *Selim III'ün Hatt-ı Hümayunları – Nizam-ı Cedıt – 1789–1807* [Imperial Edicts of Selim III-Nizam-ı Cedıt – 1789–1807]. Ankara, 1946; Karal, *Osmanlı tarihi V. Cilt, Nizam-i cedid ve tanzımat devri 1789–1861* [Ottoman History, vol. V: The Period of Nizam-i Cedid and Tanzımat]. Ankara, 1988; A. Cevdet, *Cevdet Tarihi*, 10 vols, İstanbul, 1854–1875 & *Tertib-i Cedid*, 12 vols, İstanbul, 1884–1885; S. J. Shaw, *Between Old and New: The Ottoman Empire Under Sultan Selim III, 1789–1807*. Harvard, MA: Harvard University Press, 1980; C. Findley, *Bureaucratic Reform in the Ottoman Empire: The Sublime Porte, 1789–1922*. Princeton, NJ: Princeton University Press, 1980; S. Kenan (ed.), *Nizam-ı Kadim'den Nizam-ı Cedid'e III. Selim ve Dönemi* [Selim III and His Era from Ancien Régime to New Order]. İstanbul: İslam Araştırmaları Merkezi Yayınları, 2010.
19 Shaw, *Between Old and New*, p. 42.
20 V. Mutafchieva, *Kardzhaliysko vreme* [The Age of Kircali]. Sofia: BAS, 1993; P. Mitev, 'Politicheskata aktivnost na frenskite konsulstva v Bukuresht i Yash v godinite na Direktoriyata i Imperiyata' [Political Activities of the French Consulates in Bucharest and Iasi During the Years of the Directory and Empire], *Vekove*, 4 (1988), pp. 49–58.
21 P. Petkov, *Devetnadesetiyat vek na Evropa. Ot Frenskata revolyutsiya do Parvata svetovna voyna* [The Nineteenth Century of Europe: From the French Revolution to the First World War]. Sofia: Universitetsko izdatelstvo 'Sv. Kliment Ohridski', 2012.
22 d'Allonville et al., *Mémoires tirés des papiers d'un homme d'état sur les causes secrètes qui ont déterminé la politique des cabinets dans la guerre de la révolution*, p. 241.
23 P. Kenedi, *Vazhod i padenie na velikite sili: ikonomicheski promeni i voenni konflikti XV–XX vek* [The Rise and Fall of Great Powers: Economic Changes and Military Conflicts, 15th–20th Century]. Sofia: Voenno izdatelstvo, 2011, p. 111.
24 MDT, vol. 63, AAE.
25 d'Allonville et al., *Mémoires tirés des papiers d'un homme d'état sur les causes secrètes qui ont déterminé la politique des cabinets dans la guerre de la révolution*, p. 247.
26 R. Tasheva, 'The French Republic and the Ottoman Empire: The Citoyen Descorches in Constantinople (1793–1795)', in *Power and Influence in South-Eastern Europe, 16th–19th Century*, ed. M. Baramova, P. Mitev, I. Parvev and V. Racheva. Zyrich: Lit, 2013, pp. 339–347.

27 Ibid..
28 d'Allonville et al., *Mémoires tirés des papiers d'un homme d'état sur les causes secrètes qui ont déterminé la politique des cabinets dans la guerre de la révolution*, p. 241.
29 N. Ryazyanovski, *Istoriya na Rusiya* [History of Russia]. Sofia: Kama, 2008, p. 242.
30 Belair, Mémoire contenant l'examen du divers considerations politiques et militaires sur les Turcs, les Russes et quelques autres peuples considerés sur leur divers rapports avec la France, et plusieurs puissances neutres ou belligerents, 1795, 2 (91), GR M 1617, SHD.
31 S. Iosipescu, 'Relations politiques et militaires entre la France et les principautés de Transylvanie, de Valachie et de Moldavie', *Revue historique des armées*, 244 (2006), pp. 11–21.
32 Belair, Mémoire contenant l'examen du divers considerations politiques et militaires sur les Turcs, les Russes et quelques autres peuples considerés sur leur divers rapports avec la France, et plusieurs puissances neutres ou belligerents, 1795, 2 (92), GR M 1617, SHD.
33 L'envoyé extraordinaire de la République française près de la Porte Ottomane au Citoyen Charles de la Croix, Ministre des relations extérieures (15 floréal de l'An 4/4 mai 1795) (f. 60), 1795–1802, CCC, vol. 74, AAE.
34 Extrait d'une dépêche du Cit. Verninac, envoyé à Constantinople, 22 Nivôse, An 4 (f. 18), 1795–1802, CCC, vol. 74, AAE.
35 Note (f. 53–56), 1795–1802, CCC, vol. 74, AAE.
36 L. Gallois, *Dictionnaire historique de tous les ministres depuis la Révolution jusqu'en 1827*. Paris: Charles-Béchet, 1827, pp. 10–12; Centre historique des Archives nationales, Séction des Archives privées, Fonds du général Aubert-Dubayet 170 AP [http://www.archivesnationales.culture.gouv.fr/chan/chan/AP-pdf/170-AP.pdf] (accessed 7 May 2014)
37 du Bayet, *Les généraux Aubert du Bayet, Carra Saint-Cyr et Charpentier*, p. 13.
38 *Collection des mémoires relatifs à la Révolution française. Des Véndéens et Chouances contre la République française*. Paris: Baudouin Frères, 1825; Centre historique des Archives nationales, Séction des Archives privées, Fonds du général Aubert-Dubayet 170 AP.
39 du Bayet, *Les généraux Aubert du Bayet, Carra Saint-Cyr et Charpentier*, p. 13.
40 C.-S. Gustave, *Le premier ambassadeur de La République française à Constantinople: le général Aubert Du Bayet (envoi autographe)*. Constantinople, 1904, p. 11.
41 Anderson, *The Eastern Question, 1774–1923*, pp. 23–24.
42 Gustave, *Le premier ambassadeur de La République française à Constantinople*, p. 13.
43 Ibid.
44 J. Frémeaux, 'La France, la Révolution et l'Orient. Aspects diplomatiques', *Revue du monde musulman et de la Méditerranée*, 52/53, no. 1 (1989), p. 23.
45 Aubert du Bayet au citoyen ministre des relations extérieures de la République française, 12 Fructidor an IV (29 août 1796), in du Bayet, *Les généraux Aubert du Bayet, Carra Saint-Cyr et Charpentier*, p. 13.
46 d'Allonville et al., *Mémoires tirés des papiers d'un homme d'état sur les causes secrètes qui ont déterminé la politique des cabinets dans la guerre de la révolution*, p. 241.
47 Essai sur les relations de la République Française et de l'Empire ottoman par le citoyen Jean Joseph Pain (1796), Moyens à employer par la République pour soutenir les Turcs en Europe et compensations qu'elle doit en exiger, f. 20. MD, Turquie, vol. 111, AAE.
48 'Lettre de Merlin à l'ambassadeur Aubert du Bayet sans date', in du Bayet, *Les généraux Aubert du Bayet, Carra Saint-Cyr et Charpentier*, pp. 261–262.
49 d'Allonville et al., *Mémoires tirés des papiers d'un homme d'état sur les causes secrètes qui ont déterminé la politique des cabinets dans la guerre de la révolution*, p. 250.

50 Ibid.
51 Essai sur les relations de la République Française et de l'Empire ottoman par le citoyen Jean Joseph Pain (1796) (f. 12), MDT, vol. 111, AAE.
52 Ibid., f. 20.
53 Iosipescu, 'Relations politiques et militaires'.
54 Mitev, 'Politicheskata aktivnost na frenskite konsulstva v Bukuresht i Yash v godinite na Direktoriyata i Imperiyata', p. 19.
55 Ryazyanovski, *Istoriya na Rusiya*, p. 198.
56 Mitev, 'Politicheskata aktivnost na frenskite konsulstva v Bukuresht i Yash v godinite na Direktoriyata i Imperiyata', p. 15.
57 *Vostochnyi vopros vo vneshney politike Rossii, Konets XVIII-nachalo XX v.* [The Eastern Question in Russia's Foreign Policy, End of the 18th to Beginning of 20th Century]. Moscow: Nauka, 1978, p. 34.
58 Mutafchieva, *Kardzhaliysko vreme*, p. 198.
59 Ibid., p. 199.
60 Ibid.
61 d'Allonville et al., *Mémoires tirés des papiers d'un homme d'état sur les causes secrètes qui ont déterminé la politique des cabinets dans la guerre de la révolution*, p. 256.
62 Ibid., p. 258.
63 Ibid., pp. 258–260.
64 Centre historique des Archives nationales, Séction des Archives privées, Fonds du général Aubert-Dubayet 170 AP.
65 Mutafchieva, *Kardzhaliysko vreme*, p. 197.
66 d'Allonville et al., *Mémoires tirés des papiers d'un homme d'état sur les causes secrètes qui ont déterminé la politique des cabinets dans la guerre de la révolution*, p. 269.
67 Parvev, *Balkanite mezhdu dve imperii*, p. 275.
68 *Vostochnyi vopros vo vneshney politike Rossii*, p. 55.
69 Mutafchieva, *Kardzhaliysko vreme*, p. 201.
70 Ibid., pp. 265–266.
71 Frémeaux, 'La France, la Révolution et l'Orient. Aspects diplomatiques'.
72 T. G. Djuvara, *Cent projets de partage de la Turquie (1281–1913)*. Paris: Félix Alcan, 1914, p. 345.
73 Mitev, 'Politicheskata aktivnost na frenskite konsulstva v Bukuresht i Yash v godinite na Direktoriyata i Imperiyata', p. 17.
74 Frémeaux, 'La France, la Révolution et l'Orient. Aspects diplomatiques'.
75 V. J. Puryear, *Napoleon and the Dardanelles*. Berkeley, CA: University of California Press, 1951, p. 24.
76 Djuvara, *Cent projets de partage de la Turquie (1281–1913)*, p. 338.
77 Mitev, 'Politicheskata aktivnost na frenskite konsulstva v Bukuresht i Yash v godinite na Direktoriyata i Imperiyata', p. 18.
78 'Lettres sur les hommes d'état de la France. Quatrième lettre de 1833', *Revue des deux mondes*, Vol. 4, Paris, 1833, pp. 686–725.
79 de Juchereau de St. Denys, *Histoire de l'Empire ottoman depuis 1792 jusqu'en 1844*, p. XIV.
80 E. Driault, *La politique orientale de Napoléon. Sébastiani et Gardane, 1806–1808*. Paris: Félix Alcan, 1904, p. 63.
81 Ibid., p. 60.
82 K. Jirechek, *Istoriya na balgarite* [History of Bulgarians]. Sofia: Nauka i izkustvo, 1978, p. 542.
83 Ibid., p. 347.

84 Djuvara, *Cent projets de partage de la Turquie (1281–1913)*, pp. 348–349.
85 I. Parvev, 'Iztochniyat vapros – opredelenie i nachalo' [The Eastern Question – Definition and Beginning], *Minalo*, 1 (1994), pp. 27–38.
86 Mutafchieva, *Kardzhaliysko vreme*, p. 358.
87 M. Todorova, *Angliya, Rusiya i Tanzimatat* [England, Russia and Tanzimat]. Sofia: Nauka i izkustvo, 1980, pp. 5–6.
88 P. Mitev, 'Opit za lichnosten portret na osmanskite vladeteli prez XVIII vek' [Attempt for a Personal Portrait of the Ottoman Rulers During the 17th Century], in *Lichnostta v istoricheskoto razvitie. Alternativata v istoriyata*. Sofia, 1995, p. 44.
89 Shaw, *Between Old and New*, p. 12.
90 Ibid.
91 I. Müteferrika, *Usülü'l-Hikem fi Nizamü'l-Ümem* [A Treatise on the Necessity of Military Reforms]. Istanbul: Sultanic Press, 1732; O. Sabev, *Parvoto osmansko pateshestvie v sveta na pechatnata kniga (1726–1746)* [The First Ottoman Voyage in the World of the Printed Book (1726–1746)]. Sofia: Avangard prima, 2004; Sabev, *İbrahim Müteferrika ya da İlk Osmanlı Matbaa Serüveni (1726–1746). Yeniden Değerlendirme* [İbrahim Müteferrika or the First Ottoman Printing Adventure: A Re-evaluation]. İstanbul: Yeditepe Yayınevi, 2006.
92 Tasheva, 'Definitsii na predrevolyutsionnoto minalo – Stariyat rezhim i Absolyutizmat vav Frantsiya' [Definitions of the Pre-revolutionary Past: The Old Regime and Absolutism in France], *Istrichesko badeshte*, 1, no. 3 (2003), pp. 152–171.
93 Mémoire sur la Turquie, 1794 (f. 160), MDT, vol. 15, AAE.
94 Essai sur les relations de la République Française et de l'Empire ottoman par le citoyen Jean Joseph Pain (1796), Précis historique des progrès des turcs dans les arts modernes de la guerre et course aperçu de l'état actuel de leurs forces de terre et mer (f. 11), MDT, vol. 111, AAE.
95 d'Allonville et al., *Mémoires tirés des papiers d'un homme d'état sur les causes secrètes qui ont déterminé la politique des cabinets dans la guerre de la révolution*, pp. 238–241.
96 M. Uyar and E. J. Erickson, *Military History of the Ottomans: From Osman to Atatürk*. Santa Barbara, CA: ABC-Clio, 2009, p. 121.
97 I. Mouradgea d' Osson, *Tableau historique de l'Orient*. Paris: Didot Jeune, 1804; Mouradgea d' Osson, *Tableau général de l'Empire Ottoman*. Paris: Firmin Didot, 1788–1824; Mouradgea d' Osson, *L'Histoire de la Maison Ottomane depuis Osman I jusqu'au sultan mort en 1758*. Paris, 1807 (incomplete). About him: E. A. Fraser, '"Dressing Turks in the French Manner": Mouradgea d'Ohsson's Panorama of the Ottoman Empire', *Ars Orientalis*, 39 (2009), pp. 198–230.
98 Uyar and Erickson, *Military History of the Ottomans*, p. 123.
99 Essai sur les relations de la République Française et de l'Empire ottoman par le citoyen Jean Joseph Pain (1796) (f. 19), MDT, vol. 111, AAE.
100 Ibid., f. 12.
101 Essai sur les relations de la République Française et de l'Empire ottoman par le citoyen Jean Joseph Pain (1796) (f. 11), MDT, vol. 111, AAE.
102 Traduction de la dépeche officielle du Capitan Pacha au Comité du Salut publique (f. 34–36), 1795–1802, CCC, vol. 74, AAE.
103 Rapport fait au ministre des relations extérieures sur la lettre du ministre de la marine relative à la mission du Citoyen Lesseps, consul général et envoyé de Capitan-Pacha au Gouvernement de la République française (f. 70–73), 1795–1802, CCC, vol. 74, AAE.

104 Ibid.
105 Ibid.
106 Lesseps, Chargé d'une mission du gouvernement ottoman auprès de celui de la République française au citoyen ministre des relations extérieures 14 ventose de l'An 4 (f. 37), 1795–1802, CCC, vol. 74, AAE.
107 Rapport au ministre (f. 57), 1795–1802, CCC, vol. 74, AAE.
108 Lesseps, Chargé d'une mission ottomane auprès du gouvernement de la République française au citoyen Delacroix, ministre des relations extérieures, 14 Floréal de l'An 4 (f. 51), 1795–1802, CCC, vol. 74, AAE.
109 Extrait des régistres des délibérations du Directoire exécutif du 28 Prairial an 4e/16 Juin 1795 (f. 82–83), 1795–1802, CCC, vol. 74, AAE.
110 Ibid.
111 Ibid.
112 Le ministre des relations extérieures de la République française, à Son Excéllence le Capitan-Pacha, Grand amiral des flottes ottomanes (f. 135), 1795–1802, CCC, vol. 74, AAE.
113 Note (f. 53), 1795–1802, CCC, vol. 74, AAE.
114 Panzak, *La marine ottomane*, p. 227.
115 Zorlu, *Innovation and Empire in Turkey*, p. 87.
116 Ministre de la marine et des colonies au Ministre des relations extérieures, Extrait des régistres des délibérations du Directoire exécutif du 28 Prairial de l'An 4/16 juin 1795 (f. 82–83), 1795–1802, CCC, vol. 74, AAE.
117 Ibid., f. 11.
118 Ibid., f. 12.
119 Ibid., f. 13.
120 Ibid., f. 15.
121 Zorlu, *Innovation and Empire in Turkey*, p. 84.
122 de Juchereau de St. Denys, *Histoire de l'Empire ottoman depuis 1792 jusqu'en 1844*, p. 368.
123 Zorlu, *Innovation and Empire in Turkey*, pp. 82–86.
124 Ibid., p. 85.
125 Panzak, *La marine ottomane*, p. 256.
126 Uyar and Erickson, *Military History of the Ottomans*, p. 124.

Bibliography

Archives

Archives du Ministère des affaires étrangères [Archives of the French Ministry of the Foreign Affairs]
Archives nationales [French National Archives]
Service historiques de la Défense [French Military Archives]

Primary sources

Cevdet, A., *Cevdet Tarihi*, 10 vols, İstanbul, 1854–1875 & *Tertib-i Cedid*, 12 vols, İstanbul, 1884–1885, E. Z. Karal (ed.), Ankara, 1946.

d'Allonville, A. F., de Beauchamp A., and Schubart, A., *Mémoires tirés des papiers d'un homme d'état sur les causes secrètes qui ont déterminé la politique des cabinets dans la guerre de la révolution; depuis 1792 jusqu'en 1815.* Paris: Ponthieu, 1832.

de Juchereau de St. Denys, A., *Histoire de l'Empire ottoman depuis 1792 jusqu'en 1844*, vol. 1. Paris: Guiraudet et Jouaust, 1844.

du Bayet, Fazi, *Les généraux Aubert du Bayet, Carra Saint-Cyr et Charpentier. Correspondances et notices biographiques 1757–1834.* Paris: Librairie Honoré Champion, 1902.

Gustave, C.-S., *Le premier ambassadeur de La République française à Constantinople: le général Aubert Du Bayet (envoi autographe).* Constantinople, 1904.

Müteferrika, I., *Usülü'l-Hikem fi Nizamü'l-Ümem* [A Treatise on the Necessity of Military Reforms]. Istanbul: Sultanic Press, 1732.

Revue des deux mondes, vol. 4. Paris, 1833.

Selim III'ün Hatt-ı Hümayunları – Nizam-ı Cedıt – 1789–1807.

Selim III'ün Hatt-ı Hümayunları, E. Z. Karal (ed.). Ankara, 1942.

Secondary sources

Anderson, M. S., *The Eastern Question, 1774–1923: A Study in International Relations.* London: Macmillan, 1966.

Djuvara, T. G., *Cent projets de partage de la Turquie (1281–1913).* Paris: Félix Alcan, 1914.

Driault, E., *La politique orientale de Napoléon. Sébastiani et Gardane, 1806–1808.* Paris: Félix Alcan, 1904.

Driault, E., *La question d'Orient depuis ses origines jusqu'à la paix de Sèvres.* Paris: Félix Alcan, 1921.

Findley, C., *Bureaucratic Reform in the Ottoman Empire: The Sublime Porte, 1789–1922.* Princeton, NJ: Princeton University Press, 1980.

Fraser, E. A., '"Dressing Turks in the French Manner": Mouradgea d'Ohsson's Panorama of the Ottoman Empire', *Ars Orientalis*, 39 (2009), pp. 198–230.

Frémeaux, J., 'La France, la Révolution et l'Orient. Aspects diplomatiques', *Revue du monde musulman et de la Méditerranée*, 52/53, no. 1 (1989), pp. 19–28.

Gallois, L., *Dictionnaire historique de tous les ministres depuis la Révolution jusqu'en 1827.* Paris: Charles-Béchet, 1827.

Iosipescu, S., 'Relations politiques et militaires entre la France et les principautés de Transylvanie, de Valachie et de Moldavie', *Revue historique des armées*, 244 (2006), pp. 11–21.

Jirechek, K., *Istoriya na balgarite* [History of Bulgarians]. Sofia: Nauka i izkustvo, 1978.

Karal, E. Z., *Osmanlı tarihi V. Cilt, Nizam-i cedid ve tanzimat devri 1789–1861.* Ankara, 1988.

Kenan S., (ed.), *Nizam-ı Kadim'den Nizam-ı Cedid'e III. Selim ve Dönemi* [Selim III and His Era from Ancien Régime to New Order]. İstanbul: İslam Araştırmaları Merkezi Yayınları, 2010.

Kenedi, P., *Vazhod i padenie na velikite sili: ikonomicheski promeni i voenni konflikti XV–XX vek* [The Rise and Fall of Great Powers: Economic Changes and Military Conflicts, 15th–20th Century]. Sofia: Voenno izdatelstvo, 2011.

Mitev, P., 'Opit za lichnosten portret na osmanskite vladeteli prez XVIII vek' [Attempt for a Personal Portrait of the Ottoman Rulers During the 17th Century], in *Lichnostta v istoricheskoto razvitie. Alternativata v istoriyata.* Sofia, 1995.

Mitev, P., 'Politicheskata aktivnost na frenskite konsulstva v Bukuresht i Yash v godinite na Direktoriyata i Imperiyata' [Political Activities of the French Consulates in Bucharest and Iasi During the Years of the Directory and Empire], *Vekove*, 4 (1988), pp. 49–58.

Mouradgea d' Osson, I., *Tableau historique de l'Orient*. Paris: Didot Jeune, 1804.

Mouradgea d' Osson, I., *L'Histoire de la Maison Ottomane depuis Osman I jusqu'au sultan mort en 1758*. Paris, 1807 (incomplete).

Mouradgea d' Osson, I., *Tableau général de l'Empire Ottoman*. Paris: Firmin Didot, 1788-1824.

Mutafchieva, V., *Kardzhaliysko vreme* [The Age of Kircali]. Sofia: BAS, 1993.

Panzak, D., *La marine ottomane, De l'appogée à la chute de l'Empire (1572-1923)*. Paris: CNRS Editions, 2009.

Parvev, I., 'Iztochniyat vapros – opredelenie i nachalo' [The Eastern Question – Definition and Beginning], *Minalo*, 1 (1994), pp. 27–38.

Petkov, P., *Devetnadesetiyat vek na Evropa. Ot Frenskata revolyutsiya do Parvata svetovna voyna* [The Nineteenth Century of Europe: From the French Revolution to the First World War]. Sofia: Universitetsko izdatelstvo 'Sv. Kliment Ohridski', 2012.

Puryear, V. J., *Napoleon and the Dardanelles*. Berkeley, CA: University of California Press, 1951.

Ryazyanovski, N., *Balkanite mezhdu dve imperii. Habsburgskata monarhiya i Osmanskata darzhava (1683-1739)* [Balkans Between Two Empires: Habsburg Monarchy and Ottoman State (1683-1739)]. Sofia: Universitetsko izdatelstvo 'Sv. Kliment Ohridski', 1997.

Ryazyanovski, N., *Istoriya na Rusiya* [History of Russia]. Sofia: Kama, 2008.

Sabev, O., *Parvoto osmansko pateshestvie v sveta na pechatnata kniga (1726-1746)* [The First Ottoman Voyage in the World of the Printed Book (1726-1746)]. Sofia: Avangard prima, 2004.

Sabev, O., *İbrahim Müteferrika ya da İlk Osmanlı Matbaa Serüveni (1726-1746). Yeniden Değerlendirme* [İbrahim Müteferrika or the First Ottoman Printing Adventure: A Re-evaluation]. İstanbul: Yeditepe Yayınevi, 2006.

Shaw, S. J., *Between Old and New: The Ottoman Empire Under Sultan Selim III, 1789-1807*. Harvard, MA: Harvard University Press, 1980.

Tasheva, R., 'Definitsii na predrevolyutsionnoto minalo – Stariyat rezhim i Absolyutizmat vav Frantsiya' [Definitions of the Pre-revolutionary Past: The Old Regime and Absolutism in France], *Istrichesko badeshte*, 1, no. 3 (2003), pp. 152–171.

Tasheva, R., 'The French Republic and the Ottoman Empire: The Citoyen Descorches in Constantinople (1793-1795)', in *Power and Influence in South-Eastern Europe, 16th-19th Century*, ed. M. Baramova, P. Mitev, I. Parvev and V. Racheva. Zyrich: Lit, 2013, pp. 339–347.

Todorova, M., *Angliya, Rusiya i Tanzimatat* [England, Russia and Tanzimat]. Sofia: Nauka i izkustvo, 1980.

Uyar M., and Erickson, E. J., *Military History of the Ottomans: From Osman to Atatürk*. Santa Barbara, CA: ABC-Clio, 2009.

van Regemorter, J. L., 'Commerce et politique: préparation et négociation du traité franco-russe de 1787', *Cahiers du monde russe et soviétique*, 4 (1963), pp. 232–233.

Vostochnyi vopros vo vneshney politike Rossii, Konets XVIII-nachalo XX v. [The Eastern Question in Russia's Foreign Policy, End of the 18th to Beginning of 20th Century]. Moscow: Nauka, 1978.

Zorlu, T., *Innovation and Empire in Turkey: Sultan Selim III and the Modernization of the Ottoman Navy*. London: I.B. Tauris, 2008.

5

Echoes of Tumultuous Wars: Prosperity and Poverty of the Balkan Entrepreneurial Strata (1800s–1880s)

Evguenia Davidova
Portland State University

Introduction

The 'Long Nineteenth Century' heralded vast socio-economic, political and demographic transformations of the Ottoman and post-Ottoman Balkans. Wars, revolutions and attendant violence resulted in migrations and diseases that led to impoverishment of some crafts, agricultural deterioration and community decline. An eloquent illustration presents a chronicle from Kotel (Kızğan), written by a local *abacı* (producer and/or trader in *aba*), who perceived the Crimean War (1853–1856) in terms of economic damage: 'And then [1854] the French [army] put Varna on fire and the whole çarşı [commercial street] was destroyed. They did not allow anyone to take away [goods] or put the fire down. Thus, everything was burnt and the poor merchants suffered a lot.'[1] On the other hand, the same events offered opportunities for accumulating wealth and social mobility. Another example attests to the opposite perception: 'In Stara Zagora [Eski Zağra] the Crimean War was known under the Turkish word 'muharibe' [war], which became synonymous for making a good profit. For someone who was earning well from trade, local people used to say 'he hit one muharibe'.[2] Thus, the war was a source of quick gains made through provisioning for the Ottoman and allied armies.

Most research, until recently, has emphasized the negative aspects (economic ruin, political reprisals, ethnic displacements) of such developments.[3] I take a different approach, and this chapter traces not only changes that happened during wartime but also the complex ramifications that ensued during subsequent peaceful periods. It is my contention that those cataclysmic events shaped social and ethnic reordering in the Ottoman Balkans and contributed to the emergence of broad entrepreneurial networks, which disappeared with the advent of nation-states. The new 'imagined communities' were rapidly shedding their multi-ethnic economic actors and opened up new bureaucratic avenues, though restricted to national citizens.[4] The chapter is grounded in archival materials, travelogues and memoirs and will focus mostly on examples from the Bulgarian entrepreneurial milieu in the central Balkans. In what follows, I analyse the impact of the major turbulent events in chronological order.

Wars and Revolutions in the pre-Tanzimat Period (1790s–1839)

The terminology we use today about economic actors from the past often seems to elude the layered meanings that forms of belonging had in various contexts of the late eighteenth and nineteenth century. The economic stratum was not a homogeneous body, but rather consisted of diverse ethnic, religious, linguistic and social groups with a high level of upward and downward mobility collaborating and competing with each other and with their European counterparts. For example, the terms used by the Ottoman government in issuing *tezkeres* (permits) and tax receipts reveal a broad understanding of commercial activity – around thirty different types from shopkeeper to *tüccar* (merchant).[5] The term 'portfolio capitalists' has been applied with reference to the Indian economy, and seems appropriate for other pre-industrial economic settings.[6] The use of multiple languages was another way of maintaining a rich portfolio of multiple professions and identities. It was quite common for entrepreneurs of the pre-Tanzimat era to combine different occupations, or what Fernand Braudel called the 'polyvalence' of the merchant, which was a result of non-economic factors and an inadequate volume of commercial exchange.[7] I explore local economic alliances, reflective of broader social contexts, in order to demonstrate that the level of formal and informal exchanges among various groups was quite complex and porous.[8]

These socio-economic transformations occurred alongside current political events such as the Napoleonic expansion (1798–1815), the *ayans*' (local notables) and *kırcalıs*' (brigands) despoliations (1797–1807), the Russo-Ottoman War (1806–1812), the Serbian revolts (1804–1813, 1815), the Greek War of Independence (1821–1829), accompanied by another Russo-Ottoman War (1828–1829) and wars with Egypt (1831–1833 and 1838–1839). The increased international pressure on the Ottoman Empire led to the trade convention of Balta Limanı (1838). The latter was a turning point in abandoning the previous policy of trade restrictions and monopolies. That shift, though, was not a new development but a continuation and acceleration of previous trends.[9] I will suggest that the multiple occupations, high mobility and multi-ethnic entrepreneurial webs that shaped the Balkan economy allowed for a relatively quick recovery after the devastation of war.

Various instances of combined crafts, putting-out system, tax farming, money lending and even teaching suggest hybrid occupations. Such entrepreneurial activity involved many social groups (peasants, artisans, bureaucracy, clergy as investors and/or participants), which was characteristic of the period of preindustrial economy and pre-national identities within a multi-ethnic imperial framework. It was exactly the Ottoman context in a process of both economic incorporation as well as socio-political transformations that nurtured this amalgamation of professions at the turn of the eighteenth century.

The Kırcalı and Ayan Revolts (1797–1807)

Traditionally, this period is interpreted as a time of decentralization and separatist movements; most Balkan historiographies insist on its destructive aspects. Contemporary materials, such as Prota Matija Nenadović's memoir and Sofroniĭ Vratchanski's autobiography,[10] both educated and politically engaged clergy, reinforced such perspectives on these events. Indeed, demobilization after the wars released multiple soldiers, some of whom became part of the retinues of leading *ayans*, whereas others were organized into bands (*kırcalıs*) and created chaos and destruction. The weak central state led to the rise of strong provincial power-holders such as Ali Pasha of Ioannina, Osman Pazvantoğlu of Vidin, Mehmet Buşatlı of Albania and Mustafa Bayraktar of Silistra (Silistre), to name just a few of the most prominent *ayans*. They were not a homogeneous group, though. Some studies, however, have challenged the thesis of decentralization and introduced the idea of 'localization' of Ottoman administrative and military practices by local urban elites; tax farming became a pivotal tool in this process.[11]

In fact, tax farming brought together many social groups and stimulated various forms of cooperation on both horizontal and vertical levels.[12] Many of the *ayans* purchased tax farms and not only increased their personal incomes but also entered into the flourishing contraband trade in the eighteenth century, and merchants became their natural allies.[13] Peter Sugar has interpreted the *ayans*' rule both as a stimulus for the subsequent uprisings and independent movements and a 'potential nucleus for the birth of reconstructed Ottoman Empire'.[14] For instance, it was under Ali Pasha's son's rule that the industries in Tyrnovos and Ambelakia bloomed.[15]

A good example of such profitable cooperation can be seen in the case of the Bulgarian entrepreneur hacı Khristo Rachkov of Gabrovo. The beginning of his career combined different economic activities. He started in 1782 and over the years traded in approximately 100 different commodities ranging from the export of foodstuffs, furs and silk to Bucharest and Moscow to the import of iron padlocks from Wallachia and Russia. Often in those ventures the sums invested were small. By 1791, he had participated in eight partnerships and received on average between 30 and 80 kuruş in profit. It was in the 1790s, a time that overlapped with the *kırcalıs*, that he accumulated much higher profits ranging between 1,500 and 2,000 kuruş.[16] At the same time, he moved his trading activity to Tŭrnovo (Tırnova), a larger town where he obtained a *han* (inn), which he used as a warehouse.[17]

Khristo Rachkov also organized a silk enterprise, one of the early examples of putting-out industry. Its scale was impressive: in 1796, he collected 4,868 okka raw silk, and more than 20 towns and villages around the region of Tŭrnovo and Gabrovo were incorporated into his web. In 1795, his profit from 300 okka silk was 1,500 kuruş, or 41.5 per cent. His network of partners and intermediaries included Bulgarians, Greeks and Turks. Some of his providers and partners were local ağas, quite probably *ayans* with economic interests vested in the silk production. It seems that the right to buy cocoons and silk production constituted a *mukataa* (tax farming unit) and many local ağas owned that monopolistic right. In 1802, hacı Khristo bought silk for 13,500 kuruş from Ismail ağa Trastenikliǒğlu only and in 1796 he bought 3,300 okka silk from

13 ağas in the region around Tŭrnovo.[18] By comparison, the percentage of gain was three times more than some of his contemporaries' gains from export trade in cotton to central Europe.[19] Such entrepreneurial activities in the Ottoman Empire, which included the putting-out system of silk, wool and hides yielded hefty profits. That high profit margin may also explain the reorientation of many entrepreneurs from trade within central Europe to production and commerce within the Ottoman realm where they established economic partnerships and political coalitions with local elites. Both trends were engendered by the political developments during the *kırcalı* period. On the one hand, the trade routes to central Europe became less safe; on the other hand, the *ayans* exerted their influence in local economies by collaborating with both Muslim and non-Muslim entrepreneurs.

The Serbian Revolts (1804–1813, 1815)

The First Serbian Uprising was an event that was related to the tumultuous period of the *kırcalıs*. In 1804, the Serbs in the *paşaluk* of Belgrade rose up against the four local janissary leaders, or *dahis*, who had links with Osman Pazvantoğlu.[20] Their goal was restoration of order, not political secession, and according to Prota Mateja Nenadović, the principal instigators of the First Serbian Revolt in 1804 were the families of *knezes* (village elders), the clergy and the merchants.[21] The revolt's leader, Karadjorgje, was himself a livestock trader. He was also a veteran who had served in the Austrian army.[22] Some entrepreneurs benefited substantially from the situation: Stevan Živković, a merchant who fled from Belgrade's *dahis* to Zemun, regularly supplied gunpowder and munitions to the rebels starting in 1804 and was making 130 per cent profit.[23] Although this figure is probably exaggerated, others also accumulated capital, including the merchants in Mitrovitza. They benefited from the revolt by engaging in both legal import–export trade between Austria and the Serbian lands, and illegal smuggling of arms and ammunitions.[24]

At that time, foreign and Greek merchants dominated the import trade in Serbian towns. The Serbian traders, as seen from the examples above, were also active participants in the First Revolt and many of them not only enriched themselves during the uprising but also returned to trade after that, dealing in particular in cattle, foodstuffs and salt.[25] Nikola Milićević-Lunjevica (1767–1842) presents another good illustration of the trend of accumulating capital through trade in livestock. He made deals for the sale of cattle to the value of 52,822 kuruş in 1815 and 99,221 kuruş in 1816.[26] After the Second Revolt (1815), it became easy to launch a business because it was possible to begin trade with a start-up capital of only 500 groša.[27]

After the First Serbian Revolt, the Serbian commercial hierarchy included knez Miloš Obrenović as the most powerful trader. His *ortaks* (partners) comprised: major wholesale merchants in livestock and salt; wholesalers in colonial goods; traders on commission and financially sound merchants in towns and villages; retail traders in both towns and villages; itinerant merchants; smugglers; and various brokers and *kalauz* (middlemen). There were no distinctive lines for crossing from one group to another but fierce competition was in evidence within and among those groups.[28] Thus, both revolts facilitated not only this shift in the ethnic composition of the merchants, but also the pace of accumulation of money and the emergence of broader entrepreneurial networks, which included political elites.

The Russo-Ottoman War (1806–1812)

Another turbulent event related to the economic and social transformations described above was the Russo-Ottoman War of 1806–1812. This war had a significant impact on the territories between the Danube River and the Balkan Mountains. The case of hacı Dimitraki Toshev (1780–1827) of Vratsa offers a good example of entrepreneurial and political activities embedded within the context of the war and First Serbian Uprising.[29] The success of this family-based company[30] relied on a broad network of agents and employees who worked in their shops, collected and sold goods in the Vratsa region, organized the transportation of merchandise and livestock to the Danubian ports, Bucharest and Belgrade, and regularly attended the major fairs. The Khadzhitoshevs organized putting-out productions of silk, wool and hides. Like their Serbian counterparts, the Khadzhitoshevs invested in livestock breeding and trade, and the crafts related to them. Furthermore, they established a business relationship with the Serbian Prince Miloš Obrenović who, as previously noted, was the richest livestock trader in the newly emerged neighbouring state.

The following example serves as an illustration of a flexible combination of production and trade. Hacı Dimitraki Khadzhitoshev and a furrier from Sofia formed a partnership to benefit from the demand that the war created.[31] In 1811, the former invested 3,000 kuruş and provided his *dükkân* (shop) with goods. The latter put in 1,000 kuruş and sent two servants from Sofia to Vratsa to work there. The Vratsa partner would be a treasurer and could lend money or sell goods on credit. The contract discloses a single-venture partnership with relocation of labour that combined multiple activities: production, trade and money lending. Both partners seem to belong to a more affluent urban stratum: the title hacı implies that Dimitraki Khadzhitoshev had visited Jerusalem, while the Sofia partner was possibly a master in the guild of the furriers and could afford to send two of his young apprentices to Vratsa. The invested sums also reveal available cash in sizeable quantities during the end of the Russo-Ottoman War and the First Serbian Revolt, which provided lucrative business opportunities. Moreover, hacı Dimitraki travelled to Oriakhovo on the Danube River and in 1811 wrote to ask his father in Vratsa to send him formal clothes and a 'kalpak' (hat), as well as his ring, all of which he would need for his meeting with the Russian general when he was to cross the Danube. He also gave an order: 'And try to sell because now is the right moment, one servant has to stay [in the shop] and another to bring goods here.' He also requested some rice to sell on the spot and would buy 3,000 okka of salt in Oriakhovo and trade it in Vratsa and its surroundings.[32] Hence, Dimitraki Khadzhitoshev's business, as in the other examples, expanded and diversified during the turbulent time of the war and the Serbian uprising in the neighbouring area.

However, other entrepreneurs were not as successful in making profits. The chronicle of hacı Veliko, a merchant of Shumen (Şumnu), noted how the Russians organized the siege of Shumen during the Russo-Ottoman War of 1806–1812. He lamented the fact that the army presence in the town increased the prices of food: 52 para per okka of flour, 18 para for bread, 64 para per okka of rice, 100 para per okka of cheese, 20 para for wine, etc.[33] Nonetheless, due to the blockade, many local traders were not able to benefit by selling scarce foodstuffs.

Another chronicle, that of the Arie family of Samokov (Samako), demonstrates that during this war they expanded their business not so much in trade in commodities but in banking (*sarraflık*). In 1807, Avram became a treasurer for the collection of *harac* (poll tax) in Sofia while his son stayed in Samokov and maintained their shop. Avram received 400 aspras a month. The *harac* was paid in diverse currencies. He replaced the precious coins with an equivalent amount from his salary and sent the valuable currencies to Istanbul to the banker Bohor Carmona, securing himself a profit of between 10 and 20 per cent. At the same time, he began participating in tax farming of *harac* (1808) and even brought his son to Sofia to help. However, Avram's main preoccupation remained the trade in currency.[34]

In summary, these examples are indicative of new business opportunities where entrepreneurs worked for the state, supplied foreign armies, or just sold merchandise in high demand. Furthermore, during the war, successful ventures extended beyond the regional economy and many merchants gained access to broader resources. Of course, not everyone was a part of such lucrative webs.

The Greek War of Independence (1821–1829) and the Russo-Ottoman War (1828–1829)

Many Balkan merchants supported the Greek War of Independence. Nikolai Todorov studied the Bulgarian participants and remarked that the previously mentioned Gabrovo merchant hacı Khristo Rachkov allegedly contributed financially to the revolution and, after the death of the Patriarch in Constantinople, committed suicide in 1821. There are two versions of his purported participation: first, that he hid twelve carts full of guns in his water mill in Gabrovo; second, that he donated 100,000 kuruş to the patriarchate for supporting the uprising.[35]

Another example of the link between economic career and participation in political revolution is presented in the case of the Plovdiv (Philippoupolis) Chalŭkov family, prominent merchants and *celeps* (owners and traders in cattle). One of the brothers, Stoian Todorovich Chalŭkov, was also allegedly involved with Philiki Etaireia, the secret society that organized the Greek Revolution. He had agreed to provide 10,000 armed men who were supposed to invade the Empire from Serbia – a promise that was never fulfilled. The failure of the insurrection in the Danubian Principalities did not lead a single member of the family to commit suicide. Indeed, the Chalŭkovs signed a letter, written by the Orthodox Christians in Plovdiv (1821), stating that they would remain faithful to the sultan.[36]

The above two cases link economic success with political action. The two entrepreneurs with business and administrative links with the Ottoman local elites allegedly supported an insurrection that took place in distant territory. What was their motivation? Did

Rachkov support an anti-Ottoman and political uprising or merely express Christian solidarity (hence the alleged loan to the patriarchate) against social oppression in Morea?[37] Was he afraid that he would lose his wealth and Ottoman business partners in case of reprisals against Christians? Or, on the contrary, was he hoping to increase his fortune by forsaking his Muslim partners? Was Chalŭkov merely a political opportunist? Whatever the reasons for their behaviour *vis-à-vis* the insurrection, Chalŭkov exemplifies the Bulgarian entrepreneurs who became one of the main groups of economic beneficiaries after the Greek War of Independence. On the other hand, as Socrates Petmezas has contended, the 'revolt did not serve the economic interests of the larger number of merchants and of the high Phanariot class'. It was the local and provincial notables and armed militia who benefited economically from the revolution, especially in the process of land redistribution. The traders were mainly pushed to adopt nationalist rhetoric by the rivalry of European merchants in the Mediterranean.[38]

While the Russo-Ottoman War (1828–1829) saw the emergence of the first independent nation-state in the Balkans, it also had significant economic, social and demographic ramifications in Dobruja and Eastern Rumelia. The Russian army's advance to Edirne (Adrianople) in 1829 disrupted all economic activity in present-day eastern Bulgaria and caused the out-migration of farmers to Russia. The widespread destruction (material and demographic) was described by one contemporary: 'when we passed through Dobrich on the way to Bessarabia the land was bleak and everything was deserted (*pusto razvalini*), we did not see any villages that were left intact'.[39] And yet the region experienced economic revitalization soon afterwards. Such economic prosperity was promoted by the Ottoman pro-migration and reconstruction policies coupled with effective local leadership.

Immediately upon the cessation of war hostilities in 1829, the Porte sent officials to restore stability and security in Rumelia and to assess conditions. Municipal notables asked them to protect the population from itinerant criminal gangs. Even in 1830, the Metropolitan of Edirne travelled to Iambol (Yanbolu) and Sliven (Islimiye) to convince the peasants not to leave the Ottoman Empire. Thus, local authorities contributed to the formulation of state-organized projects that offered multiple material incentives to stop migration, to attract return migrants from the Russian Empire, and to resettle the displaced *reaya* (tax-paying subjects). Bulgarian return settlers were presented with privileges not usually given to populations living in the Ottoman Empire, such as tax-free agricultural loans, property guarantees, input into local decision-making and governance, a crackdown on corrupt tax farmers, administrative assistance, amnesty to those who had sided with the Russians during the war, and tax exemptions.[40] As a result, Ottoman Rumelia and Dobruja experienced an impressive demographic and economic revival in the 1830s. A lot of those incentives, as Andrew Robarts convincingly argues, predate the Tanzimat reforms.

The Era of Reforms: the Tanzimat (1839–1876)

The loss of the Russo-Ottoman War (1828–1829), the subsequent emergence of the first independent state in Rumelia and the wars with Egypt (1831–1833 and 1838–1839) increased international pressure on the Ottoman Empire. The trade convention of Balta Limanı (1838) and the edict of Gülhane, which initiated the Tanzimat, were the Ottoman responses to those losses. The Tanzimat (and wars) added further tensions among various groups who competed for representational positions on a local level[41] as well as a redistribution of economic resources.

The Crimean War (1853–1856)

The Crimean War is usually interpreted as a significant political event that also had serious economic repercussions. The war created temporary inflation but also contributed to accumulation of capital. Commercial correspondence reveals that close attention was paid by local entrepreneurs to diplomatic and military developments. For example, the beginning of the Crimean War was commented on as follows:

> We are still worrying about the political [events]. Rumors say that Omer Pasha will invite prince Gorchakov to vacate Moldo-Wallachia in 21 days ... The *cambials* [bills of exchange] and currencies are going up and down. I am forced to let you know that all your money will be calculated in metal, as I have already announced that to all other friends.[42]

In order to minimize the risk of loss due to a lack of cash and unstable currency rate during the war, the above quoted merchant redirected most of his financial operations through Vienna. Other entrepreneurs listed the names of stable partners and limited their business contacts with people on the list.[43] Still others bribed local pashas to transport merchandise through the Danube during the quarantine. For example, Khristo Tŭpchileshtov, an Istanbul-based entrepreneur who imported tallow (*çerviş*) from Bucharest, wanted to receive it through Svishtov because he had good connections with the Tŭrnovo pasha while the pasha in Rusçuk wanted more butter as a 'gift'.[44]

As the above concerns show, one of the major economic consequences was the so-called 'silver disease', or lack of available cash, which saw a rise in interest rates. Its impact was felt in all economic transactions. For example, the Uzundzhovo (Uzuncova) fair experienced high supply but lower demand. One shrewd entrepreneur sold his goods before the opening of the fair on condition he got his payment in 'three months'. Initially, he was ridiculed but his colleagues who did not sell in advance suffered economic damage.[45] That unstable situation was accompanied by multiple bankruptcies in 1857–1859 that had a domino effect.

Trade in grain and *çerviş* was quite profitable business during the Crimean War. The region around Pleven and Svishtov specialized in livestock and trade in hides, meat and *çerviş*. Many local companies thrived and accumulated capital. Even in 1854 all export of Gabrovo *çerviş* was banned, as it was reserved for the needs of the army.[46] As for grain, there are indications that it was exported from Eski Zağra, Svishtov and Lom to Istanbul in 1854.[47] A sign of post-war prosperity, or 'muharibe', was reflected in increased contributions to support education, and often women's education. For example, the obituary of hacı Ilia hacı Nikolov of Eski Zağra shows that he designated his donation of 15,000 kuruş for such a school in 1856.⁴⁸

As noted earlier, the Aries began *sarraflık* during the war of 1806–1812 by selling various coins in the Ottoman capital. This business was even more profitable during the Crimean War but it seems that they were sidelined by the big bankers in Istanbul. Thus, in 1853 *mubağcılık* (the right to buy old coins at fixed prices) was bought by an Armenian family in Istanbul. They sent a certain Bedroz in Samokov who hired Avramaci for 400 kuruş monthly pay.⁴⁹ While medium-level entrepreneurs still benefited from banking business during the war, the lion's share went into the hands of the Galata bankers.

Tax farming of *öşür* (tithe) during the Crimean War was very lucrative due to subfarming, which included a wide web of participants and led to a trickling down of the profits. In 1854, the previously mentioned entrepreneur Tŭpchileshtov was farming out the Svishtov *kaza* with two Bulgarian merchants in Tŭrnovo.⁵⁰ It seems that he had contacts with *mültezims* (tax farmers) in Edirne who had also bought the tithe there but could not deliver the required amount. Thus, Tŭpchileshtov negotiated a collaboration between his Tŭrnovo and Edirne partners to combine the delivery in Ruse (Rusçuk).⁵¹ As Murat Çizakça has suggested, such a portfolio of multiple enterprises was aimed at risk aversion rather than capital pooling.⁵² Usually, the payments in instalments were sent to Istanbul as bills of exchange. The abovementioned case, however, shows payment in kind and/or redistribution of the surplus of foodstuffs to another region. The documents are silent about government orders for such transactions and it might be a local arrangement related to the increased need for food during the war. Similarly, in 1853, the Gavriel brothers bought the delivery of grain for the Ottoman army; it was delivered in Silistra and Ruse. They appointed a trusted person, Elianucho Arie, to oversee the matter there for 750 kuruş per month.⁵³

Most of the examples also demonstrate that the same tax collectors were engaged in a portfolio of tax collections. Other instances of various tax collections occurred in Svishtov: in the late 1840s and early 1850s, hacı Mincho hacı Tsachev tax farmed the *beğlik* (sheep tax) of Svishtov *kaza* and the taxes of *suvats* (pastures), both with Tŭpchileshtov's surety.⁵⁴ He collaborated with hoca Maksut and hoca Misak. In 1853, the sum was 1,931,000 kuruş.⁵⁵ The accounts of Tŭpchileshtov manifest a steady growth of his capital during the war and immediately after it: from 437,391 kuruş in 1851 to 1,014,771 kuruş in 1854 and to 4,102,151 kuruş in 1857 – or it increased 2-, 3- and four-fold, respectively.⁵⁶ Most of his profits were derived from tax farming. Another Tŭrnovo entrepreneur ended up with capital of one million kuruş after the war.⁵⁷

Often tax collections were linked to state deliveries, as in the examples from the Crimean War. When one correspondent wanted to sign a subcontract with Tŭpchileshtov for a state delivery of rams, he wrote: 'I could make a contract with you for rams, but this is not a business for you because you don't know it. The conditions of such a contract are the same as what I have with the government now and they are quite severe.'⁵⁸ Both tax farming and state deliveries were organized through partnerships that encompassed large multi-ethnic networks. Often the regional actors were the same persons who concurrently participated in diverse enterprises and were also involved in the circulation of local and regional money in Istanbul. The formation of multi-ethnic business coalitions in various geographical areas closely linked to the Ottoman capital contributed not only to the enrichment of provincial entrepreneurs but also shaped their investment strategies, social behaviour and political preferences. Such endeavours were also appealing because they privileged alliances of local merchants at the expense of their foreign counterparts.

The Tumultuous Years (1875–1878)

Political events during the late 1870s led to dramatic economic and social changes. In the 1860s and 1870s, the Balkan states attempted various acts against the Ottoman Empire, which materialized in the uprisings in Crete (1866–1868), Bosnia and Herzegovina in 1875 and the subsequent Serbo-Montenegrin-Ottoman War, and the Bulgarian Uprising in 1876. The Russo-Ottoman War of 1877–1878 and the Berlin Congress (1878) redrew the map of the peninsula, creating two independent states (Serbia and Rumania), an autonomous Ottoman province of Eastern Rumelia, and a Bulgarian Principality under Ottoman suzerainty. Important events were unfolding within the Ottoman Empire as well: the adoption of a constitution in 1876 and an election of parliament in 1877. The political developments were accompanied by a moratorium on external debts followed by the establishment of the Ottoman Public Debt Administration in 1881. In what follows, I examine some significant economic and social shifts that resulted from the wars.

All the above mentioned political upheavals jeopardized the economic prospects for many Ottoman entrepreneurs. The period was also marked by the international price depression during 1873–1896. According to Dobre Ganchev's memoirs, around ten Bulgarian families were still living in Istanbul in 1878, mostly people who could not collect their debts. Almost all of them were ruined by the war with the exception of Ivan Dochoğlu, who multiplied his wealth because he delivered butter, cheese and smoked dried meat to the Ottoman army. He was supposed to have a wealth of 200,000–300,000 Ottoman liras, but it was all in assignations (*havale*) and that was how his fortune melted away.[59] It is no surprise that most of the impoverished Ottoman entrepreneurs left Istanbul; many of them reinvented themselves as new bureaucratic elites. Out of the 279 Bulgarian commercial families with a medium-size volume of business mentioned in the sources around 1870s, only 62 survived the turbulent war years.[60]

One possible explanation for these diminished numbers is that there was a shift from trade to factory production, as manifested by the case of Ivan Kalpazanov of Gabrovo. In the 1860s, he organized a putting-out system for production of wool, and especially *şayak* (type of *aba* or cloth) and *gaitan* (braid made of wool), which he traded in Anatolia, Bosnia and Wallachia. In the 1870s, he not only retained his membership in the *gaitan*'s guild but also became its master. During the Russo-Ottoman War of 1877–1878, there was a high demand for basic necessities and Kalpazanov opened a shop selling candles, sugar, rice and coffee, and made about 150–200 per cent profit. When the situation changed in 1879, he began building a spinning factory in Gabrovo.[61] In 1878, the Tŭrnovo entrepreneur Stefan Karagiozov died and left a silk factory to his heirs.⁶² These examples suggest that since the 1870s many economic actors transitioned to manufacturing and factory production. In some cases, this shift was an extension of the trade that they were familiar with (as with Kalpazanov); in others, it was a new venture. Other merchant families, such as the Aries, moved into finance and even established a bank 'Avram Arie' in Istanbul, a trend that began with the war of 1806–1812.⁶³

As in every war, some entrepreneurs were quick to secure contracts for food delivery to the army. For instance, the Georgiev brothers who owned *moşie* (big farms) in Wallachia sold wheat to the Russian army. Although their business was predominantly in the field of banking, during the 1877–1878 war they accrued more profits from trade in foodstuffs.⁶⁴ On the other hand, the war also brought a lot of misfortune. The *abacıs* in Sliven were required to sell their *aba* to the army at a lower price. The government delayed its payments and at the beginning of 1878 it still owed 500,000 kuruş to the Sliven *abacı* guild. Moreover, a fire destroyed around 800 *dükkans* in the central part of the town.⁶⁵

The prospect of easy property acquisition at the expense of the departing Muslims marked social and economic interactions in the early 1880s. Similar processes of land redistribution and the concomitant social reshuffling had occurred earlier in Greece and Serbia. In Greece, the state nationalized the former Turkish properties and prevented the formation of a stratum of big landowners. The prevailing smallholdings became instrumental for the expansion of the production of currants.⁶⁶ This social shift is usually interpreted in terms of agrarian ownership. For example, Michael Palairet has contended that the Bulgarian economy after 1878 became 'Serbianized' and turned into a mass smallholder society while the urban sector declined.⁶⁷

Yet these property transfers happened in urban areas as well. For instance, Ruscho Mirkovich of Sliven was buying estates from the departing Muslim residents in Sliven and its vicinity. In 1880, he acquired a house with a barn from Ruhçuoğlu Osman effendi.⁶⁸ A list of his immovable properties in 1881–1882 included: eight houses, three shops and four *hans*, whose value was estimated by the Sliven's financial council at a total of 100,000 kuruş. His income from those properties was 37,300 kuruş.⁶⁹

Thus, the events in the late 1870s entailed not just economic but also ethnic redistribution of resources at the expense of migrating Muslims in both rural and urban environments. Those processes reflected not only shifts in the economy but also changes in the social fabric, and in legal, political, ideological and cultural norms. The shifting economic landscape in the Ottoman Empire in the 1870s and the 1880s diminished the previously lucrative opportunities for multi-ethnic tax farming and state deliveries. Yet other economic and financial alternatives were not as profitable and many minority entrepreneurs began looking for new possibilities in the emerging nation-states.

Conclusion

The standard narrative contends that Balkan entrepreneurs were promoters and staunch supporters of national revolutions, or constantly suffered from devastation, wars and administrative malpractices. However, the evidence of economic and political coalitions calls into question such a black-and-white picture painted from the ideological perspective of the nation-state. Wars and uprisings, and concomitant violence, acted as catalysts to significant socio-economic, ethnic and political reordering as well. And yet throughout the whole century a couple of changes persisted: the intermingling of local economic and administrative elites and increasing state visibility within the economic sphere; neither one in conflict but both often mutually constitutive.

During the pre-Tanzimat period, the *ayans'* revolts and *kırcalıs'* depredations enabled risk-taking local entrepreneurs to accumulate fortunes through partnerships with Muslim landlords and administrators. Such business collaborations allowed provincial elites to insert themselves into local economic structures. At the same time, wars with Russia and Austria extended profitable opportunities to the larger non-Muslim commercial strata through both participation in contraband trade and deliveries to the Ottoman army. Last, the Serbian uprisings and the Greek Revolution paved the way to ethnic reshuffling. In the late 1870s, this trend became fully manifested when the Muslim out-migration in tandem with the Berlin Congress' redrawing of the map of the region led not only to territorial redistribution but also turned the national middle class into the main beneficiary of this resource rearrangement.

Looking through the lens of entrepreneurial strategies of wealth accumulation during times of conflict offers a more nuanced perspective on the role of the state in processes of socio-economic re-stratification. The Porte's taxation and pro-migration policies during the pre-Tanzimat period as well as afterwards facilitated the emergence of regional multi-ethnic economic coalitions. These alliances simultaneously invested in multiple endeavours, such as trade, tax farming and deliveries for the army and the state. These developments were particularly visible during the Crimean War when the scale of the transactions increased and their geographic scope was extended. Often financial players from Istanbul were major stakeholders, which added an additional layer to the relationships between the centre and peripheries. The post-Ottoman nation-states were also pivotal in fostering a national middle class either by protectionist measures or by staffing the enormous bureaucratic apparatuses. The process of de-Ottomanization was accompanied not only by new economic opportunities in the field of manufacturing but also by the disappearance of these multi-ethnic alliances and of the Ottoman markets. However, the subsequent wars and conflicts that punctuated the end of the nineteenth and the beginning of the twentieth century brought more destitution than prosperity.

Notes

1 Ventseslav Nachev and Nikola Fermandzhiev, *Pisakhme da se znae. Pripiski i letopisi* [We Wrote to be Known: Marginal Notes and Chronicles]. Sofia: Izdatelstvo na Otechestvenia front, 1984, p. 315.
2 Atanas Iliev, *Spomeni* [Memoirs]. Sofia: Pechatnitsa P. Glushkov, 1926, p. 21.

3   For example, Barbara Jelavich, *History of the Balkans: Eighteenth and Nineteenth Centuries*, vol. 1. Cambridge: Cambridge University Press, 1983; John Lampe and Marvin Jackson, *Balkan Economic History, 1550–1950: From Imperial Borderlands to Developing Nations*. Bloomington, IN: Indiana University Press, 1982. For a more nuanced picture, see Michael Palairet, *The Balkan Economies c. 1800–1914: Evolution Without Development*. Cambridge: Cambridge University Press, 1997; Halil Inalcık and Donald Quataert, eds., *An Economic and Social History of the Ottoman Empire, 1300–1914*. Cambridge: Cambridge University Press, 1994; Evguenia Davidova, *Balkan Transitions to Modernity and Nation-States through the Eyes of Three Generations of Merchants (1780s–1890s)*, Leiden: E.J. Brill, 2013.
4   Andrei Pippidi, 'The Development of an Administrative Class in South-East Europe', in *Ottomans into Europeans: State and Institution Building in South-East Europe*, eds. Alina Mungiu-Pippidi and Wim Van Meurs. New York: Columbia University Press, 2010, pp. 111–133.
5   Nikolai Todorov, *The Balkan City 1400–1900*. Seattle, WA: University of Washington Press, 1983, pp. 395–396.
6   Sanjay Subrahmanyam and C.A. Bayly, 'Portfolio Capitalists and the Political Economy of Early Modern India', *Indian Economic and Social History Review*, 25, no. 4 (1988), pp. 410–424.
7   Fernand Braudel, *The Wheels of Commerce: Civilization & Capitalism 15th–18th Century*, vol. 2. New York: Harper & Row, 1982, p. 149.
8   For more details, see Davidova, *Balkan Transitions*.
9   Donald Quataert, 'The Age of Reforms, 1812–1914', in *An Economic and Social History of the Ottoman Empire*, vol. 2, *1600–1914*, eds. Halil Inalcık and Donald Quataert. Cambridge: Cambridge University Press, 1994, p. 825.
10 Prota Matija Nenadović, *The Memoirs of Prota Matija Nenadović*, trans. Lovett F. Edwards. Oxford: Oxford University Press, 1969; Sofroniĭ Vratchanski, *Zhitie i stradania greshnago Sofronia* [Life and Sufferings of Sinful Sofronii], ed. Nikolaĭ Dilevski. Sofia: Nauka i izkustvo, 1989.
11 Dina Rizk Khouri, 'The Ottoman centre versus provincial power-holders: an analysis of the historiography', in *The Cambridge History of Turkey*, vol. 3, ed. Suraiya N. Faroqhi. Cambridge: Cambridge University Press, 2006, pp. 136–137.
12 Linda Darling, *Revenue Raising and Legitimacy: Tax Collection and Finance Administration in the Ottoman Empire 1500–1660*. Leiden: E.J. Brill, 1996, p. 136.
13 Deena R. Sadat, 'Rumeli Ayanlari: The Eighteenth Century', *Journal of Modern History*, 44, no. 3 (1972), pp. 349, 354.
14 Peter F. Sugar, *Southeastern Europe under Ottoman Rule, 1354–1804*. Seattle, WA: University of Washington Press, 1977, p. 240.
15 Todorov, *The Balkan City*, pp. 272–274.
16 Plamen Mitev, 'Dŭrzhavna reglamentatsia na gradskoto stopanstvo v bŭlgarskite zemi prez XVIII v.' [State Regulation of the Urban Economy in the Bulgarian Lands in the Eighteenth Century], in *Sŭzdavane i razvitie na moderni institutsii v bŭlgarskoto vŭzrozhdensko obshtestvo*, ed. Plamen Mitev. Sofia: Universitetsko izdatelsvo 'Sv. Kliment Okhridski', 1996, pp. 77–78.
17 Petŭr Tsonchev, *Iz stopanskoto minalo na Gabrovo* [From Gabrovo's Economic Past]. Gabrovo: 'Otvoreno Obshestvo', 1996, pp. 598–599.
18 Svetla Ianeva, 'Stopanski praktiki prez Vŭzrazhdaneto v tŭrgovskia tefter na h. Khristo Rachkov. Opit za mikroanaliz' [Economic Practices During the Revival Seen Through the Commercial Ledger of h. Khristo Rachkov: An Attempt at Microanalysis], *Istoricheski Pregled*, 3–4 (2003), pp. 30–67.

19 For more details, see Davidova, *Balkan Transitions*, p. 26.
20 Jelavich, *History of the Balkans*, pp. 125, 196.
21 Nenadović, *The Memoirs of Prota Matija Nenadović*, pp. 18, 47.
22 Jelavich, *History of the Balkans*, p. 209. L.S. Stavrianos, *The Balkans Since 1453*. New York: New York University Press, 2000, p. 213.
23 Nenadović, *The Memoirs of Prota Matija Nenadović*, pp. 58, 72, 88.
24 Slavko Gavrilović, 'Mitrovački trgovci i prvi srpski ustanak (Povodom 175-godišnjice prvog ustanka)' [Merchants from Mitrovac During the First Serbian Uprising (On the Occasion of 175 Years)], *Zbornik matice srpske za istoriju*, 20 (1979), pp. 109–111.
25 Danica Milić-Miljković, *Trgovina Srbije (1815–1839)* [Serbia's Trade (1815–1839)]. Beograd: Nolit, 1959, pp. 17–22, 31.
26 Danica Milić, 'O delatnosti jednog istaknutog nosioca trgovačkog kapitala' [On the Deeds of a Well-known Bearer of Commercial Capital], *Zbornik Muzeja prvog srpskog ustanka*, Beograd, 1960, pp. 56–57.
27 Milić-Miljković, *Trgovina Srbije*, p. 122.
28 Milić-Miljković, *Trgovina Srbije*, pp. 271–273.
29 For recent research, see Evelina Razhdavichka, 'People of Wealth and Influence: The Case of the Khadzhitoshev Family (1770s–1880s), in *Wealth in the Ottoman and post-Ottoman Balkans: A Socio Economic History*, ed. Evguenia Davidova. London: I.B. Tauris, 2016, pp. 30–50.
30 Traian Stoianovich has attributed the success of the Balkan Orthodox merchants to the family-based model of business. Traian Stoianovich, 'The Conquering Balkan Orthodox Merchant', *Journal of Economic History*, 20, no. 2 (1960), pp. 295–296.
31 Kirila Vŭzvazova-Karateodorova et al., eds., *Semeen Arhiv na Khadzhitoshevi (1751–1827)* [Archive of the Khadzhitoshev Family (1751–1827)], vol. 1. Sofia: Izdatelstvo na Bŭlgarskata akademia na naukite, 1984, p. 408.
32 Vŭzvazova-Karateodorova, *Semeen Arhiv na Khadzhitoshevi*, pp. 107–109.
33 Nachev and Fermandzhiev, *Pisakhme da se znae*, pp. 303–304.
34 MS-NA, Khronika, 11, a.e. 1, 112–116.
35 Tsonchev, *Iz stopanskoto minalo*; Nikolai Todorov, *Filiki eteria i Bŭlgarite* [Filiki Etaireia and the Bulgarians]. Sofia: Izdatelstvo na Bŭlgarskata academia na naukite, 1963, pp. 60, 85.
36 Andreas Lyberatos, 'Men of the Sultan: The *Beğlik* Sheep Tax Collection System and the Rise of a Bulgarian National Bourgeoisie in Nineteenth-Century Plovdiv', *Turkish Historical Review*, 1 (2010), pp. 57, 65, 72.
37 Information about the insurrection of the Bulgarians around Tŭrnovo in support of what was going in Morea exists in Serbian documents. AS-KK, XXI, 229, 231.
38 Socrates D. Petmezas, 'The Formation of Early Hellenic Nationalism and the Special Symbolic and Material Interests of the New Radical Republican Intelligentsia (ca. 1790–1830)', *Historein*, 1 (1999), pp. 67–68.
39 Cited in Andrew Robarts, 'Reconstruction, Resettlement, and Economic Revitilization in Pre-Tanzimat Ottoman Bulgaria', in *Wealth in the Ottoman and post-Ottoman Balkans: A Socio-Economic History*, ed. Evguenia Davidova, London: I.B. Tauris, 2016, p. 72. My discussion here was derived mostly from Robarts' analysis.
40 Robarts, 'Reconstruction', pp. 77–78.
41 Halil Inalcık, 'Application of the Tanzimat and its Social Effects', *Archivum Ottomanicum*, V (1973), pp. 100–101.

42 Khristo Tŭpchileshtov to Khristo Georgiev, 22 September 1853. BIA-NBKM, f. 7, 2, a.e. 1421, 36–37.
43 BIA-NBKM, IA 854; IA 956; f. 7, a.e. 1423, 71–72.
44 BIA-NBKM, f. 7, a.e. 1421, 44–47.
45 David Koen, 'Bankerskata deĭnost na kŭshtata 'Evlogi i Khristo Georgievi' v bŭlgarskite zemi do Osvobozhdenieto' [The Banking Activity of the Company 'Evlogi i Khristo Georgievi' in the Bulgarian Lands Before the Liberation], *Istoricheski pregled*, 6 (1975), pp. 65–66.
46 Tsonchev, *Iz stopanskoto minalo*, pp. 359–378.
47 BIA-NBKM, IA1836, IA 1843; Simeon Damianov, *Lomskiat krai prez Vŭzrazhdaneto. Ikonomicheski zhivot i politicheski borbi* [Lom Region During the Revival: Economic Life and Political Struggles]. Sofia: Otechestven front, 1967, p. 76.
48 Rumiana Radkova, *Posmŭrtni materiali za bŭlgarski vŭzrozhdenski deĭtsi* [Obituaries about Bulgarian Revival Activists]. Sofia: Akademichno izdatelstvo 'Marin Drinov', 2003, p. 63.
49 MS-NA, Khronika, 11, a.e. 1, 234.
50 BIA-NBKM, f. 6, IA 1840.
51 BIA-NBKM, f. 307, a.e 8, 9–10.
52 Murat Çizakça, *A Comparative Evolution of Business Partnerships: The Islamic World and Europe, with Specific Reference to the Ottoman Archives*. Leiden: E.J. Brill, 1996, p. 173.
53 MS-NA, Khronika, 11, a.e. 2, 88–89.
54 BIA-NBKM, f. 307, a.e. 6, 49; a.e. 5, 58.
55 BIA-NBKM, f. 307, a.e 2, 2; a.e 12, 75–76; a.e. 3, 35.
56 BIA-NBKM, IIA 7907; IA 27412; IA 9017, 1–2.
57 Dimitŭr Kosev, *Lektsii po nova bŭlgarska istoria* [Lectures on Modern Bulgarian History]. Sofia, 1951, p. 121.
58 Khristo Tŭpchileshtov to D. Papazoğlu and Sons, 28 June 1865. BIA-NBKM, f. 6, IA 8987, 8–10.
59 Dobre Ganchev, *Spomeni 1864–1887* [Memoirs 1864–1887]. Sofia: Pridvorna pechatnitsa, 1939, p. 195.
60 Zhak Natan, ed., *Ikonomikata na Bŭlgaria* [Economy of Bulgaria]. Sofia: Nauka i izkustvo, 1969, p. 375.
61 Khristo Gandev, *Problemi na Bŭlgarskoto Vŭzrazhdane* [Notes on the Bulgarian National Revival]. Sofia: Izdatelstvo Nauka i izkustvo, 1976, pp. 437–452.
62 Georgi Pletniov, 'Stopanska deĭnost na tŭrnovskiia fabrikant Stefan Karagiozov prez Vŭzrazhdaneto' [Economic Activity of the Tŭrnovo Manufacturer Stefan Karagiozov During the Revival], *Istoricheski Pregled*, 33, no. 1 (1977), p. 71.
63 MS-NA, 11, a.e. 1. 272.
64 Koen, 'Bankerskata deĭnost', p. 73.
65 Simeon Tabakov, *Opit za istoria na grad Sliven* [History of Sliven], vol. 2. Sofia: Komitet za istoria na grad Sliven, 1929, pp. 316–317.
66 Christos Hadziiossif, 'Class Structure and Class Antagonism in Late Nineteenth-Century Greece', in *Greek Society in the Making, 1863–1913: Realities, Symbols and Visions*, ed. Philip Carabott. Aldershot: Ashgate Variorum, 1997, p. 5.
67 Palairet, *The Balkan Economies*, p. 171.
68 BIA-NBKM, f. 169, a.e. 3, 118.
69 BIA-NBKM, f. 169, a.e. 3, 139. See also Evguenia Davidova, 'Business Partnerships and Practices from the 19th-Century Ottoman Balkans', *Turcica*, 44 (2012–2013), p. 235.

Bibliography

Primary sources

Arhiv Srbije – Knjažeska kancelarija (AS-KK), XXI.
Bŭlgarski Iistoricheski archiv, Narodna biblioteka 'Sv. Kiril i Metodii' (BIA-NBKM), f. 6, 7, 169, 307.
Muzei Samokov – Nauchen Arkhiv (MS-NA), Khronika na semeistvo Arie, Inv. No. 11.

Secondary sources

Braudel, Fernand, *The Wheels of Commerce: Civilization & Capitalism 15th–18th Century*, vol. 2. New York: Harper & Row, 1982.
Çizakça, Murat, *A Comparative Evolution of Business Partnerships: The Islamic World and Europe, with Specific Reference to the Ottoman Archives*. Leiden: E.J. Brill, 1996.
Damianov, Simeon, *Lomskiat krai prez Vŭzrazhdaneto. Ikonomicheski zhivot i politicheski borbi* [Lom Region During the Revival: Economic Life and Political Struggles]. Sofia: Otechestven front, 1967.
Darling, Linda, *Revenue Raising and Legitimacy: Tax Collection and Finance Administration in the Ottoman Empire 1500–1660*. Leiden: E.J. Brill, 1996.
Davidova, Evguenia, *Balkan Transitions to Modernity and Nation-States through the Eyes of Three Generations of Merchants (1780s–1890s)*, Leiden: E.J. Brill, 2013.
Davidova, Evguenia, 'Business Partnerships and Practices from the 19th-Century Ottoman Balkans', *Turcica*, 44 (2012–2013), pp. 219–249.
Ganchev, Dobre, *Spomeni 1864–1887* [Memoirs 1864–1887]. Sofia: Pridvorna pechatnitsa, 1939.
Gandev, Khristo, *Problemi na Bŭlgarskoto Vŭzrazhdane* [Notes on the Bulgarian National Revival]. Sofia: Izdatelstvo Nauka i izkustvo, 1976.
Gavrilović, Slavko, 'Mitrovački trgovci i prvi srpski ustanak (Povodom 175-godišnjice prvog ustanka)' [Merchants from Mitrovac During the First Serbian Uprising (On the Occasion of 175 Years)], *Zbornik matice srpske za istoriju*, 20 (1979), pp. 103–112.
Hadziiossif, Christos, 'Class Structure and Class Antagonism in Late Nineteenth-Century Greece', in *Greek Society in the Making, 1863–1913: Realities, Symbols and Visions*, ed. Philip Carabott. Aldershot: Ashgate Variorum, 1997, pp. 3–18.
Ianeva, Svetla, 'Stopanski praktiki prez Vŭzrazhdaneto v tŭrgovskia tefter na h. Khristo Rachkov. Opit za mikroanaliz' [Economic Practices During the Revival Seen Through the Commercial Ledger of h. Khristo Rachkov: An Attempt at Microanalysis], *Istoricheski Pregled*, 3–4 (2003), pp. 30–67.
Iliev, Atanas, *Spomeni* [Memoirs]. Sofia: Pechatnitsa P. Glushkov, 1926.
Inalcık, Halil, 'Application of the Tanzimat and its Social Effects', *Archivum Ottomanicum*, V (1973), pp. 97–127.
Inalcık, Halil and Donald Quataert, eds., *An Economic and Social History of the Ottoman Empire, 1300–1914*. Cambridge: Cambridge University Press, 1994.
Jelavich, Barbara, *History of the Balkans: Eighteenth and Nineteenth Centuries*, vol. 1. Cambridge: Cambridge University Press, 1983.
Khouri, Dina Rizk, 'The Ottoman centre versus provincial power-holders: an analysis of the historiography', in *The Cambridge History of Turkey*, vol. 3, ed. Suraiya N. Faroqhi. Cambridge: Cambridge University Press, 2006, pp. 133–156.
Koen, David, 'Bankerskata deĭnost na kŭshtata 'Evlogi i Khristo Georgievi' v bŭlgarskite zemi do Osvobozhdenieto' [The Banking Activity of the Company 'Evlogi i Khristo

Georgievi' in the Bulgarian Lands Before the Liberation], *Istoricheski pregled*, 6 (1975), pp. 63–74.
Kosev, Dimitŭr, *Lektsii po nova bŭlgarska istoria* [Lectures on Modern Bulgarian History]. Sofia, 1951.
Lampe, John and Marvin Jackson, *Balkan Economic History, 1550–1950: From Imperial Borderlands to Developing Nations*. Bloomington, IN: Indiana University Press, 1982.
Lyberatos, Andreas, 'Men of the Sultan: The *Beğlik* Sheep Tax Collection System and the Rise of a Bulgarian National Bourgeoisie in Nineteenth-Century Plovdiv', *Turkish Historical Review*, 1 (2010), pp. 55–85.
Milić, Danica, 'O delatnosti jednog istaknutog nosioca trgovačkog kapitala' [On the Deeds of a Well-known Bearer of Commercial Capital], *Zbornik Muzeja prvog srpskog ustanka*, Beograd, 1960, pp. 43–63.
Milić-Miljković, Danica, *Trgovina Srbije (1815–1839)* [Serbia's Trade (1815–1839)]. Beograd: Nolit, 1959.
Mitev, Plamen, 'Dŭrzhavna reglamentatsia na gradskoto stopanstvo v bŭlgarskite zemi prez XVIII v.' [State Regulation of the Urban Economy in the Bulgarian Lands in the Eighteenth Century], in *Sŭzdavane i razvitie na moderni institutsii v bŭlgarskoto vŭzrozhdensko obshtestvo*, ed. Plamen Mitev. Sofia: Universitetsko izdatelsvo 'Sv. Kliment Okhridski', 1996, pp. 75–82.
Nachev, Ventseslav and Nikola Fermandzhiev, *Pisakhme da se znae. Pripiski i letopisi* [We Wrote to be Known: Marginal Notes and Chronicles]; Sofia: Izdatelstvo na Otechestvenia front, 1984.
Natan, Zhak, ed. *Ikonomikata na Bŭlgaria* [Economy of Bulgaria]. Sofia: Nauka i izkustvo, 1969.
Nenadović, Prota Matija, *The Memoirs of Prota Matija Nenadović*, trans. Lovett F. Edwards. Oxford: Oxford University Press, 1969.
Palairet, Michael, *The Balkan Economies c. 1800–1914: Evolution Without Development*. Cambridge: Cambridge University Press, 1997.
Petmezas, Socrates D., 'The Formation of Early Hellenic Nationalism and the Special Symbolic and Material Interests of the New Radical Republican Intelligentsia (ca. 1790–1830)', *Historein*, 1 (1999), pp. 51–74.
Pippidi, Andrei, 'The Development of an Administrative Class in South-East Europe', in *Ottomans into Europeans: State and Institution Building in South-East Europe*, eds. Alina Mungiu-Pippidi and Wim Van Meurs. New York: Columbia University Press, 2010, pp. 111–133.
Pletniov, Georgi, 'Stopanska deĭnost na tŭrnovskiia fabrikant Stefan Karagiozov prez Vŭzrazhdaneto' [Economic Activity of the Tŭrnovo Manufacturer Stefan Karagiozov During the Revival], *Istoricheski Pregled*, 33, no. 1 (1977), pp. 27–71.
Quataert, Donald, 'The Age of Reforms, 1812–1914', in *An Economic and Social History of the Ottoman Empire*, vol. 2, *1600–1914*, eds. Halil Inalcık and Donald Quataert. Cambridge: Cambridge University Press, 1994.
Radkova, Rumiana, *Posmŭrtni materiali za bŭlgarski vŭzrozhdenski deĭtsi* [Obituaries about Bulgarian Revival Activists]. Sofia: Akademichno izdatelstvo 'Marin Drinov', 2003.
Razhdavichka, Evelina, 'People of Wealth and Influence: The Case of the Khadzhitoshev Family (1770s–1880s), in *Wealth in the Ottoman and post-Ottoman Balkans: A Socio Economic History*, ed. Evguenia Davidova. London: I.B. Tauris, 2016, pp. 30–50.
Robarts, Andrew, 'Reconstruction, Resettlement, and Economic Revitalization in Pre-Tanzimat Ottoman Bulgaria', in *Wealth in the Ottoman and post-Ottoman Balkans: A Socio-Economic History*, ed. Evguenia Davidova, London: I.B. Tauris, 2016, pp. 71–85.

Sadat, Deena R., 'Rumeli Ayanlari: The Eighteenth Century', *Journal of Modern History*, 44, no. 3 (1972), pp. 346–363.
Sofroniĭ Vratchanski, *Zhitie i stradania greshnago Sofronia* [Life and Sufferings of Sinful Sofronii], ed. Nikolaĭ Dilevski. Sofia: Nauka i izkustvo, 1989.
Stavrianos, L.S., *The Balkans Since 1453*. New York: New York University Press, 2000.
Stoianovich, Traian, 'The Conquering Balkan Orthodox Merchant', *Journal of Economic History*, 20, no. 2 (1960), pp. 234–313.
Subrahmanyam, Sanjay and C.A. Bayly, 'Portfolio Capitalists and the Political Economy of Early Modern India', *Indian Economic and Social History Review*, 25, no. 4 (1988), pp. 410–424.
Sugar, Peter F., *Southeastern Europe under Ottoman Rule, 1354–1804*. Seattle, WA: University of Washington Press, 1977.
Tabakov, Simeon, *Opit za istoria na grad Sliven* [History of Sliven], vol. 2. Sofia: Komitet za istoria na grad Sliven, 1929.
Todorov, Nikolai, *Filiki eteria i Bŭlgarite* [Filiki Etaireia and the Bulgarians]. Sofia: Izdatelstvo na Bŭlgarskata academia na naukite, 1963.
Todorov, Nikolai, *The Balkan City 1400–1900*. Seattle, WA: University of Washington Press, 1983.
Tsonchev, Petŭr, *Iz stopanskoto minalo na Gabrovo* [From Gabrovo's Economic Past]. Gabrovo: 'Otvoreno Obshestvo', 1996.
Vŭzvazova-Karateodorova, Kirila et al., eds., *Semeen Arkhiv na Khadzhitoshevi (1751–1827)* [Archive of the Khadzhitoshev Family (1751–1827)], vol. 1. Sofia: Izdatelstvo na Bŭlgarskata akademia na naukite, 1984.

6

The Final Phase of the Greek Revolution: Delimitation, Determination and Demarcation of the First Greek Borders in Ottoman Sources

Dilek Özkan
University of Oxford

Introduction

It is widely acknowledged that the Greek Revolution had a marked impact on the Ottoman reforms.[1] Although the years of insurrection were considered a 'revolution' by European and Greek intellectuals from the very beginning, the Ottoman authorities were not so eager to afford the events the same esteem.[2] However, it would not be long before the Ottomans had to address revolutionary terms.[3] During the discussions to finalize the Greek-Ottoman border and the political status of the Greek State, Ottoman authorities' encounters with the terms used by the European representatives challenged them in many ways. Moreover, during this period, not only their acquaintance with revolutionary terms but also the whole demarcation process of the first Greek borders challenged the Ottoman power of diplomacy.

In this chapter, I will revisit the official discussions regarding the agreeing of the Ottoman-Greek boundary through documents that are kept in the Ottoman archives. The main focus will be on the last meetings of the Ottoman and European representatives to finalize the Greek border (i.e. the Conference of Constantinople).[4] From the beginning of the Greek Revolution until the determination of its borders and political status almost ten years later, the Ottoman Porte accepted the border negotiations and sat at the table with the representatives of the Great Powers, and thus used its diplomatic power with great effectiveness for the first time. This provides an opportunity to survey the Ottoman approach to the Greek affair and to assess the gamut of Ottoman arguments. In addition, these discussions provide an opportunity to comment on Ottoman terminology, which changed as a result of the whole affair.

The borders of the Ottoman Empire are a topic of great interest for present-day Ottoman historians. Hungarian scholars are leading the way; owing to centuries of interactions between Ottoman-Austro-Hungarians, they have investigated the imperial borders extensively.[5] From the Ottoman borders in the nineteenth century, the Albanian-Montenegrin borderlands have received much scholarly attention, in discussions on Ottoman centralization and modernization and their effects on the borderlands and frontiers.[6]

Among the works dealing with the finalizing of the Ottoman-Greek border, three approaches come to the fore in no particular order. The first approach sees the Ottoman border as an area of competition between the Ottoman Empire and Greece, viewing the border as a tool of ethnic and nationalist claims. This approach does not allow for the neighbouring states to work in cooperation for the management of border-related issues. Veremis and Dakin are the precursors to this approach.[7] The second approach highlights the Ottoman geopolitical situation in the nineteenth century. The expansion of Russia and the admittance of the Ottoman Empire, with the support of France and Britain, into the European continental powers led many scholars to claim that the stability of the Ottoman borders was guaranteed by the European powers. They claimed that the Ottomans had to militarize their borders as mandated by the European powers to prevent territorial disputes between neighbouring states and other great powers such as Russia.[8]

Nevertheless, the first Ottoman-Greek border and borderlands received less attention. One of the earliest and most comprehensive studies is that of Koliopoulos, who dealt with the 'brigandage' – the most serious and longest running problem of the region – and its role in the Greek irredentist intentions.[9] The book also highlighted for the first time the continuity of the traditional military elements of the region in the form of captainships (chiefs of irregular bands), which continued to exist after the borders were agreed, by maintaining new positions as border guards. Monographs focusing directly on Ottoman-Greek borderlands have come to the fore more recently. For instance, Anne Couderc's research on the first Ottoman-Greek boundary emphasizes the establishment of a national state, primarily from a Greek perspective, through consultation of French consular reports.[10] Gavrilis, in contrast, treats the Greek-Ottoman boundary as an institution, and examines how and when it was transformed into a grey-military zone.[11] Although Örenç's book is one of the earliest works on the history of the Greek Revolution, focusing on the exile of the Muslim population at that time, he includes discussion on the formation of the Ottoman-Greek border referring to the Ottoman sources have felt under the nationalist tendencies of its author.[12]

Encountering the Greek Boundary Problem

Following the constant uprisings and revolts in the Peloponnesus which were the precursor to Greek independence, the authorities and 'protectors' of the new Greek State encountered several major problems during its establishment. The agreeing of the frontiers was one such issue, observable through discussions on various occasions between European and Ottoman representatives.[13] Following the destruction of the Ottoman fleet at Navarino Bay by the Great Powers and defeat in the war with Russia, the Porte was forced in 1830 to negotiate and recognize the Greek State. However, the frontiers of Greece remained a complex issue that the Great Powers had yet to resolve. Questions of the exact location of the Greek boundaries, together with those of the limits of the state and which territories to include, as well as the concomitant justifications, were paramount during the process.

Indeed, the exact borders of the newly established Greek State formed a central part of negotiations at the time. Theories abounded as to what ought to prescribe demarcation, one of which included the ancient Greek world. What were the boundaries of ancient Greece? No frontier dividing the ancient Greeks from their enemies ever truly existed. The boundaries tended to be natural obstacles which prevented ease of approach by enemies. In the same manner, the first theory proposed during border discussions referred to the classical mountains, considered to be Parnassus and Cithaeron, and even possibly expansion to include Pelion, Ossa and Olympus. The limits available to the Great Powers to set the boundaries of Greece were much more approximate than immutable. It was expressed on one occasion, for example, 'how little of the territory it might be sufficient to demand, in order to constitute a state capable of going on, under the guarantee of the three powers, without any reasonable danger of such collisions, as might compromise the security of the commerce of nations in the Levant'.[14] Furthermore, for the wider international community of the time, the boundaries of the Greek State would include territories from which the Greek people had freed themselves from Ottoman domination under the decisive influence of a *de facto* principle.[15]

In addition to disregarding the demands of the Greek representatives, the approach of the European powers to the issue of suitable borders for the new state showed little in the way of coherence or a clear trajectory. Each had diverse proposals for those territories claimed by Greece. Russia, for instance, looked to allot the maximum amount of territory, whereas Britain insisted on a limited and 'secure' territory (i.e. the Peloponnesus and the islands). Finally, upon Greek representative Kapodistrias' insistence, a frontier stretching from the Gulf of Volos to Arta was considered the most appropriate. Its aim, however, to maintain a complete separation of the Greek and Muslim populations was, without dispute, not negotiable. Similar attempts at separation would continue in the following century, especially as nationalism took centre stage in the formation of the Greek State. Who would be regarded as Greek? How far would the borders of Greece expand? These were among the questions that would occupy Greek intellectuals and politicians in perpetuity.

Before 1832, the Ottomans had negotiated, agreed, signed and accepted the demarcation of many borders.[16] They issued *sınırname/hududname* widely to establish the imperial borders. They used *hudud* to refer to their borders, which is a plural version of the Arabic term *hadd*, meaning something sharp like the blade of a knife, as the limits to the sphere of action of a person. However, the term *sınır*, which is of Greek origin, is thought to have been used in the fifteenth and sixteenth centuries to indicate the state border, and *hudud* to indicate other borders, such as that of a province. From the eighteenth century, we see both terms being used synonymously, and many documents combined both in one term: *hudud ve sınır*.[17] However, the Treaty of Karlowitz (1699) was different. Scholars consider the signing of the treaty and demarcation of the border to be a turning point for the Ottomans, as they had to accept leaving aside the theory of 'a permanent state of war' between *dar-ül islam* (House of Islam) and *dar-ül harb* (house of war), which in practice was the motive behind Ottoman expansion in Europe. In other words, by Karlowitz, Ottoman perceptions of 'borders' – pushing forward the borders of Islam in the Christian world – came to an end.[18] The Treaty of Karlowitz halted Ottoman expansion to the west through fortification of the border; that is why this border was long considered to be the dividing line between East and West, the Christian and Muslim worlds. However, as Costantini and Koller have suggested, Karlowitz could also be seen as a process of Ottoman integration into the Western border policy system. From the late seventeenth and eighteenth centuries, the European states and Ottoman Empire began to consider their border as a remote perimeter that required armed reinforcement. Thus, following the Treaty of Karlowitz, the Empire began to reinforce its borders with its Western neighbours by constructing costly new fortifications.[19]

Out of discussions of how to decide upon the borders of the Greek State, there was the question of the Ottoman-Greek border becoming a new dividing line between Muslims and Christians separating the Greek Orthodox from the Muslim Ottoman world. For the Ottoman Porte, it was already understood that the territory of Greece would be Morea, Attica and the territories lost by the war, extending to the classical mountains. By accepting the mediation of the Great Powers, the Porte expected to resolve the issue in order to prevent any future territorial clashes with Greece. However, as later developments have shown, the guarantee of the Great Powers fell short of the mark from an Ottoman perspective.[20]

During this period, the European ambassadors communicated in the main with the *Reissülküttap*, or Reis Efendi (a foreign ministry position). The then *Reissülküttap*, Pertev Efendi, represented the Ottoman Porte.[21] Pertev Efendi maintained good relations with, and was much valued by, Sultan Mahmud II, not least on account of his firm policy towards the Greek issue. He fervently refused all offers of negotiation by the Great Powers on the basis that the 'Greek affair' was an internal problem and would be solved on the basis of the Empire's laws and religion. International intervention was, therefore, uncalled for and indefensible. Nevertheless, it would be contrary to the Ottoman constitution to settle terms requested by the European powers with a group of rebel '*reaya*'. Such proposals were against the religious and political rights of the Ottoman Empire. Additionally, he insisted that their war with the Greeks was not one based on religious differences.

During the Russo-Turkish war of 1828–1829 [the Porte had tried to solve the Greek affair in its own way, by declaring an amnesty for the insurgent Greeks to submit their allegiance to the sultan whereby they would regain their properties and status (23 March 1828)], the British, French and Russian ambassadors to the Porte continued their work at Poros where they discussed analytically the issue of borders. At the conference of Poros in 1828, the 'natural frontier' argument became prominent, which required a clearly defined border that was easy to defend, and contained a reasonable proportion of the Greek population, which was rebelling against Ottoman rule.[22]

> a 'natural frontier' clearly defined, easy of defence, containing a reasonable proportion of the Greek population which was really in a state of insurrection against the Porte; lately, traced in such a manner, as to afford the least possible risk of any subjects of dispute arising between its inhabitants and those of the adjoining Turkish [Ottoman] provinces.[23]

Eventually, a line that would advance from the Gulf of Arta to the passes of Macrinoros on the one side, and on the other to Mount Othrys, near the entrance of the Gulf of Volos, was agreed in the London Protocol of 22 March 1829. By September 1829, when the Russian armies were close to the Ottoman capital, the Porte signed the treaty of Adrianople, which required its strict adherence to the stipulations of the 1826 Treaty of London (1826) and similarly the 1829 London Protocol.

Immediately following the signing of the Treaty of Adrianople, the Ottoman Foreign Minister, Reis Efendi, communicated with the ambassadors on 25 September expressing other concerns why the limits of the new state should not be extended beyond the isthmus (Korinthos). Upon this suggestion, the ambassadors stated that the three powers would settle the boundary question 'without asking the consent or the recognition of the Porte'.[24] The following excerpt, taken from the Reis Efendi's letter, vividly expresses the Porte's discomfort regarding the proposed boundary from the Gulf of Arta to the Gulf of Volos:

> To say we will have the limits of the Morea to extend from the Gulf of Zeitoun to that of Arta, because that delimitation appears the best adapted to the defence of the country, would be the same thing as saying all the islands of the Archipelago must be united with the Cyclades, because the latter are too weak to defend themselves.[25]

In the aftermath of the Ottoman defeat, high ranking officers of the Porte saw Pertev Efendi as the sole source of misguidance to the Ottoman sultan. However, until his dismissal from the office of Reis, just after Greece's declaration of independence, he had fought zealously to reduce the territory granted to Greece by the protocol of 22 March. Indeed, to some degree, he succeeded. The London Protocol of 3 February 1830 stipulated that Greece would be an entirely independent country but, in light of the Reis Efendi's objections, reduced its claim to territories to the Aspropotamos-Spercheios line. As a result, aware this would create an atmosphere of unease among the Greek public, the European representatives sought to smoothen the effects of declaring a fully independent Greek State.

The Greeks objected strongly to this development. The Greek president, Kapodistrias, issued dozens of dispatches to convince the ambassadors and the representatives of this, before his assassination in October 1831. Finally, the London Protocol of 26 September 1831 asserted that the Aspropotamos-Spercheios line would not be adopted because of 'material errors' found on it.[26] It was decided to finalize the border at the conference in Constantinople.

Indeed, the Great Powers had already agreed to return to the Arta-Volos line, proposed by the protocol of 22 March 1829; however, the Porte had to be convinced of that. The Great Powers observed that two regions – Aetolia and Acarnania – were arid and poor lands and it would be of no benefit to the Porte to retain them since their inhabitants had never fully submitted to Ottoman rule. Thus, they would use this argument to secure compensation for these regions.

By the summer of 1831, the Ottoman Porte and the European ambassadors began their negotiations to finalize the Greek border. This discussion can be traced through documents kept at the Ottoman archives in Istanbul, registered in the *Hatt-ı Hümayun* folders, and all dated 10 June 1831.[27] What is more significant concerning these sources are the personal notes of the Ottoman Sultan (Mahmud II) in his own handwriting, giving directions concerning the methods to be followed by the Ottoman authorities in negotiating the frontier. Many times he expressed his exhaustion with the whole affair and his desire to conclude the issue by agreeing a 'middle way' with his European counterparts.[28]

Determining the Boundary: The Constantinople Conferences

By the winter of 1831–1832, as the ambassadors arrived to the Porte for negotiations,[29] they found the new Reis, Necip Efendi, disinterested in the issue as can be determined from the particularly lax scheduling of the 20 February meeting.[30] In this first meeting, the ambassadors began by citing their grievances, claiming a lack of response on the part of the Porte regarding their new border proposals, and that they expected the issue to be resolved at the meeting. Although an Ottoman reporter noted that the Ottoman representatives[31] saw such a statement as a threat, the Porte explained that the delay was due to a lack of time. The Ottoman delegates protested that as all discussions regarding the border had been concluded, and as agreements had been made that the existing frontier would provide only the necessary order and security, there were reasons to try and improve upon it.[32] The Porte claimed that the reasons for proposing another frontier were vague. In addition, the answers supplied by the ambassadors were deemed unsatisfactory by the Ottoman delegates. Therefore, the ambassadors foresaw that the issue could not logically be concluded in a single meeting lasting three hours.

The ambassadors aimed to clarify the new line on a map they brought with them, claiming that the map was prepared according to a recent survey along the border region. The Ottoman delegates compared this map, which was likely used during earlier discussions, with their own. They discovered that the two maps were identical except for a line drawn on that of the ambassadors, showing the new proposed frontier. Realizing that the two maps were the same, the Ottoman delegates began to complain about the European representatives' undertakings.[33] The Ottoman delegates reminded the *Düvel-i selase* that during discussions about the previous border, they would have been barred by the powers from dispatching experts to the area to conduct a similar survey.[34] They also entreated them to be reasonable, considering the Porte's losses as a result of the *Rum maslahatı* (Greek Affair). In response, the European representatives, stating their awareness of the Porte's losses, insisted that *emniyet ve asayiş* (security and order) would be provided for by the proposed frontier. The Ottoman delegates expressed in no uncertain terms that they did not intend to reject the proposal outright, but wished to find a 'middle way', which, according to them, would take the form of another line between the old and new suggested frontiers. Moreover, the Ottoman delegates clarified to the ambassadors that the issue could not be resolved at a single meeting due to economic and political matters. For the Ottoman delegates, the existing frontier was a convenient border between two states that was a natural line passing through mountain chains and rivers. However, this line had to pass through various villages, dividing them down the middle. The line the European delegates proposed would be situated further north, leaving a territory (according to Ottoman estimates) equal to 40 hours' walking distance in total to the Greek Kingdom. The amount of compensation requested by the Ottoman delegates was more than that considered appropriate by the European representatives.[35]

As the discussions continued, the Ottoman delegates' disapproval of the proposal became more evident. Their denouncement was now directed towards the conference in London, at which the proposals for the new line had originated. According to them, the Great Powers had made the proposal alone, without an Ottoman representative present who would have participated had one been invited. In response, the words of the English ambassador are telling: 'there were not even Greek representatives in the conference'. Such a reply drew an aggressive reaction from the Ottoman delegates, as the ambassador had entailed that the Ottoman state and the Greek government were being ascribed equal weight. Understanding the Ottoman delegates' position on the issue, the English ambassador explained that he did not consider them equal; however, since the Greeks' independence was approved, it was necessary to treat them differently.[36]

Upon the ambassadors' insistence of immediate approval from the Porte, the Ottoman delegates requested an approximate estimate of the time taken to finalize the proposal in front of them. The reply was less than comforting given the extremely quick turnaround which the European powers had demanded from the Porte – two years. The Porte berated the expectation that they be required to approve something immediately that took two years to draw up. The Russian ambassador, however, then claimed that the Porte had already accepted the terms of the Treaty of Adrianople containing an article on the Greek issue, thus obliging them to accept the new proposal. The Ottoman delegates stated their view that the aforementioned treaty was signed and fully completed, and therefore they assumed that the new frontier proposal was a separate negotiation.

Thus, the first conference with the European ambassadors in the Ottoman capital gave the Porte an opportunity to express strong disapproval with the European powers' mediation in solving the Greek affair by imposing their plans. It is clear from the records that, for the Porte, any further territorial loss would not be permissible; their losses from the whole affair were already immense. They were also aware of the fact that if the Great Powers had decided as such, they would not have a chance to change it at all. The strategy for the Ottoman delegates was to argue their cause to the greatest possible extent.

Meanwhile, the representatives of the Great Powers gave particular weight to the considerations of the Greeks as per the establishment of an alternative frontier, not least of which stemmed from communications between Kapodistrias and Prince Leopold regarding the territories to remain under Ottoman control in the border region according to the London Protocol of 3 February 1830. In addition, Greek sentiments were catapulted to the fore following the assassination of Kapodistrias in October 1831 and the subsequent unrest.

At the end of April 1832, the second conference began with Ottoman proposals for a frontier situated somewhere in the middle of the two lines. The ambassadors, however, rebuked this frontier on account of the lack of surrounding mountains in the proposed plan.[37] This repudiation of the Ottoman delegates' plan sparked discussion as to the nature of what ought to separate two states: 'natural frontiers' or 'legal borders'. On the one hand, the ambassadors based their arguments on the grounds that they had formulated the most suitable natural boundary (i.e. the Arta-Volos line), which provided the maximum 'security and order' possible for the region. On the other hand, the Ottomans refuted this proposal on the grounds that, if it was security and order which the ambassadors sought to ensure, this would be accomplished more practically and assuredly via legislation and not by a natural frontier. Their rationale was that should one state decide to attack the other, a natural boundary would not necessarily forestall such activities; legislated borders, in contrast, would provide a more accountable means of security and order.[38]

In agreement, the ambassadors claimed that a legislated line based on a natural frontier would be the optimal solution. From these discussions, and in the face of Ottoman proposals to send their own survey team to assess where the line should fall, the English ambassador stated that, having seen the area for himself, he was convinced that there were no other suitable places for the frontier than that which their proposal provided for.[39]

In another attempt to prove the superiority of a legislated border, the Ottoman delegation used the example of the Arta Gulf. According to the proposal, the frontier would pass through the middle of the gulf. The Greeks, advanced in navigation, would threaten Ottoman fisheries and security in that area. The Ottomans directed a question to the ambassadors as to what they should do in such circumstances, to which they answered that such trespass ought necessarily be met with punitive measures. This answer provided the opportunity to prove that legislation was a more appropriate solution than a natural frontier.[40]

Believing that they had convinced the ambassadors, the Ottoman delegation proposed continuing the discussions following a break; they were reconvened with a new Ottoman proposal. Although this time it was closer to that of the ambassadors, they faced the same question as before: *'bunda tabii hudud olabilecek yerler var mı?'* (Are there places that would be natural frontiers?). The Ottoman delegation responded that their plan did indeed include some *derbends* (mountain passes) and rivers; however, they requested that the ambassadors drop their insistence on a natural frontier (*şu tabii hudud lakırdısını elçi beylerin terk etmesini iltimas ederiz*) on account of the fact that not all states maintained borders that could be considered natural frontiers.[41]

During subsequent discussions on 11, 21 and 26 May, the Ottoman delegates firmly set out their objections to the proposed border based on unacceptable losses of territory, citing the centrality of the Izdin or Zeitoun (Lamia) and Padracık or Badracık (Gr. Ypati) districts.[42] Acceptance of the proposed border, they maintained, was incompatible with Ottoman legislation. In addition, it violated the Şeri'at to maintain a territory the population of which consisted mainly of *ahali-yi İslam*, and on the basis of which the objections to the secession of Izdin and Padracık districts were based. In reply to the Ottoman objections, however, the European representatives produced a recent population survey of these districts which indicated that, over the last four to five years, the Muslim population had in fact dispersed and thereby obviated any claims of validity based on the presence of a majority Muslim community.[43] The Ottoman delegates countered that, during the Greek Revolution, the residents of Lamia did not collaborate with the insurgent *reaya* and, in fact, maintained their allegiance to Ottoman authority. As such, the secession of those areas would be inappropriate and contrary to the general stipulations of the boundary.[44]

Moreover, the Ottoman delegates' momentary endorsement of the suggestion of the English Ambassador that the Zeitoun district be allotted to the Ottoman Empire and the Ypati district to the Greek Kingdom, was soon withdrawn.[45] Despite discrepancies between the European and Ottoman maps, the Ottoman delegates later acknowledged that the line had not included Izdin port, instead dividing the district down the middle. Although the Ottoman delegates persistently requested its modification, claiming that the district without its port would not make sense, the European representatives disagreed and repeated their aim to agree a border that would pass along mountain peaks and reach the sea from two sides – east to west. With such issues at play, any possibility for modification in favour of the Ottoman demands were quashed. This problem and the Ottoman insistence on assurances from the European delegates regarding Izdin continued as the focal point throughout the third conference without resolution. Finally, the parties agreed that these issues would be decided at the London conferences.

By the same token, the line would pass from the foot of Mt. Makrynoros, and the *derbend* (mountain pass) of the same name would be given to the Greeks. The Ottoman delegates agreed that their officials would explore the possibility that if the *derbend* in question was as worthless for the Porte as the ambassadors claimed, there would be no apparent problem in allowing it to be given to the Greeks. As such, negotiations regarding the frontier concluded in Istanbul, leaving aside the issue of Izdin, on 9–21 July 1832. The Porte assigned a certain Nabi Efendi to conduct a survey on the ground, and Hüseyin Bey from Voniçe (Gr. Vonitsa) as Ottoman representative to the committee for border demarcation, meeting in Nafplio at the time. By the end of August 1832, Hüseyin Bey met with other members of the border commission in Preveza.

At the end of negotiations in Istanbul, grand vizier Reşit Paşa wrote an official note to Sultan Mahmud II on 17 August 1832, only a week before talks ended in London. There he evaluated the latest developments and agreements concluded in the Ottoman capital regarding the Greek frontier and suggested to the Sultan acceptance of the terms and the need to finalize the matter of the frontier. While these terms appeared iniquitous, he highlighted that a change in favour of the Ottoman state was not possible. According to him, in the future, a time would present itself to take revenge. He suggested increased efforts to take both sides of the Gulf of Arta, in spite of losing the Zeitoun and Badracık districts.[46]

The Treaty of London dated 30 August 1832 gave Izdin to the Greek Kingdom. Jean Mavroyanni, having represented the Porte at the conference in London, submitted a memorandum (tezkere) to the representatives of the Great Powers, harshly criticizing their conduct. Mavroyanni's memorandum repeated the views of the Porte regarding Izdin, which was often written as 'Zeitoun':

On what pretext could Zeitoun be separated from the Ottoman Empire? The Greek inhabitants of that district have taken no part in the revolt: they are mixed up and live in peace with the Musulmans, who also inhabit that part of the Ottoman dominions. War having never broken out between the two populations of Zeitoun, they are not divided by any recollection of bloodshed, by any thought of reaction. Therefore, there is no moral necessity to separate them. These are facts which cannot be contested. Up to the present time, no one amongst those who have studied the nature of the localities to establish a line of demarcation going on the hypothesis of the limits being from Volo to Arta, no one, we say, has thought of including Zeitoun in those limits. Some have pointed out the line which takes in Thermopylea and Macrinoros, others the course of Sperhius from its source at mount Hellona to its mouth in front of Thermopile; but no one has conceived the idea of going beyond that river, and of encroaching upon Thessaly. General Church himself, that warm friend of the Greeks, who has commanded their troops, and particularly examined the ground, declared in a report sent to the conference, that the true line of boundary, that which combined conditions equally advantageous for both countries, and completely took in every part of continental Greece, was that line to the left of Macrinoros and to the right of Thermophile.[47]

At the same time, the Porte had received news that a Greek general with 300 soldiers had occupied the contested areas of Zeitoun, forcing the *ahaliyi İslam* to take refuge in the fortresses.[48] The representatives of the Great Powers were informed of the development and asked to intervene against the illegal act of the Greek army. In expectation that the outcome of the conference of London would change the status of Zeitoun in favour of the Porte, the Ottoman commissioner Hüseyin Bey refused to collaborate with the commissioners, deeming their work inapplicable on many occasions.

Discussions conducted between the Ottoman authorities and the European representatives on the Greek border question bring another important issue to the surface – the cartographic knowledge of the Ottoman authorities and even Ottoman cartographers. As was noted on several occasions during these discussions, the Ottoman authorities had difficulty understanding the geographic and cartographic explanations of the European representatives. They used different maps. The map of the Ottoman delegates failed to indicate geographical landscapes, such as mountains and rivers. On the other hand, the map of the European representatives was probably based on the work of Pierre Lapie in 1822, which was improved in 1826. In fact, the geography and topography of the Greek lands were not new to the European representatives. European travellers largely visited the Greek lands from the late eighteenth century. While they were mainly interested in the archaeological remnants of ancient civilizations, their detailed descriptions of geographical features, the locations of towns and villages, etc., helped later cartographers.[49] For instance, William Martin Leake, who was a member of the British Royal Geographical Society, was sent to the Peloponnesus by the British army in the early nineteenth century to gather geographical and strategic information about the region.[50] In fact, the first cartographic maps of the Peloponnesus based on new scientific developments of the time, accredited to French cartographer Barbié du Bocage, were largely used by travellers.⁵¹ Therefore, they initiated a new means of communication among travellers, geographers and cartographers. For instance, Pouqueville, during his travels in northern Greece, made extensive use of Barbié's map, and later for his travelogue helped Pierre Lapie create better maps of the region.⁵² However, Lapie's main provider of geographic features and landscapes of the region was French general Armand Charles Guilleminot, who later served as French ambassador in Istanbul from 1824 to 1831. In contrast, Ottoman cartography from the same period was unable to keep up with such developments; the Ottomans did not possess a map that was at all as accurate as the one the Europeans had. This likely mitigated their power of negotiation during discussions on the border.⁵³

Ottoman Terminology during the Negotiations

From these discussions, it is possible to observe transformations in Ottoman terminology regarding the Greeks, principally the terms *Rum* (Roman, Greek Orthodox) and *Yunan* (Hellen, Greek).⁵⁴ It is widely acknowledged that the Ottoman authorities, prior to the Greek insurrection, predominantly used the terms *Rum taifesi* or *Rum milleti* to refer to the Greek Orthodox community.⁵⁵ The term *Yunan* (Greek), still in use in modern Turkish, was not used until the Greek uprisings. It was revived from the Greek term *Ιων*, which first appeared in ancient Persian texts, and then later in Arabic and Ottoman Turkish, and was used to refer to the Ionians and indirectly to the Hellenes of ancient times. Up to the point of the insurrection, Ottoman chroniclers, historians and intellectuals deliberately used the term *Yunan* only in reference to the ancient Greeks. However, during the uprisings, prominent figures among the revolutionary movement, such as Ypsilantis and Kapodistrias, wrote many texts in which they addressed the Greeks using the term *hellenes*, inciting the movement for the independence of 'Hellas'.⁵⁶ Ottoman translators reflected these terms in Ottoman Turkish with the term *Yunan*. Soon thereafter, especially in the records of the conferences, phrases such as *zuhur-u devlet-i Yunan* (formation of Greek state), *Yunan hükümeti* (Greek government), *Yunan hududu* (Greek boundary) and so on, emerged regarding the provincial Greek government. In fact, the Ottoman chronicler Şanizade⁵⁷ wrote about the first years of the Greek uprisings using the term *Rumistan*⁵⁸ as a translation for 'Hellas'; -İstan is the common Turkish ending to denote a geographical area of a distinct ethnic community or geographical feature, such as Dağistān. However, its scant appearance in other Ottoman sources indicates that the Porte for the Greek Orthodox people of the empire and the subjects of Greece worked well for political discourse in the Ottoman Empire. Its practicality was to continue during the republican period until it fell from favour. Furthermore, referring to the Greek state as *Rumistan* would have been misleading for the Empire's Greek Orthodox subjects, who continued to be called *Rum*. The term *Yunan* proved more equivalent to the term Hellen, and eventually became the term most widely used.

Interestingly, in response to the Greek uprisings, the Porte encouraged, if not demanded, that the terms appropriated to describe related events reflected this intent. In the early years of the uprisings, while European texts described the events as 'rebellion, uprising, or insurgency', Ottoman sources used distinct terms such as *Rum isyanı* (rebellion), *Rum usātı* (rebels), *tuğyan* (revolt) and *fetret* (secession). Following the independence of Greece, and the concomitant changes in the political and socio-economic order, such terminology proved incompatible with European views. After Greek independence in 1830, dispatches by European ambassadors began to include the term 'revolution'. The change in connotation was reflected in the manner in which the Europeans approached negotiations with the Porte and its delegates, seemingly unaware of the fact that their counterparts had not changed their own attitudes to events. They soon understood that their expectations were in vain. During the conferences of Constantinople, the manner of the Ottoman delegates reflected not only their reluctance to settle boundary disputes with the Greeks, but also their continuing grievance with the Great Powers taking the side of the Greeks and advocating their cause, therefore doing their best to sabotage the timely outcome of the discussions.

Documents dated to 1830 use the designation *Yunan taifesi muvakkat hükümeti* (The temporary government of Greeks) to refer to the Greek government, and thereafter *Yunan hükümeti* (Greek government); while in a previous document, dated to 1828, Greek representatives are referred to as *Rum taifesinin vekilleri* (representatives of the Greek Orthodox community). In reference to the Greek people, Ottoman officials used the terms *Rumlar* (Greek Orthodox Community) and *Yunanlılar* (Hellenes, Greeks) interchangeably; while their country as a territorial unit (i.e., Greece) appears as *Yunan memaliki*. The term used for the 'Greek affair' was either *Yunan maddesi* or *Yunan maslahatı*. The Greek Revolution appears in these documents as *Yunan ihtilali*. During the conferences held in Istanbul, the Ottoman authorities, by and large, used the term *Yunan hududu* (Greek boundary) to denote their common boundary.

Demands by the then British delegate, Stratford Canning, that following Greek independence the Greeks deserved a whole new manner of recognition were dismissed by the Ottoman representatives. From the Ottoman perspective, they would not regard the Greeks as being equivalent to other states and they expected the Europeans to adopt the same approach to the issue. On another occasion, Canning insisted on the urgent resolution of the boundary issue in order to halt the Greek uprisings. The Ottoman delegates responded by stating that the use of such words could not be countenanced.[59] In their view, such a stance would give the impression that the Ottoman representatives had downgraded the new dimensions of the Greek Revolution; therefore, they continued to define the events as they had done previously. The same approach was also reflected in subsequent periods. Texts from Ottoman and Turkish historians continued to define the events as uprisings, not as revolution, which was commonly done when referring to the French Revolution.[60]

Demarcation of the Border

George Philip Baker, who was one of the commissioners for the boundary, published his memoirs in 1837. His article on the frontier first appeared in the *Journal of the*

Royal Geographical Society. On thirty-one pages, he detailed where markers denoting the border were placed. He also identified cases where villagers found themselves on the side of the border that they did not wish to be on.[61]

The map of Greece's northern frontier originated from such operations conducted by the commissioners of the three allied powers (i.e. Great Britain, France and Russia), and monitored by the Greek and Turkish sides to ensure accuracy and to prevent errors on the existing maps. The wild, mountainous, and inaccessible character of the border was not the only issue impeding the commissioners from executing their duties in an appropriate manner. As Baker states, the completion of their work was also prevented by political disputes. While the boundary was examined and determined during the autumn of 1832, the surveys and redrawing of maps continued until the spring of 1835. The frontier extended 137 miles in total and was defined by 95 stone markers (pyramids), two of which were destroyed by locals (Turks, according to the text).

Wherever the boundary intersected inhabited districts, the local people sought to profit from the opportunity that the new territorial divisions presented. The case of Gianitzou exemplifies this. The villagers, after learning that the new boundary had divided their homes from their most valuable land, moved their entire village of 60 houses across the border to the Greek side, stone by stone, despite the objections of the Ottoman authorities.

Baker also mentions that the border was to be based mainly on natural features such as rivers and mountain summits. Although it would not separate Christians and Muslims as it had been designated to do, Baker thought it would suffice since the Muslims of the region mainly resided in larger towns, while rural districts were entirely under the care and cultivation of the Christian *reaya*. Muslims and Christians had formerly lived alongside one another in towns like Ypati and Lamia; however, following the revolution, the Turkish-speaking Muslims left their towns and sold off their properties. Thus, according to Baker, with the exception of the occasional visit of the *dervend ağa* and tax collectors, no Ottoman authorities were to be seen in the frontier region.

The commissioners noted that many descriptions provided to them did not reflect the geographical features of the region. One such case was that of Mount Veluchi, described as being the intersection of the Ceta, Othrys and Pindus mountain chains. In reality, they found this place to be a hill and the real intersection of the three mountain chains to be further north, at Zacharaki Vrisi; they therefore decided to mark the boundary there.

Another place that did not comply with the instructions was Graditzas. The English commissioner, Baker, asserted that there was no such place 'as described by Sir William Gell, both in his map and itinerary, as well as in Mr. Dodwell's tour and copied thence into Lapie's map'.[62] Baker also mentions that the villages along this part of the frontier – Gardiki, Gura and Surbis (in southern Magnesia/Thessaly) – had been plundered by bandits and were not habitable. Half of the houses were in ruins and had been abandoned, as they provided no security or protection for their former inhabitants.[63]

In May 1833, upon the arrival of Hüseyin Bey at the Porte, following completion of demarcation of the frontier, the issue of violations re-emerged on the agenda.[64] The Reis Efendi requested an explanation from the ambassadors regarding such claims.

Their response was that they had not been informed of the matter but would pursue it immediately. Meanwhile, they noted their expectation of a *ferman* on the approval of the entire border. Ottoman claims of violations were further exacerbated by the delivery of a map prepared by the border commissioners, who had met with the Reis Efendi at his residence in Istanbul.[65] Hüseyin Efendi was also present and the time had come to investigate the claims. Two major violations had supposedly occurred: the first concerned changes made to Veluchi, submitted to Zacharaki Vrisi; the second concerned the misspelling of Granitzas as Graditza. The commissioners laid out their reasons for the changes and defended their arguments, as mentioned earlier.

The commissioners also stressed that the main purpose of their visit was to submit the map, adding that its acceptance by the Ottoman authorities would be confirmation of its validity. The Ottoman authorities, while wanting to keep the map, did not want to assent to its validity. As the map exists in the Ottoman archives and in another document, it is evident that the Reis Efendi gave orders to students of the Engineering School (*Muhendishane*) to examine the map on account of the violations. It appears the map remained in the hands of the Ottoman authorities. The Ottoman engineers most probably prepared the map that we can see today, dated to 1836. I believe that it is a copy of Lapie's map of 1828, which was the map used during the conferences to determine the boundary. If we compare the two maps, the similarities are evident.

Following the departure of the commissioners, the Reis Efendi communicated with the ambassadors again to further investigate the violations based on the available evidence. In response, the ambassadors claimed that the commissioners had the right to use *ekseriyet-i ārā* (the majority manner) applicable in controversial circumstances. They therefore had not created something contrary to regulations or agreements. The Reis Efendi, however, found these explanations unsatisfactory, since should they proceed to draw the border elsewhere, such as Yenişehr-i Fenar (Larissa), it would then be possible to use the same reasoning of *ekseriyet-i ārā*. Moreover, the violation regarding Veluchi was equal to 20 hours' distance in total and proved more crucial owing to the existence of taxable goods and inhabitants.[66] Thus, it was not an isolated place as the commissioners had claimed it to be; additionally, it meant granting another territory, non-contractually, to Greece.

In the end, responsibility for dislocation of the border was attributed to the representatives of the European powers, as they had not sent an expert as per the proposals of the Porte, likely because of their lack of familiarity with the landscape.[67] On the other hand, it was declared that for the second violation – that regarding the spelling of Granitzas – at the eastern edge of the frontier, they could be more tolerant. With this in mind, the Porte refused to give its assent to the frontier and ordered a re-examination of its controversial parts by the commissioners.

According to a document in the Greek archives, the Porte referred the issue to the Paşa of Thessaly, who communicated with the Greek government on 24 November 1834.[68] Summarizing Ottoman claims on the violations, it affirmed that a new Ottoman commissioner had arrived in the town (probably Trikala) and was awaiting other commissioners, then resident in Zakinthos, to come to the town of Lamia to re-demarcate the controversial part of the border. The Greek authorities responded to this document stating that as far as they and the commissioners were concerned, the frontier had already been settled.[69]

Ottoman claims of violations, without any concrete resolution, ceased for some years with the exception of a few emergent, minor incidents according to the sources. It thus appears that the Porte unwillingly accepted the demarcated border and the maps related to it. Alongside the border issue, when banditry became more of a concern, the anxieties of both the Ottoman and Greek authorities towards illegal movements on the boundary were expressed more strongly in these sources. In the years between 1833 and 1838, the Porte was preoccupied more with the rebellion of the Albanian beys and especially of the Derbend Ağa, Tafil Bouzi.[70]

The border violation issue would again resurface in 1842, following the appointment of the first Ottoman ambassador to Athens. The ambassador, Constantinos Mousouros, informed the Porte on 27 October 1842 of the border violation claims by the Greek government, announced a few months earlier in a semi-official newspaper. According to the source, the Ottoman authorities had seized a small, uninhabited, barren island in the Gulf of Arta, that of Vouvala. Situated a considerable distance from the Greek coast, the Greek government tried to enforce its rights to the island for two years. As the island had fisheries connections, the Greeks looked to use its supplies for their own purposes. The news, which was spread across all Greek newspapers and various French and German outlets, consisted of comments and malicious remarks against the Sublime Porte, which apparently also came to the attention of the representatives of the Great Powers.[71]

From the records, Mousouros suggested inspection of the map of the Greek border that was in the Porte's archives. Attaching the commissioners' documentation related to Vouvala, Mousouros stated that it was within the boundaries of the Greek state. In addition, the island in question was the property of a *reaya* resident at Preveza. Mousouros questioned whether the Greek government had, having made such an evocative protest for an otherwise insignificant, barren and uninhabited island, the right to claim it back when a substantial part of Ottoman territory had been appropriated by the Greek government at the hands of the commissioners. He referred to the sixth session of the commissioners, when they discussed the line between the 22nd and 23rd frontier points. He traced this part of the border, comparing it with a recently published Greek map, and drew with 'scrupulous accuracy' to show that the aforementioned violations indeed had taken place.[72]

Moreover, Mousouros asserted that the River Karitsa, which served as a border between the two countries, had been appropriated by the Greek state. In fact, the area contained a considerable portion of Ottoman territory, including the village of Karitza, two other villages close to it, and a valley consisting of very fertile land that ran along the border. Once more, Mousouros referred to the sixth meeting of the border demarcation commissioners, at which the said river was determined as part of the boundary on account of it being a natural barrier. According to him, the river could not provide such a natural barrier, and therefore no safety for either state. Referring to the bandit attacks a year earlier in Greece, he claimed that bandits could take refuge on the Ottoman side, passing the river easily. In short, Mousouros' suggestion was that if the Greek government laid claims to the small island of Vouvala, then the Porte could also do so based on the aforementioned violations of the Greek government in Karitsa.

Although the Porte refused to give assent to the frontier in the first instance, the request for a re-examination of its controversial parts never materialized. The demarcated border and the maps related to it were inadvertently accepted, and claims regarding the violations, without taking any definitive action, ceased for many years, until 1856. The issue of territorial violations was exacerbated again in the aftermath of the insurrections of 1854–1855, when the Greek and Ottoman states signed a convention to act together to suppress banditry. An overview of the borders on the existing maps was ordered, with the intention of agreeing new border stations; thus, the forgotten issue of violations once more occupied the Porte.

Conclusions

The borders of the Ottoman Empire during the nineteenth century were in constant flux owing to territorial losses as a result of several wars. Ottoman withdrawal towards the centre was concluded at the end of the First World War; however, the first major rupture emerged following the Greek Revolution and was sealed with the establishment of the Greek Kingdom. As one of the most important issues to occupy the political agenda of both states following the Greek Revolution, the demarcation and delimitation of the first Ottoman-Greek border challenged the Ottomans' power of diplomacy in the early nineteenth century, and led to the creation of a greater diplomatic service. Nonetheless, the negotiations regarding the first Ottoman-Greek border conceal the tensions in Ottoman-Greek relations, which would rise to the surface by the end of the century.

Notes

1 For instance, as an impetus to change the political mind-set of the Ottoman ruling elite and the sultan, see Şükrü Ilıcak, 'A Radical Rethinking of Empire: Ottoman State and Society during the Greek War of Independence 1821–1826', PhD dissertation, Harvard University, 2012; Hakan Y. Erdem, 'The Greek Revolt and the End of the Old Ottoman Order', in *The Greek National Revolution: A European Event*, ed. Petros Pizanias. Athens: Kedros, 2009, pp. 281–288.
2 William Martin Leake, *An Historical Outline of the Greek Revolution*. London: J. Murray, 1825; Edward Blaquiere, *The Greek Revolution, Its Origin and Progress: Together with Some Remarks on the Religion, National Character, &c. in Greece*. London: G. & W.B. Whittaker, 1824.
3 Erdem, 'The Greek Revolt and the End of the Old Ottoman Order'.
4 *Başbakanlık Osmanlı Arşivi* (BOA), *Hatt-ı Hümayun* (HAT) collection. Earlier works on the Greek-Ottoman boundaries largely applied European sources; for instance, Thanasis Christos provides an overview of discussions concerning the territorial limits of the Greek state using a collection of various archival documents from the Greek state. Thanasis Christos, *Ta Sinora tou Hellenikou Kratous kai oi Diethneis Sinthikes*

(1830-1847) [The Frontiers of the Greek State and the International Treaties (1830–1847)]. Athens: Dimiourgia, 1999; Georgios K. Th. Lelis, 'Praktika orothetikis grammis (1832) tou Neosistatou Ellinikou Kratous, Proskinio Paraskinio, Fthiotiki Istoria', *Praktika 3ov Sinedriou Fthiotikis Istorias*, 4–6 November 2005, Lamia, 2007. For elaboration of the European and specifically French archival sources: Anne Couderc, 'États, nations et territoires dans les Balkans, Histoire de la première frontière gréco-ottomane, 1827–1881', unpublished PhD dissertation, Université Paris I, 2001. For a general overview of the Greek 'frontier' question, see Malcolm Wagstaff, *Independent Greece: The Search for a Frontier, 1822–35*. Cambridge: Cambridge University Press, 1999.

5   Pál Fodor and Dávid Géza, *Ottomans, Hungarians, and Habsburgs in Central Europe: The Military Confines in the Era of Ottoman Conquest* Leiden: Brill, 2000; Gábor Ágoston, 'A Flexible Empire: Authority and its Limits on the Ottoman Frontiers', in *Ottoman Borderlands: Issues, Personalities, and Political Changes*, ed. K. Karpat and R. Zens. Madison, WI: University of Wisconsin Press, 2003, pp. 15–32. Another piece of work by Ágoston is also essential for an integrated understanding of the Ottoman-Habsburg frontier: Ágoston, 'Where Environmental and Frontier Studies Meet: Rivers, Forests, Marshes and Forts Along the Ottoman-Habsburg Frontier in Hungary', in *The Frontiers of the Ottoman World, Proceedings of the British Academy*, ed. A.C.S. Peacock. Oxford: Oxford University Press, 2009, pp. 57–79.

6   Isa Blumi, Thwarting the Ottoman Empire: Smuggling through the Empire's New Frontiers in Ottoman Yemen and Albania, 1878–1910', in *Ottoman Borderlands: Issues, Personalities and Political Change*, ed. K. Karpat and R. Zens. Madison, WI: University of Wisconsin Press, 2003, pp. 255–274. Also see Blumi, 'Translating Imperial Failures into Smugglers' Gold: The Boundaries of State in Ottoman Albania and Yemen, 1872–1908', in *Boundaries in Depth and in Motion*, ed. I. William Zartman. Athens, GA: University of Georgia Press, 2010, pp. 73–100; Blumi, 'The Frontier as a Measure of Imperial Power: Local Limits to Empire in Yemen, 1872 to 1914', in *The Frontiers of the Ottoman World*, ed. A.G.C. Peacock. Oxford: Oxford University Press, 2009, pp. 289–304; Frederick Anscombe, 'Continuities in Centre–Periphery Relations 1789–1915', in *The Frontiers of the Ottoman World*, ed. A.C.S. Peacock. Oxford: Oxford University Press, 2009, pp. 235–251; Maurus Reinkowski, 'Double Struggle, No Income: Ottoman Borderlands in Northern Albania', in *Ottoman Borderlands: Issues, Personalities, and Political Changes*, ed. K. Karpat and R. Zens. Madison, WI: University of Wisconsin Press, 2003, pp. 239–253.

7   George Gavrilis, *The Dynamics of Interstate Boundaries*. Cambridge: Cambridge University Press, 2008, p. 67; Thanos Veremis, 'From the National State to the Stateless Nation, 1821–1910', in *Modern Greece: Nationalism and Nationality*, ed. Matin Blinkhorn and Thanos Veremis. Athens: Sage-Eliamep, 1990, pp. 9–22; Douglas Dakin, *The Unification of Greece, 1770–1923*. New York: St. Martin's Press, 1972.

8   Roderic H. Davison, 'The Ottoman–Greek Frontier Question, 1876–1882, from Ottoman Records', In *Nineteenth Century Ottoman Diplomacy and Reforms*. Istanbul: Isis Press, 1983, pp. 239–256; Üçyol Rıfat, 'The Border Dispute between the Ottoman Empire and Greece: Rearranging the Border According to the Berlin Treaty of 1878 and Giving Land to Greece (1878–1881)', *Revue Internationale d'Histoire Militaire*, 67 (1988), pp. 119–139; Ali Fuat Türkgeldi, *Mesail-i Muhimme-i Siyasiyye*, vol. 2. Ankara: Türk Tarih Kurumu. 1957; Georgia Ioannidou-Bitsiadou, 'The Bavarian Loans and Chancellor Bismarck's Intervention in the Greek-Turkish Dispute over Greece's Borders (1878–1881)', *Balkan Studies*, 34, no. 1 (1993), pp. 73–83; F.A.K. Yasamee,

Ottoman Diplomacy: Abdulhamid and the Great Powers, 1878–1888. Istanbul: Isis Press, 1996; M. Murat Hatipoğlu, *Yunanistan'daki Gelişmelerin Işığında Türk-Yunan ilişkilerin 101. Yılı.* Ankara: Türk Kültürünü Araştırma Enstitüsü, 1998.

9 John Koliopoulos. *Brigands with a Cause: Brigandage and Irredentism in Modern Greece 1821–1912.* Oxford: Clarendon Press, 1987; Koliopoulos, 'Brigandage and Insurgency in the Greek Domains of the Ottoman Empire, 1853–1908', in *Ottoman Greeks in the Age of Nationalism*, ed. Dimitri Gondicas and Charles Issawi. Pennington, NJ: Darwin Press, 1999, pp. 143–160.

10 Couderc, 'États, nations et territoires dans les Balkans'.

11 Gavrilis, *The Dynamics of Interstate Boundaries.*

12 Ali Fuat Örenç, *Balkanlarda ilk Dram: Unuttuğumuz Mora Türkleri ve Eyaletten Bağımsızlığa Yunanistan* [The First Drama in the Balkans: The Forgotten Turks of Morea and Greece from a Province to its Independence]. Istanbul: BYK, 2009.

13 Henry Phillpotts, 'The Greek Question', *The Quarterly Review*, 43 (1830), pp. 495–553; Great Britain Foreign Office 1826–1828, *Papers Relative to the Greek Question.* London, 1828; Edouard Driault and Michel L'heriter, *Histoire Diplomatique de la Grece de 1821 a nous Jours.* Paris: Les Presses Universitaire de France, 1925; Gabriel Noradounghian Effendi, *Recueil d'actes internationaux de l'Empire Ottoman 1897–1903*, 2 vols. (1789–1856). Paris: F. Pichon, 1903.

14 Phillpotts, 'The Greek Question', p. 498.

15 Mikulas Fabry, 'The International Society and the Establishment of New States: The Practice of State Recognition in the Era of National Self-Determination', unpublished PhD dissertation, University of British Columbia, 2005, p. 22.

16 See, for instance, Dariusz Kalodziejczyk, *Ottoman-Polish Diplomatic Relations (15th–18th Century).* Leiden: Brill, 1999.

17 Maria Pia Pedani, 'The Border from the Ottoman Point of View', in *Tolerance and Intolerance on the Triplex Confinium: Approaching the 'Other' on the Borderlands, Eastern Adriatic and Beyond 1500–1800*, ed Egidio Ivetic and Drago Roksandic. Padova: CLEUP, 2007, pp. 195–214.

18 Rıfa'at Ali Abou-E-Haj, 'The Formal Closure of the Ottoman Frontiers in Europe, 1699–1703', *Journal of the American Oriental Society*, 89, no. 3 (1969), pp. 467–475.

19 Suraiya Faroqhi, *The Ottoman Empire and the World Around It.* New York: I.B. Tauris, 2006, p. 28.

20 The role and usage of terms such as 'guarantee' and the 'protection of the great powers' has received no shortage of critical examination by scholars, and the usefulness of such discussion is incorporated into the present work. Katerina Gardika. *Prostasia kai Eggiiseis: stadia kai mithoi tis ellinikis ethnikis oloklirosis (1821–1920)* [Protection and Guarantee: Stages and Myths of Greek National Completion, 1821–1920]. Thessaloniki: Banias, 1999; James Headlam-Morley, *Studies in Diplomatic History.* London: Taylor & Francis, 1930, p. 121.

21 There are limited sources on Pertev Paşa: Carter V. Findlay, *Bureaucratic Reform in the Ottoman Empire: The Sublime Porte, 1789–1922.* Princeton, NJ: Princeton University Press, 2012; Özhan Kapıcı, 'Tanzimat Yolunda bir Osmanlı Devlet Adamı: Mehmed Said Pertev Paşa', unpublished master's thesis, Hacettepe University, 2006.

22 Great Britain Foreign Office, *1828 Protocol of Conference held at Poros, between the Representatives of Great Britain, France and Russia on 12th of December 1828: Presented to both Houses of Parliament, June 1830.* London: J. Harrison, 1839; Thomas Erskine Holland (ed.), *The European Concert in the Eastern Question: A Collection of Treaties and Other Public Acts.* Oxford: Clarendon Press, 1885, pp. 28–30.

23 Great Britain Foreign Office, *1828 Protocol of Conference held at Poros*, p. 25.
24 Ibid., p. 194.
25 The translation of the note declared by Reis Efendi, on 25 September 1829; ibid., p. 186.
26 C.J. Crawley, *The Question of Greek Independence: A Study of British Policy in the Near East*. Cambridge: Cambridge University Press, 1930, p. 205.
27 BOA. HAT 935-40460; HAT 939-40556; HAT 1218-47688; HAT 896-39466D; HAT 1218-47685. It is stated in the Conference of London proceedings (16 November, 1831) that 'negotiations relative to the improvement of the frontiers of Greece shall be opened immediately upon the arrival of Sir Stratford Canning at Constantinople'. Again, at the conference dated 14 February 1832, it was asserted that 'negotiations are about to be opened at Constantinople'; and finally, at the conference of 26 April 1832, it is mentioned that the negotiations had recently opened with the Porte for the execution of the Protocol of 26 September 1831. See *British and Foreign State Papers, 1831–1832*, Hertslet, p. 1834.
28 For instance: '[…] *bu yunan maddesine gelince bunlarin üçü ittifakat maslahatına giriyorlar*' [In this Greek matter, these three [great powers] entering alliance] BOA. HAT. 890-39310, '[…] *bu elçilere şu madde-i mekruha için şimdiye dek söylemedik söz kalmadı, yine bildiklerinden ayrılmazlar, ne diyeyim Allah belalarını versin*' [(…) There is nothing left to say to these ambassadors on this matter; again, they do not change their mind about what to say – may God give them troubles] HAT 47689. '*Reis bu babda güzel mukabele etmiş ne çare insafane dinleyüp kabul etmiyorlar ki bir ortasını bulub da bitirilsün bu madde*' [Reis replied to them beautifully on this subject, alas, they do not listen and accept it mercifully, so a middle way can be found to complete it] HAT 922-40082. '*hiç bir devlet yoktur ki kendü memleketinden ahra isteyerek bir mahal terk eyleye ama bu kaide bu maddede düvel-i selasenin birleşüp ittifakata ilhaç ve iramları vakı' olmakta olduğundan bu maddenin bir ucu ortası bulunup* [No state will leave a territory willingly; it is a fact that three states united with alliance for this matter – a middle way should be found] HAT 935-40460.
29 Sir Stratford Canning replaced British ambassador Sir Robert Gordon in August 1831 because of illness. He reached the Ottoman capital at the end of January 1832, and remained there until the end of his mission in August 1832. D. Urquhart was also a member of Stratford's staff during this time. France was represented by M. de Varenne and Russia by M. de Bouténief at these conferences. Crawley, *The Question of Greek Independence*, p. 249.
30 Driault and L'heriter, *Histoire Diplomatique de la Grece de 1821 a nous Jours*, p. 89.
31 The Ottoman delegates were Reis Necip Efendi, Behcet Efendi and translator Istefenaki Vogorides.
32 HAT 891-39350-A.
33 HAT 891-39350-A, p. 1.
34 Following signing of the protocol of 3 February 1830, the Porte assigned Nayab Efendi as a border commissioner and sent him to the Greek lands to meet with the other commissioners; however, after waiting some months without any answer regarding the beginning date of their survey, he returned to Constantinople. See Ahmet Lütfi Efendi, *Lütfi Tarihi*, vols. 2–3. Istanbul: Yapıkredi Yayınları, 1999, p. 327.
35 HAT 891-39350A.
36 '*İngiltere elçisi vâkı'a taraf-ı Devlet-i 'Aliyyeden me'mûr bulunmadı, lâkin Rumların dahi me'mûru yoğidi demekle beri taraftan elçi beyin bu kelâmı bayağı mûcib-i teessür olunur bir sözdür Devlet-i Aliyye ile onları muvâzene mi ediyor deyu redd-i cevab olundukda*

Elçi-i mersûm çünki taraf-ı saltanat-ı seniyyeden Rumların istiklâli tasdîk olunmağla şimdi onlara başka nazarla bakılmak îcâb eder, yoksa Devlet-i Aliyye ile muvâzene ma'nasına değildir yollu i'tizâr ederek yine eski sözlerini tekrâr ile bu meclisde cevâb-ı kat'î i'tasına ısrâr eylediklerine' [Upon the British ambassador saying that there was not an Ottoman officer [at the conference], nor did the Greeks have one; our side rejected this reply saying that such an expression saddened us as it meant that you were equalising the Sublime Porte with them [Greeks]; upon this answer the aforementioned [British] ambassador repeating his previous sayings objected to it, saying that the approval of the independence of the Greeks required a different treatment to be taken towards them and it did not mean equalizing [the Greeks] with the Sublime Porte]. HAT 891-39350A.

37 For the proceedings of the second meeting held at Constantinople, see BOA HAT 891-39350 B. '... *bu gösterilen mahal dağsız olduğundan hudud olamaz diyerek lakırdıya savurmalarıyla beru tarafdan haritadan anlaşılan bazı dağlar idare ile işte bunlar dedikleriniz gibi hudud-u tabii olunabiliyor*' [... as they commented on the indicated place saying that it cannot be a boundary because it does not have mountains, our side replied, 'apparently these can be considered a 'natural boundary' as you say showing some mountainous places on the map...']. The second conference was delayed because of Ramadan celebrations; there was also a change in the office of reis. Akif Efendi was appointed the new reis, and directed the negotiations with the European representatives. Driault and L'heriter, *Histoire Diplomatique de la Grece de 1821 a nous Jours*, p. 90.

38 '*Beri tarafdan elçi beyler dirâyetli âdemler olmağla bilirler, bunca devletleri hudûd mu te'mîn eder yoksa bâ'is-i te'mîn olan ahd ü şart mıdır denildikde cümle indinde eşlem olan kudret-i ilâhiyye ile yapılmış şey midir yoksa mahlûkun yapdığı mıdır diyerek güya yapdıkları hudûd-ı cedîdenin muhassenât-ı tabîîsini îma ve ahd ü şart mahlûkun işidir, lâkin buraları hudûd içün halk olunmuş gibiyle vâdîsinde sözler ile müddeâlarını îzâh ü inba' etmeleriyle beri tarafdan gûya oralar Yunan hududu içün yaradılmış suretine konulup öylece iddia olunması teslîm olunur mevâddan olmayıp ol mahalleri Cenâb-ı hak Devlet-i Aliyye-i Osmaniyye'nin silk-i mülküne idhâl buyurmuş olmağla şimdi kavâid-i düvelliyye muktezasınca bize göre hıfzı içün elzem olan uhûd u şurûtdur ve bir devlet devlet-i diğerle muhâbere edecek olsa hudûdda bulunan dağlar mı hâil olur yoksa ahd ü şart muktezâsı mı mâni'dir denildikte*' [From our side, it is said that 'as being skilful men ambassadors know that which secures all these states – is it border or agreement conditions?' Upon this, they asked: 'is something made by God or by human better?' In spite of this, 'they wanted to imply the 'natural character' of the border that they were proposing, because the agreements/conditions are man-made. Continuing with sentences like these places are almost created to be borders', they began to explain and insist on their arguments. From our side, it is not acceptable to consider that those places are created to be the Greek borders; those places were included in the domination of the Sublime Porte by God's will, and for us now as the regulations of the state's system requires, it is important to comply with agreements/conditions. And, it is asked whether agreements or the mountains are obstacles when one state enters into war with other state.] BOA HAT 891-39350 B.

39 '*Mersûmlar teslîm ü itirafdan gayri lakırdı bulamayarak fakat ahd ü şart tâbî olan şeyi tevâfuk eylediği halde daha güzel olur dediklerinde beri tarafdan esâs bu vechile karargîr olunsun da tâbî sûreti dahi mahalinde bi'l-iltizâm tevsiyesine bakılır denildikde İngiltere elçisi bu çekdiğiniz hatt-ı hudûd ile def'-i müşkilât mümkin olamayarak bizim çekdiğimiz hatt-ı hudûddan gayri çâresi yokdur buraları ben kendim gördüm ve*

harîtadan müstefâd olduğu üzere şu enhârın cerayânı ve cibâlin irtifâı hudûd-ı tabiiyye olduğunu isbât eder demesiyle' [The ambassadors could not find other words than accepting their confession; upon which they said that agreements/conditions are better when they synchronize with the natural ones. From our side it is said 'let us agree on this principle, and the natural one can be checked on the side'. The British ambassador said that 'it is not possible to remove the obstacles with this border line that you proposed. There is no other solution than our proposed border. I personally visited these places, and from the map it is evident that this mountain's height is the 'natural border".] BOA HAT 891-39350 B.

40 'Beri tarafdan hudûd-u tâbiiyye bâ'is-i emniyyet olmadığı müdelleden söylenmiş olduğundan yalnız mes'ele arâzi üzerinde kalıyor ve yine lakırdıyı tekrâr edelim ki farzâ Yunanîler beri tarafa tecâvüz edecek olsalar dağlar yol vermez diyerek mi terk ederler yoksa düvel-i selâsenin kararına muhâlif olur diye mi terk ederler yollu lede'l-istifsâr evvelce verdikleri müzekkerede hudûd-ı tabiiyyenin sebeb ü keyfiyyeti mestûr olduğunu îrâd eylediklerini cerhan' [Asking from our side, 'it has already been said and proven that the natural frontier cannot provide the security; the problem remains on the ground. And let us repeat our words for the sake of argument – if the Greeks trespass in our territory, will they give up their intention because the mountains do not allow them the way or will it be against the agreements of the great powers?' And they said that because in their [ambassador's] previously submitted memorandum, the reason of the 'natural border' was hidden.] BOA HAT 891-39350 B.

41 'Bunda tabîî hudûd olabilecek yerler var mı demeleriyle beri tarafdan derbend ve nehirler gibi yerler vardır bi'l-farz olmasa bile şu tabîî hudud lakırdısını elçi beylerin terk etmesini iltimâs ederiz, her devletin hudûdu tabîî hudûd denilecek yerler olmayarak ba'zısında olsa bile ekserisi açık mahallerdir ve asıl hudûd-u şurût ve uhûddur denildikte ...' [after their asking whether there was any place that can be a 'natural border', our side answered 'there are places like passages and rivers' and even if there is not [a place to be natural border], we may request messieurs ambassadors to quit this argument of 'natural border', as each state's borders are not 'natural borders'; some of them have 'natural borders' whereas the majority of the borders [of states] are open fields, and the real borders are terms and conditions [of an agreement].] BOA HAT 891-39350 B.

42 In Ottoman Turkish both Zeytun (Zeitoun) or Izdin appellations were used for Lamia town.

43 'Elçi-i mersûm cebinden bir müzekkere çıkarıp ana bakarak dört beş sene oluyor ki İzdin'in ehl-i İslâm ahâlisi dağılmış ve evâilde ehl-i İslâm ve reâyâsı şu kadar bu kadar iken şimdi mikdâr-ı cüz'iye tenzil etmişdir diyecek' [The aforementioned ambassador pulled some notes from one of his pockets and looking at them said that the Muslim population of İzdin [Zeytun] was dispersed and the Muslim and Christian population of the region were that much previously and he said that the Muslim population was diminished now.] BOA HAT 891-39350.

44 'Bizim mesâlihimiz yalnız usûl-i düveliyye ile görülemeyerek dînimiz iktizâsınca şer'-i şerîf ahkâmına tatbik olunmak dahi lâzım gelir. Bu cihetle İzdin, Badracık gibi mevtın-ı ehl-i İslâm olan mahallerin terki şer'an caiz olmayacağından peşin bunu ifâde edelim denilmeğin' [Our affairs cannot be performed only based on state systems, according to our religious requirements; it is also necessary to comply with the Islamic law. Hence, we should express that according to Islamic law, the abandonment of territories like İzdin, Padracık, that have a settled Muslim population is unacceptable.] BOA HAT 891-39350.

45 'İngiltere elçisi haritada göstererek fakat İzdin'in taraf-ı Devlet-i Aliyye'ye terkiyle Badracık Yunaniler tarafında kalmak üzere hudûd kat'ını söylemekle beri tarafdan haritada frengi olduğundan biz anlayamıyoruz elçi bey yine müzâkere olunmak üzere bir hat işaret eylese denildikde merûm bi'l-muvâfaka kurşun kalemle hatt-ı hududu çekerken elçi beyin elini daha ötelere çekelim yollu vâki' olan latifeye mersûm dahi refiklerim elimi berilere çekiyorlar diyerek bi'l-mukabele Badracık kazâsı öte tarafda ve İzdin kasabası beride kalarak ikisinin beyninde Narda körfezine doğru bir hatt-ı müstakim çekmiş olduğundan' [While showing it on the map, the British ambassador was explaining the border demarcation line leaving İzdin to the Sublime Porte and Padracık to the Greeks, from our side it was said that 'because the map is in a European language, we cannot understand it. May we request that monsieur ambassador mark a line to be discussed?' Upon agreeing to that, when the ambassador drew a border line with a pencil, from our side it was said jokingly 'shall we pull the hand of monsieur ambassador a bit further up?' Following that [the ambassador] while saying that 'my friends are pulling my hand to this side', at the same time had drawn a straight line towards the Gulf of Narda leaving Badracık district on the side [of the Greeks] and the district of İzdin on the other side of the line.] BOA HAT 891-39350.

46 'Narda körfezinin iki canibinin dahi berü tarafda bırakılması mümkün olabildiği halde pek çok faidemiz olacağından zikr olunduğu üzre İzdin ile Padracık'ın öte tarafda olan arazisi gider ise gitsün. Hala şu nehir-i mezkurun berü tarafıyla zikr olunan körfezin taraf-ı devlet-i aliyyeye bırakılması mümkün olabildiği halde icrasına himmet buyrulması lazım geleceği beyanıyla' [Upon mentioning that we would have many benefits if it could be possible to have both sides of the Gulf of Narda to us, let territories of İzdin and Padracık on the other side remain there; it will be necessary to make it possible to have the other side of that river still, and the aforementioned Gulf remained on the side of Sublime Porte.] BOA. HAT 1219-47727 C (17 August 1832).

47 25 September 1832, Constantinople, Memorial of the Sublime Porte addressed to the conference assembled in London on the subject of the Greek affair. (Protocol of Conference of 13 November 1832).

48 BOA. HAT 878-38886. 20 August 1832.

49 Evangelos Livieratos explains this phenomenon very well. See Evangelos Livieratos, *Chartografikes peripeteies tis Ellados 1821–1919*. Athens: ELIA, 2009, pp. 52–63.

50 Livieratos, *Chartografikes peripeteies tis Ellados 1821–1919*, p. 53.

51 Ibid., p. 52.

52 Ibid., p. 58.

53 Ottoman cartography and its comparison with that of the Europeans requires further consideration which cannot be handled here. For more specialized evaluations: Giorgos Tolias, *Challenged Frontiers: Cartographies of Greece and the Levant During the Ottoman Era*. Istanbul: Isis Press, 2010; Athanassios E. Karathanassis, 'Some Observations on the European Cartographers with regard to 15th–18th Century Macedonia', *Balkan Studies*, 32, no. 1 (1991), pp. 5–17.

54 In the 1856 edition of Redhouse Ottoman & English dictionary, the entries related to these terms are as follows: *Yunan*: a Greek (of the little kingdom); an ancient Greek; *Yunani*: the ancient Greek language.

55 For various theories on usage of the term millet in the Ottoman text, see Benjamin Braude, 'Foundation Myths of the *Millet* System', in Benjamin Braude, 'Foundation Myths of the *Millet* System', in *Christians and Jews in the Ottoman Empire: The Functioning of a Plural Society*, ed. Benjamin Braude and Bernard Lewis. London:

Holmes & Meier Publishers, 1982, p. 70; Paraskevas Konortas, 'From Ta'ife to *Millet*: Ottoman Terms for the Ottoman Greek Orthodox Community', in *Ottoman Greeks in the Age of Nationalism*, ed. D. Gondicas and C. Issawi. Princeton, NJ: Darwin Press, 1999, p. 171; Dimitris Stamatopoulos, 'From Millets to Minorities in the 19th-Century Ottoman Empire: An Ambiguous Modernization', in *Citizenship in Historical Perspective*, ed. S.G. Ellis, G. Hálfadanarson and A.K. Isaacs. Pisa: Edizioni Plus – Pisa University Press, 2006, pp. 253–273. See also Roderic H. Davison, *Reform in the Ottoman Empire, 1856–1876*. Princeton, NJ: Princeton University Press, 1963, p. 56.

56 Hakan Y. Erdem, 'Do Not Think of the Greeks as Agricultural Labourers: Ottoman Responses to the Greek War of Independence', in *Citizenship and the Nation-state in Greece and Turkey*, ed. Faruk Birtek and Thalia Dragonas. London: Routledge, 2005, pp. 67–84.

57 Şani-zade Mehmed Atâullah Efendi (1771–1826), who was a member of a prosperous Ottoman intellectual family, occupied the official Ottoman historian position during the years between 1819 and 1825, and recorded the events of 1806–1822. Şanizade Mehmet Atanullah, *Tarih-i Şanizâde, cild-i salis*. Istanbul: Ceride-i Havadis Matbaası, 1867.

58 The translation of this term would be 'country of Romans'.

59 '*mersûmlar taraf-ı Devlet-i Aliyye'den bu def'aki hudûda muvâfakat olmadıkça Yunan'ın ihtilâli kesilmeyerek âsâyiş ü emniyyet hâsıl olamayacağından düvel-i selâse bu hudûda karar verdiler diyicek beri tarafdan Yunan ihtilâli bizim bileceğimiz şey değildir, kaldı ki devletler saltanat-ı seniyyeye böyle nâ-hâk teklifi edeceklerine mukaddemki karara bi'l-farz Yunan denilenler râzı olmasalar dahi edebsizlik etmeyin biz böyle karar verdik demiş olsalar iş biterdi*' [After ambassadors saying that if they did not determine the borders [with Greece] the Greek Revolution would not calm down, and security would not be established, that is why three powers agreed on this [proposal]; from our side 'Greek Revolution' is not something we would say; besides, [three] states in spite of offering such an unjust proposal to the Sublime Porte, if they previously had told those so-called Greeks – even if they did not comply with it – 'do not misbehave, we decided as such' –this affair would have been closed.] BOA. HAT 891-39350 A.

60 Erdem, 'Do Not Think of the Greeks as Agricultural Labourers'.

61 George Philip Baker, *Memoir of the Northern Frontier of Greece*. London: J. Backhouse, 1837. The border demarcation commission consisted of Russian general A. de Scalon, French Colonel J. Barthélemy, who was the head of the French topographic group, Expédition, which was formed in March 1829, and the British Colonel George Baker. See Livieratos, *Chartografikes peripeteies tis Ellados 1821–1919*, p. 93.

62 Baker, *Memoir of the Northern Frontier of Greece*, pp. 28–29. Here we understood that the commissioners' main description of the regions was based on two main sources: William Gell's maps and Mr. Dodwell's tour, which was also used by Lapie to produce his map of Greece in 1828. William Gell, 1777–1836, was an English classical archaeologist and illustrator. From 1804 to 1806 he travelled in Ottoman Greece, the neighbouring islands and coastal Asia Minor. His work on Greece was used as a travel guide for other European travellers in the region. See William Gell, *The Itinerary of Greece, with a Commentary on Pausanias and Strabo, and an Account of the Monuments of Antiquity at Present Existing in that Country, Compiled in the Years 1801, 2, 5, 6 etc.* London: T. Payne, 1810 [2nd ed. containing a hundred routes in Attica, Boeotia, Phocis, 1827]. Edward Dodwell (1767–1832) toured Ottoman Greece from 1801 to 1806. See Edward Dodwell, *A Classical and Topographical Tour through Greece, During the Years 1801, 1805, and 1806*, vol. I. London: Rodwell & Martin, 1819. French

cartographer and engraver Pierre M. Lapie's (1779–1850) map of Greece was largely used during the negotiations. Pierre M. Lapie, *Atlas Classique et Universel de Geographie Ancienne et Moderne dressé pour l'Instruction de la Jeunesse et Servant à l'Intelligence tant de l'Histoire que de Voyages dans les différentes Parties de Monde*, 4th edn. Paris: Chez Anselin, Successeur de Magimel, 1828.

63 Baker, *Memoir of the Northern Frontier of Greece*, p. 29.
64 BOA, HAT 1220-47756 A (19 May 1833).
65 BOA, HAT 932-40381 (28 April 1835).
66 Ibid.
67 'Divan-ı hümayun tercümanı esbak İshak Efendi ve Koniçeli Hüseyin Bey [iktisabat?] olunarak sefera-yı selaseye bu söylediklereniz hududu biz bilmiyoruz lakin bilen adamlarımız vardır meclis celb edelim de onların yanında söyleşelim deyu teklif olundukda sefara-yı selase bir vecihle kabul etmeyüp istedikleri gibi yazdılar çizdiler suh-u mukamet var ise kendilerinindir bize ne diyebilürler.' BOA HAT 932-40381 (28 April 1835).
68 AYE. 1834, 1:1 3:2 4:1 No: 3662, 9 December 1834. Lelis, 'Praktika orothetikis grammis (1832) tou Neosistatou Ellinikou Kratous, Proskinio Paraskinio, Fthiotiki Istoria', pp. 336–337.
69 Ibid., p. 337.
70 In 1833, Tafil Buzi (Tafilboz in Ottoman sources), together with other influential Albanian military chiefs, gathered some thousands of men around them, and rebelled against the Ottoman government's new reforms on taxation, conscription and provincial administration. Threatened with the attacks of the rebel Albanian chiefs, the governor of Trikala, Mustafa Nuri Paşa, offered him the post of *Derbend Superintendent* of the Agrafa and Dömeke districts in order to prevent further attacks on the region. Tafil Buzi might have remained as *derbend* superintendent of these regions for a short period of time. HAT 419-21694 1833; HAT 420-21703-C 1833; HAT 421-21715 1833.
71 Gennadius Library Archives, The Musurus Papers, Folder 3, no. 53, Musurus to Sarim Efendi, 27 October/8 November 1842.
72 Ibid.

Bibliography

Primary sources

Başbakanlık Osmanlı Arşivi (BOA), Hatt-ı Hümayun Collection.
Diplomatikou kai Istorikou Archiou Ipourgiou Eksoterikou tis Elladas (AYE).
Gennadius Library Archives (GLA), Mousouros Papers.

Secondary sources

Abou-E-Haj, Rıfa'at Ali, 'The Formal Closure of the Ottoman Frontiers in Europe, 1699–1703', *Journal of the American Oriental Society*, 89, no. 3 (1969), pp. 467–475.
Ágoston, Gábor, 'A Flexible Empire: Authority and its Limits on the Ottoman Frontiers', in *Ottoman Borderlands: Issues, Personalities, and Political Changes*, ed. K. Karpat and R. Zens. Madison, WI: University of Wisconsin Press, 2003, pp. 15–32.

Ágoston, Gábor, 'Where Environmental and Frontier Studies Meet: Rivers, Forests, Marshes and Forts Along the Ottoman-Habsburg Frontier in Hungary', in *The Frontiers of the Ottoman World, Proceedings of the British Academy*, ed. A.C.S. Peacock. Oxford: Oxford University Press, 2009, pp. 57–79.

Ahmet Lütfi Efendi, *Lütfi Tarihi*, vols. 2–3. Istanbul: Yapıkredi Yayınları, 1999.

Anscombe, Frederick, 'Continuities in Centre–Periphery Relations 1789–1915', in *The Frontiers of the Ottoman World*, ed. A.C.S. Peacock. Oxford: Oxford University Press, 2009, pp. 235–251.

Baker, George Philip, *Memoir of the Northern Frontier of Greece*. London: J. Backhouse, 1837.

Blaquiere, Edward, *The Greek Revolution, Its Origin and Progress: Together with Some Remarks on the Religion, National Character, &c. in Greece*. London: G. & W.B. Whittaker, 1824.

Blumi, Isa, 'Thwarting the Ottoman Empire: Smuggling through the Empire's New Frontiers in Ottoman Yemen and Albania, 1878–1910', in *Ottoman Borderlands: Issues, Personalities and Political Change*, ed. K. Karpat and R. Zens. Madison, WI: University of Wisconsin Press, 2003, pp. 255–274.

Blumi, Isa, 'The Frontier as a Measure of Imperial Power: Local Limits to Empire in Yemen, 1872 to 1914', in *The Frontiers of the Ottoman World*, ed. A.G.C. Peacock. Oxford: Oxford University Press, 2009, pp. 289–304.

Blumi, Isa, 'Translating Imperial Failures into Smugglers' Gold: The Boundaries of State in Ottoman Albania and Yemen, 1872–1908', in *Boundaries in Depth and in Motion*, ed. I. William Zartman. Athens, GA: University of Georgia Press, 2010, pp. 73–100.

Braude, Benjamin, 'Foundation Myths of the *Millet* System', in *Christians and Jews in the Ottoman Empire: The Functioning of a Plural Society*, ed. Benjamin Braude and Bernard Lewis. London: Holmes & Meier Publishers, 1982, pp. 69–88.

Christos, Thanasis, *Ta Sinora tou Hellenikou Kratous kai oi Diethneis Sinthikes (1830–1847)* [The Frontiers of the Greek State and the International Treaties (1830–1847)]. Athens: Dimiourgia, 1999.

Couderc, Anne, 'États, nations et territoires dans les Balkans, Histoire de la première frontière gréco-ottomane, 1827–1881', unpublished PhD dissertation, Université Paris I, 2001.

Crawley, C.J., *The Question of Greek Independence: A Study of British Policy in the Near East*. Cambridge: Cambridge University Press, 1930.

Dakin, Douglas, *The Unification of Greece, 1770–1923*. New York: St. Martin's Press, 1972.

Davison, Roderic H., *Reform in the Ottoman Empire, 1856–1876*. Princeton, NJ: Princeton University Press, 1963.

Davison, Roderic H., 'The Ottoman–Greek Frontier Question, 1876–1882, from Ottoman Records', In *Nineteenth Century Ottoman Diplomacy and Reforms*. Istanbul: Isis Press, 1983, pp. 239–256.

Dodwell, Edward, *A Classical and Topographical Tour through Greece, During the Years 1801, 1805, and 1806*, vol. I. London: Rodwell & Martin, 1819.

Driault, Edouard and Michel L'heriter, *Histoire Diplomatique de la Grece de 1821 a nous Jours*. Paris: Les Presses Universitaire de France, 1925.

Erdem, Hakan Y., 'Do Not Think of the Greeks as Agricultural Labourers: Ottoman Responses to the Greek War of Independence', in *Citizenship and the Nation-state in Greece and Turkey*, ed. Faruk Birtek and Thalia Dragonas. London: Routledge, 2005, pp. 67–84.

Erdem, Hakan Y., 'The Greek Revolt and the End of the Old Ottoman Order', in *The Greek National Revolution: A European Event*, ed. Petros Pizanias. Athens: Kedros, 2009, pp. 281-288.

Fabry, Mikulas, 'The International Society and the Establishment of New States: The Practice of State Recognition in the Era of National Self-Determination', unpublished PhD dissertation, University of British Columbia, 2005.

Faroqhi, Suraiya, *The Ottoman Empire and the World Around It*. New York: I.B. Tauris, 2006.

Findlay, Carter V., *Bureaucratic Reform in the Ottoman Empire: The Sublime Porte, 1789-1922*. Princeton, NJ: Princeton University Press, 2012.

Fodor, Pál and Dávid Géza, *Ottomans, Hungarians, and Habsburgs in Central Europe: The Military Confines in the Era of Ottoman Conquest* Leiden: Brill, 2000.

Gardika, Katerina, *Prostasia kai Eggiiseis: stadia kai mithoi tis ellinikis ethnikis oloklirosis (1821-1920)* [Protection and Guarantee: Stages and Myths of Greek National Completion, 1821-1920]. Thessaloniki: Banias, 1999.

Gavrilis, George, *The Dynamics of Interstate Boundaries*. Cambridge: Cambridge University Press, 2008.

Gell, William, *The Itinerary of Greece, with a Commentary on Pausanias and Strabo, and an Account of the Monuments of Antiquity at Present Existing in that Country, Compiled in the Years 1801, 2, 5, 6 etc*. London: T. Payne, 1810.

Great Britain Foreign Office 1826-1828, *Papers Relative to the Greek Question*. London, 1828.

Great Britain Foreign Office, *1828 Protocol of Conference held at Poros, between the Representatives of Great Britain, France and Russia on 12th of December 1828: Presented to both Houses of Parliament, June 1830*. London: J. Harrison, 1839.

Hatipoğlu, M. Murat, *Yunanistan'daki Gelişmelerin Işığında Türk-Yunan ilişkilerin 101. Yılı*. Ankara: Türk Kültürünü Araştırma Enstitüsü, 1998.

Headlam-Morley, James, *Studies in Diplomatic History*. London: Taylor & Francis, 1930.

Holland, Thomas Erskine (ed.), *The European Concert in the Eastern Question: A Collection of Treaties and Other Public Acts*. Oxford: Clarendon Press, 1885.

Howe, Samuel G., *An Historical Sketch of the Greek Revolution* New York: White, Gallaher & White, 1828.

Ilıcak, Şükrü, 'A Radical Rethinking of Empire: Ottoman State and Society during the Greek War of Independence 1821-1826', PhD dissertation, Harvard University, 2012.

Ioannidou-Bitsiadou, Georgia, 'The Bavarian Loans and Chancellor Bismarck's Intervention in the Greek-Turkish Dispute over Greece's Borders (1878-1881)', *Balkan Studies*, 34, no. 1 (1993), pp. 73-83.

Kalodziejczyk, Dariusz, *Ottoman-Polish Diplomatic Relations (15th-18th Century)*. Leiden: Brill, 1999.

Kapıcı, Özhan, 'Tanzimat Yolunda bir Osmanlı Devlet Adamı: Mehmed Said Pertev Paşa', unpublished master's thesis, Hacettepe University, 2006.

Karathanassis, Athanassios E., 'Some Observations on the European Cartographers with regard to 15th-18th Century Macedonia', *Balkan Studies*, 32, no. 1 (1991), pp. 5-17.

Koliopoulos, John, *Brigands with a Cause: Brigandage and Irredentism in Modern Greece 1821-1912*. Oxford: Clarendon Press, 1987.

Koliopoulos, John, 'Brigandage and Insurgency in the Greek Domains of the Ottoman Empire, 1853-1908', in *Ottoman Greeks in the Age of Nationalism*, ed. Dimitri Gondicas and Charles Issawi. Pennington, NJ: Darwin Press, 1999, pp. 143-160.

Konortas, Paraskevas, 'From Ta'ife to *Millet*: Ottoman Terms for the Ottoman Greek

Orthodox Community', in *Ottoman Greeks in the Age of Nationalism*, ed. D. Gondicas and C. Issawi. Princeton, NJ: Darwin Press, 1999, pp. 169–180.

Lapie, M. Pierre, *Atlas Classique et Universel de Geographie Ancienne et Moderne dressé pour l'Instruction de la Jeunesse et Servant à l'Intelligence tant de l'Histoire que de Voyages dans les différentes Parties de Monde*, 4th edn. Paris: Chez Anselin, Successeur de Magimel, 1828.

Leake, William Martin, *An Historical Outline of the Greek Revolution*. London: J. Murray, 1825.

Lelis, Georgios K. Th., 'Praktika orothetikis grammis (1832) tou Neosistatou Ellinikou Kratous, Proskinio Paraskinio, Fthiotiki Istoria', *Praktika 3ov Sinedriou Fthiotikis Istorias*, 4–6 November 2005, Lamia, 2007.

Livieratos, Evangelos, *Chartografikes peripeteies tis Ellados 1821–1919*. Athens: ELIA, 2009.

Noradounghian, Gabriel, *Recueil d'actes internationaux de l'Empire Ottoman 1897–1903*, 2 vols. (1789–1856). Paris: F. Pichon, 1903.

Örenç Ali Fuat, *Balkanlarda ilk Dram: Unuttuğumuz Mora Türkleri ve Eyaletten Bağımsızlığa Yunanistan* [The First Drama in the Balkans: The Forgotten Turks of Morea and Greece from a Province to its Independence]. Istanbul: BYK, 2009.

Pedani, Pia Maria, 'The Border from the Ottoman Point of View', in *Tolerance and Intolerance on the Triplex Confinium: Approaching the 'Other' on the Borderlands, Eastern Adriatic and Beyond 1500–1800*, ed Egidio Ivetic and Drago Roksandic. Padova: CLEUP, 2007.

Phillpotts, Henry, 'The Greek Question', *The Quarterly Review*, 43 (1830), pp. 495–553.

Reinkowski, Maurus, 'Double Struggle, No Income: Ottoman Borderlands in Northern Albania', in *Ottoman Borderlands: Issues, Personalities, and Political Changes*, ed. K. Karpat and R. Zens. Madison, WI: University of Wisconsin Press, 2003, pp. 239–253.

Rıfat, Üçyol, 'The Border Dispute between the Ottoman Empire and Greece: Rearranging the Border According to the Berlin Treaty of 1878 and Giving Land to Greece (1878–1881)', *Revue Internationale d'Histoire Militaire*, 67 (1988), pp. 119–139.

Şanizade Mehmet Atanullah, *Tarih-i Şanizâde, cild-i salis*. Istanbul: Ceride-i Havadis Matbaası, 1867.

Stamatopoulos, Dimitris, 'From Millets to Minorities in the 19th-Century Ottoman Empire: An Ambiguous Modernization', in *Citizenship in Historical Perspective*, ed. S.G. Ellis, G. Hálfadanarson and A.K. Isaacs. Pisa: Edizioni Plus – Pisa University Press, 2006, pp. 253–273.

Tolias, Giorgos, *Challenged Frontiers: Cartographies of Greece and the Levant During the Ottoman Era*. Istanbul: Isis Press, 2010.

Türkgeldi, Ali Fuat, *Mesail-i Muhimme-i Siyasiyye*, vol. 2. Ankara: Türk Tarih Kurumu. 1957.

Veremis, Thanos, 'From the National State to the Stateless Nation, 1821–1910', in *Modern Greece: Nationalism and Nationality*, ed. Matin Blinkhorn and Thanos Veremis. Athens: Sage-Eliamep, 1990, pp. 9–22.

Wagstaff, Malcolm, *Independent Greece: The Search for a Frontier, 1822–35*. Cambridge: Cambridge University Press, 1999.

Yasamee, F.A.K., *Ottoman Diplomacy: Abdulhamid and the Great Powers, 1878–1888*. Istanbul: Isis Press, 1996.

7

Petko Voivoda: A Re-evaluation of Nineteenth-Century Bulgarian Military History

Assia Nakova
Princeton University

From 'Primitive Rebels' to *Haiduks*: Theoretical Background and a Framework for Discussion

Eric Hobsbawm, who has left an indelible mark on twentieth-century historical writing, albeit from a Marxist point of view, first proposed a framework of study for what he called 'primitive rebels'.[1] His exploration of 'archaic forms of social movements in the nineteenth and twentieth centuries' tracks the pre-history of modern revolutionary labour and peasant societies, even as the analysis probes 'banditry of the Robin Hood type, rural secret societies, various peasant revolutionary movements of the millennarian sort, and pre-industrial urban "mobs"'.[2] His framework seems also to accommodate the phenomenon of the Bulgarian *haiduks*, or irregular fighters against the Ottoman authorities of the nineteenth century.[3]

Hobsbawm further develops his ideas on the subject in his *Bandits*, first published in the 1960s, a book which establishes the field of study for the pre-industrial and pre-revolutionary 'social' rebels, as he designates them. These 'social' bandits are 'peasant outlaws whom the lord and state regard as criminals, but who remain within peasant society, and are considered by their people as heroes, champions, avengers, fighters for justice, perhaps even leaders of liberation, and in any case as men to be admired, helped and supported. In those cases where a traditional society resists the encroachments and historical advance of central governments and states, native and foreign, they may be hired and even supported by local lords.[4] 'Social' bandits are to be found, Hobsbawm argues, wherever in an agricultural society the peasants or landless labourers are ruled, oppressed or exploited by some lord, government or even banks and tax collectors. The types themselves are said to fall into three categories: the noble robber, such as the legendary Robin Hood; the 'primitive' resistance fighter or guerrilla, a perfect example of which is the nineteenth-century Bulgarian *haiduk*; and any terror-bringing avenger of wrongs committed against his people.

Relying exclusively on folk songs and poetry for his primary evidence, Hobsbawm draws an exceedingly and almost entirely attractive and positive picture of 'social banditry'. Yet this is his theme – though not the only one – to have attracted immediate criticism. Despite pointing out that *haiduks* and other 'social rebels' tended to use violence – after all, robbery and kidnapping were their main means of support – Hobsbawm maintains that peasants and even some lords tolerated the violence which 'social' bandits engaged in and lauded it as the price of their supposed protection.

Scholars criticizing Hobsbawm's depiction of *haiduks* and other 'social bandits' saw his work as supporting what they perceived as a somewhat picturesque representation of 'social' banditry, which, they urged, actually obscured the bandits' unsavoury behaviour, including their exploitation of peasants and other subordinated groups. As Hobsbawm's critics pointed out, 'social bandits' in fact propped up rather than subverted the political and economic power structures within which they operated, especially by creating opportunities for the expression of vendettas and financing themselves by violence, instead of trying in some fundamental way to change the structure and modes of operation of their society.

Anton Blok, for instance, in 'The Peasant and the Brigand: Social Banditry Reconsidered' (later updated as part of *Honor and Violence* (2001)), argues, with apparent correctness, that Hobsbawm places undue focus on a supposed connection between assumed class conflict and certain forms of banditry, among them *haidukdom*. Blok demonstrates that bandits often terrorized those from whose ranks they had managed to emerge, in effect helping to suppress them. This and other uncomfortable aspects of the breed known as the bandit, brigand, *klepht, celali, haiduk* and other 'social' rebels or highwaymen, while mentioned by Hobsbawm, are not seriously analysed. In fact, they remain more or less ignored as Hobsbawm's tendency is to interpret new information only in terms of his original model.[5] It follows, Blok stresses, that 'if we agree on political mobilization as a process through which people seek to acquire more control over the social conditions of their lives, it may be argued that bandits do not seem the appropriate agent to transform any organizational capacity among the peasants into a politically effective force'. Blok thus rejects entirely Hobsbawm's tendency to view at least a certain category of bandit as a 'social rebel' who expresses the exasperations, desires and ambitions for a better life of those who are oppressed and exploited in society, including the peasantry.

Kim A. Wagner likewise finds worrisome various aspects of Hobsbawm's description of 'social' banditry. Her re-examination of the bandit-as-social-rebel phenomenon, however, seeks to establish a more nuanced analysis rather than a complete and polemical deconstruction of Hobsbawm's model. In tackling the concept of thuggee in early nineteenth-century colonial India, Wagner sets its practice in its appropriate social context and shows the need for a more detailed and systematic methodology than Hobsbawm provides, or one grounded more securely in empirical materials. Her study demonstrates the complexity of the idea of thuggee, or the act of robbing and killing travellers on the road after tricking them into trusting their undeclared assailants, and the difficulty of viewing and interpreting their behaviour along lines of social protest. Wagner focuses on 'the construction of knowledge of banditry, the differing views of authorities and rural populations and the bandit's self-perception and myth'.[6] This line of argument seems a worthwhile and fruitful approach to analysing the phenomenon of thuggee and indeed that of nineteenth-century Bulgarian *haiduks*.

How information about various bandits, including *haiduks*, was accumulated, and knowledge about them produced and codified, is in fact the focus and starting point of Nathan Brown's analysis in his 'Brigands and State-Building in Modern Egypt'. Even though his discussion of Egypt's bandit problem in the second part of the nineteenth century predates Kim Wagner's analysis of Indian thuggee, Brown's and Wagner's approaches may be seen as similar in their appropriate use of documentation and their questioning of the differing views of officialdom – both local and colonial – as well as the views of the bandits themselves, when they left written records. Brown shows how even though banditry was for centuries an on-going phenomenon in Egypt, it became a focal point of official repression only with the arrival of British occupation in 1882. At that point, 'the definition of banditry as a national problem became an integral part of state-building in Egypt'.[7] Brown argues that 'banditry as a national problem was invented as a political weapon by Egypt's rulers as a part of the process of creating a stronger, centralized state apparatus and as an effort to keep that apparatus out of British hands'.[8] Peasants were thus almost entirely passive during this period, fearing both the state and bandits, and lacking the resources or will to oppose either. They certainly did not see bandits as expressing any sort of social protest on their behalf, or so Brown makes clear.

Karen Barkey explores a similar inability of peasants to express protest through bandits, or *celali*, in the Ottoman heartland version of the bandit as irregular fighter. In her study *Bandits and Bureaucrats: The Ottoman Route to State Centralization* (1994), she traces the trajectory of Ottoman state-building and centralization from the sixteenth to the eighteenth centuries through co-opting and negotiation with bandits. During this process, Barkey points out, the brigand developed a new persona, which involved being 'disloyal to his origins and even helping to repress the members of his village'.[9] To a great extent the brigand was thus a new entity created by the state 'through direct employment in state armies or indirect employment by local power holders'.[10] The result, contrary to what Hobsbawm describes in his model of the 'social' bandit, was that 'vagrants turned into mercenaries and became organized along state-military lines'.[11] Throughout this process of centralization and greater control over territory through negotiation with Ottoman bandits, or *celali*, the state certainly never came close to collapsing. Nor was it the goal of brigands to destabilize it. Instead, Barkey asserts, the *celali* sought to 'derive as much utility from society and the state as possible'.[12] Whatever the mischief that rebellious bandits got up to, their activities did not represent a collective action in any traditional sense because they did not seek to change societal structures. In fact, the fear of lawlessness occasioned by their activities was often used as a means of promoting the state's increased interference in society and a consolidation of state power.

Perhaps the strongest dissent from Hobsbawm's argument that *haiduks* and other irregular fighters and bandits were engaged in primitive forms of social protest is to be found in John Koliopoulos' careful and detailed study of brigandage and irredentism in modern Greece during the period 1821–1912. Koliopoulos examines the stages and connections between Greek bandits' activities with those of irregular fighters, or *klephts* and *armatoles*, and the development of the modern Greek State. He sees the practice of allowing a certain amount of banditry as a convenient way for the state to provide disaffected, disgruntled or simply unemployed citizens with an opportunity to 'let off steam'. Another way for the state to reduce tensions was for it tacitly to encourage the *klephts* and *armatoles* to engage in irredentist activities.[13] It is also worth remembering that in its early stages the modern Greek State struggled to control the size of its territory. Its tactics for handling the *klephts* thus created a 'semblance of legitimacy in the exercise of non-state authority and at the same time rendered such pursuits as less dangerous to the security of the state'.[14]

This may be an appropriate point to suggest that despite the ongoing scholarly debate on a suitable framework of discussion about bandits in their various manifestations, as *haiduk*, *celali* or *klepht*, Bulgarian historians have largely failed to engage with them in an evidence-supported way. What is clear is that, like Hobsbawm's approach to the subject, but rooted in nationalist strivings, the Bulgarian historical establishment, for so it may still be described, has relied on and perpetuated a romantic, uncritical account of the Bulgarian *haiduk*, much along Hobsbawm's apparently inadequate lines.

Haiduk Activities: An Alternative Approach

The *haiduks*, or irregular fighters who took to the mountains to fight Ottoman authority in response to injustices perpetrated on the Bulgarian population, remain part and parcel of Bulgarian national folklore. To this day, any mention of their actual names (Petko Voivoda, Hadji Dimitar, Velko Voivoda and the occasional female such as Sirma Voivoda) provokes expressions of admiration. This reaction is echoed in professional historical circles.[15] In fact, the well-known modern narrative tends also to follow familiar or typical folktale lines: an oppressed Bulgarian man – there seem to have been very few, if any, women involved as hero-types in these stories – reaches a breaking point in respect to what he feels he can handle in his politically, socially and economically depressed life. He decides to remove himself from this life altogether, and heads into the Bulgarian mountains, long famous for offering opportunities for escape from desperate circumstances. About him he gathers a small but trusted group of friends, and soon begins to harass the Ottoman authorities, defending, as he sees it, the Bulgarian population of his region. As he does so, he comes to be regarded, and indeed regards himself, as having preserved his 'Bulgarianness', a term often left conveniently undefined, but understood as having contributed significantly to the liberation struggle of Bulgarians everywhere.[16]

Peter Kiriakov (1844–1900), or as he was commonly known, Petko Voivoda, became one of the most famous of these types of men, or *haiduks*, and is therefore a figure appropriate for consideration here. Born in the village of Dogan Hisar, or Aisymi in present-day Greece, by 1953 he had become the subject of some 130 publications devoted in various ways to his life and exploits. These included memoirs and articles authored by friends and acquaintances, many of which expanded, often far too extravagantly it seems, on his adventurous and politically significant career.[17] It should also be understood that since the 1950s, the quantity of these publications has increased exponentially.[18] An overview of them, however, quickly reveals that not much has been done in the way of analysing his exploits critically, or taking up a few of the less savoury, unpleasant, and even violent aspects of his life and those of the men who may be counted as his supporters, along with their unquestionably illegal, or quasi-legal, other activities.[19] Kiriakov's approach to organizing an initially small band of followers and fellow *haiduk* fighters – at first only seven to nine men joined him in 1863, though their number later increased to some three hundred during and after the Russo-Turkish War of 1877–1878 – has, for instance, simply been lauded as a new stage in the Bulgarian national struggle.[20] In essence, it must be admitted, lavish praise may be appropriate: Kiriakov's contribution to the cause of Bulgarian freedom was certainly invaluable. On the other hand, what, it may be asked, about the illegitimacy, possible inhumanity and likely indefensible cruelty of the types of local governing practices that he certainly encouraged in the course of his military campaigns? Have their vices as well as virtues been properly vetted, or even professionally and honestly discussed? In Kiriakov's widely recognized imitation of the behaviour of the hero of the Italian unification movement, Garibaldi, it should also be wondered whether he did not engage in questionable if not disreputable tactics and methods.

The proposition which seeks advancement here is that a more balanced and systematic approach to what should become a more authentic account of the history of the *haiduks* in the period following the Russo-Turkish War, which signalled the beginning of the formation of the modern Bulgarian nation, is certainly overdue. This is to say that any real understanding of Kiriakov's career is bound to reveal that far too much emphasis has been placed on the injustices, economic and other problems, and the outright murders and massacres that the Bulgarian people suffered during this period to lead to anything like a complete description of what indeed became a national struggle.[21] The disaster which took place at the village of Batak, for instance, and which is often cited sympathetically by Bulgarian writers dealing with their own history, stands out in any such analysis as the *raison d'être* for Bulgarian revenge exacted from often quite innocent populations of Turks, Jews, Greeks and Armenians.[22] To be sure, the Kiriakov-supportive attitude of modern historians is easily understood, and is probably common enough among historians generally in respect to war and violence, in which patriotism can easily replace soundness of investigation. Nonetheless, it is appropriate today to take a more sober and balanced view of the crimes committed by Bulgarians against Turks and other minorities in the aftermath of the war of 1877–1878. If such a reconsideration is attempted, it must, I would suggest, be conceded that Bulgarian historians have distorted their accounts of the events following the war against the Turks, as well as getting wrong important episodes and implications of the Bulgarian-Turkish conflict, perhaps especially in respect to the Bulgarian treatment of Turks, Jews, Armenians and Greeks.[23]

What seems clear is that at times a familiar, patriotic Bulgarian project, as it may be termed – whose goal has been to preserve Bulgarian predominance in the political, cultural and economic life of the various Bulgarian provinces, especially after the Berlin Congress of 1878 – has been mainly concerned not just with history but with preserving a vague if jingoistic idea of 'Bulgarianness'. This mysterious national essence continues to play a definite role in the political life of the country, often, in the political arena, taking the form of manipulating the national electoral process, as was the case in the first elections for the national assembly held in both Bulgaria and Eastern Rumelia in 1878. At other times, a manipulation of history has played a more horrific role, as when the property of Turks and other ethnic minorities, who may have fled to Turkey and later attempted to return to the Bulgarian towns and villages which were often their places of origin, was seized by Bulgarians who then resisted returning their homes and other valuables. Nor is crucial evidence lacking in respect to this behaviour. During the post-war period on 24 June 1879, the English representative to the European Commission in Eastern Rumelia – a territory including what is today the southern part of Bulgaria, along with the Balkan mountains – Thomas Mitchell, reported to Robert Gascoyne-Cecil, Lord Salisbury, the British Foreign Secretary, that 'twenty Jewish families left Carlovo yesterday, having received an official invitation to return to their homes. They were conducted to a house, which was soon surrounded by about 2,000 people, among whom were a large number of women. These broke open the door, pulled down a wall, and attacked the Jews, wounding three women.'[24] On other even more distressing occasions, entire Turkish villages were wiped out by Bulgarian-initiated arson and vandalism, as well as murder.[25] This was the case with the two villages which Petko Voivoda and his men regarded as having collaborated with the Ottoman authorities and which, therefore, or according to their own article 12 of the set of rules of Petko's *cheta*, or band of irregular fighters, deserved to be razed to the ground: 'Outsiders agitating, spying, collecting weapons to fight against the *druzina* (or *cheta*) are punishable by death' [my translation]. These rules were first published in *Maritsa*, an important Plovdiv newspaper, on 27 May 1877. Its stipulation, which governed Petko's *druzina* or *cheta*, actually came to be used as a justification for exacting revenge on the basis of the presumed collective guilt of several Muslim villages, which were offered no due process in law, or a chance for their inhabitants to defend themselves against the violence thrown their way. One may reasonably infer that such atrocious behaviour amounted at best to legalized vigilantism, yet scholarly and popular discussions of these and similar events, if they mention them at all, treat them only in terms of the 'righteousness' of the Bulgarian cause and gloss over Bulgarian-initiated violence as a natural reaction to the many injustices suffered by Bulgarians at the hands of Turks during the five hundred years of Ottoman rule.

There can, of course, be no denying that Bulgarians endured hardships and injustices during the Ottoman period. Peter Kirkov Petkov, or Petko Voivoda, was himself a victim of it, losing two family members, his brother Matthew (Matei) and his cousin Velcho, the latter of whom was killed in 1861 by the local Ottoman representative in his home-village, when Petko was seventeen. No doubt such savagery, and the absence of any legal or other normal recourse to justice for his family, left deep marks on him as a young man. This seems clear from the fact that instead of continuing his education as he had dreamed he might, and as he had urged his father to allow him to do, he soon took to the mountains with six or seven friends, seeking the revenge that he felt he deserved for the loss of his brother and cousin. His subsequent capture by Ottoman authorities, his being sentenced to a term in prison, and his escape in 1864 seem to have prompted him to seek his fortune, together with additional education, at a military school in Athens, possibly at the invitation of the Greek revolutionary committee, which was preparing an uprising in Crete.[26] It is important to note that this phase of

Petko's education and experience only became possible because of his knowledge of modern Greek. It also seems clear that he did not stay long in Athens – or for only one academic year, from September 1864 to July 1864 – and that he soon returned to the Rhodope mountains, possibly hoping to be able to organize an uprising that would coincide with yet another uprising planned in Crete.[27]

In Athens he is said to have developed a wider view of the struggle for Bulgarian liberation from Ottoman rule when he witnessed the Ottoman suppression of the Greeks and learned about other national movements for unification and popular self-realization farther afield, in Europe. The Italian surge towards freedom, for instance, and the bold behaviour of its most important leader, Guiseppe Garibaldi, likewise seem to have offered Petko a promising model for emulation. As a result, and after deciding that an uprising could not yet be organized in the Rhodope region, a conclusion which he arrived at during his tours of the area, he travelled to the island of Caprera, where Garibaldi was recovering from wounds he had suffered in 1862 at Aspromonte. It is of considerable interest that Petko visited with Garibaldi for three months. While few details of his stay at the Italian revolutionist's villa are known, Garibaldi himself has written about his sympathy for 'the little people of the Balkans' and the young Bulgarian visiting with him, Petko Kiriakov. Petko himself attests in his memoirs that he learned a great deal about the nature of the struggle for national unification, and the violence that he thought it would require, from Garibaldi, and that he certainly put it to use in his struggle against Ottoman rule. He supplies few details about what he learned, but it seems clear that a bond of trust emerged between him and the Italian: he was given command of Garibaldi's group of some two hundred and twenty fighters, or the Garibaldi 'legion', as it was dubbed, which took part in the uprising in Crete in 1866.

This well-known episode in the Italian rebellion proved a failure, but following it Petko found himself travelling across Europe for three years, between 1866 and 1869 (starting in Egypt, in Alexandria). On his return to Bulgaria, he formed yet another *druzina*, or group of irregular fighters, and established himself in the region bordering the Maritsa River, which runs through the city of Plovdiv and cuts southern Bulgaria roughly in two. By 1870 he and his men had begun to develop themselves officially, designing and having made an official-appearing stamp, showing the name of their *cheta*, which Petko used for signing letters and other missives emanating from his revolutionist headquarters. A couple of years later, in 1873, his famous 'set of rules', comprising some seventeen articles, or judicial points, was written up and approved by the *druzina*. These contained the two articles on the basis of which he and his men came to regard the burning of the two Turkish villages cited above as a legitimate step in their struggle for the 'moral and political defence of the Bulgarian people in their struggle to free themselves from Ottoman rule' (article I of the set of rules of the *druzina*). More specifically, article XIV states that 'if any villages or several villages rise against the *druzina*, those initiating the revolt are punishable by death, and the village(s) with heavy fines or destruction, depending on the severity of their actions'.

It thus seems clear that a far too drastic approach to a perceived and not clearly proved transgression against the *druzina* amounted not so much to a rebellion against an unjust and vicious Turkish imperialism as to acts of vengeance undertaken by vigilantes. Over a century later, the destruction of these Turkish villages remains a fact that it is unpleasant to contemplate and that seems to cry out for a more even-handed discussion of Bulgarian liberation. Such a revised account ought to be set against the revised larger picture of the realities of life in Bulgaria and Eastern Rumelia during a period of upheaval which offered both hope and ill fortune to most of those living there, whether they were Bulgarian, Greek, Jewish, Muslim or Armenian, following on from the Russo-Turkish War of 1877–1878. It is to be hoped that a start towards achieving that goal can be understood as having been made possible by this inquiry.

Notes

1. Prior to Hobsbawm's efforts, no comprehensive studies of the phenomenon existed. Cf. G. Rosen, *Die balkan Haiduken im Beitragzur innern Geschichte des Slawenthums*. Leipzig, 1878; J.W. Baggally, *The Klephtic Ballads in Relation to Greek History, 1715–1821*. Oxford: Oxford University Press, 1937; and P.S. Spandonidis, 'Le clefte', *L'hellenisme contemporain*, January/February (1954), pp. 3–18, as L.S. Stavrioanos cites them in his discussion 'The Antecedents to the Balkan Revolutions of the Nineteenth Century', *Journal of Modern History*, 29, no. 4 (1957), pp. 335–348, which offers only an incomplete discussion.
2. Eric Hobsbawm, *Primitive Rebels: Studies in Archaic Form of Social Movement in the 19th and 20th Century*. New York: W.W. Norton, 1965, p. 1.
3. *Haiduks* were reported as early as 1528. My focus here is likewise on the nineteenth century.
4. Hobsbawm, *Primitive Rebels*, p. 20.
5. Blok, Anton, 'The Peasant and the Brigand: Social Banditry Reconsidered', *Comparative Studies in Society and History*, 1, no. 4 (1972), p. 496.
6. Kim A. Wagner, 'Thuggee and Social Banditry Reconsidered', *The Historical Journal*, 50, no. 2 (2007), p. 354.
7. Nathan Brown, 'Brigands and State-Building: The Invention of Banditry in Modern Egypt', *Comparative Studies in Society and History*, 32, no. 2 (1990), p. 259.
8. Ibid., p. 260.
9. Karen Barkey, *Bandits and Bureaucrats: The Ottoman Route to State Centralization*. New York: Cornell University Press, 1994, p. 183.
10. Ibid., p. 176.
11. Ibid.
12. Ibid.
13. The 1830 international treaty which established the modern Greek State left more Greeks outside its boundaries than inside them. This led to expanding irredentist ambitions and activities, especially in Macedonia, where Greeks and Bulgarians frequently clashed.
14. John Koliopoulos, *Brigands with a Cause: Brigandage and Irredentism in Modern Greece, 1821–1912*. New York: Oxford University Press, 1987, p. ix.
15. The historiographic literature on *haiduks* in Bulgarian is extensive. The topic seems to lend itself easily to the creation of a 'national mythology', or the type of myth known as 'creation-of-the-nation'. Nikolai Aretov tackles the question of Bulgarian mythology engagingly and informatively in his *Natsionalna mitologia i natsionalna literatura: siuzeti izgrazdashti bulgarskata natsionalna identichnost v slovensnostta ot XVIII i XIX vek* [National Mythology and National Literature. Literary Plots in the Creation of

Bulgarian National Identity and Literature from the Eighteenth and Nineteenth Centuries]. Sofia: 'Kralitsa Mab' Publishing House, 2006.

16 Relevant scholarly investigations fail to discuss or try to provide a definition of 'Bulgarianness'. A number of recent studies demonstrate that Bulgarians did not tend to think of themselves as belonging to a clearly defined nation until well past the middle of the nineteenth century. See Mark Mazower, *The Balkans: A Short History*. New York: Modern Library, 2002 and Raymond Detrez, *Ne Tersiat gertsi, a romei da bedat* [They Do Not Seek to be Greek but Rumeli: Orthodox Christian Cultural Identity in the Ottoman Empire, Fifteenth to Nineteenth Centuries]. Sofia: 'Kralitsa Mab' Publishing House, 2015.

17 Cf. Bulgarian Historical Review, 6, 1973, 29–48.

18 At a recent unveiling of a Petko monument, the president of Bulgaria, Rosen Plevleniev, urged everyone to follow his example. See *Thracian Review*, 2014, p. 210. As is perhaps to be expected, Petko Voivoda has always been painted in the bright colors of a national hero. This image is bolstered by a popular book, *Captain Petko Voivoda* (1974), by Nikolai Haitov, one of Bulgaria's best known authors, as well as by a well-acted and -directed eponymous television series which followed the book's publication in the 1980s, and which is still often shown in Bulgaria.

19 See, for instance, *Petko Voivoda: Sbronik ot statii, dokumenti i materiali* [Petko Voivoda: Collection of Articles, Documents and Materials]. Sofia, 1954, pp. 7–9.

20 A more modern approach to documenting their activities would probably explore how the organizing of the *cheta*, or the group of men under Petko's guidance and following a set of rules, may provide a better organized and fairer understanding of the otherwise irregular methods of the famous *haiduks*. Scholars tend to locate the seeds of Petko's desire for organized methods of operation in his brief but significant military education in Athens, and particularly in his stay with the hero of Italian unification, Garibaldi.

21 The debate over the use of the term 'yoke', for example, to describe the years of Ottoman rule in Bulgaria continues in Bulgarian academic and civil society and offers a case in point. Accusations of a lack of patriotism on the part of those dissenting from the 'official' view, which continuously invokes the image of the 'yoke', are often levelled at those who suggest that a less emotionally charged and perhaps more accurate term might better serve any sensible discussion of this period of Bulgarian history.

22 By contrast, the near complete destruction of the village of Batak by bashi-bouzuks, or Turkish irregular fighters, caused an international uproar. British prime minister Benjamin Disraeli's pamphlet, 'Bulgarian Horrors and the Question of the East' (1876), popularized the 'Bulgarian Question', as it came to be called. Cf. *History Review*, 50 (December 2004).

23 The role of the Greeks and Greek culture and language in particular as cultural colonizers of Bulgaria is a major touchstone and basis of the story of the Bulgarian struggle for liberation in the nineteenth century. Some recent studies, such as Raymond Detrez's *They Do Not Seek to be Greek but Rumeli*, may be regarded as providing major advances in this area and seen as contributing to a deeper analysis and paring down of a somewhat ossified and long overdue position.

24 See Turkey, Blue Book, No. 5, Dispatch No. 2.

25 Daniel Iurukov, *Spomeni iz politicheskia zivot na Balgarija* (Memoirs of Bulgarian Political Life). Sofia: Hudoznik, 1932, p. 135.

26 See D.G. Shishmanov, Xaidushko-buntovnicheski revoliutsionni deinost na Petko Voivoda sreshtu turksoto robstvo (1861-1877), in *Petko Voivoda*, p. 35.
27 See Filip Simidov, in *Petko Voivoda*, p. 152 and ibid., p. 35.

Bibliography

Aretov, Nikolai, *Natsionalna mitologia i natsionalna literatura: siuzeti izgrazdashti bulgarskata natsionalna identichnost v slovensnostta ot XVIII i XIX vek* [National Mythology and National Literature. Literary Plots in the Creation of Bulgarian National Identity and Literature from the Eighteenth and Nineteenth Centuries]. Sofia: 'Kralitsa Mab' Publishing House, 2006.

Baggally, J.W., *The Klephtic Ballads in Relation to Greek History, 1715-1821*. Oxford: Oxford University Press, 1937.

Barkey, Karen, *Bandits and Bureaucrats: The Ottoman Route to State Centralization*. New York: Cornell University Press, 1994.

Blok, Anton, 'The Peasant and the Brigand: Social Banditry Reconsidered', *Comparative Studies in Society and History*, 1, no. 4 (1972), pp. 494-503.

Brown, Nathan, 'Brigands and State-Building: The Invention of Banditry in Modern Egypt', *Comparative Studies in Society and History*, 32, no. 2 (1990), pp. 258-281.

Detrez, Raymond, *Не Търсят Гърци, а Ромеи да Бъдат, Православна Културна Общност в Османската Империя. XV-XIX в* [They Do Not Seek to be Greek but Rumeli: Orthodox Christian Cultural Identity in the Ottoman Empire, Fifteenth to Nineteenth Centuries]. Sofia: 'Kralitsa Mab' Publishing House, 2015.

Ellis, John, *A Short History of Guerrilla Warfare*. New York: St. Martin's Press, 1976.

Haitov, Nikolai, *Капитан Петко Войвода* [Captain Petko Voivoda]. Sofia, 1974.

Haitov, Nikolai, *Хайдути, Родопски Властелини* [Haiduks, Rhodopi Mountain Heroes]. Sofia: Evro Press, 2000.

Hobsbawm, Eric, *Primitive Rebels: Studies in Archaic Form of Social Movement in the 19th and 20th Century*. New York: W.W. Norton, 1965.

Hobsbawm, Eric, *Bandits*. London: Weidenfeld & Nicolson, 2000.

Iurukov, Daniel, *Spomeni iz politicheskia zivot na Balgarija* (Memoirs of Bulgarian Political Life). Sofia: Hudoznik, 1932.

Koliopoulos, John, *Brigands with a Cause: Brigandage and Irredentism in Modern Greece, 1821-1912*. New York: Oxford University Press, 1987.

Mazower, Mark, *The Balkans: A Short History*. New York: Modern Library, 2002.

Petko Voivoda: Sbronik ot statii, dokumenti i materiali [Petko Voivoda: Collection of Articles, Documents and Materials]. Sofia, 1954.

Rosen, G., *Die balkan Haiduken im Beitragzur innern Geschichte des Slawenthums*. Leipzig, 1878.

Seal, Graham, *Outlaw Heroes in Myth and History*. London: Anthem Press, 2011.

Spandonidis, P.S., 'Le clefte', *L'hellenisme contemporain*, January/February (1954), pp. 3-18.

Stavrioanos, L.S., 'The Antecedents to the Balkan Revolutions of the Nineteenth Century', *Journal of Modern History*, 29, no. 4 (1957), pp. 335-348.

Wagner, Kim A., 'Thuggee and Social Banditry Reconsidered', *The Historical Journal*, 50, no. 2 (2007), pp. 353-376.

Wilson, Stephen, *Feuding, Conflict and Banditry in Nineteenth-Century Corsica*. New York: Cambridge University Press, 1988.

8

Uprisings, Revolutions and Wars: Visual Representations in the Bulgarian Illustrated Press at the End of the Nineteenth and Early Twentieth Century[1]

Dobrinka Parusheva
University of Plovdiv/Institute of Balkan Studies, Bulgarian Academy of Sciences

Introduction

Considering the vast number of books on uprisings and wars in the Balkans, one might assume that almost everything has already been said leaving but a few uncharted areas. Yet, as far as the iconography is concerned, only a few studies have made a contribution. The reason lies, I believe, in the continuing perception of the visual mainly from the point of view of its illustrative value while neglecting its ability to tell us stories. In 2001, Peter Burke pointed to the invisibility of the visual for most historians.[2] Despite listing early examples such as some of Philippe Ariès' studies, Burke stated that it was only in the 1980s when a *pictorial turn* occurred. A concern for the importance of the visible in the humanities and social sciences (that is, the *pictorial* or the *visual turn*) since the 1980s is widely shared.[3] As for wars and revolutions, during the last decade, on the occasion of the centenary of the First World War, a plethora of research has been published, including analyses of visual representations: scholars from France, Portugal and elsewhere provide elaborate discussions of the role of visual materials in war's representation.[4]

Yet, if one looks at the Balkans and scholars of Balkan history, the interest in the visual seems to be very limited. An overarching temporal and spatial academic discussion of the visual culture in the region, with an emphasis on the religious realm, was recently offered by Karl Kaser;[5] there are also a number of texts analysing some particular phenomena.[6] However, when the revolutions and wars in the Balkans are the focus of attention, particularly those that happened during the (long) nineteenth century, one can find just a few examples.[7] Hence, this chapter's attempt to contribute to the field of visual studies in the history of the Balkans by shedding light on the way the Bulgarian illustrated press represented events like uprisings and wars.

At the turn of the nineteenth century, there were few illustrated journals in Bulgaria, only two of which referred to this characteristic explicitly: *Ilyustratsiya Svetlina*

(Illustration Light) and *Savremenna Ilyustratsiya* (Contemporary Illustration). The latter was published between 1910 and 1914 but remained largely unknown outside the capital Sofia, while the former was launched in 1891 and ran without a break for more than 40 years. The first issue of *Ilyustratsiya Svetlina* was published in March 1891 and from that point on it appeared once a month until 1934; only during wartime in the 1910s was there some occasional irregularity in its appearance. This is one reason why I focus on *Illustration Light* here.[8] In addition, it was the first illustrated journal to be published in the Bulgarian language and by a Bulgarian, Yordan Mihaylov. I analyse the issues of *Light* from its launch in 1891 to the end of the First World War and provide information and illustrative material in an attempt to answer such questions as: What sort of coverage of uprisings and wars did this herald of the Bulgarian illustrated press offer its readers? What role did the images play in this coverage, and what types of images predominated? Were women visible or were they absent from the war and violence narrative in both words and pictures? How were Self and the Other (or allies and enemies) depicted? The answers to these questions will be presented in three main sections which follow the chronology: first, I discuss the visual representation of uprisings and wars on the *Light*'s pages in the 1890s and 1900s; next, I analyse the coverage of the Balkan wars in 1912–1913; finally, the visual presence of the First World War is scrutinized.

Turn of the Century

The journal *Light* was launched about 12 years after the Russo-Ottoman War of 1877–1878, which the Bulgarian people considered a war of liberation because it resulted in the re-establishment of the Bulgarian State. At that time, in the early 1890s, people's memory of the period before liberation was still vivid and that was the reason, in my reading, for the absence of many publications, whether of texts or images, related to events before 1878. I can list only one example related to the April 1876 uprising and particularly of the Batak massacres: two photographs by Dimitar Kavra, one of the prominent photographers at the end of the nineteenth century in Plovdiv, were published in October 1894 – *The bones of the victims of Batak* and *Batak. A commemoration at the place of the massacre*.[9]

In addition, we find the publication of pictures which reminded readers of the successful outcome for Bulgarians of the Serbo-Bulgarian War of 1885.[10] In 1893, in 1896 and again in 1907, a few reproductions of paintings by the Polish artist Antoni Piotrowski were published.[11] They showed Bulgarian troops entering the Serbian town of Pirot, the battle near the town of Tsaribrod and its aftermath, the Bulgarian army next to the town of Slivnitsa and the important battle there, and so on.[12] Piotrowski did his paintings in the first half of the 1890s and they were published in *Light* shortly after that, with the following explanation by the publisher: '[A]s we know the famous Polish artist Mr A. Piotrowski monumentalized with his successful paintings our war with our *brothers Serbs*.'[13] All of them but especially the last one published at the end of 1907 (*Bulgarian forces chase the enemy behind Pirot. The November victory over the Serbs* [Ill. 1])[14] commemorated the victory of the Bulgarian army in the autumn of 1885. Apart

Visual Representations of Uprisings, Revolutions and Wars 151

Ill. 1: 1907, no. 11–12, pp. 20–21 – *Bulgarian forces chase the enemy behind Pirot. The November victory over the Serbs*, painting by Antoni Piotrowski.

from Piotrowski's paintings, another reminder of the Serbo-Bulgarian war found its way onto the pages of *Light*: a photograph of the Bulgarian students who participated in the war taken by an unknown photographer.[15] This picture recalled the enthusiasm of the Bulgarian people in general and of Bulgarian students abroad in particular who returned to the country to defend the unification of Eastern Rumelia with the Bulgarian Principality. Interestingly, there were no visual materials memorizing the act of unification but only the few mentioned above which were a reminder of the war in its defence.

Uprisings: 'ours' and distant

One of the topics that attracted the attention of the readers of *Light* was the massacre of the Armenians in the Ottoman Empire in the mid-1890s. These events were pictured in the journal on several occasions. On the one hand, visual material representing the atrocities of the Ottoman forces was published, mainly drawings with captions like *Atrocities in Armenia, Armenian Rebellion in Stambul, Massacres in Trebizund* (Ill. 2) and so on.[16] On the other hand, the fate of the Armenian refugees in Bulgaria was also the focus of attention, depicted in a couple of photographs.[17] In a brief explanatory text offered about 30 pages after a picture of refugees in Varna, the publisher praised the good will of the Bulgarian government in welcoming the Armenians and supplying the poorest with food. The contrast in the representation of the massacres (by drawings)

Ill. 2: 1896, no. 1, p. 5 – *Massacres in Trebizund*.

and peaceful moments experienced by the refugees in Bulgaria (by photographs) is obvious. This is easy to explain bearing in mind the level of development of the photographic technique at the time and impossibility to 'catch' moving pictures like the ones we see in the drawings.

Another issue that was of great importance for Bulgaria and its people was the fate of the population in Macedonia. Many drawings, paintings and some photographs appeared in *Light* at the beginning of the twentieth century. In almost every issue in 1903, visual materials either depicted the situation of the population in the region or followed developments during the uprising in the summer of 1903.[18] Here I should point to the difference in the forms of representation: while mainly drawings and reproductions of paintings were used to depict street scenes of the Armenian massacres, the images representing the events in Macedonia often offered a more close-up view, even acts of extreme brutality.

As an example I use an engraving, evidently taken from a photograph, named *Heroes and trophies. Macedonian events*. It depicts six men standing in uniforms, in fezzes, with their rifles raised. The six men in front of the camera stand behind three severed heads (supposedly of rebels) displayed on a pedestal (Ill. 3).[19] This picture presents just one of many images of severed heads published in West European illustrated newspapers and journals in 1903. It was reproduced a number of times in different journals (such as *La vie illustrée*, *Berliner illustrierte Zeitung* and St. Petersburg's *Novoye Vremya*) after it had appeared on the cover of the French journal

Ill. 3: 1903, no. 3, p. 13 – *Heroes and trophies. Macedonian events*.

L'Illustration on 28 February 1903 with the title *Les evénements de Macédoine*. A detailed caption explained that at a mere 40 hours' distance from Paris, reproductions of photographs like this were on the windows of bookshops in Salonica and Monastir. As Edhem Eldem, one of the authors of a recent study on photography in the Ottoman Empire frames it: 'The message was clear and meant to be shocking. At a distance of only forty hours from civilization, barbarism had reached such a degree of banality that it had become a curiosity item, on display in shops.'[20] Eldem also questions the reason for the almost simultaneous use of these images in the Western illustrated press: was it a chain reaction from one periodical to another, or was it, perhaps, a result of 'a concerted effort of Macedonian freedom fighters or their supporters to bombard the Western public with hard evidence of atrocities committed in the region.'[21] One way or another, photographs like this undoubtedly had a profound influence on public opinion. Especially so in the case of the Bulgarian reading public, where the distance to the events – or rather the lack of emotional distance – was mirrored in the way the events were represented on the pages of *Light*.

Light continued to pay attention to the developments in Macedonia also in the years after the 1903 uprising: in July 1904 a photograph of the inspector-general of the Macedonian gendarmerie in Thessaloniki, General di Giorgis, was published;[22] in the autumn of 1906 some local victims and also the death of one of the leaders of the new rebels were represented again in two photographs, the latter one by Georg Woltz.[23] And once more, the fate of the refugees was of interest and hence represented on the pages of the journal.[24] About these people we read on the pages of *Light* the following: 'The Macedonian refugees endured the hardship of destitution and winter; the Bulgarians from the principality did not leave them without food and clothes; the brotherly welcome [...] They will remember and narrate to their people how Bulgaria thought and took care of them.'[25]

In contrast to the attention paid to Macedonia, I should underline that the journal devoted very little attention to the Young Turk Revolution of 1908, referring to it as 'events in Turkey' with a focus on what was happening in Macedonia again.[26] The visual materials in this issue (1908, no. 7–8) were accompanied by a text that requires no further discussion of the mood in Bulgaria at the time:

> **The events in Turkey.** Macedonia and all the Turkish Empire triumph and celebrate the proclaimed freedom. After years long tortures by the despotic regime the country wakes up and restores. Under the lead of the Turkish liberals, the Christian population in the empire finally gains its rights [...] In this issue we publish most interesting photos of the events in Macedonia, photos representing scenes between the dates of the tyrannical regime and the morning of freedom; scenes which are the break, the line that divided the dark from the light. On the previous day we see the rebel on the gallows or tyrannized from one prison to another, and on the next morning the contrast of the proclaimed constitution shines: [...][27]

This quotation alludes to the main concerns of the Bulgarian people, or one may call it the Bulgarian sore point – that is, Macedonia. To illustrate: the fact that Bulgaria declared its independence from the Ottoman Empire in September 1908 was represented by just two caricatures on the pages of *Light*,[28] while the fate of the population in the region of Macedonia continued to be the focus of attention of the publisher after the Young Turk Revolution, although not in every issue as it was in 1903–1904.[29]

Before turning my attention from uprisings and revolutions to wars, let me add just one more point to the account: I have so far discussed which important events, 'inner' to Bulgaria and to a certain extent to the Balkans, were represented visually on the pages of the journal *Light*. No 'foreign' matters of this kind were considered, with one single exception, the Russian Revolution in 1905 – it was depicted in one drawing published in September 1906.[30]

Wars: worldwide

Each and every important war event all over the globe, no matter how close or distant it was to Bulgaria, found visual coverage in the journal *Light*. Yet, the wars at the turn of the century were still represented almost exclusively by drawings or reproductions of paintings and not by photographs. The sequence of wars covered started with the Greco-Turkish war of 1897. This event was depicted by a few drawings and a couple of caricatures.[31] In both the May and June issues of 1897, the journal expressed sympathy with the Greeks having eventually lost the war: 'But the result of this war is sad and disastrous for Greece. If it is not the autonomy of Crete, one may say, Greece has not won anything else but its moral and material destruction.'[32]

During the next couple of years, the Spanish-American War (1898) regarding the fate of Cuba and the English-Transvaal War (1899–1900) were the focus of attention. Drawings appeared on the pages of *Light* as a means of representing these two wars also. The Spanish-American War saw the end of Spain as a colonial and navy power. Visual material depicted sea battles and their results,[33] military equipment of both armies,[34] portraits of military and state leaders,[35] as well as landscapes.[36] *Light* also reproduced a few photographs of people, including children, suffering hunger as a result of the war in Cuba.[37] These are probably the most striking illustrations in the journal, after the severed heads of the rebels in 1903. The English-Transvaal War received less attention than the Spanish-American War.[38] It is interesting to point to a comparison with Bulgarian history made by the editor of *Light*:

> **Transvaal war.** The motives of the English men to provoke the war with the Republic of Transvaal are not more relevant than the ones that were used by Milan to attack Bulgaria. For this reason the luck was not on the side of England in this reckless adventure [...][39]

Comparing the way war events were represented at the end of the nineteenth century, the Greco-Turkish War of 1897, despite the fact it was closer to Bulgaria, did not attract any more attention than the Spanish-American War or English-Transvaal War. The most prolific coverage, however, was reserved for the Russo-Japanese War. After it started in early February 1904, all issues of *Light* until October 1905 (the war finished in September) contained visual materials related to the war. In the first months they were more numerous but then began to gradually diminish.[40] In the main, it was the movements and victories of the Russian army that were presented,[41] despite the fact Russia suffered numerous defeats at the hands of the Japanese and eventually lost the war, which somehow remained unclear to the readers of *Light*. Along with drawings depicting military manoeuvres and battles, some peaceful (and even cheerful) moments were presented too, like the one depicting Cossacks and Russians dancing at the Khabarovka train station.[42] Two explanations can be offered for this prolific coverage: first, the development of visual culture elsewhere provided the publisher of *Light* with a huge reservoir of materials to borrow from; and second, the participation in this war of Russia, considered the liberator of Bulgaria after the Russo-Ottoman War of 1877–1878. Perhaps both played a role but, I am inclined to think, the latter mattered more. To support my belief, I will focus attention on the visual report of the existence of a Bulgarian hospital in Gandzhulin. It was published in the journal in 1905 (issue no. 5) and presented three photographs: *One corner of the healing rooms*; *View from the outside*, and *A Japanese officer receiving treatment in the hospital*. They were accompanied by a brief text which appeared two pages later: 'Bulgarian hospital in Gandzhulin. Only Bulgaria from all Slavic countries had the honour to establish its hospital in Manchuria. The pictures on p. 29 give us an idea about this hospital that functions in full order and continues to offer good services to the wounded Russians.'[43]

As already pointed out, the visual materials used as a means of communication had until now consisted mainly of reproductions of paintings, drawings and caricatures. Yet, photography was making headway – slowly but irreversibly – despite the fact the 'traditional' ways of visual representation prevailed. Photography is assumed to be a 'modern' instrument of communication worldwide and played a major role in the 'late visual revolution' in the Balkans in particular, to use the words of Karl Kaser.[44] The time for photographs and their domination was to come in Europe's southeast corner during the Balkan Wars of 1912–1913, which are considered by many to be the first 'modern' European wars at the end of the 'Long Nineteenth Century'. They mark the transition from traditional forms of visual coverage of events (paintings, cartoons, lithographs, postcards) to documentary media that will dominate the entire twentieth century: press photography (and photo reportage) and the documentary film.[45] This change started to become evident with the Turkish-Italian War of 1911–1912. A large number of illustrations related to the war were published in *Light*, many of them photographs.[46] In one issue a brief note starting '[T]he *Turkish-Italian war* is the most important event today for all of Europe'[47] underlined the importance of this war, often considered a prologue to the Balkan Wars.

Balkan Wars

The First Balkan War was a war between the Balkan League (formed by Bulgaria, Greece, Montenegro and Serbia) and the Ottoman Empire, in which Bulgaria and its neighbours were allies, if not friends. During the Second Balkan War, those allies became enemies. The pages of *Light* depicted both the euphoria at the beginning of the First Balkan War after the military victories of the Bulgarian army, and the stark change in relationship between the former allies.

'The Great War of Liberation'

Light began reporting the First Balkan War in issue no. 8–10, which appeared in early November 1912. Almost two-thirds of the pages in this issue were devoted to the war and almost half of them (17 out of 40) contained visual material – photographs, drawings, reproductions of paintings; some text was also present, although in most cases it did not relate to the pictures. A photograph of very poor quality of the Bulgarian King on horseback appeared on the cover page, but instead of a caption a sentence from the Manifesto to the Bulgarian people about opening the war against the Ottoman Empire was reproduced: 'We command the brave Bulgarian army to enter the Turkish territories.'[48] Although the entire Manifesto appeared on page 2, already on page 1 an announcement was made that fitted perfectly the discourse of the Manifesto: this war was 'the Great war of liberation of Macedonia and region of Adrianople'.[49] All further coverage of developments followed this idea: the war of 1912 was regarded as a continuation of the Russo-Ottoman War of 1877–1878 which restored the Bulgarian State after centuries-long Ottoman rule. The ideological preparation for this 'Second Liberation War' had started long before 1912[50] but when the war began the idea was used as a means of propaganda in the media for mobilization of the population. As one Bulgarian colonel pointed out, 'We will fight with the bodies of our peasants, but first we have to take their souls.'[51] Closely related to the idea of the liberating character of the First Balkan War, a special section called 'New Lands' appeared in several issues of *Light*, where pictures from places liberated by the Bulgarian army were published, including a photograph of the parade organized on 13 January 1913 in Seres (today in Greece) on the occasion of its liberation from Ottoman rule, photos from the town of Solun (Thessaloniki), etc. These photographs were accompanied by short explicatory texts.[52] The places where these photos were taken were part of the Bulgarian Principality for a very short time only because as a result of the Second Balkan War, they went to Greece. Nevertheless, their liberation was celebrated by Bulgarian society and its joy was mirrored on the pages of *Light*.

The first wartime issue of *Light* (1912, issue no. 8–10) established a kind of model that would be adhered to in the following months. The main topic of interest would be victories of the Bulgarian army. Many photographs by Dimitar A. Karastoyanov[53] and the already mentioned Georg Woltz, as well as those of known or unknown Bulgarian officers and soldiers, made their way onto the pages of *Light*. The siege of Adrianople (which began in early November 1912 and ended in late March 1913) and particularly the battle that resulted in the city being taken by Bulgarian (and Serbian) troops acquired a lot of space and attention in almost every issue of the journal (Ill. 4).[54] The journal failed to note the participation of the allied troops, despite the fact that at least

Ill. 4: 1913, no. 3, p. 28 – *Before the siege of Odrin* (Edirne), photo by Ivan Mihaylov.

47,000 Serbian soldiers fought on the battlefield, alongside the Bulgarian army (more than 100,000 troops). This omission, in my view, resulted directly from the main purpose of the media, namely propaganda and glorification of the victories of the Bulgarian army. The depiction of the battle at Lozengrad (Kırklareli) and the liberation of the town of Mustapha Pasha (nowadays Svilengrad) served the same ends.[55] In addition, a special rubric 'Bulgarian military leaders' presenting portraits of Bulgarian officers was published in the first war issue.[56] In the next volume of the journal (1913, issue no. 1–2), two other rubrics could be found: 'Heroes of the Liberation War' and/or 'Heroes fallen in the Great War' (Ill. 5).[57] The titles were often used interchangeably, since most of these men were victims of war, only a few survived.

Ill. 5: 1913, no. 1–2, p. 33 – *Heroes fallen in the Great War.*

The siege of Adrianople was the perfect event on which to publish many photographs of quite good quality. News from the point of view of the history of photography would have been coverage of the use of an airplane for the first time in military operations: during the attack of Adrianople, the city was bombarded from above by an aircraft.[58] Dimitar Karastoyanov, Georg Woltz and Georgi Georgiev took many pictures depicting the development of Bulgarian military aircraft, early aviators and their actions during the successful taking of the city of Adrianople, but none were published in *Light* or in any other media at the time. One explanation for this was wartime censorship. There was a complex set of rules relating to the activity of the press and the way war developments were represented was strictly controlled: there was a ban on any announcements relating to army movements or activities, fatalities, wounded soldiers, or text with an anti-war content.[59] Thus it could be claimed that the photographs published in *Light*, along with any text, were part of the official campaign that sought to mould the way people understood the war. The facts were presented selectively with the aim of encouraging active participation and self-sacrifice. Both the visual and textual messages aimed to produce an emotional rather than rational response in its readers.

Light's war coverage paid attention not only to the front line but also to the home front, where women also had a presence, the idea being that this war was a war for the whole nation, not only the Bulgarian army. In issue no. 3 of 1913, one Bulgarian female author used the following expressive language to convey this idea: 'the war of the cross against the crescent', 'the war against the Asian tigers, bearers of darkness and ignorance'.[60] Although rarely so, Bulgarian women did appear in the journal pictured in their roles as mothers or wives, nurses (Ill. 6), providers of clothing for men at the front line, heroes dealing with the agricultural challenges at home, and so on.[61]

During 'the Great War of Liberation', *Light* offered its readership a variety of visual materials aimed at further inspiring the Bulgarian people, including drawings and reproductions of paintings representing the brave behaviour and heroism of the soldiers at the front with their attendant captions, such as *Turkish defeat at Lozengrad* (Ill. 7) and *The decisive fight at Seliolu*, and caricatures mocking the cowardice of the enemy and featuring brave Bulgarian solders.[62] However, despite these materials, it was photographs that prevailed as a means of communication in the presentation of developments.[63]

Friends turn foes: the Second Balkan War

Not only the mood but also the mode of war coverage in *Light* changed during the Second Balkan War. This change took many directions. First, the number of photographs diminished considerably leaving more space for paintings and drawings. One possible explanation for this is that the Bulgarian army – though invincible on the battlefield – had to return to Bulgarian lands. Photos of glorious battles would be replaced by representations of refugees (not only Bulgarian) (Ill. 8).[64] The second major change was in relation to former allies who turn into enemies, a change that deserves a bit more attention. Interestingly, the activities of Bulgaria's allies during the First Balkan War found little room on the pages of *Light*. Only once did the journal publish the portraits

Ill. 6: 1913, no. 1–2, p. 53 – *The Heroes: Treatment at the Red Cross Hospital – Sofia.*

Ill. 7: 1912, no. 8–10, p. 4 – *Turkish defeat at Lozengrad.*

Ill. 8: 1913, no. 11–12, p. 4 – *Photos of refugees*.

of the four heads of the allied states (Greece, Bulgaria, Serbia and Montenegro) (Ill. 9) underlining the power of the alliance in the caption: 'The power of the Balkan states is in the union.'[65] Apart from this single allusion to the alliance, there were just one caricature of the Montenegrin inheritor of the throne and one painting representing the Montenegrin troops entering the town of Shkodër (historically known as Scutari; today in Albania).[66] The absence of the Greek and Serbian allies resulted, in my opinion, from the complicated situation that was the future division of Macedonia – the problem that was the cause of the Second Balkan War.

In the first issue of *Light* after the start of the Second Balkan War (August 1913, no. 7–8), there were several illustrations devoted to friends-turned-foes. On the one hand, the bravery of the Bulgarian army was promoted once more, alongside the cowardly behaviour of the former allies: *Bulgaria fights heroically her perfidious allies. Bulgarian artillery sowing death in the Serbian positions at Kotchani* (Ill. 10) or *Stampede of the Greeks along the valleys of Pehtchevo after their defeat by the right wing of the Bulgarian army*.[67] In addition, the atrocities of the Greek army were explicitly pictured a few times: *The Greek 'heroism' against Bulgarian military unit in Thessaloniki*; *The Greek*

Ill. 9: 1913, no. 1, p. 60 – *The force of the Balkan states is in the agreement* (portraits of the four heads of the allied states).

Ill. 10: 1913, no. 7–8, p. 1 – *Bulgaria fights heroically her perfidious allies. Bulgarian artillery sowing death in the Serbian positions at Kotchani.*

massacres upon Bulgarian people in Kukush. Devious lies of the Greek King (Ill. 11); *Greek cruelty against a boy*.[68] On the other hand, the humane treatment of the Serbian war captives was underlined by publishing a couple of photographs picturing them in Sofia, unlike the non-humane 'barbarian' reception the Bulgarian war captives suffered in Belgrade.[69]

The bitter dissatisfaction of the Bulgarian people with developments in the wars and their outcomes was widely shared by the editor of *Light*. Along with the bitterness,

Ill. 11: 1913, no. 7–8, p. 29 – *The Greek massacres upon Bulgarian people in Kukush. Devious lies of the Greek King.*

however, there was a shared hope for the future: 'The Bulgarian army has carried on a one-year irrepressible war, fighting at several fronts at once, against five enemies, and after numerous victims remained yet invincible. This non-exhausting energy of the Bulgarian upholds him at untouchable heights in the eyes of the whole world. The future belongs to the brave peoples.'[70] The jump from the point of deep dissatisfaction with the results of the Balkan Wars to the appearance of a wish for revenge was very short. An attempt at this, both unsuccessful and devastating, was made during the First World War when Bulgaria joined the Central Powers.

The Great War

The Great War descended on the Bulgarian reading public only shortly after having experienced the Balkan Wars. In 1912–1913, as already discussed, two major changes occurred: first, photo reportage from the front line was used for the first time in the Balkans; second, and also for the first time, special arrangements were introduced for journalists and photographers. As a result, there was a proliferation of visual materials covering developments but their publication was the subject of wartime censorship. This continued to be the case during the First World War and it seems reasonable to ask the question whether the coverage of war in *Light* – and the visual coverage in particular – in 1912–1913 established a model to be followed in 1914–1918; in other words, was there a continuity in the way war was represented visually.

The coverage of the Great War in general followed an already established pattern. Yet, some differences in the way of presenting the events at the beginning of the war and after October 1915 when Bulgaria entered the fray can be traced. For this reason, I will briefly elaborate on the first period and then pay more attention to the years of Bulgaria's involvement.

At the outset of war in 1914, the journal *Light* first referred to the German-French war, Russian-German war, etc.; its captions then changed to reflect a European war or Great Inter-European war; and finally, from early 1916, it became the Great War. From the point of view of the visual, there were two main characteristics. First, many pictures showed 'the horrors of war', both at the Western and Eastern front: wounded Germans in the city of Lyon, French peasants being shot by German soldiers, British billiard players with just one arm, etc.[71] Some materials depicting everyday life at the front as well as behind the lines were also published.[72] Second, reminders (both textual and visual) of the glorious victories of the Bulgarian army during the First Balkan War appeared. This is not surprising: despite the diplomatic defeat after the Second Balkan War, the military victories of the Bulgarian army continued to be a source of national pride for the Bulgarian people. There were reminders not only of successful battles such as at Bulair[73] and Adrianople[74] but also commemorations of heroes of the 'Great War of Liberation'.[75] All this disappeared from the pages of *Light* with the entry of Bulgaria into the war in October 1915, only to reappear in March 1917 on the occasion of the Bulgarian military actions in Dobrudzha in late 1916, with the aim of recalling the previous direct confrontation between the Bulgarian and Romanian armies in 1913.[76]

During the initial period of the war, often there were just captions and no explanations related to the visual representations – neither texts, nor a few lines below or next to the illustrations. This is in contrast to the practice during the Balkan Wars, when at the end of all issues of *Light* there were brief explanatory notes related to the visual material published on the pages before. After Bulgaria entered the war and from issue no. 8 of 1915, one can find once more short texts along with the pictorial representations. Despite the timing, I am very cautious in looking for a direct connection between this change of pattern and Bulgaria entering the war. Rather, I see it as a result of the influence of the illustrated press in Central Europe, in Germany and Austria-Hungary in particular.

'All under arms!'

On 14 October 1915, King Ferdinand's Manifesto for declaring war on Serbia was issued. The need for mobilization and enhancement of the military spirit of the Bulgarian people and army resulted in a media campaign, in which the journal *Light* took part. The focus on the need for and requirements of propaganda may be seen as one of the main similarities with the Balkan Wars. Mobilization of the public spirit through recall of the glorious past made way to another strategy, already adopted in 1912–1913: first, call-up to the army was praised in various ways, then immediately after that there appeared glorification of previous successful military actions by the Bulgarian army. Pictures played their role too. For example, in the autumn of 1915, several photographs representing the excitement of the Bulgarian people were published, with suitable captions: *All under arms. Our heroes going to the field of honour and glory are sent with blessings and acclamations by the people*; *Mobilized Bulgaria. A group of reserves of the eldest age who participated in the first war in which they covered their foreheads with laurels*; *To the border. A group of infantry all in flowers and singing heads to the border*; *Bulgarian State Railways provides for the glorious Bulgarian heroes*, and so on.⁷⁷

The main theme became the victorious activities of the Bulgarian army. There are many examples of texts and photographs, reproductions, drawings, etc., with short captions next to them showing the successful exploits of Bulgarian troops. Special attention was paid to the actions of the Bulgarian army (Ill. 12) and administration in the occupied territories in Macedonia.⁷⁸ The return of the representatives of the Bulgarian church was also discussed and presented visually, including the photograph captioned *Mitropolit Gerasim coming back to the town of Tikvesh*.⁷⁹

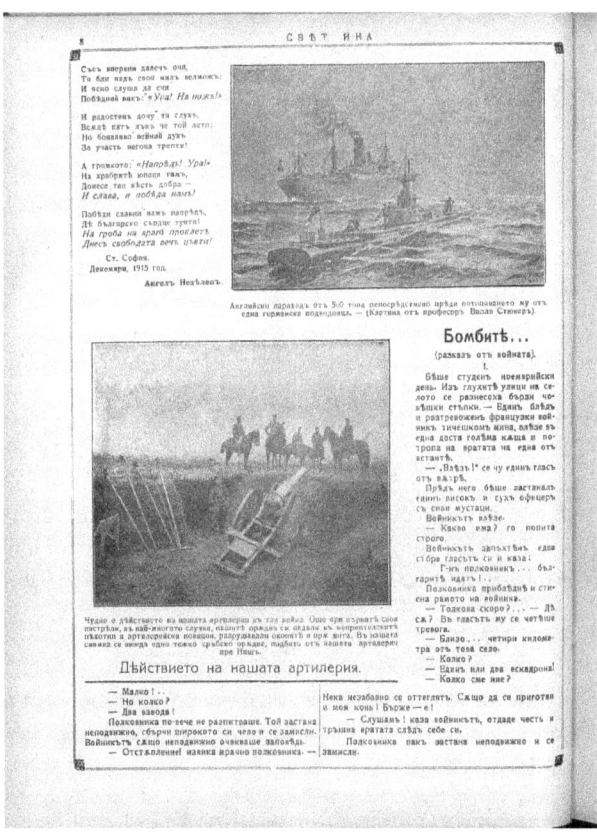

Ill. 12: 1916, no. 3, p. 8 – *The actions of our artillery*.

Ill. 13: 1916, no. 9–10, p. 5 – *The tandem of pilots Captain Ivanov and Lieutenant Vakafchiev.*

The media also presented the achievements of Bulgarian airmen. They had already attracted the attention of the press, both at home and abroad, at the time of the siege of Adrianople in 1913. During the First World War, the readership of *Light* admired again the tandem of pilots Captain Ivanov and Lieutenant Vakafchiev (Ill. 13); a group of the first class of the Bulgarian Airplane School (1915–1916); and Lieutenant Manov, who was awarded an order of honour for his bravery.[80] Furthermore, similar to the time of the Balkan Wars, throughout the First World War a lot of information was accompanied by images of Bulgarian military heroes, most fallen in battle.[81]

Allies[82]

There was one significant difference in the visual war coverage between the Great War and the Balkan Wars: contrary to the sporadic presence of Bulgaria's allies on the pages of *Light* in 1912–1913, during the First World War the opposite is apparent. During the first year of the war when Bulgaria remained neutral, the presence of both fighting coalitions tended to be balanced. Immediately after Bulgaria entered the war, the attention devoted to Bulgaria's allies increased enormously; consequently, the space that remained for enemies gradually diminished. Most often the Germans were the focus of attention, followed by the Austro-Hungarians, while the Turks reached the pages of *Light* in exceptional circumstances only.

Let me introduce a few pictures that directly promote the idea of alliance. At the beginning of 1916, a photograph of seven officers, walking arm-in-arm in the street, was published. This picture had the title *The Central Alliance* and appeared twice in the same issue in early 1916, both on the cover and inside the journal (Ill. 14).[83] The same allusion to alliance was drawn in the summer of 1916: 'The German illustrations offer the upper interesting photo called by them *The Balkan train*. These are German, Austrian, Hungarian, Bulgarian and Turkish officers in Wiesbaden, whose order follows the order of the states which the Balkan train crosses. The Bulgarian officer is Captain Trayko Kotsev.'[84]

Regardless of whether they were on the front or behind the lines, during the First World War the allies of Bulgaria could be found in almost all issues of *Light*: either portraits of their heads of states and military leaders, or coverage of some of their military achievements and victories. Most frequent 'visitors' to the journal were Field Marshal August von Mackensen (Ill. 15)[85] and Marshal Paul von Hindenburg (Ill. 16),[86]

Ill. 14: 1916, no. 2, p. 12 – *The Central Union*.

Ill. 15: 1916, no. 11–12, p. 13 – *General August von Mackensen at the Dobrudzha front.*

although Bulgarians were introduced to other officers of the German and Austro-Hungarian armies also.[87] These allied officers were often accompanied by senior officers of the Bulgarian army or by King Ferdinand and/or Bulgarian prime minister Radoslavov.[88] The victories of the German army received, as one would expect, a lot of attention and were followed strictly by the publisher in both text and pictures.[89] In addition, information about some cultural events, such as the Bulgarian exposition in Berlin, was also presented to the readership of the journal.[90]

It is quite curious the way in which the alliance with the Ottoman Empire, the centuries-old enemy, was presented. Information regarding the activities of the Ottoman army was almost absent. In fact, the Ottomans appeared only when all of Bulgaria's allies were the focus of attention, as in the group photographs mentioned above. Apart from this, the editor of *Light* drew the attention of its readers to this not-particularly-loved-ally of Bulgaria only twice during the whole war: first, on the occasion of the murder of Naum Tyufekchiev, when next to his portrait another photograph was published reminding readers of the role he played in negotiating the Ottoman-Bulgarian agreement in 1915;[91] and second, when the battles in the area of the Suez Canal took place, in which Turkish forces also participated.[92]

Ill. 16: 1916, no. 1, p. 12 – *Field Marshal Paul von Hindenburg in front of his headquarters at the Eastern front.*

Enemies

Unlike her allies, Bulgaria's enemies did not frequent the pages of *Light* very often. In addition, they were represented in a very different manner. The directly drawn allusion to black ('Negroes') and dirty should be outlined immediately. Images of 'Negroes' were published a few times, and introduced, for example, as *Types of Anglo-French culture at the Macedonian front* (Ill. 17)[93] or, alternatively, with an accompanying note: 'Our readers know that the French army is a mixture of different races. Here one Sudanese is presented, a French soldier, interrogated by a German officer in the presence of one more who-knows-of-which-state-and-race French soldier.'[94] Readers' attention was focused in a similar way on the dirtiness of captured Russian soldiers: the editor pointed to the contrast before and after they had a bath (Ill. 18).[95]

Special attention was reserved for Bulgaria's neighbours, all of which – except the Ottoman Empire – were on the other side of the front line. Similar to the case of the Second Balkan War, during the Great War any direct confrontation resulted in an

Ill. 17: 1915, no. 9–12, p. 21 – *French 'culture' at the Macedonian front*.

increase in attention. This was particularly true when Bulgarian troops engaged in battles with the Romanians in Dobrudzha in late 1916. On the cover page of the autumn issue of that year, a photograph was published under the title *The Wallachian massacres in Dobrudzha* (Ill. 19), accompanied by the following text:

> Powerless against the powerful attack of our troops the Wallachian people poured all their anger over the Bulgarian population in Dobrodzha. The population of entire villages was slaughtered, property robbed and burned. Dobrich, Baldzha, Kali Petrovo and several other settlements experienced the cruelty of the Wallachian armed mobs. Our photo shows the corpses of Bulgarians killed in Dobrudzha by the Wallachians and their accomplices, Russians and Serbians. Above them are the relatives of the victims who mourn.

The same picture appeared again in the following issue, but this time only with a caption, without any text.[96] The juxtaposition of the two drawings *The heroism of Mamuligarescu in 1913* and *His inglorious escape in 1916* in one of the first issues of

Ill. 18: 1916, no. 1, p. 8 – *Russian captives at the time of their capture* vs. *Cleaned by the Germans after capture.*

1917 also does not come as a surprise.[97] Victories of the Bulgarian army and the return of Dobrudzha were considered by the editor of *Light* – as well as by the majority of the Bulgarian people at the time – as compensation for the drama experienced three years previously. A similar message was communicated by photographs of some Romanian officers, prisoners of the Bulgarian army.[98] Despite the reduction in the number of photographs and augmentation of reproductions of paintings and drawings on the pages of *Light*, not many stereotypical images were reactivated and used as a means of wartime propaganda, compared with some satirical journals and newspapers in which many caricatures of Serbs, Greeks and Romanians appeared.[99]

Conclusion

To wrap up, I would like to go back to the questions asked at the start of this chapter. Some of them have been explicitly addressed: I have tried to show the kind of coverage of uprisings and wars that the journal *Light* offered to its readership, and I have looked at the different ways in which allies and enemies (or self and the other) were portrayed.

Ill. 19: 1916, no. 9–10, p. 1 – *The Wallachian massacres in Dobrudzha*.

It might appear to some as if the question of the visibility of women remained unanswered. Yet, it has been tackled too. The fact is that in contrast to the female Bulgarian author who appeared in issue no. 3 of 1913 and a few pictures of nurses at the front or in hospitals during the Balkan Wars, there was nothing on the pages of *Light* to list during the First World War. Bulgarian women were totally absent, and only two pieces of information regarding women appeared at the end of 1917/early 1918, which dealt respectively with one Russian female military unit and a few American women who volunteered for the USA navy.[100] And that is about it regarding the visibility of women during wartime in both text and photographs in the illustrated journal *Light*. Women and children were present in some drawings that depicted violence, such as those visualizing the massacres of Armenians at the end of the nineteenth century, or those portraying the cruelty of Greek troops during the Second Balkan War. I believe the poor visibility of women in the representation of uprisings and wars was mainly due to their absence from the front line.

Last but not least, one of the questions deserves special attention: the types of images – or means of communication – that predominated, as well as the more general question about the role of images in the coverage. From the point of view of the visual,

Ill. 20: 1916, no. 4, p. 12 – *Theatre at the front*.

the uprisings and wars were covered in the Bulgarian illustrated press, exemplified here by its herald *Light*, by a mix of 'traditional' and 'modern' representations. Drawings and reproductions of paintings, lithographs and cartoons[101] were used alongside the new means of representation, press photography, as is evident on the pages of *Light*. At the turn of the century, the photographs were of wars far from Bulgaria's borders. With the wars in the 1910s, the use of photography increased significantly. And it was not only professional photographers such as brothers Dimitar and Ivan Karastoyanov as well as Georg Woltz who were reporting from the front line. Some officers were also taking pictures and submitting them for publication, including Lieutenant Minkov and Lieutenant Maleev, solder Ivan Mihailov and the military engineer L. Valchev. The new forms of visual media (photography but also the documentary films screened for the first time during the Balkan Wars) pretended to reproduce reality and truth. However, as Peter Burke states, it would be 'unwise to attribute an 'innocent eye', in the sense of a gaze which is totally objective, free from expectations or prejudices of any kind'[102] to these means of communication. Particularly so in the case of the military photographers who were constrained by wartime censorship.

In terms of types of images and which media was used to depict what kind of events, one opposition should be outlined: time at rest at the front line was depicted mainly by photographs (Ill. 20),[103] whereas drawings and reproductions of paintings were used to depict battles and violent scenes of uprisings. One possible explanation for this could involve 'technology': although photo reportage was used for the first time in the Balkans during the Balkan Wars, the photographic technique was not advanced enough to allow battles to be photographed in real time. That is why photography was used to depict mainly periods of calm on the front – in short, all what was visible before and after a battle – while any fighting was left to the pencil and brush of the artists.[104]

As for the role of images, the visual material was used by the editor of *Light* in two main ways, the first of which was as a tool for maintaining the collective memory. The aim was to commemorate important *lieux de mémoirs* (à la Pierre Nora) in the recent history of the Bulgarian people and state, for example, recalling the Serbo-Bulgarian war of 1885 during the 1890s or reminding the readership of the victorious battles of the Bulgarian army in the First Balkan War during the Great War. Second, it was used as a means of communicating news about contemporary events. This way of using the visual gradually turned into a major feature of representation at the time of the Balkan Wars. Of course, to the extent one monthly journal like *Light* could pretend to provide its readers with an in-time coverage from the front lines.

Although I base my conclusions on only the visual material in *Light* – and this was clearly emphasized throughout the text – I would like to clarify that, on the one hand, one could consider *Light* a case study but, on the other hand, there was no other illustrated journal of the time in Bulgaria that could be compared with it. There were other visual representations of various uprisings and wars in other printed outlets and these too would have had an impact. However, they were too dispersed, appearing in various newspapers and journals rather accidentally, and a discussion of them all was not possible here.

In a brief chapter such as this, one can only cover a limited selection of research questions. I am fully aware of the fact that there are more aspects that could have been addressed, such as the audience – the readership of *Light* – since the meaning of an image depends a great deal on what the public constructs with it. Here I can only speculate, although that speculation is based on observation and accumulated expertise: during wartime, visual materials were used extensively for mobilization of the population and propaganda and bearing in mind the existence of censorship, we may assume that what the editor of the journal *Light* made its Bulgarian readership take notice of was exactly what the Bulgarian government wanted the Bulgarian people to pay attention to.[105]

Notes

1   Some of the ideas discussed here – particularly those related to the Balkan Wars – have already been developed elsewhere. See D. Parusheva, 'Light on War: Visual Representation of Wars and Violence in Bulgaria, End of the Nineteenth and Early Twentieth Century', *Bulgarska etnologiya* [Bulgarian Ethnology], 3 (2014), pp. 275–298 [in Bulgarian].
2   P. Burke, *Eyewitnessing: The Uses of Images as Historical Evidence*. London: Reaktion Books, 2001, p. 9 ff.

3   For example, B. Brennen and H. Hardt, 'Introduction', in B. Brennen and H. Hardt (eds.), *Picturing the Past: Media, History, and Photography*. Urbana, IL: University of Illinois Press, 1999; M. Jay, 'Cultural Relativism and the Visual Turn', *Journal of Visual Culture*, 1, no. 3 (2002), pp. 267-278.
4   Just a few examples: J. Beurier, *Images et violence: 1914-1918. Quand le miroir racontait la Grande Guerre*. Paris: Nouveau monde, 2007; Beurier, 'Information, Censorship or Propaganda? The Illustrated French Press in the First World War', in H. Jones, J. O'Brien and C. Schmidt-Supprian (eds.), *Untold War: New Perspectives in First World War Studies*. Leiden: Brill, 2008, pp. 293-324; C. Marty, 'Un point de fuite dans le réel? Les représentations de combats dans les journaux illustrés (1914-1918)', *Matériaux pour l'histoire de notre temps*, 3 (2008), pp. 62-66; A. Lafon, La photographie mobilisée 1914-1918', *Annales de Bretagne et des Pays de l'Ouest*, no. 123-3 (2016), pp. 33-49; H. Lima and J. Pedro Sousa, 'A ilustração portuguesa e cobertura da Primeira Guerra Mundial (1914-1918): imagens da guerra em contextos de censura e propaganda', in *A Grande Guerra (1914-1918): problemáticas e representações*. Porto: CITCEM, 2015. Cf. M Griffin, 'The Great War Photographs: Constructing Myths of History and Photojournalism', in B. Brennen and H. Hardt (eds.), *Picturing the Past: Media, History, and Photography*. Urbana, IL: University of Illinois Press, 1999, pp. 122-157.
5   K. Kaser, *Andere Blicke. Religion und visuelle Kultur auf dem Balkan und im Nahen Osten*. Vienna: Böhlau Verlag, 2013.
6   See, for example, the following edited volumes: T. Sindbaek and M. Hartmuth (eds.), *Images of Imperial Legacy: Modern Discourses on the Social and Cultural Impact of Ottoman and Habsburg Rule in Southeast Europe*. Münster: Lit, 2011; and E. Pistrick, N. Scaldaferri and G. Schwörer (eds.), *Audiovisual Media and Identity Issues in Southeastern Europe*. Newcastle upon Tyne: Cambridge Scholars Publishing, 2011. See also: M. Özen, 'Visual Representation and Propaganda: Early Film and Postcards in the Ottoman Empire, 1895-1914', *Early Popular Visual Culture*, 6, no. 2 (2008), pp. 145-157; A. Anagnostopoulos, 'Picturing Public Space: Ethnicity and Gender in Picture Postcards of Iraklio, Crete, at the Beginning of the 20th Century', in E. Pistrick, N. Scaldaferri and G. Schwörer (eds.), *Audiovisual Media and Identity Issues in Southeastern Europe*. Newcastle upon Tyne: Cambridge Scholars Publishing, 2011, pp. 171-191; A. Kassabova, 'Inclusion and Exclusion: The Role of Photography in the Nation-Building Process in Bulgaria from Approximately 1860 to World War I', in D. Demski, I. Kristóf and K. Baraniecka-Olszewska (eds.), *Competing Eyes: Visual Encounters with Alterity in Central and Eastern Europe*. Budapest: L'Harmattan, 2013, pp. 112-139.
7   Among them, K. Kaser, 'Visualizing the Balkans: The Balkan Wars, the Great War and Visual Modernity', *Balgarska etnologia* [Bulgarian Ethnology], 3 (2014), pp. 332-351 [in Bulgarian], with a focus on photography and cinema, and Parusheva, 'Light on War'. See also K. Kaser, Visual Modernity and the Balkan Wars, 1912-13', in Dimitris Stamatopoulos (ed.), *Balkan Nationalism(s) and the Ottoman Empire*, vol. II: *Political Violence and the Balkan Wars*. Istanbul: Isis Press, 2015, pp. 143-164.
8   I shall refer to it as *Light*, for the sake of presentation.
9   1894, no. 9-10, p. 152.
10 This war was closely related to another memorable event in Bulgarian history, the unification of the Principality of Bulgaria with the province of Eastern Rumelia in September 1885 – an event which some scholars read through the lens of uprising though I personally am more inclined to think of it as a political scenario successfully performed by the Bulgarian elites in the Principality and in Eastern Rumelia.

11 Antoni Piotrowski (1853-1924) arrived in Bulgaria in 1879 as a correspondent of the British journals *Graphic* and *Illustrated London News*, and of the French *Illustration* and *Le monde illustré*. During the Serbo-Bulgarian war he volunteered for the front line. His nine paintings depicting scenes from the war have been obtained by the Bulgarian State and now hang in the National Museum of Military History in Sofia.
12 See 1893, no. 3, p. 53; 1893, no. 4, pp. 108-109; 1893, no. 6, p. 125; 1893, no. 6, p. 128; 1896, no. 6, p. 83; 1896, no. 7, p. 103.
13 1896, no. 6, p. 95 (italic in the journal – D.P.).
14 1907, no. 11-12, pp. 20-21.
15 1896, no. 12, p. 181.
16 1895, no. 5, p. 68; 1896, no. 1, p. 4; 1896, no. 1, p. 5; 1896, no. 9-10, p. 133.
17 1896, no. 11, p. 137; 1896, no. 12, p. 177.
18 I will list the captions of the visual materials related to the Macedonian Question because they – or at least most of them – speak volumes: 1903, no. 1, p. 5 – three photographs, all under the same caption *Macedonian movement: A gunfight at Macedonian border, Macedonian Bey in a bad mood* and *Macedonian woman from the region of Debar*; p. 9 –*Rebellion in Macedonia. The battle at the village of Kresna* – drawing by Mr. Berberov; p. 13 – three studio photographs under a common caption *Diplomacy and the Macedonian Question: Prime Minister Dr. S. Danev, Mr. G. Westman, Russian representative in Plovdiv*, and *Dr. D. Stantchov, King's plenipotentiary in Petersburg*; 1903, no. 3, p. 13 – *Events in Macedonia*: two photographs, *Macedonian refugees in Rila Monastery* and *Heroes and trophies* (see the description in the text); 1903, no. 4, p. 1 – one drawing representing men with yataghans killing people in the street with the ironic title *In Turkey everything is calm*; p. 5 – four portraits of *Macedonian heroes*: General Tsontchev, Colonel Nikolov, Boris Sarafov and Colonel Yankov; 1903, no. 5, p. 13 – two photographs, *Macedonia: Their village was burned* and *A street in Skopje*; 1903, no. 9, p. 21 – a photograph (?) with the caption *In the heart of Macedonia. The speech of the chieftain*; p. 29 – a drawing, *Fighters for Macedonian freedom. A break*; 1903, no. 11-12, p. 9 – a drawing, *Macedonian villages. Devastation by fire and sword*; p. 17 – a drawing, *At Bitola train station. The sentenced to exile*; p. 21 – a photograph by Berberov, *In the heart of the Pirin Mountains. Rebellions and refugees*; p. 33 – a drawing, *Funeral procession in Sofia. Commemoration of Macedonian victims*.
19 1903, no. 3, p. 13.
20 E. Eldem, 'Powerful Images – The Dissemination and Impact of Photography in the Ottoman Empire, 1870-1914', in Z. Çelik and E. Eldem (eds.), *Camera Ottomana: Photography and Modernity in the Ottoman Empire 1840-1914*. Istanbul: Koç University Press, 2015, pp. 120-121.
21 Ibid., p. 127.
22 1904, no. 7, p. 21.
23 1906, no. 10-11, p. 1; 1906, no. 12, p. 1. Georg Woltz (1857-?) was a prominent photographer in Sofia at the beginning of the twentieth century. Some have claimed he was a court photographer of King Ferdinand; however, there is very little reliable information about him.
24 1904, no. 5, p. 9 (two photographs).
25 1904, no. 5, p. 31.
26 1908, no. 7-8, p. 5 – two photographs with a common title, *Events in Turkey*; p. 25 – three photographs under the caption *Freedom in Macedonia: Macedonian people welcome the freedom with songs and dances, On the way to the prison. One day before*

the putsch and *The last gallows*; p. 29 – one photograph, *The people of Thessaloniki acclaim the proclaimed constitution*, and a portrait of the major Enver Bey (drawing).

27   1908, no. 7–8, p. 31.
28   1908, no. 9, p. 32 and 1909, no. 2, p. 28.
29   For example, 1910, no. 7–8, p. 5 – two photographs, *The most recent Macedonian refugees* and *Macedonian people tortured by the Turkish authorities*.
30   1906, no. 9, p. 9; text on p. 31.
31   For example, 1897, no. 5, pp. 8–9 – three drawings by different authors: *The correspondents of the foreign newspapers in the Greek lager, View of the town of Larisa* and *Battle of the Greek forces next to Farsala*; 1897, no. 6, p. 9 – *Greek-Turkish War, the decisive battle at Velestino* (drawing). Caricatures: 1897, no. 6, p. 16; 1898, no. 4, p. 16; 1898, no. 12, p. 16.
32   Quotation from 1897, no. 6, p. 16.
33   1898, no. 4, p. 9; 1898, no. 5–6, p. 11; 1898, no. 7, p. 9.
34   1898, no. 5–6, p. 13; 1898, no. 7, p. 15; 1898, no. 8, p. 5.
35   1898, no. 5–6, p. 21; 1898, no. 7, p. 9.
36   1898, no. 8, p. 9.
37   1898, no. 5–6, p. 17 – four photographs: *Spanish-American war. The hunger in Cuba*.
38   1899, no. 11–12, p. 5; 1900, no. 4, pp. 8, 10; 1900, no. 6, p. 12.
39   1899, no. 11–12, p. 20.
40   1904, no. 2 – three drawings (pp. 8, 9, 29) and three caricatures (pp. 30, 32); 1904, no. 3 – four drawings (pp. 1, 17, 24, 25); 1904, no. 4 – nine drawings on pp. 1, 9 (two), 13 (two), 17, 21, 25 and 29; 1904, no. 5, p. 5 – one drawing; 1904, no. 6 – one photograph (p. 1) and one drawing (p. 29); 1904, no. 7 – one drawing (p. 1) and two caricatures (p. 32); 1904, no. 8–9 – three drawings (pp. 5, 9, 17); 1904, no. 11 – two drawings (pp. 1, 17); 1904, no. 12 – two drawings (pp. 21, 25). In 1905, visual material appeared less often but was still present: 1905, no. 1, pp. 1, 9; 1905, no. 2, pp. 1, 9, 20, 21, 25; 1905, no. 3, p. 25; 1905, no. 5, pp. 13, 29; 1905, no. 10, pp. 9, 29, 32.
41   For example, 1904, no. 4, p. 21; 1904, no. 5, p. 29; 1904, no. 8–9, p. 5.
42   1904, no. 8–9, p. 9.
43   1905, no. 5, pictures on p. 29 and text on p. 31. The hospital was established under the leadership of the Bulgarian military doctor Colonel Dimitar Kiranov; a few more doctors and three nurses took part. See K. Bankova, 'Bulgarian Sanitary Mission in the Russo-Japanese War], *Voennoistoricheski sbornik* [Military Historical Collection], 2 (2004), pp. 43–49 [in Bulgarian].
44   Kaser, *Andere Blicke*, p. 131 ff.
45   Kaser, 'Visualizing the Balkans', pp. 336–341.
46   1911, no. 9–10, p. 24 – two photographs, p. 25 – a drawing; 1911, no. 11–12, p. 1 – two photographs, p. 4 – two photographs; 1912, no. 1, p. 1 (photograph), p. 17 (photograph). See also 1912, no. 8–10, p. 24 – two pictures (it is unclear whether they are drawings or photographs) of the last battles in Tripoli, after the first Balkan War had started.
47   1911, no. 11–12, 31.
48   1912, no. 8–10, cover page.
49   Western Europe used the name Adrianople for the biggest city in Eastern Thrace at the time (its Roman name); the Turks called it Edirne, while the Bulgarian name for the city was Odrin.
50   A patriotic mood was deliberately created and maintained in the schools and in the army. Naum Kaychev offers a comparison between the Bulgarian and Serbian cases

with respect to these developments. See N. Kaychev, *Macedonia Coveted... Army, School, and the Building of Nation in Serbia and Bulgaria (1878-1912)*. Sofia: Paradigma, 2003 [in Bulgarian].

51 Quoted after A. Kassabova, 'Identities in Frame: Photography and the Construction of a 'National Body' in Bulgaria (approx. 1860 to World War I)', in P. Hristov (ed.), *Migration and Identity: Historical, Cultural and Linguistic Dimensions of Mobility in the Balkans*. Sofia: Paradigma, 2012, pp. 73–86.

52 1913, no. 4, p. 20; 1913, no. 4, p. 21.

53 Dimitar Atanasov Karastoyanov (1856-1919) was born in the family of Anastas Nikolov Stoyanovich/Karastoyanov in 1856 in Samokov. Dimitar learned the craft from his father, the court photographer in Belgrade in the 1860s and 1870s. After 1878 he and his brother Ivan inherited his father's photographic studio – one of the first studios in Sofia. From 1886 they operated in separate studios but both were among the most prominent photographers in Bulgaria. During the Balkan Wars, D. Karastoyanov was military photographer with the headquarters of the Bulgarian army. For more information about his life and work, see P. Boev, 'Dimitar Karastoyanov 1856-1919', *Balgarsko foto* [Bulgarian Photo], 7 (1973), pp. 28–30.

54 1912, no. 8-10, pp. 1, 8 (photos by Karastoyanov), p. 33 (photo by Woltz), pp. 4, 8; 1913, no. 1-2, p. 53 (drawing); 1913, no. 3, pp. 17, 20, 21, 24, 25, 28, 29; 1913, no. 4, pp. 1, 5, 12, 13, 16, etc.

55 1912, no. 8-10, p. 4 (battle at Lozengrad, drawing by Shoylev), pp. 25, 32 (about Mustapha pasha).

56 1912, no. 8-10, pp. 34-35; 1913, no. 1-2, p. 52; 1913, no. 3, p. 25 etc.

57 1912, no. 8-10, p. 37; 1913, no. 1-2, pp. 33, 48; no. 4, p. 17; no. 5, p. 17; no 7-8, p. 17; no. 9, p. 7, etc.

58 The lack of information led the Bulgarian public to believe that Bulgarian pilots were the first who made an aerial bombardment whereas, in fact, it was the Italian Giulio Gavotti during the Turkish-Italian War in 1911.

59 For further elaboration on this topic, see Y. Konstantinova, '"Political Propaganda in Bulgaria During the Balkan Wars', *Etudes balkaniques*, 2, no. 3 (2011), pp. 79–116 and K Peeva, 'Military Correspondents Against Censorship During the Balkan War', in *Svilengrad i Balkanskite voyni*. Veliko Tarnovo: Faber, 2013, pp. 210–233 [in Bulgarian].

60 1913, no. 3, pp. 19-20 – E. Dryanovska, 'The role of the Bulgarian woman in the Balkan Liberation war'.

61 See, for example, the photograph by Ivan Karastoyanov in 1913, no. 1-2, p. 1.

62 See, respectively: 1912, no. 8-10, p. 4 (drawing by Shoylev); 1913, no. 3, p. 1; 1913, no. 3, p. 32 (caricature by Andro).

63 1913, no. 3, pp. 4, 17, 21, 24, 25, 28, 29; 1913, no. 4, pp. 5, 12; 1913, no. 5, p. 8, etc.

64 1913, no. 11-12, p. 4; 1913, no. 11-12, p. 10. Some poetry devoted to these people was also published. See 1913, no. 11-12, p. 5 ('To the refugees', 'On the sad way').

65 1913, no. 1, p. 60.

66 1912, no. 8-10, p. 40 and 1913, no. 5, p. 13.

67 1913, no. 7-8, pp. 1 and 25.

68 1913, no. 7-8, pp. 21, 29 and 1913, no. 11-12, p. 17.

69 1913, no. 9, pp. 8 and 20.

70 1913, no. 9, p. 21.

71 For example, 1915, no. 4, p. 5 – five photographs under the caption *The Horrors of the War*.

72 See, for example, 1915, no. 5–6, p. 21 – *Grandfather blesses his grandson-soldier, Easter entertainment at Russian positions. Playing with bottles on the head, Letter to the father-solider* [drawing], etc.
73 1914, no. 10–12, p. 33 (two photographs, with text on pp. 34–35).
74 See 1915, no. 3, pp. 5, 8, 25 and 28. The majority of the photos from Adrianople were taken by Dimitar Karastoyanov.
75 For example, 1914, no. 8–9, p. 8; 1915, no. 4, p. 16; 1915, no. 8, p. 5.
76 1917, no. 3, p. 4 – *The heroism of Mamuligarescu in 1913* [drawing]. Mamuligarescu is a pejorative name for Romanian people, stereotypically used by Bulgarians at the time.
77 1915, no. 9–12, pp. 4, 5, 8, 9.
78 For example, 1916, no. 2, p. 8 – *Battles in Veles*; 1916, no. 3, p. 8 – *The actions of our artillery* [ill. 12]; 1916, no. 3, p. 4 – *Our forces next to Ohrid*; 1917, no. 5, p. 12 – *A fest in the New Bulgaria*, etc. The term 'occupied' is used by the editors of the journal.
79 1916, no. 7, p. 8.
80 1916, no. 9–10, p. 5; 1916, no. 11–12, p. 1 (same picture on the cover also); 1916, no. 11–12, p. 4 – *The downloaded plane* (five photographs with text; one of them represents Lieutenant Manov).
81 1916, no. 6, p. 13; 1917, no. 2, p. 5; 1917, no. 5, p. 4; 1918, no. 7–8, p. 9, etc.
82 Here *allies* denotes Bulgarian allies in the First World War and not the name of the other war coalition, the Allies (based on the Triple Entente).
83 1916, no. 2, cover and p. 12.
84 1916, no. 7, p. 8.
85 In October 1915, August von Mackensen took command of all German, Austro-Hungarian and Bulgarian armies fighting against Serbia; in the autumn of 1916, he commanded the successful campaign of German, Ottoman and Bulgarian troops against Romania. For his presence in *Light*, see 1915, no. 9–12, cover page; 1916, no. 1, p. 13; 1916, no. 11–12, p. 13 [ill. 15]; 1917, no. 2, p. 9; 1917, no. 3, p. 12; 1917, no. 4, p. 12, etc.
86 Paul von Hindenburg commanded the Headquarters of the German army from 1916 on; later he was President of Germany (1925–1934). As an example of his photos in *Light*, see 1916, no. 1, p. 12.
87 For example, 1918, no. 6, cover – *Mr Colonel von Massov military mandatary of the HM German Emperor*.
88 1916, no. 2, pp. 1, 4; 1916, no. 4, pp. 5, 13.
89 For example, 1915, no. 8, p. 17 – *Russian defeat*.
90 1916, no. 7, p. 13.
91 1916, no. 5, p. 13 – *Tallat Bey, Naum Tyufekchiev, Halil Bey and Enver Pasha in the salon of the Enver Pasha's palace, after the banquet on the occasion of signing the Turkish-Bulgarian agreement*.
92 1916, no. 8, p. 13.
93 1915, no. 9–12, p. 21 – four photographs of 'Negroes' (put together in one picture).
94 1916, no. 6, p. 8.
95 1916, no. 1, p. 8 – *Russian captives at the time of their capture* vs. *Cleaned by the Germans after capture*.
96 1916, no. 9–10, p. 1 and 1916, no. 11–12, p. 12.
97 1917, no. 3, p. 4.
98 1916, no. 9–10, p. 10 – *Romanian officers captured near Tutrakan*; 1917, no. 3, p. 1 – *Wallachian officers on the way to Sofia rest at Kaspichan train station*.

99 Cf. D. Parusheva, 'Bulgarians Gazing at the Balkans: Neighboring People in Bulgarian Political Caricature at the Beginning of the Twentieth Century', in D. Demski, I. Kristóf and K. Baraniecka-Olszewska (eds.), *Competing Eyes: Visual Encounters with Alterity in Central and Eastern Europe*. Budapest: L'Harmattan, 2013, pp. 418–437.
100 See 1917, no. 9, p. 8 and 1918, no. 3, p. 13.
101 Caricatures and cartoons depicting war developments were present on the last page of each number of *Light*. They can and should be a separate object of research, as those in other Bulgarian journals and newspapers have been.
102 Burke, *Eyewitnessing*, p. 19.
103 1916, no. 1, p. 5 – *Musical entertainment of soldiers in the occupied lands*; 1916, no. 4, p. 12 – *Theatre at the front*; 1916, no. 5, p. 9 – *The life of our soldiers at the front. Letter to family*; 1916, no. 8, p. 9 – *Barbershop at Macedonian front*, etc.
104 For example, 1914, no. 10–12, p. 17 – *Cossack attacks in Galicia* (drawing); p. 20 – *Battle between Serbs and Austrians in Bosnia* (drawing); p. 21 – *The battle in the Carpathian Mountains* (drawing); p. 24 – *The German attack at Ostend* (drawing), and many more examples in the next war years.
105 This is a reference to José Ortega y Gasset's idea (1968) that people don't pay attention to an object because they see it; on the contrary, they see only what they take notice of.

Bibliography

Anagnostopoulos, A., 'Picturing Public Space: Ethnicity and Gender in Picture Postcards of Iraklio, Crete, at the Beginning of the 20th Century', in E. Pistrick, N. Scaldaferri and G. Schwörer (eds.), *Audiovisual Media and Identity Issues in Southeastern Europe*. Newcastle upon Tyne: Cambridge Scholars Publishing, 2011, pp. 171–191.

Bankova, K., 'Balgarskata sanitarna misia v Rusko-Yaponskata voyna' [Bulgarian Sanitary Mission in the Russo-Japanese War], *Voennoistoricheski sbornik* [Military Historical Collection], 2 (2004), pp. 43–49.

Beurier, J., *Images et violence: 1914–1918. Quand le miroir racontait la Grande Guerre*. Paris: Nouveau monde, 2007.

Beurier, J., 'Information, Censorship or Propaganda? The Illustrated French Press in the First World War', in H. Jones, J. O'Brien and C. Schmidt-Supprian (eds.), *Untold War: New Perspectives in First World War Studies*. Leiden: Brill, 2008, pp. 293–324.

Boev, P., 'Dimitar Karastoyanov 1856–1919', *Balgarsko foto* [Bulgarian Photo], 7 (1973), pp. 28–30.

Brennen, B. and H. Hardt (eds.), *Picturing the Past: Media, History, and Photography*. Urbana, IL: University of Illinois Press, 1999.

Burke, P., *Eyewitnessing: The Uses of Images as Historical Evidence*. London: Reaktion Books, 2001.

Eldem, E., 'Powerful Images – The Dissemination and Impact of Photography in the Ottoman Empire, 1870–1914', in Z. Çelik and E. Eldem (eds.), *Camera Ottomana: Photography and Modernity in the Ottoman Empire 1840–1914*. Istanbul: Koç University Press, 2015, pp. 106–153.

Griffin, M., 'The Great War Photographs: Constructing Myths of History and Photojournalism', in B. Brennen and H. Hardt (eds.), *Picturing the Past: Media, History, and Photography*. Urbana, IL: University of Illinois Press, 1999, pp. 122–157.

Jay, M., 'Cultural Relativism and the Visual Turn', *Journal of Visual Culture*, 1, no. 3 (2002), pp. 267–278.

Kaser, K., *Andere Blicke. Religion und visuelle Kultur auf dem Balkan und im Nahen Osten.* Vienna: Böhlau Verlag, 2013.

Kaser, K., 'Vizualizatsiata na Balkanite: Balkanskite voyni, Parvata svetovna voyna i vizualnata modernizatsia' [Visualizing the Balkans: The Balkan Wars, the Great War and Visual Modernity], *Balgarska etnologia* [Bulgarian Ethnology], 3 (2014), pp. 332–351.

Kaser K., 'Visual Modernity and the Balkan Wars, 1912–13', in Dimitris Stamatopoulos (ed.), *Balkan Nationalism(s) and the Ottoman Empire*, vol. II: *Political Violence and the Balkan Wars*. Istanbul: Isis Press, 2015, pp. 143–164.

Kassabova, A., 'Identities in Frame: Photography and the Construction of a 'National Body' in Bulgaria (approx. 1860 to World War I)', in P. Hristov (ed.), *Migration and Identity: Historical, Cultural and Linguistic Dimensions of Mobility in the Balkans*. Sofia: Paradigma, 2012, pp. 73–86.

Kassabova, A., 'Inclusion and Exclusion: The Role of Photography in the Nation-Building Process in Bulgaria from Approximately 1860 to World War I', in D. Demski, I. Kristóf and K. Baraniecka-Olszewska (eds.), *Competing Eyes: Visual Encounters with Alterity in Central and Eastern Europe*. Budapest: L'Harmattan, 2013, pp. 112–139.

Kaychev, N., *Makedoniyo, vazzhelana . . . Armiata, uchilishteto i gradezhat na natiata v Sarbia i Balgaria (1878–1912)* [Macedonia Coveted . . . Army, School, and the Building of Nation in Serbia and Bulgaria (1878–1912)]. Sofia: Paradigma, 2003.

Konstantinova, Y., 'Political Propaganda in Bulgaria During the Balkan Wars', *Etudes balkaniques*, 2, no. 3 (2011), pp. 79–116.

Lafon, A., 'La photographie mobilisée 1914–1918', *Annales de Bretagne et des Pays de l'Ouest*, no. 123-3 (2016), pp. 33–49.

Lima, H. and J.P. Sousa, 'A ilustração portuguesa e cobertura da Primeira Guerra Mundial (1914–1918): imagens da guerra em contextos de censura e propaganda', in *A Grande Guerra (1914–1918): problemáticas e representações*. Porto: CITCEM, 2015.

Marty, C., 'Un point de fuite dans le réel? Les représentations de combats dans les journaux illustrés (1914–1918)', *Matériaux pour l'histoire de notre temps*, 3 (2008), pp. 62–66.

Ortega y Gasset, J., *The Dehumanization of Art and Other Essays on Art, Culture, and Literature*. Princeton, NJ: Princeton University Press, 1968.

Özen, M., 'Visual Representation and Propaganda: Early Film and Postcards in the Ottoman Empire, 1895–1914', *Early Popular Visual Culture*, 6, no. 2 (2008), pp. 145–157.

Parusheva, D., 'Bulgarians Gazing at the Balkans: Neighboring People in Bulgarian Political Caricature at the Beginning of the Twentieth Century', in D. Demski, I. Kristóf and K. Baraniecka-Olszewska (eds.), *Competing Eyes: Visual Encounters with Alterity in Central and Eastern Europe*. Budapest: L'Harmattan, 2013, pp. 418–437.

Parusheva, D., 'Svetlina varhu voynata. Vizualno predstavyane na voynata i nasilieto v Bulgaria, kraya na XIX i nachaloto na XX vek' [Light on War: Visual Representation of Wars and Violence in Bulgaria, End of the Nineteenth and Early Twentieth Century], *Bulgarska etnologiya* [Bulgarian Ethnology], 3 (2014), pp. 275–298.

Peeva, K., 'Voennite korespondenti sreshtu tsensurata po vreme na Balkanskata voyna' [Military Correspondents Against Censorship During the Balkan War] in *Svilengrad i Balkanskite voyni* [The Town of Svilengrad and the Balkan Wars]. Veliko Tarnovo: Faber, 2013, pp. 210–233.

Pistrick, E., N. Scaldaferri and G. Schwörer (eds.), *Audiovisual Media and Identity Issues in Southeastern Europe*. Newcastle upon Tyne: Cambridge Scholars Publishing, 2011.

Sindbaek, T. and M. Hartmuth (eds.), *Images of Imperial Legacy: Modern Discourses on the Social and Cultural Impact of Ottoman and Habsburg Rule in Southeast Europe*. Münster: Lit, 2011.

9

Under a Gun: Eugen Kumičić on the Austria-Hungarian Occupation of Bosnia and Herzegovina

Klara Volarić
Loughborough University

Introduction

The nineteenth-century (Ottoman) Balkans always draw the attention of scholars interested in nationalism because they are the ideal case for testing various theories and exploring nationalism in all its manifestations. The dismantlement of the Ottoman Empire, aggressive nation-building in the newly created Balkan states, and endless migrations of primarily the Muslim population to their Ottoman-Turkish 'fatherland' were often seen as something peculiar to this part of Europe. This was well demonstrated in the works of those scholars who borrowed Edward Said's *Orientalism* and applied it to the Balkans.[1] The wars and revolutions in the Ottoman Empire and the Balkans were traditionally explained through its decline and inability to modernize itself as well as through national movements that spread throughout its territory. On the other hand, wars and revolutions in Western and Central Europe were not defined through apocalyptic versions of violence and the effect it had on mass populations but through clashes of the Great Powers and national awakening.

However, in recent historiography (including this volume) the Ottoman Empire is not portrayed exclusively as *The Sick Man of Europe* but as an active and modernizing participant on both the domestic and international scene. Therefore, the revolutionary movements and wars in the Ottoman Empire should not be seen as an isolated phenomenon but as part of a larger European context where wars and revolutions also took place. The social uprisings in Bosnia and Herzegovina in 1875, the Russo-Ottoman War, Berlin Congress and, finally, Austro-Hungarian occupation of Bosnia and Herzegovina in 1878 should not be analysed solely as one more proof of the decline of the 'weak' Ottoman Empire, but should be seen in the wider context where all the empires throughout the nineteenth century experienced waves of crises. And it wasn't just the Ottoman Empire that saw a shift in its internal politics (such as the introduction of *Tanzimat* after the Greek War of Independence) after military defeats and revolutions, as the same was true of the Great Powers. For instance, throughout the nineteenth century France shifted back and forth from empire to republic, and revolutionary events and wars led Habsburgs to the dual monarchy.

In this chapter, I investigate the effect that one such event had on an ordinary man. I will focus on the Austrian occupation of Bosnia and Herzegovina, experienced through the eyes of Croatian intellectual Eugen Kumičić, who described his experience in a novel entitled *Under a Gun* (*Pod Puškom*) and whose experience arguably shaped his future political career and writings. In order to better understand Kumičić's writings and political thought, I review extensively what the occupation meant for the Croatian political context and, furthermore, how the two leading Croatian intellectuals – Josip Juraj Strossmayer and Ante Starčević, around whom all the other intellectuals gathered – reacted to this occupation. Hence, the main goal of the chapter is to show how grand events like wars and revolutions shape national political thought in general and personal political and intellectual paths in particular.

The Croatian Question and the Occupation of Bosnia and Herzegovina

After the Napoleonic Wars and the Congress of Vienna in 1815, all Croatian lands[2] came under Habsburg rule. These lands were not unified but were divided between direct Austrian patronage in Vienna and Croatian *ban* in Zagreb. Until the dissolution of the Habsburg State, the so-called 'Croatian Question' – or unification of all the Croatian lands – became the main theme of Croatian politics, accompanied by resistance to the growing Hungarian nationalist tendencies. Although the Hungarian Revolution of 1848–1849 failed because of Russia's intervention, the Hungarians managed to strengthen and equalize their position *vis-à-vis* the Austrians through the 1867 Austro-Hungarian Compromise. This Compromise introduced dualism and turned the Habsburg monarchy into Austria-Hungary, which consequently made Croatian demands for unification more difficult. Namely, the provinces of Istria and Dalmatia ended up under the Austrians while *Banian* Croatia with Slavonia became a Hungarian adjunct. The following year, the Hungarians and Croats signed an agreement in an attempt to regulate both their joint and independent affairs, but due to manipulations and political games the agreement made Croatian autonomy less likely because it was virtually placed under Hungarian control.[3]

Practically up until the dissolution of Austria-Hungary, the Croats were trying to remedy this position within or outside the monarchy and also revise their agreement with the Hungarians, both unsuccessfully. Thus it was not a surprise that news of the Austrian occupation of Bosnia and Herzegovina was well received. The Croatian public and most of the politicians optimistically thought that the occupation would lead not just to the unification of Croatian lands and Bosnia and Herzegovina, but also the large number of South Slavs would see a reconfiguration of the state. Because of this, Austria-Hungary decided to occupy Bosnia and Herzegovina in a way that did not jeopardize dualism or encourage South Slav federalist movements. Thus in 1881, Bosnia and Herzegovina was placed under joint rule of the Ministry of Finance in Vienna, though maintained a separate position within the state.[4]

Croatians versus Serbs

Both Croatian and Serbian intellectuals began an intense propaganda campaign in Bosnia and Herzegovina during the 1860s with the intention of reminding local inhabitants of their Serbian or Croatian national roots. In Bosnia there was an especially active Croatian bishop – Josip Juraj Strossmayer – a prominent Croatian politician, intellectual and benefactor whose diocese in Đakovo (Croatia) also extended over Bosnian Catholics. These activities drew the attention of the Ottoman governors who, in their reports to Constantinople, showed that they were well-informed of the ideological initiatives coming from the neighbouring Slavic lands and propaganda activities conducted by the Croats and Serbs. In one letter dated 6 April 1868, Bosnian governor Şerif Osman pasha wrote to the Ottoman government that the Bosnian Franciscan Grgo Martić was leaving for Constantinople on the orders of Strossmayer. Martić was supposed to inspect the financial affairs of Constantinople's Franciscans but the governor believed it amounted to more than that:

> [Strossmayer] is the bishop in the town of Čakovar in Austrian territory who leads the pan Slavic movement and who seems to have unofficial spiritual power over our friars. When the political situation requires, he consults with them [...] Although the departure of the named is officially motivated like this, still it could be understood that they aspire to gain some privileges in order to ideologically foster pan Slavism. We have found out that for this occasion the Serbian Principality gave him [Martić] 2,000 ducats in the greatest secrecy.[5]

News about the uprising in Bosnia and Herzegovina was warmly welcomed and both Serbian and Croatian periodicals agreed that Bosnia and Herzegovina should be taken from the Ottomans. However, while the Croatian press defended the thesis that it did not matter who took Bosnia, the Serbs were adamant that Bosnia should be theirs alone or otherwise left within the Ottoman domain.[6] After Serbia's defeat and Russia's entry into the conflict, various Croatian assemblies and press supported Russia and expressed the hope that Austria-Hungary would not jeopardize this mission.[7] The discussion between Croatia and Serbia over Bosnia intensified, but because it became evident that neither of the two would participate in solving the Bosnian Question, the discussion revolved around national issues. Who had the right to Bosnia and Herzegovina was no longer the issue, but instead who were Bosnian inhabitants – that is, were they Croats or Serbs? All Bosnian Catholics were identified as Croats whereas all members of the Orthodox church were considered Serbs. Naturally, the Muslim population was claimed by both.[8]

It is evident that not just the Great Powers but also the small and unrealized Balkan nations such as Serbia and Croatia approached the situation of Bosnia and Herzegovina exclusively from their own national programmes and interests – the specific position of Bosnia and Herzegovina and its Muslim inhabitants was neglected, as well as their right to self-determination. For Serbia, Bosnia and Herzegovina represented a step towards the realization of the great nationalistic expansion; for Croatia it was the possibility to resolve the Croatian Question and open the way for federalist reconfiguration of the monarchy.[9]

After the shock that the Croatian public received when the separate status of Bosnia and Herzegovina within Austria-Hungary was revealed, Croatian intellectuals turned to Russia as the only power that could really help solve the Croatian Question. This was the stance in particular of the Croatian Party of Rights, which became especially prominent after the outcome of the Great Eastern Crisis and expulsion of Croatian soldiers and officials serving in Bosnia during the occupation but who were dismissed later from the service as a precaution to curb eventual Slavic movement. One of the party's periodicals stated:

> For us Croats it is of the outmost importance to resolve this matter. We must monitor what is going on in the East and be prepared for anything so that the events do not jump on us as happened in 1848. We must use any convenient opportunity that cannot be far away and secure unification and freedom of our homeland Croatia.[10]

Ante Starčević and Josip J. Strossmayer

After the *Spring of Nations* (1848–1849), two prevalent political ideas soon crystallized in Croatia around which most intellectuals gathered: the South Slavism/Yugoslavism of Josip Juraj Strossmayer and Croatian nationalism led by Ante Starčević. These ideas advocated diametrically opposed means of resolution of the Croatian and Eastern question, although shared some common ground when it came to the Austrian occupation of Bosnia and Herzegovina.

South Slavism as a cultural concept (which unlike Yugoslavism included Bulgaria) can be traced back to the 1830s. During 1848, it was very influential as an ideology and remained so until the 1870s when Croatian intellectuals like Strossmayer and Franjo Rački, who were its main proponents, began to abandon it. South Slavism was seen as a means to resolve the Croatian Question within the federalist Habsburg state (so-called *Austroslavism*) but also to help culturally unite with other South Slavs, thus reinforcing the political South Slav/Croatian position when it came to any decision-making. This cultural unification would primarily mean the coming together of Catholic and Orthodox, on which Bishop Strossmayer worked especially diligently. In its nature, the concept was anti-Ottoman.[11] However, because of the complex political situation and the (un)balanced relations between the Powers, Strossmayer's political views were prone to change. This was normal in Croatian politics because many parties and politicians changed their stance based on the current political situation. After the unsuccessful revision of the Croatian-Hungarian agreement in 1873, Strossmayer officially abandoned politics and became completely disillusioned with the present Austria-Hungarian State. Yugoslavism, which until then Strossmayer had only advocated as a cultural concept (South Slavism, which included Bulgaria, was eventually discarded, as was *Austroslavism*), slowly turned into a political concept and therefore the resolution of the Croatian Question was seen to lie outside the borders of Austria-Hungary.[12]

Even after retiring from politics, Strossmayer continued to fight the Croatian cause. Because Croatian politicians did not participate in any decision-making when it came to state policy and were deprived of participating on the international diplomatic stage, Bishop Strossmayer acted as a *de facto* Croatian diplomat – his contacts with many European politicians and intellectuals enabled him to promote Croatian political and cultural interests abroad, which otherwise would not have been brought up owing to the dominance of the Austrian and Hungarian diplomats. This was especially visible during the Great Eastern Crisis.[13] During the uprising in Bosnia and Herzegovina, Strossmayer corresponded with British politician Gladstone with whom he shared the view that the Ottoman Empire should be removed from Europe because it was unable to modernize or ensure the safety and intellectual progress of its subjects. Moreover, Strossmayer believed that the removal of the Ottoman Empire would allow the South Slavs to unite. Regarding the position of Bosnia and Herzegovina, Strossmayer reasoned it would be best to leave it to Serbia because 'this Principality did the most in a fight for this holy matter'.[14] Strossmayer mocked the Croatian public and politicians who welcomed Austrian occupation of Bosnia and Herzegovina because, in his opinion, Croatia depended entirely on Hungary, so it was illogical to expect any help on their part regarding Bosnia.[15]

Unlike Strossmayer, who sought the resolution of the Croatian Question first among Austrians and then among Serbs, Ante Starčević, another influential politician and Father of the Croatian Nation, reasoned from the very beginning that the greatest threat to Croatia came from Vienna and Belgrade, although in his earlier political thought Russia was also seen as a danger. The politician was not sure what was worse for Croatia – to unite with Russians in the same state or be part of some sort of federal agglomeration, because according to Starčević, Russia also behaved as a typical great power, which did nothing to enhance the position of the South Slavs. Hence, he believed that independence was the best option for the Croats.[16]

After 1848, Starčević became a Croatian nationalist with a visible pro-Ottoman stance and he eagerly opposed South Slavism and later Yugoslavism. Starčević explained his pro-Ottoman stance in the following way: 'We do not care for Turkey as a European state, or as our neighbour. We care and we must care for Turkey because it is the state in which live millions of people of the purest and the noblest Croatian blood.'[17] However, as much as Starčević was full of praise for Bosnian Muslims, he was also full of criticism for Bosnian Christians. While Starčević described Orthodox inhabitants as faulty conspirators who only learned how to hate their sovereign, make rebellions and then run, Catholics in contrast were moral but 'flabby'.[18] Starčević opposed the idea of joining Bosnia and Herzegovina with Austria-Hungary because Bosnia should join instead an independent Croatia or remain within the Ottoman Empire. He reasoned: 'If you are in prison alone or with your comrades, you are still enslaved. If Bosnia will be under Austria as an independent crown or one crown with us, it does not matter because this is the same.'[19]

Not hard to predict, the idea of breaking the monarchy and achieving a completely independent Croatia was, in the present circumstances, an isolated view advocated by only a few individuals. Starčević was one of the few Croatian politicians to stay loyal to his political principles, regardless of the current political flow – he advocated Croatian independence irrespective of whether or not it was possible to achieve. Furthermore, Starčević considered his Party of Rights not just a political party but a national movement that should 'awaken' Croats and mobilize them to fight for their independence.[20]

Before the start of the Bosnian uprising, Starčević warned Bosnian Christians not to be taken in by foreign propaganda campaigns or Russian and Austrian 'apostles' who promised assistance. He commented on the 1870s uprising in the following way:

> The current uprising, along with past and future uprisings, came to Turkey from the outside. [...] As long as the rebellion comes from outside and as long as the Bosnian people accept it, there will be no peace and with every new uprising the Bosnian raja will only aggravate their own position. Even if they come under another government, it will not make them better unless they change themselves. [...] Thus, in my opinion, no available combination at the moment can resolve the Eastern Question but only perplex it and turn it into a European Question. With the present rebellions and the position of its subjects, Turkey cannot improve or strengthen itself in any possible way. However, at this moment there is no one in this region who can replace Turkey.[21]

Similar to Strossmayer, Starčević condemned the Austrian occupation of Bosnia and remained consistent in his views. Furthermore, he accused the Bosnian Christians of anti-Ottoman activities and for the uprising that resulted in their occupation without realizing that any other occupier would be less palatable than the Turks.[22] According to Starčević, the Ottoman Empire had to be released from foreign interference and should be given the chance to conduct reforms in peace. However, if this were to fail – that is, if the Ottoman Empire proved not to be up to the job – then the Ottomans should be replaced.[23] Until then, Starčević advocated the *status quo* and was convinced that political action in the present circumstances was not possible – it would be possible only after crushing dualism and the Austria-Hungarian State. In this respect, Starčević was convinced that the 'Cossack hoof' that crushed the 1848 Hungarian revolution should also crush Austria-Hungary as a means to obtain Croatian independence.[24]

Eugen Kumičić's *Under a Gun*: A Personal Narrative

So far, I have sketched the general stance of the Croatian press and of two prominent Croatian intellectuals who were influential on the political and public stage, none of whom, however, directly witnessed the events during the occupation of Bosnia and Herzegovina. Most were armchair thinkers who debated how the present Great Eastern Crisis could be used to help solve the Croatian Question. Therefore, I now turn my attention to Eugen Kumičić, a Croatian writer and politician who had witnessed the events in Bosnia and described them in his novel *Under a Gun*.

Eugen Kumičić was born in 1850 in Istria province. He was educated in Rijeka, Kopar and Zadar, mainly in the Italian language. In Prague he studied medicine, but soon he transferred to Vienna to study history, philosophy and geography until 1873. Kumičić worked shortly as a teacher in Zadar and Split before moving to Paris in 1875, where he spent two years as a student preparing for the French examination, and then to Venetia, where he prepared for the Italian examination. While in Paris, Kumičić became familiar with Emile Zola's work, which was to greatly influence his future literary work. After the occupation of Bosnia and Herzegovina in 1878 he returned to Zagreb, where he worked as a high school teacher and at the same time pursued a career in literature. In 1883, with the beginning of *ban* Khuen-Hedervary's regime and Magyarization, Kumičić involved himself in politics, which, along with literature, became his primary occupation.[25]

Kumičić was an ardent supporter of Ante Starčević, whose Party of Rights was the most popular Croatian political party in the second half of the nineteenth century, which stood for an independent Croatian state. In the 1880s, the party attracted large numbers of followers and sympathizers because of disillusionment with the current state of politics, whereby mainstream political parties were unable to resolve the Croatian Question. The main disseminators of the party's ideas were students at the newly formed University of Zagreb. They established the paper *Sloboda* (Freedom) in 1878 with the blessing of Starčević, in the first edition of which they set out the main principles of the Party of Rights. That meant obtaining an independent Croatian state based on its historical and natural right because, according to them, the current position of Croatia within Austria-Hungary was illegal.[26]

Since this main goal was an obvious betrayal in the context of Austria-Hungary, the Croatian Party of Rights did not have a clearly developed programme. Its programme was based on the current political situation and varied depending on the given circumstances. This pragmatism in politics was in fact a constant facet of most Croatian politicians, except Ante Starčević, who remained strongly devoted to his political beliefs. Because of this, Starčević was more than once left isolated on the Croatian political scene, even in his own party. This is also the reason why the Party of Rights did not have a clear stance towards the occupation of Bosnia and Herzegovina. While some members saluted the occupation, the bard of the party Starčević was against it and did not hide his inclination towards the Ottoman Empire and Muslims and his disdain of the Serbs. Thus the lack of a clear political programme often resulted in contradictory and uneven articles in the party's official political paper.[27]

As already mentioned, Kumičić pursued a career in literature alongside his political interests. He is one of the most distinguished Croatian writers of the second half of the nineteenth century, known for introducing naturalism into Croatian literature with which he became acquainted through Emile Zola's works in Paris. *Under a Gun*, which he wrote under the pseudonym Jenio Sisolski, was also published in this tone. Indeed, Kumičić's introduction of naturalism into Croatian literature had a clear political goal. Namely, throughout the nineteenth and twentieth centuries, Croatian politics and literature were closely related and this was especially evident in the works of intellectuals who were prominent politicians and writers of the time. Milan Marjanović wrote in 1913: 'For Croats everything was politics and politics was everything.'[28] Therefore, through literary works Kumičić persistently propagated Croatian self-consciousness, statehood and the need for change. It was literature that performed a national function.

Unlike bourgeoisie writers, the followers of the Croatian Party of Rights such as Kumičić and Ante Kovačić, another distinguished Croatian writer, used literature to present and confirm Starčević's view that Croatia's current situation under the monarchy was an absolute evil. Therefore, it is not surprising that Kumičić introduced naturalism into Croatian literature when by doing so writers could analyse and critique the Croatian reality of that time and become a voice of all those who were disaffected with the socio-political situation in the country. Their criticism covered almost all the questions concerning the Croatian political and cultural scene, including dualism, trialism, the Frankopan-Zrinski cult, clericalism and so on.[29] For instance, Kumičić's novel *Olga and Lina* published in 1881 was written as an allegory in which exemplary Olga represented Croatia and corrupted Lina stood for Austria. The same was true of his historical novel *The Zrinski-Frankopan Conspiracy* published in 1893, where he further popularized the cult of Petar Zrinski and Fran Krsto Frankopan, portraying them as national heroes who fought for the national cause.[30] In other words, literature became a means for mobilizing the Croatian public and propagating certain political goals. This was apparent in *Under a Gun* as well.

Kumičić published *Under a Gun* in the *Balkan* magazine in Zagreb in 1886, eight years after the beginning of the occupation. Although Kumičić took notes in Bosnia and Herzegovina, he mentioned in the novel that he had lost his notes during the battle for Ključ in which he participated.[31] The loss of his notes might be the reason why the novel was published eight years later, although it is difficult to predict whether his portrayal would have been the same if it had been published shortly after the occupation.

In the early 1880s, Kumičić became actively involved in politics as a member of the Croatian Party of Rights and a diligent follower of Ante Starčević. Although historians agree that the factual part of his writings on battles and logistical problems is correct, his description of the inhabitants of Bosnia should be viewed with more caution.[32] Even the last paragraph of the novel highlights the current political situation and his disdain of the Hungarians:

> Around me nothing but the flat country, desolate and sad, covered with snow like a death cloak. Some of the Hungarians were beating the Vlach whom I heard screaming, while the others were struggling to pull their carriage out of the mud. I ran to the Sava River, hoping the screams would stop and the Hungarians would remain stuck in the dirt.[33]

Kumičić received a recruitment letter in Vienna in July 1878 when he immediately but involuntarily went to Zagreb. From there he moved to Sisak and Stara Gradiška where he crossed the Sava River and entered Bosanska Gradiška, most likely on 29 July. Kumičić did not record dates very often, so it is only certain that he embarked from Vienna in late July and a few days later he was in Bosnia. He was a member of a regiment which went to Banja Luka. He described the regiment's march from one village to another, hampered by heavy rain and the mountainous and hilly landscape.

> The next day around five in the afternoon we crossed the Sava River and stepped onto Bosnian soil in Bosanska Gradiška. [...] We walked through the main street. People were already accustomed to seeing our army so no-one paid attention to us. Merchants were sitting in front of their little shops and smoking čibuk. I saw many women with beautiful faces. [...] We were in Bosnian Posavina, such a sad and

deserted place. We were walking on a crumbling road and to the left and right there was nothing but mire which mirrored the reddish sky. When the dark began to descend, black clouds surrounded us and it started to rain. The rain appeared like a huge wall, blocking our way into Bosnia. Lightening was filling the sky and thunder surrounded us. Everything around us was quiet and bleak. We marched silently. In the night, the cold wind and rain drove into us. Where to go? The dark, you cannot see even a finger in front of your eyes. [...] We are trudging through mud, falling into the mire; some are cursing, some scolding themselves but no-one prays to God. [...] The field is getting narrow. Through forest, up and down a hill, and here we are on the field of Banja Luka. [...] A great army occupies the field. When I noticed it, I immediately thought: 'Count Andrassy was not telling the truth when he said that he will send to Bosnia only two companies with a military band.' Here we find our regiment too. The same day we were placed in different companies, to fill the place.[34]

Kumičić stated several times that soldiers were treated poorly, beaten by their superiors and dying from illness and exhaustion. Sometimes they didn't eat for days. The Austrians obviously did not expect such resistance from the local Orthodox (whose resistance Kumičić failed to mention) and Muslim population. The harsh terrain also added to the situation, so the atmosphere among the troops was tense.

The captain divided the company into several units and scattered us around the hill to help the horses and to push the carriages to higher ground. When we reached the top of the hill, we had to run down again to catch the carriages. Push, pull, sweat, let the bones break. [...] Soldiers passed next to us tired, drained from the walk, sweaty and thirsty and they did not even notice us. Their superiors were angry, they were yelling and ordering the team to go faster. I saw a young officer whipping a soldier who led two loaded horses. His face was covered with blood but he did not utter a word. Discipline! The sun was harsh, everything was burning hot. [...] I watched those exhausted people, those sad, pale and wet faces and asked myself: where is their home, where are they going? They were walking in silence, heads bent, dragging their legs, broken and crushed. One tall blonde fellow just collapsed and – blackened. The doctor ran to him and noticed right away there was nothing that could be done. He said in German: This one is the third already.[35]

In Banja Luka, thanks to his education and language skills, Kumičić was employed as scribe and court interpreter, translating from Bosnian to German and vice versa. At Banja Luka, however, he was again recruited and sent south, namely to Čađavica, and then participated in the battle for Ključ (7–9 September). His description of the battle is an especially touching testimony of loss and suffering because Kumičić's closest friend was killed right in front of him.

In the early Saturday morning, with the first sunlight, Mohammedans greeted us with bullets. In just a second, from all the sides of the valley you could hear weapons' roar. Tired, hungry and thirsty we did nothing but sneaking up and down, from hill to hill, advancing, retreating and shooting the whole day. Our colonel was shot twice that day. The commander in chief was Wirtemberg. Mohammedans started to retreat around noon, pressed by a more powerful force. They were hiding within their forests and gorges. [...] The shooting was with each moment more intense. I could see smoke from the forest, the whole valley was under attack, and I heard the screaming of the injured. I finally became intoxicated with all this roar and mess and started to fire rapidly towards the forest. My gun was hot, I was out of ammunition but others who had it supplied those who were short. Again I was shooting, too high, too low, it doesn't matter. Everything that kept me occupied was more than welcome because I didn't want to have time to think about anything else.

Ernesto was laying on his left hip, with his back turned. Suddenly he asked me if I had bullets. I threw him a couple. He then got up to fire but the gun fell out of his hands, he turned abruptly to me, looking at me shivering, and then collapsed on his back. The blood was pumping from his left temple. In a second I was by his side and took his hand into mine. He pressed it and opened his mouth to tell me something and then he brokenly jerked. 'Ernesto, Ernesto!' I screamed.

We were firing late into the night. Ernesto lay on the same spot where he died. I looked at him in shock and in disbelief. We dug him grave later and placed him into it, me and two other soldiers. Today I cannot not describe how I felt in my heart when I was placing soil on his beautiful and tortured face.[36]

A few weeks after the battle at Ključ, Kumičić was again transferred to Banja Luka as an interpreter where he mostly dealt with Vlachs accused of robbery, murder and so on. He spent a few months there before, on 23 December, he was dismissed from the army and was free to go home.[37]

Many scholars have addressed the national identification of the Bosnian population and how various agents from neighbouring states were sent to instil a specific 'national consciousness' into local inhabitants. However, even during the occupation, that is twenty years after the agents began to operate intensively in the area, the situation was pretty much the same. During his service as a scribe and interpreter, Kumičić became aware of it too.

I have asked hundreds of people, and not many would know, what is the name of their language.
I don't know, 'Vlach' would reply.
How don't you know? Do you speak Turkish?
I do not know Turkish. Look, this is how I am crossing myself.
Do you speak Serbian?
No, I don't.
How do you speak then?
Like you, or like this fellow, he would say, pointing to another defendant.
Do you speak Bosnian?
Oh, yes, this must be it, yes, Bosnian.
This is how the people who lived in villages between the mountains replied to me. Some Mohammedans told me they speak Croatian. When I would ask a

burgher 'Vlach', for instance a merchant from Banja Luka, he would reply immediately that he speaks Serbian.

And who tells you that you speak Serbian?

Who tells me!? Man, our pastor is no fool![38]

It is evident that Kumičić simplified events in Bosnia and Herzegovina – that is, portrayed characters in black and white in order to fit his political thought. What is striking is that Kumičić did not describe Muslims as the enemy, although in his novel they were characterized as the only ones who were resisting. They were described as brave and proud heroes, in absolute epithets. For instance, two village leaders whom his regiment encountered and later executed over the false accusation of participating in the attack on the Austrian soldiers were described in the following way:

In front of the door were sitting two men and they were looking at the green garden as if they did not hear our steps. The elder of the two was around forty-five; he was tall and had a moustache, with dark eyes and noble features, a rock, handsome man. His dress was clean and decent, almost aristocratic, like at beg's. Later I found out that he was the leader of one of the strongest families of this village. The other was his son, young as a drop and healthily strong with a strange dark look. You could see in his eyes the flames of creeping anger. Hundreds of lives simmered in the eyes of this wonderful young man.[39]

On the other hand, Orthodox inhabitants whom Kumičić simply referred to as Vlachs were not described as resistors but as conspirators who were informing the Austrians of the whereabouts of the rebellious Mohammedans (i.e. Muslims) and what they were planning to do. They were traitors and war profiteers, always portrayed in an objectionable way. For instance, one of them was portrayed as

... especially odious and he was the one who most often spoke with the captain. He was medium height, a bit bent; he could be around forty. His head was big and flat, blonde hair ragged and muddy, face pimpled, nose broad and ruinous, and his mouth huge, stretched from one ear to another. His little grey eyes impudently and cunningly wander beneath a low forehead.[40]

The resemblance between Kumičić and Starčević's views is striking when it comes to Muslims and Vlachs (i.e. Serbs). Like Starčević, Kumičić thought that Bosnian Muslims ought to be admired while Serbs were to be despised. Similarly, the occupation is also perceived as something that was forced upon him and as something he did not support. Actually, the novel has a strong anti-war flavour and faithfully describes how the subaltern element, not just the local inhabitants but soldiers as well, were unwillingly subjected to the imperial politics of the Great Powers. In one passage, Kumičić describes the horror he felt when he was forced to take part in a firing squad.

We were surprised when we saw ten fellows bring us two Mohammedans, a father and son, who were captured at their home. [...] We were immediately on our feet. They stopped in front of us. The captain counted, there were eight of us. I froze and looked at Ernesto. He was pale. The captain ordered that we prepare for the shooting, and said to the Mohammedans to sit down in front of us. They obeyed. My heart stopped. The company was watching us, the other captives were watching us, the old man who was a father and grandfather to those sitting in front of us was watching us. The rules were that we had to be three steps removed from the captives and the four of us had to shoot at one of them. My head was spinning, I took a step back and dropped my gun. The captain pointed a gun at my chest and yelled in German that I was a coward. I took my gun again and looked at those poor people. They sat next to each other, one moment watching us and the next the sky. What a fine people they were, in their prime, still seeing their old father and grandfather and the sun up in the sky. The silence surrounded us. [...] The captain looked at me fiercely, with his gun still pointing. I stood in front of the old Mohammedan and Ernesto in front of his son. I turned my face away, as I did not want to see them alive. Somehow I pointed my gun at the older one, my hands shaking. The captain was ready to hit me with his fist, but I could not see anything, I did not know what was going on. I just wanted to die. My heart stiffened, my throat became dry, the darkness took me, everything around me stopped...

At the captain's command eight guns fired. [...] Ernesto took my hand and asked me if I felt unwell. I was chocking, was unable to breathe or utter a word. My friend took me to company that was ready to depart. Then, I looked at the old man who witnessed how we had buried his son and grandson. His grey head was bent, his long beard was shaking. [...] 'Oh you miserable cowards', he spoke in a small voice, 'today a black day came over us! Aidža, my little smiley, your father is no more, there he lays next to your brother! Oh my poor eyes, what did you just witness!'

I covered my eyes with my hands so that I couldn't see him. What a horrible night! Oh, you unfortunate Aidža, lovely and poor girl, on a bare hill, on a stormy night I found out your name from your grandfather, devastated with grief, tiredness and hunger! [...] You are always in front of my eyes! Where are you today? Did you find the strength to move forward? Did you find their graves? Did you curse me in those desolate fields?

Aidža, you were born in the hilly landscape of sad Bosnia, I was born along the rugged coast of the Croatian sea, your father did nothing to me, nor I anything to him. I did not even know you lived under the sun, and now you curse me! You poor girl, if you are still alive, I do not believe your smile will return to your lips again! Your soul will be grief-stricken when you remember that day, which is always on your mind. I am full of sadness too and I will be haunted by that day for the rest of my life. [...] But Aidža learn this, the moment before our guns were fired, your father looked at me compassionately and please know, your father forgave me...[41]

Conclusion

Under a Gun, written in a naturalistic style, is the testimony of a young man who took part in one of the many nineteenth-century war events. It is a testimony of subaltern peoples caught in the middle of international politics and who suffered the most because of it. Although it has many flaws and some parts may be disputed (such as black-and-white characterization), the events described in the book are convincing. Also, Kumičić's anti-war sentiments and disapproval of the Austria-Hungarian occupation, as well as his inclination towards Muslim inhabitants, are quite unambiguously stated in this novel. Nevertheless, the main intention of this chapter was to move from the macro level in which wars and revolutions affect states and international equilibrium, and to show how local political thought and ordinary people were obviously affected as well. In this sense, I find this autobiographical novel intriguing – it presents concrete experiences of people who otherwise would remain mostly silent.

Notes

1. See Maria Todorova, *Imagining the Balkans*. New York: Oxford University Press, 1997.
2. 'Croatian lands' refers to autonomous Croatia and Slavonia (governed by Croatian *ban*; in the rest of the text referred to as Croatia), Dalmatia and Istria (after the dissolution of the Venetian Republic, both provinces came under direct Austrian rule), and the Military Frontier (demilitarized in 1873 and abolished in 1881). All these lands formed the basis of the medieval Kingdom of Croatia, which, in 1102, entered into personal union with the Hungarian Kingdom and in 1527 with the Habsburg Monarchy. Nineteenth-century Croatian politicians used this as a historical right when it came to the question of Croatian unification and the strengthening of its position within the Habsburg state.
3. On concise history of this period, see Ivo Goldstein, '1790–1918: Development of the Middle Class', in *Croatia: A History*. London: C. Hurst & Co., 1999, pp. 54–107.
4. Stijn Vervaet, *Centar i periferija u Austro-Ugarskoj* [Centre and Periphery in Austria-Hungary]. Zagreb: Synopsis, 2013, pp. 42–44.
5. Ibid., p. 265.
6. Ibid., p. 439.
7. Mirjana Gross and Agneza Szabo, *Prema hrvatskome građanskom društvu* [Towards Croatian Bourgeoisie Society]. Zagreb: Globus, 1992, pp. 456–457.
8. Ibid., p. 459; Dragutin Pavličević, *Hrvati i Istočno pitanje (Croats and the Eastern Question)*. Zagreb: Golden Marketing-Tehnička knjiga, 2007, pp. 444–445.
9. Gross and Szabo, *Prema hrvatskome građanskom društvu*, pp. 462–463.
10. Josip Mihaljević, 'Odnos Stranke prava prema okupaciji Bosne i Hercegovine 1878. i 1879. godine u listu 'Sloboda'' (The Relation of the Croatian Party of Rights Towards the Occupation of Bosnia and Herzegovina in the Paper 'Sloboda' in 1878–1879), *Bosna franciscana*, 16, no. 28 (2008), p. 146.
11. Ibid., pp. 42–43.
12. Željko Karaula, 'Pisma crnogorskoga pjesnika, svećenika i diplomata Jovana Sundečića bosansko-đakovačkom i srijemskom biskupu Josipu Jurju Strossmayeru (1881.–1887.)' [The Letters of Montenegrin Poet, Priest and Diplomat Jovan Sundečić to Josip Juraj Strossmayer, the Bishop of Bosnia, Đakovo and Srijem (1881–1887)], *Diacovensia*, 17 (2009), pp. 96–97.
13. Zoran Grijak, 'Uspomene i Razgovori s biskupom Strossmayerom Izidora Kršnjavoga kao povijesni izvor' [Memoirs and Conversations with Bishop Strossmayer by Izidor Kršnjavi as a Historical Source], *Scrinia Slavonica*, 11 (2011), p. 98.

14 Ibid., p. 110.
15 Gross and Szabo, *Prema hrvatskome građanskom društvu*, pp. 458–459.
16 Pavličević, *Hrvati i Istočno pitanje*, pp. 451–452.
17 Zlatko Hasanbegović, 'Hrvatske nacionalno-integracijske ideologije i istočno pitanje' [Croatian National Integration Ideologies and the Eastern Question], in *Zbornik radova 1*, ed. Dušan Musa. Široki Brijeg: Suton, 2009, p. 48.
18 Pavličević, *Hrvati i Istočno pitanje*, p. 459.
19 Ibid., p. 453.
20 Tomislav Markus, 'Društveni pogledi Ante Starčevića' [The Social Views of Ante Starčević], *Journal of Contemporary History*, 41, no. 3 (2010), p. 831.
21 Pavličević, *Hrvati i Istočno pitanje*, p. 460.
22 Hasanbegović, 'Hrvatske nacionalno-integracijske ideologije i istočno pitanje', p. 51.
23 Ibid., p. 52.
24 Markus, 'Društveni pogledi Ante Starčevića', p. 832.
25 Eugen Kumičić, *Istrapedia*. Available at: https://www.istrapedia.hr/hrv/1433/kumicic-eugen/istra-a-z/.
26 Mihaljević, 'Odnos Stranke prava prema okupaciji Bosne i Hercegovine 1878. i 1879. godine u listu 'Sloboda'', p. 131.
27 Ibid., p. 131.
28 Vinko Brešić, 'Literatura kao ideologem. Ante Kovačić i pravaštvo' [Literature as an Ideologue. Ante Kovačić and the Croatian 'Pravaštvo' Movement], *Umjetnost riječi*, 35, no. 1 (1991), p. 47.
29 Ibid., p. 49.
30 Eugen Kumičić, *Hrvatska enciklopedija*. Available at: www.enciklopedija.hr/Natuknica.aspx?ID=34604#top.
31 Eugen Kumičić, *Pod puškom (Under a Gun)*. Available at: www.orlovac.eu/knjige/pod-puskom.pdf, p. 59.
32 Pavličević, *Hrvati i Istočno pitanje*, pp. 492–494.
33 Kumičić, *Pod puškom*, p. 74.
34 Ibid., pp. 8–9.
35 Ibid., pp. 10-11.
36 Ibid., pp. 55–57.
37 Ibid., pp. 3–74.
38 Ibid., p. 70.
39 Ibid., p. 28.
40 Ibid., pp. 24–25.
41 Ibid., pp. 33, 35, 36.

Bibliography

Brešić, Vinko, 'Literatura kao ideologem. Ante Kovačić i pravaštvo' [Literature as an Ideologue. Ante Kovačić and the Croatian 'Pravaštvo' Movement], *Umjetnost riječi*, 35, no. 1 (1991), pp. 47–53.
Goldstein, Ivo, '1790–1918: Development of the Middle Class', in *Croatia: A History*. London: C. Hurst & Co., 1999, pp. 54–107.
Grijak, Zoran, 'Uspomene i Razgovori s biskupom Strossmayerom Izidora Kršnjavoga kao povijesni izvor' [Memoirs and Conversations with Bishop Strossmayer by Izidor Kršnjavi as a Historical Source], *Scrinia Slavonica*, 11 (2011), pp. 97–181.

Gross, Mirjana and Agneza Szabo, *Prema hrvatskome građanskom društvu* [Towards Croatian Bourgeoisie Society]. Zagreb: Globus, 1992.
Hasanbegović, Zlatko, 'Hrvatske nacionalno-integracijske ideologije i istočno pitanje' [Croatian National Integration Ideologies and the Eastern Question], in *Zbornik radova 1*, ed. Dušan Musa. Široki Brijeg: Suton, 2009, pp. 39–55.
Karaula, Željko, 'Pisma crnogorskoga pjesnika, svećenika i diplomata Jovana Sundečića bosansko-đakovačkom i srijemskom biskupu Josipu Jurju Strossmayeru (1881.–1887.) [The Letters of Montenegrin Poet, Priest and Diplomat Jovan Sundečić to Josip Juraj Strossmayer, the Bishop of Bosnia, Đakovo and Srijem (1881–1887], *Diacovensia*, 17 (2009), pp. 91–156.
Kumičić, Eugen, *Pod puškom (Under a Gun)*. Available at: www.orlovac.eu/knjige/pod-puskom.pdf (last accessed 23 July 2015).
Kumičić, Eugen, *Hrvatska enciklopedija*. Available at: www.enciklopedija.hr/Natuknica.aspx?ID=34604#top (last accessed 1 August 2015).
Kumičić, Eugen. *Istrapedia*. Available at: https://www.istrapedia.hr/hrv/1433/kumicic-eugen/istra-a-z/ (last accessed 9 October 2018).
Markus, Tomislav, 'Društveni pogledi Ante Starčevića' [The Social Views of Ante Starčević], *Journal of Contemporary History*, 41, no. 3 (2010), pp. 827–848.
Mihaljević, Josip, 'Odnos Stranke prava prema okupaciji Bosne i Hercegovine 1878. i 1879. godine u listu "Sloboda"' (The Relation of the Croatian Party of Rights Towards the Occupation of Bosnia and Herzegovina in the Paper 'Sloboda' in 1878–1879), *Bosna franciscana*, 16, no. 28 (2008), pp. 127–149.
Pavličević, Dragutin, *Hrvati i Istočno pitanje (Croats and the Eastern Question)*. Zagreb: Golden Marketing-Tehnička knjiga, 2007.
Todorova, Maria, *Imagining the Balkans*. New York: Oxford University Press, 1997.
Vervaet, Stijn, *Centar i periferija u Austro-Ugarskoj* [Centre and Periphery in Austria-Hungary]. Zagreb: Synopsis, 2013.

10

War, Intellectuals and the Balkan States: French Intellectuals' Perception of Serbia and Serbs in the Great War[1]

Aleksandra Kolaković
Institute for Political Studies, Belgrade

Introduction

This case study aims to research and understand the role of intellectuals in war and their impact on national issues, especially the national issues of 'small' nations who were in the geopolitical squall of events. The Great War brought large changes in the balance of power, but it also left a legacy of enlarged national plans and instability, especially in the Balkans. Throughout the entire twentieth century, the Balkan nations were trying to solve their national issues. In relation to the Serbian nation and the cooperation of French and Serbian intellectuals, I discuss here the role of those intellectuals in the war, as reflected in the Balkan region.

Since the late nineteenth century, newspapers, through means of large circulations and visualization of text (photos and caricatures), had been relaying information to the masses and quickly became a prominent force that had a significant impact on society. Paris had grown into the propaganda centre of Europe. The years between 1871 and 1914, known as 'the golden age' of the French press, when circulations were at their highest, was also a period of 'despicable corruptibility'.[2] *Le Petit Journal*, *Le Petit Parisien*, *Le Matin* and *Le Journal*, with a circulation of 4 million copies between them, were channelling public opinion.[3] *Le Journal des Débats*, *La Revue des Deux Mondes*, and *La Revue de Paris* had circulations of approximately 20,000 copies and their readerships comprised statesmen, politicians, academics and business people. Scholars, writers and artists, active in social and political life, were also associates of these reputable newspapers and journals. Serbian intellectuals, educated since the mid-nineteenth century in reputable European universities, especially in France, and active in political and public life in Serbia at the end of the nineteenth and turn of the twentieth century, sought a way to further Serbian interests in the Balkans in cooperation with French intellectuals.[4] They believed that cooperation with French intellectuals in shaping public opinion could influence the political decision-makers in France to understand the interests of such a small nation in the Balkans.

On the other hand, French society, wounded by its defeat in the Franco-Prussian war, sought revival, and French intellectuals looked to return France to the top table of international relations as a means of resisting the rise of Germany. French intellectuals saw the possibility of the defence of French interests through cooperation with Serbian intellectuals.[5] With the Ottoman Empire in its twilight years and Europe characterized by a complex set of relations between the Great Powers, as well as instability that would lead to the Great War (1914–1918), the Serbian intelligentsia believed the conditions were right to change Serbia's foreign political outlook in order to accomplish the idea of liberation and unification. The change of Serbian foreign policy, which began in the last decade of the nineteenth century, was confirmed by the passing of the Serbian throne to the Karadjordjević Dynasty in 1903. Serbian politicians and intellectuals sought to facilitate liberation from economic dependence, development of the state and the national idea, by edging away from Serbia's reliance on Austria-Hungary.[6] The main task of Serbian ambassadors, diplomats, scholars and journalists was to present Serbia as the most developed state in the Balkans ready to move away from the Ottoman Empire, but a state that also required aid to resist the Germanic threat (which was also beneficial to French interests). Therefore, the growing influence of public opinion became a means for a small Balkan nation to highlight its interests to the Great Powers.

French Intellectuals and the Balkans

On the eve of the Great War (1914–1918), French intellectuals were a heterogeneous group in terms of their political attitudes and ideals. However, they were the generation formed after France's defeat in the war against Prussia (1871) and they shared strong patriotic feelings. Ernest Denis (1849–1921), Emile Haumant (1858–1942), Charles Loiseau (1861–1945), Auguste Gauvain (1861–1931), Albert Malet (1864–1915), Victor Bérard (1864–1931), André Chéradame (1871–1948), Henry Barby (1876–1935), Auguste Boppe (1862–1921) and Pierre Lanux (1887–1955) grew up and were educated in a country that was striving to overcome its weakened position in international relations by relying on rapid economic and cultural development, despite its decaying reputation and a stormy political scene.[7] The development of industry, agriculture and transport, as well as the expansion of financial activities and the money market, enabled the French to focus on the organization of the state. France was caught in a process of laicization. Under the influence of the republicans and supporters of colonial expansionism, Jules Ferry extended this process to the realm of education. Colonial policy in Tunisia, Egypt and Indochina was seen as 'a means of reviving the French energy and gaining a new imperial pride'.[8] Ferry introduced into political practice a belief in the cult of progress, opposition to the participation of the masses in politics, and the end of the influence of the Church in science and the education system as a path to progress.[9] His school reforms included the introduction of compulsory, free and secular education, focused on civic education, the development of secular morality, moral values and patriotism. Ferry laid the foundations for the education of those generations of French intellectuals who were influential in the social sphere of the early twentieth century.

The Third Republic was marked by civil unrest (Boulangism, social problems, the struggle against clericalism, the Dreyfus Affair), which made it difficult for France to regain her previous position in European politics.[10] After 1891, the introduction of a more aggressive policy of Germanization in Alsace and Lorraine spurred vehement French revanchism. The generation of the philosopher Julien Benda, Charles Maurras – the principal ideologist of *Action française* (French Action) – as well as the supporters of Catholicism, such as Paul Claudel and Charles Péguy, depicted Germans in a negative light.[11] The insistence on the development of a Greater German nationalism was a major concern for French intellectuals at the time of Boulangism, the Dreyfus Affair and the subsequent international crises over Morocco. However, French patriotism did not result in intellectual isolation from German society. While pursuing the sources for the reformation of the historical method, philosophy and social sciences, French intellectuals sought to gain insight into the German intellectual scene and state. Ernest Lavisse, a French historian and a positivist, devoted himself to the study of Prussia's history and its education system with the intention of devising – by comparing and adopting the best features of the Prussian model – a suitable system that would enable spiritual and, consequently, overall progress in France.[12] As a professor and the author of numerous books, textbooks and manuals, Lavisse used national history as a framework for the study of the past and a means of strengthening national and civic awareness – that is, patriotism – in France. When developments arising from the Dreyfus Affair threatened to create a rift in the unity of the French nation, Lavisse directed his students to study international relations.[13]

Drawing on a patriotic school system, in the ruling ideologies of the late nineteenth and early twentieth century there emerged an effort on the part of French intellectuals towards securing the position of France. The growing power of Germany, the First and the Second Moroccan Crises, the Annexation Crisis and the Balkan Wars were signs of an impending worldwide conflict. Beginning in 1894, with the official entry into force of the agreement between France and Russia, which marked the beginning of the formation of the Triple Entente, French intellectuals turned their attention to Russia and its spheres of interest: the end of Turkish rule in the European territories of the Ottoman Empire.[14] Late in the nineteenth century, there existed a group of scholars in France who continued the tradition of Slavic studies, initiated in 1840 within the Department of Slavic Languages and continued in 1873 within the School of Oriental Languages. Albert Malet, Victor Bérard, Charles Loiseau, André Chéradame, Auguste Gauvain, Emile Haumant and Ernest Denis were part of this French intellectual elite who focused their attention on Serbia and the Serbs.[15]

The aforementioned French intellectuals lived at a time when the consequences of the Franco-Prussian War of 1870–1871 was the main concern of intellectual circles, which shaped their interests.[16] With the apparently growing power of Germany and the pan-Germanist movement, an interest in Austria-Hungary, which relied on Germany in its international affairs, was also becoming more relevant. As Austria-Hungary was interested in the Balkans, especially in Bosnia and Herzegovina and the future partition of the Ottoman territories in Europe, French intellectuals also took an interest in internal relations within the Habsburg Empire, as well as in its relations with Serbia. Charles Loiseau, a French diplomat, politician and publicist, believed that since the establishment of the Franco-Russia alliance in 1893, it was in the interests of France to adopt a benevolent policy towards Italy and the unification of the Slavic peoples.[17] For him, the history of the South Slavs was part of the perpetual struggle for Pan-Germanism, and Kallay's regime was considered an expression of Austria's support for German expansion.

The interest of French intellectuals in the Balkans was also fostered by collaboration with their Balkan counterparts, based in part on the fact that some young intellectuals from Serbia (Milovan Milovanović, Jovan Žujović, Bogdan Popović, Jovan Skerlić, Milenko Vesnić, Grgur Jakšić and so on) were educated in France.[18] Victor Bérard, the Secretary General of the prestigious *La Revue de Paris* between 1904 and 1911, embarked on a detailed study of the Serbs and he supported Serbian interests when the Balkans were troubled by the Annexation Crisis of 1908.[19] Furthermore, tenacious diplomatic activity and propaganda by the Balkan countries in Paris stimulated interest among the French intellectuals. Bérard, together with Ernest Denis and Emil Haumant, both professors at the Sorbonne, drew the attention of the French public to the widespread antagonism among Serbs towards the authorities of the Austrian occupation, adopted the idea of a Yugoslav movement among the South Slavs, and delivered public lectures in Paris, Lille, Saint-Quentin, Besneville and Reims.[20] The development of international relations in the aftermath of the Annexation Crisis, which highlighted the path of Germany's breakthrough in the East, as well as a new political map of the Balkans established in the Balkan Wars, fostered closer and more vigorous cooperation between French and Serbian intellectuals.

Intellectual Cooperation

The strengthening of ties between France and Serbia and the idea of political reliance on France were also supported by Serbian ambassadors in Paris: Stojan Novaković, Andra Nikolić and Milenko Vesnić.[21] Their collaboration with Albert Malet, Ernest Denis, Charles Loiseau, Auguste Gauvain and Émile Haumant, together with the fact that in France public opinion had a powerful impact, persuaded Serbian intellectuals to make Paris the centre of Serbia's propaganda activities. As Serbia's informal press attaché in Paris, Grgur Jakšić had the opportunity to become acquainted and bond with French intellectuals who moved in journalists' circles.[22] Therefore, he suggested in a letter sent to Nikola Pašić that Serbian orders should be awarded to journalists working for *Le Temps*, *L'Echo de Paris*, *Le Journal des Debats*, *Le Petit Journal* and *L'Opinion* 'because great accomplishments could be made in Paris owing to orders and decorations, particularly in the press'.[23] At the same time, Henry Barby, a journalist and correspondent for the Paris newspaper *Le Journal* during the Balkan Wars (1912–1913), and André Chéradame, a French scholar, pointed out that it was in the interests of France to keep the alliance of Balkan states on an anti-German line.[24]

The cooperation of French and Serbian intellectuals resulted in a number of papers in French about Serbia and the Serbs, numerous lectures aimed at promoting Serbian issues to the French public, and a joint diplomatic and propaganda effort that paved the way for the political rapprochement between France and Serbia on the eve of the First

World War. The Association of Slavic and French Students in Paris brought together prominent political journalists and university professors to deliver lectures and engage in discussions where, on the eve of the Balkan Wars and the Great War, the concept of Yugoslavism was the focus. This association sought to develop a sense of unity among the Slavs, along with 'a more limited national awareness', and for the South Slavs it became 'a true school of rapprochement and solidarity'.[25] Its members believed in the need to establish 'a Yugoslav *La Revue des Deux Mondes*', which would 'offer space for literature and the arts, for politics and social life, and for economics and philosophy, as well as for any topical discussion, even on extremely specialized areas of knowledge'. The magazine was to be 'a source of light to all Yugoslavs' and it ought to create 'a unified Yugoslav national consciousness'.[26] Another urgent requirement was 'a Yugoslav journal in French', which would inform international public opinion about the Yugoslav nation and publish translations into French of important works of the Yugoslav genius that would inform a global audience.

Changes to French Public Opinion Towards the Serbs from 1894 to 1913

Serbian Francophiles and intellectuals who had studied in France sought to develop and organize the Serbian state, resist the pressures of Austria-Hungary, rely politically on Russia and France, become culturally closer to the family of developed European countries and affirm Serbian interests in European public opinion.[27] At the turn of the twentieth century, besides analysis of Serbia's foreign policy, the political, economic and cultural development of Serbia featured in the writings of French intellectuals. These French intellectuals noticed that Serbia was going through tumultuous changes and challenges. Focusing on the specifics of the development of both Serbian society and state, the period between 1894 and 1914 witnessed a significant change in the image of Serbia in France. Although the interest of French intellectuals in Serbia and the Serbs had grown considerably since 1894, the prevailing image of Serbia among the French public was based largely on unreliable information, travelogues and popular epic poetry.[28] The French authors of travelogues saw Serbia, the Serbs and Belgrade as part of the mystical and exotic East, though Serbia had gained independence in 1878. While preparing for their journeys into the lands inhabited by Serbs they had a feeling that they were visiting a civilization that lacked any elements of Western society and culture. Similar views prevailed in diplomatic reports.[29]

Significant changes in public opinion occurred during the Annexation of Bosnia and Herzegovina and the Balkan Wars, with a growing understanding of the problems, when French intellectuals supported the interests of the Serbs. The geographer and ethnologist Paul Labbé, the secretary-general of the Norman Geographical Society, travelled throughout Serbia and the Balkans during the Annexation Crisis. Upon returning from his journey, he published the text *A travers la Serbie. Impressions d'un récent voyage* (Through Serbia: Impressions from a Recent Trip), and delivered many lectures in Paris and other cities in France. Being themselves patriots, French intellectuals both valued and emphasized the patriotism of the Serbs and 'the fully justified pride of a people who had been for centuries spilling their own blood for independence'.[30] Reporters from the Balkan battlefields (1912–1913) wrote that 'the Serbian race [was] amazingly resistant' and brisk at crucial moments.[31] This created an awareness among the French public that the Serbs could be expected to act as a worthy ally in any upcoming conflict. French intellectuals argued that the Serbs had to be given the chance to master the skills of solving their problems and achieving their goals. The Balkan Wars showed that the Serbs had gained the necessary degree of political maturity and civilizational – that is, economic and social – progress to take responsibility for the fate of their nation and the state.[32]

A photographic record in the Balkans and in Serbia was organized in Paris as part of a project under the patronage of the well-to-do, scholars and lovers of art. Albert Kahn, a banker and patron of the arts, was among the first to understand the importance of colour photographs.[33] In 1912, Kahn initiated a photographic record that was to form the project *Les Archives de la Planète* (Archives of the Planet). He appointed Jean Brunhes as project director, head of the Department of Social Geography at the Collège de France.[34] As a focus for his research and photography, Brunhes chose the European southeast, an area that was mostly known through works of fiction. On the one hand, such a photographic record demonstrated the true culture of the Balkans, Serbia and Serbs, while on the other it stirred the imagination of authors of books of fiction. The image of Serbs among the French public during the Balkan Wars changed for the better due to political and economic cooperation, as well as the texts of these French intellectuals.

Intellectuals in War: From Sympathy to Affirmation of the Serbian National Aims

When Serbia was hit by an epidemic of typhus fever after the first victories in the Great War, humanitarian organizations in France, backed by the support of French intellectuals and indirectly supported by the state, played an important role.[35] The French-Serbian Committee, or the Committee for Emergency Help to the Serbs, with the assistance of Victor Bérard, collected monetary donations, food, clothing and medications. Early in January 1915, the organization *La nation serbe en France* (The Serbian Nation in France) was founded in the home of the scholar Victor Bérard. Simultaneously, Serbian pupils and students began to arrive in France: 'The first reception of our students in France was cordial, warm and parental. And the official authorities and whole citizenship welcomed our students ceremonially in all areas, in which they came for schooling. The school administration greeted them with speeches, which touched the hearts.'[36]

At the same time, Serbian intellectuals established in Paris a centre of Serbian academic war propaganda. Auguste Gauvain, editor of the foreign policy section of prominent French magazine *Le Journal des Débats* (*The Journal of Debates*), was a member of L'Institut de France and one of the French intellectuals who had a significant impact on public opinion. Already in the late nineteenth century, when he was the French representative to the Danube Commission, Gauvain established connections with Serbs.[37] His articles that portrayed in depth the causes for the Great War were published (1917–1923) in 14 volumes, entitled *L'Europe au jour le jour* (*Europe from Day to Day*). During the war, the former French student Jovan Žujović, who had been president of the Serbian Royal Academy since 1915, became a special envoy of the Serbian government to Paris and he dedicated himself to organizing education for Serbian refugee schoolchildren and students in France.[38] A group of eminent French scholars (Denis, Bérard, Haumant, Loiseau and Gauvain) collaborated with Žujović, Grgur Jakšić, Milenko Vesnić and others.[39]

Together with the humanitarian aid, French intellectuals contributed to the affirmation of Serbian victories and engendering sympathy for the Serbs among international public opinion. Academic Dragoljub Živojinović emphasizes that change of situation and reflects on how the Great Powers, at the time of the First World War, often 'provoked earthquakes, disbelief, misunderstandings, aloofness, open criticism and even distrust, but also fear and anxiety among the small countries, their allies'. Thus the support of the French intellectuals was crucial for the affirmation of Serbian interests.[40] The booklet *La Serbie* (*Serbia*), written by Victor Bérard and published in April 1915 by the renowned publishing house Armand Colin in celebration of Serbian Day in French schools, was propagandist in character. Bérard depicted war as a conflict between 'the national and victorious, independent and parliamentary, tolerant and democratic Serbia against feudal, police-driven and inquisitorial Austria-Hungary'.[41] Ernest Denis, an expert on Central Europe, a 'Serbian friend', and member of the *Études et documents sur la guerre. Comité du publication* (Studies and Documents on the War. Committee for Publication), published *La grande Serbie* and believed that it was in the interests of France to establish a barrier formed by Slavic states that would protect the rest of Europe from the German world and its expansionist aspirations.[42] Auguste Gauvain saw the Serbs as warriors and Serbia as a country 'with a mission which had to fight, to strive for the national liberation and to unite with liberated brothers into one community. He presented us to European public opinion as such warriors and he followed us throughout our struggle for liberation and unification.'[43] Also, Poul Labbé, head of the committee for propaganda *L'effort de la France et de ses alliés* (The Effort of France and Its Allies), whose activities included four thousand lectures, dedicated great attention to Serbia in 1916, especially in his lecture titled *L'Effort Serbe* (Serbian Effort), which received a huge public response.

Auguste Boppe, the French ambassador to Serbia during the Great War, after the joint offensive of the German, Austrian and Bulgarian troops in Serbia, followed the retreat of the Serbian army through Albania to Corfu.[44] With the support of the French Ministry of Foreign Affairs, he published a book, *À la suite du Gouverment Serbe de Niš à Corfu* (Following Serbian Government from Niš to Corfu). Boppe described the situation in Serbia, the retreat of the army and civilians, and their expectations of the allies, giving also an account of his memories of an earlier visit to the region and historical data about Serbian monasteries (Studenica, Dečani, the Patriarchate of Peć), as a testimony to Serbia's rich history. 'The struggle for bread has begun and there is no flour. The overburdened authorities cannot manage to supply soldiers and refugees. The lack of petty cash has additionally aggravated an already difficult situation,' wrote Boppe.[45] Along with Auguste Boppe, Henry Barby, the correspondent of *The Paris*

Journal since the Balkan Wars, also paid testimony to the hardship of the Serbs, the high numbers of the wounded and sick and the great famine that afflicted the retreating army and civilians. Barby described hunger and marching through the snow and ice without food: 'exhausted by fatigue and the lack of food', 'numb from the lack of sleep', 'the more we are advancing, the more our suffering is becoming unbearable'.[46]

Besides the hunger and suffering of the Serbs, Barby and Boppe noted Serbian expectations of the allies. Barby emphasized: 'The Serbian army was aware of the effort endured by the Frenchmen on their battlefield. They turned their anxious eyes towards the Russians and the Englishmen, from whom they expected help. They hoped until the last moment! Until the last moment they believed that the Allies would relieve them by providing sufficiently strong aid', and the lack of sufficient ammunition and weapons was also a problem.[47] At the same time, Boppe highlighted French support for Serbia and Serbs:

> Poor Serbs! Their suffering excuses the state of mind that overcame them when they saw their demise. They suffered for weeks and France sent them flour and toast which saved them from dying from hunger in Scutari (Skadar, Shkodër); France managed to save their army from falling prisoner to Austrians and Bulgarians by transporting soldiers from Albania. The dissent among the Serbs has ceased.[48]

In French texts, the crossing of Albania and transfer of the Serbian army and people to a place of safety, showed the Serbs to be durable, brave and heroic: 'Without revolt or slackening, not only soldiers, but everybody, the old men, women and even small children, fought to the last moment against a fatal destiny.'[49] Boppe described the arrival of the Serbs in Corfu and Tunisia as just a breather in the attempt to free their homeland:

> Hence the Serbian army will be saved, and the deliverance has once again come from France. Upon hearing that the evacuation had begun, the liveliest joy could be observed among the soldiers; they initially showed some aversion to the idea of being transported across the sea; now, they express their satisfaction that they are going to Tunisia, already imagining that they would return in a few months to liberate their homeland.[50]

Jovan Jovanović noted: 'By his book, his word, and his official work, Boppe influenced France to believe in the Serbs, and to largely rely upon them in its Eastern policy.'[51] This view of Boppe's activities during the Great War was also applied to Barby, as well as Denis, Haumant, Gauvain, Loiseau and other French intellectuals. The image of Serbia disseminated through the French education system in more than 100,000 schools on 26 March 1915 was aimed at strengthening patriotism. The celebration of Serbian Day in French schools (1915, 1916) was in line with the French policy of the 'Holy Unity' proposed by President Raymond Poincaré to erase all political divisions in France with the aim of achieving national unity in a time of war.[52] Yet during the war, the cult of gratitude to France began to build, which was manifested in the form of feelings of sincere and permanent alliance – 'eternal friendship' of the French and Serbs in the years after the war, that remained strong even during the twentieth century.⁵³

Exploring the history of small nations, potential allies in a future battle with the Germanic world, was important for French science and politics. Pierre Lanux, in his book *Yugoslavia: France and the Serbs* (1916), said that, until the First World War, French policy towards the Serbs and the Slavs in the Balkans was based on the 'fantasies' of famous French authors, including Pierre Loti and his glorification of the Turks. Emphasizing that it was necessary to visit Belgrade and create an objective image, Lanux pointed out:

> The Yugoslav world begins a mere 500 kilometres from our borders. It is the distance that divides our Savoy of the first Slovenian villages. We cannot continue to not know about it. I can already hear one persistent objection: – Actually, whether the Serbs can be perceived as uncultured highlanders? Or, even worse, 'Orientals', unreliable, careless, unreachable? ... Is it possible to rely on them? ... That's what many Parisians judge about the Balkans through operetta performances, and is not so scary. All foreigners have given us the operatic heroes ... But expressing a judgment about the Serbs, that has for so long been in circulation, is not a product of Paris: I object for it is a creation of the Austro-Hungarian people. Prepared and established opinion on Serbia was created in Vienna, and our tabloid reporters were only their porters.⁵⁴

Furthermore, Lanux said: 'At the present moment not a small number of French see the Balkans as a land of ambushes, diplomatic mischief, to sum it up in one word: betrayal. But one should stop this superficial view ... There is no Balkan unity, as we have already said. It should spare our allies, the Serbs, from being shoved into the same bag with the Bulgarians and with others, neutral people.'⁵⁵ At the time of the Great War, the perspective of French intellectuals concentrated on the whole Balkans was changed by the increasing significance of the Serbian factor in this part of Europe.

'My Serbian Patriotism Follows Behind My French Patriotism'

Serbs' wartime bravery was recognized as a model by the French intellectuals. Before the beginning of the Great War, Malet was appointed Secretary General of L'Alliance Française, and when war came, he volunteered for service despite his age.⁵⁶ In early summer 1915, Malet, former educator of Serbian king Aleksandar Obrenović, and well-known friend of several Serbian intellectuals (Grgur Jakšić, Jovan Žujović, Milenko Vesnić), began to free Alsace and Lorraine, just as he had dreamed of doing. Before he died in the trenches in September 1915, in support of Serbia's fight, he wrote to his Serbian friends: 'What wonderful people you are! My Serbian patriotism follows behind my French patriotism.'⁵⁷ He wove his patriotism in exploring the Serbs and Serbia at the turn of the twentieth century, which gradually grew into cooperation with Serbian scholars, diplomats and politicians on matters of mutual interest to France and Serbia, as well as the fight against their common enemy in 1914. At the same time,

Alphonse-Désiré Magrou, another teacher of King Aleksandar Obrenović wrote: 'There is no nation who fought for their independence with fearless energy, a nation who resents being enslaved and humiliated in life, who has brought more energy into the achievement or defending of its ideals [...] in particular let's not forget that the Serbs are the only Balkan nation which was liberated by their own means.'[58] French intellectuals had high regard for the patriotism of the Serbs and 'completely justifiable pride of a nation, a nation who was shedding blood for the cause of its own independence throughout the centuries'.[59]

French intellectuals observed the role played by folk heroic songs, memories of the glorious mediaeval Serbian State and the Kosovo legend on the formation of Serbian identity and patriotism. Magrou emphasized the importance of Serbian national folk poetry:

> The goal of Serbian poetry was to pass on those heroic memories, to save the popular tradition, to preserve the soul of Serbia. That is, no more than any other folk poetry, the one who reflects the spirit, the genius, fate of the whole nation; in it one can feel the flickering of heart [...] Poetry was the voice of the Homeland, without her, a new history of the Serbs wouldn't be able to be understood [...] Nothing is more noble than the patriotism which breathes this monumental Iliad. This is not the kind of patriotism inclined to hate, aggressive, desirous to propagate broad hegemony of one nation to the whole planet. It is a sense of pride because it was a fighter for the holy matter.[60]

At the same time, Magrou did not neglect the importance of Kosovo in the process of engendering the patriotism, sacrifice and courage shown by the Serbs from the Balkan Wars, and later in the First World War: 'The memory of Kosovo has perhaps further impassioned their patriotic belief because the glory of the victims was more noble than the celebration of triumph.'[61] At the beginning of the First World War, Viktor Berard also emphasized the importance of Serbian folk songs, and connections of Serbian heroism in the wars from 1912 with the consecration of the Kosovo and Serbian heroes, Emperor Dušan and Prince Lazar respectively.[62] French and other writers wrote about the hero of ancient Serbian legends – Marko Kraljević called him Roland of the South Slavs. 'They sing about him, in the hearts of all soldiers of the old King Peter, folk songs which from Serbia have made Thermopiles gorge. These sad and tragic, true war songs, in the end celebrate the victory, imminent and near one.'[63]

Conclusion

During the Great War (1914–1918), scholars, writers and artists were getting involved in politics in greater numbers than ever before and were eager to publicly express their opinions on various social issues. Due to the rapid development of the press, their words had the power to change beliefs and attitudes, with varying effects in shaping the ideas of French policy-makers. The starting point of the French intellectuals educated in a patriotic spirit was the return of France to a position of importance in international relations, whereas Serbia and the Serbs, who became the subject of their considerable interest, especially after the Annexation Crisis (1908) and the Balkan Wars (1912–1913), served during the Great War as a pretext for rekindling the spirit of French patriotism. The involvement and the significant role of scholars in the Great War, as well as the importance of the struggle in the area of propaganda, the image of Serbia and the Serbs created by French intellectuals shaped French-Serbian and, later, French-Yugoslav relations. By highlighting the hardship and heroism of the Serbs during the war, French intellectuals instilled faith in French soldiers on the battlefield, maintained the national unity and indirectly ensured for France a prominent role in international relations after the Great War. At the same time, by affirming the Serbian issue, Serbia received support for the idea of single Yugoslavia. This case study shows that away from the front in the Great War, the role of the intellectuals was crucial in moulding public opinion. For less than two decades the Serbs, a small Balkan nation, became a symbol of wartime courage and morals for French intellectuals. And the most important thing was that the French decision-makers believed that Serbs were capable of resisting German aggression. In wartime, the strength of intellectuals was recognized as more effective than weapons, and it had a decisive influence on the implementation of national plans of small nations.

Notes

1   This contribution is a part of the project *The Democratic and National Capacities of Serbia's Institutions in the Process of International Integrations*, supported by the Ministry of Education, Science and Technological Development of the Republic of Serbia (Grant no. 179009).
2   S. Vitanović and G. Vitanović, *Francuska civilizacija* [French Civilization]. Beograd: Geopolitika, 1996, p. 139; P. Alber, *Istorija štampe* [History of the Press] Beograd: Plato, 1998, pp. 64–66; M. Bjelica and Z. Jevtović, *Istorija novinarstva* [History of Journalism]. Beograd: Megatrend, 2006, pp. 81–82, 93–97.
3   A. Brigs and P. Berk, *Društvena istorija medija* [Social Media History]. Beograd: Clio, 2006, p. 266.
4   A. Kolaković, *U službi otadžbine: saradnja francuskih i srpskih intelektualaca 1894–1914* [For the Homeland: Cooperation of French and Serbian Intellectuals 1894–1914]. Beograd: Institut za političke studije, 2016.
5   A. Kolaković, 'War and Propaganda in 1915: French Intellectuals and Actualisation of Serbian Issues', in *The Great War in 1915*, ed. Denda Dalibor and Mario Christian Ortner. Belgrade: Heeresgeschichtliches Museum/Militärhistorisches Institut Strategic Research Institute Belgrade, 2017, pp. 330–352.
6   A. Kolaković, 'French Intellectuals on the Austro-Hungarian Interest in the Balkans 1894–1914', in *Balkan Entanglements – Peace of Bucharest*, ed. Matei Gheboianu and Cosmin Ionita. Bucharest: Universitatii din Bucuresti, 2016, pp. 13–29; Kolaković, 'Intelektualci, srpsko pitanje i velike sile (1894–1918)', in *Srbija i politika velikih sila 1914–2014*, ed. Djurić Živojin and Miloš Knežević. Beograd: Institut za političke studije, 2014, pp. 371–399; Kolaković, '– Road to Great War – Serbian Intellectuals and Austro-Hungarian Policy in the Balkans (1894–1914)', *Serbian Political Thought*, 1 (2014), pp. 67–89.

7   ANF [Les Archives nationales de France – Site de Paris]: AJ/16/113, AJ/16/6019, Dossier Emile Haumant; F/17/26707, Dossier Victor Bérard; AJ/16/6074, Dossier Mallet; F/17/2987a; ASANU [Archives of SASA], Inheritance Loazo – Vojinović, no. 14427, III-1, Memoirés I Partie (1880–1914), 1, 94; A. Scheikevitch, *André Chéradame et son oevre*. Paris: Impr. du Réveil économique, 1928, p. 4; J.-M. Mayeur, *La vie politique sous la Troisième République 1870–1940*. Paris: Éditions du Seuil Points-Histoire, 1984, pp. 27–34; M. Winock, *La fièvre hexagonale. Les grandes crises politiques 1871–1968*. Paris: Éditions du Seuil, 1999, pp. 80–82.

8   A. Dž. P. Tejlor [A.J.P. Taylor], *Borba za prevlast u Evropi 1848–1918* [The Struggle for Mastery in Europe]. Sarajevo: Veselin Masleša, 1965, p. 279; Mayeur, *La vie politique*, p. 71; M. Winock, *La France politique XIXe–XXe siècle*. Paris: Éditions du Seuil, 2003, pp. 94–96.

9   M. Ković, *Zapadnoevropske ideje u Srpskom književnom glasniku 1901–1914* [The Western European Ideas in the *Serbian Literary Gazette* 1901–1914], master's thesis, Belgrade University, 2003, pp. 35–37; Ž. Diga [J. Dugast], *Kulturni život u Evropi na prelazu iz 19. u 20. vek* [Cultural Life in Europe at the Turn of the Nineteenth and Twentieth Centuries]. Beograd: Clio, 2007, p. 147.

10 Mayeur, *La vie politique*, pp. 73, 95, 124; Winock, *La fièvre hexagonale*, pp. 117–123; Dz. Roberts [J. Roberts], *Evropa 1880–1945* [Europe 1880–1945]. Beograd: Clio, 2002, pp. 171–174; M. Peri [M. Perry], *Intelektualna istorija Evrope* [An Intellectual History of Modern Europe]. Beograd: Clio, 2000, pp. 339–340.

11 Pierre Renouvin, *Evropska kriza i Prvi svjetski rat* [European Crisis and World War I]. Zagreb: Školska knjiga, 1965, p. 64; Diga, *Kulturni život u Evropi*, pp. 53, 55.

12 P. Nora, 'Lavisse, instituteur national', in *Les lieux de mémoire*, vol. 1, ed. C.-R. Ageon and P. Nora. Paris: Gallimard, 1997, pp. 239–275.

13 Nora, 'Lavisse, instituteur national', pp. 239–275; S. Sretenović, *Francuska i Kraljevina Srba Hrvata i Slovenaca* [France and the Kingdom of Serbs, Croats and Slovenes]. Beograd: Institut za savremenu istoriju, 2008, p. 36; Sretenović, '*Srbija* Viktora Berara: jedan pogled na doprimnos Srbije zajedničkim naporima saveznika 1915. godine' [*Serbia* by Viktor Berard: A View of the Contribution of the Joint Efforts of the Allies of Serbia in 1915], in *Prvi svetski rat balkanski čvor* [The First World War and Balkan Knot], ed. I. Pantelić, J. Milanović and M. Gatalović. Beograd: Institut za savremenu istoriju, 2014, p. 579.

14 Sretenović, *Francuska i Kraljevina Srba Hrvata i Slovenaca*, pp. 33–37; A. Kolaković, 'French Intellectuals and the French Policy Change in the Balkans (1912–1913)', *Journal of Turkish World Studies*, XII, no. 2 (2012), pp. 199–212.

15 A. Kolaković, *Francuski i srpski intelektualci: saradnja i uticaji (1894–1914)* [French and Serbian Intellectuals: Cooperation and Influences (1894–1914)], doctoral dissertation, Beograd, 2015.

16 ANF, AJ/16/6074 (Dossier Mallet); ANF, F/17/2987a (A. Mallet – *Mission en Macédoine études éthnographiques*, 1902); F/17/26707 (Dossier Berard); AJ/16/113, AJ/16/6019 (Dossier Haumant); F/17/25832 (Dossier Leger); A. Scheikevitch, *André Chéradame et son oevre*, pp. 4–9; L. Eisenmann, 'André Chéradame et la question d'Autriche', *Revue historiorque*, LXXIX (1902), pp. 5–8; J. Žujović, 'Ernest Deni' ['Ernest Denis'], *Godišnjak SKA*, XXIX (1920), pp. 206–209; K. Spasić, 'Srpska javnost o četvorici poznatih francuskih istoričara' [Serbian Public Opinion on the Four Famous French Historians'], in *Jugoslovensko-francuski odnosi* [Franco-Yugoslav Relations], ed. Slavneko Terzić. Beograd: Istorisjki institute, 1990, p. 234; M. Vojvodić, *Izazovi srpske spoljne politike (1791–1918) ogledi i rasprave* [The Challenges of Serbian

Foreign Policy (1791–1918): Essays and Studies]. Beograd: Istorijski institute, 2007, p. 409.
17 Ch. Loiseau, *Le Balkan slave et la crise autrichienne* [The Slavic Balkans and the Austrian Crisis]. Paris: Perrin, 1898.
18 D.T. Bataković, 'Francuski uticaji u Srbiji 1836–1914. Četiri generacije Parizlija' [French Influence in Serbia 1836–1914: Four Generations of Parisians], *Zbornik Matice srpske za istoriju*, 56 (1997), pp. 73–95; M. Vojvodić, *Putevi srpske diplomatije* [Paths of Serbian Diplomacy]. Beograd: Clio, 1999; Lj. Trgovcević, *Planirana elita* [Scheduled Elite]. Beograd: JP Službeni glasnik, Istorijski institut, 2003; M. Pavlović, *Od Esklavonije do Jugoslavije* [From Esklavonia to Yugoslavia]. Sremski Karlovci, Novi Sad: Izdavacka knjižarnica Zorana Stojanovića, 1994, pp. 187, 297; A. Kolaković, 'L'Élite serbe et le modèle culturel français dans la revue "Delo" (L'Oevre) de 1894 à 1915', in *La Serbie et la France – une alliance atypique*, ed. D.T. Batakovic. Belgrade: Institute for Balkan Studies, SASA, 2010, pp. 205–216.
19 V. Bérard, 'Questions extérieures. Entente Austro-Russe', *La Revue de Paris*, 15 March (1908), pp. 416–448; Bérard, 'Indépendance Serbe', *La Revue de Paris*, 15 January (1909), pp. 436–448.
20 NBS [National library of Serbia], Hartije Grgura Jakšića [Papers Gregory Jaksić], P558/IX/618; É. Haumant, *En Bosnie*. Paris: Impr. de P. Brodard, 1906; A. Mazon and A. Livondelle, 'Émile Haumant – Nécrologie', *Revue des études slaves*, 21, no. 21-1-4 (1944), pp. 174–179.
21 Stojan Novaković was Serbian Minister in Paris 1900. He was a historian, scholar, literary critic and translator; he was also President of the Serbian Academy of Sciences and Arts, head of the National Library, the Prime Minister of the Kingdom of Serbia, Minister of Education, Minister of the Interior and leader of the Progressive Party. Andra Nikolić was a lawyer, writer, historian of literature, diplomat and politician; he was also Minister of Education, Minister of Foreign Affairs, Minister of Justice, State Counsellor, President of the National Assembly of the Kingdom of Serbia (1909–1918) and Serbian Minister in Paris in 1902 and 1913. Milenko Vesnić was a politician and diplomat, Minister of Justice (1904), Prime Minister and a member of the People's Radical Party. Vesnić was appointed Serbian Minister in Paris in 1904, a post he held for almost 17 years in various terms. After the Balkan Wars, Vesnić was a member of the Serbian Delegation at the Conference of Ambassadors in London (1912–1913). (AS [Archives of Serbia], MID [Ministry of Foreign Affairs], Poslanstvo u Parizu [Mission in Paris], f. 1, pov. no. 880, 10.03.1899; MID – Poslanstvo u Parizu, Izveštaj [Raport], 12.07.1900; Ibid, f. 2, no. 4831, 27.12.1902; M. Vojvodić, *Stojan Novaković u službi nacionalnih i državnih interesa* [Stojan Novakovic in the Service of National and State Interests]. Beograd: Srpska književna zadruga, 2012; M. Radojević, 'Milenko Vesnić', in *Srpska enciklopedija* [Serbian Encyclopaedia], vol. 2. Novi Sad, Beograd: Matica srpska, Srpska akademija nauka i umetnosti, 2013, p. 306.
22 Kolaković, 'Intelektualci, srpsko pitanje i velike sile (1894–1918)', pp. 371–399.
23 NBS, Hartije Grgura Jakšića, P558/IX/618.
24 *Dokumenti o spoljnoj politici Kraljevine Srbije 1903–1914* [Documents on foreign affairs of the Kingdom of Serbia 1903–1914], t. V, v. 3, SANU, Beograd, 1986, no. 50, 80, 83, 86; H. Barby, *Les Victoires serbes*. Grasset, Paris, 1913; H. Barby, *Brégalnitza. La guerre serbo-bulgare*. Paris: Grasset, 1914; A. Chéradame, *Douz ans de propagande en faveur des peuples balkaniques*. Paris: Plon, 1913.
25 M. N., 'Omladina na strani' [Youth Abroad], *Slovenski jug*, no. 49, 4.12.1910, pp. 385–386.

26 P. Mitrović, 'Dvije prijeke potrebe' [Two Pressing Needs], *Slovenski jug*, no. 27, 02.7.1911, p. 209.
27 M.Ković, 'Civilizatorska misija Austrougarske na Balkanu: pogled iz Beograda (1901–1914)' [Civilizing Mission of Austria-Hungary in the Balkans: A View from Belgrade (1901–1914)], *Istraživanja*, 22 (2011), pp. 365–379; M. Radojević and Lj. Dimić, *Srbija u Velikom ratu* [Serbia in the Great War]. Beograd: Srpska književna zadruga, 2014, pp. 25–30; Kolaković, '– Road to Great War –', pp. 67–89.
28 M. Pavlović, *Jugoslovenske teme u francuskoj prozi* [Yugoslav Themes in French Prose]. Beograd: Institut za književnost i umetnost, 1982, p. 14; J. Veyrenc, 'Histoire de la slavistique française', *Beiträge zur Geschichte der Slawistik in nichtslawischen Ländern*, 1985.
29 A. Malet, *Dnevnik sa srpskog dvora. – Journal de Serbie: 1892–1894*. Beograd: Clio, 1999, p. 70.
30 A. Mouzet, *Aux pays balkanique: Monténégro Serbie Bulgarie*. Paris, 1912; 'Beleške' ['Note'], *Srpski književni glasnik* [Serbian Literary Gazette], book XXIX, v. 11, 01.01.1912, p. 875; *Srpski književni glasnik*, book XXXI, v. 1, 01.7.1913, p. 79.
31 *Srpski književni glasnik*, book XXXI, v. 8, 16.10.1913, p. 635.
32 Barby, *Brégalnitza*, p. III.
33 *Albert Kahn: photographies, films, jardins. Un monde aux portes de Paris*. Paris: Musée Albert-Kahn, Conseil Général des Hauts de Seine, 2006; D. Okuefuna, *The Wonderful World of Albert Kahn: Colour Photographs from a Lost Age*. London: BBC Books, 2008.
34 N. Broc, *Regards sur la géographie française de la Renaissance à nos jours*. Paris: Presses Universitaires de Perpignan, 1995; J.-L. Tissier, 'Brunhes (Jean)', in *Dictionnaire des intellectuels français*, dir. J. Julliard, M. Winock. Paris: Seuil, 1996, pp. 195–196.
35 B. Popović, *Ogist Goven (1861–1931) i Viktor Berar (1864–1931)* [Auguste Gauvin (1861–1931) and Victor Bérard (1864–1931)]. Beograd: Narodna štamparija, 1931, p. 24.
36 Ibid., pp. 28–29.
37 Ibid., pp. 10, 12.
38 V.M. Djordjević and M. Stojadinović, *Sećanje na Bolije* [Memory of Beaulieu]. Beograd: Drag. Grefotića, 1930, pp. 15–16; L.J. Trgovčević, *Naučnici Srbije i stvaranje Jugoslavije 1914–1920* [Scholars of Serbia and the Creation of Yugoslavia 1914–1920]. Beograd: Srpska književna zadruga, 1987, p. 141.
39 The main initiator and coordinator of Serbian 'academic propaganda' was Jovan M. Jovanović, who was also a French student.
40 D. Živojinovic, *Nevoljni ratnici: Velike sile i Solunski front 1914–1918* [Unwilling Warriors: The Great Powers and the Salonika Front 1914–1918]. Beograd: Zavod za udžbenike, 2010, p. x.
41 V. Bérard, *La Serbie*. Paris: Librairie Armand Colin, 1915, p. 14.
42 Žujović, 'Ernest Deni', pp. 206–209; E. Denis, *La grande Serbie*. Paris: Librairie Delagrave, 1915; Denis, *Du Vardar à Sotcha*. Paris: Bossard, 1923, pp. 111–112; M. Ekmečić, 'Francuska nauka i Srbi 1914' [French Science and Serbs in 1914], *Letopis Matice srpske*, book 460, 5 (1997), pp. 665–674; Vojvodić, *Izazovi srpske spoljne politike (1791–1918)*, pp. 409–411.
43 Popović, *Ogist Goven (1861–1931) i Viktor Berar (1864–1931)*, p. 13.
44 Boppe began his diplomatic career at the French Embassy in Belgrade and Cetinje (at the beginning of the 1890s). Already at that time he had made numerous acquaintances among Serbian intellectuals.

45 A. Boppe, *Za srpskom vladom od Niša do Krfa* [A la suite du Gouverment Serbe de Niš à Corfu]. Ženeva: Štamparija Ujedinjenja, 1918, p. 30.
46 H. Barby, *Avec l'armée serbe: de l'ultimatum autrichien à l'invasion de la Serbie*. Paris: Albin Michel, 1916, p. 33.
47 Ibid., p. 11.
48 Boppe, *Za srpskom vladom od Niša do Krfa*, p. 33.
49 Barby, *Avec l'armée serbe*, pp. 14–15.
50 Boppe, *Za srpskom vladom od Niša do Krfa*, p. 79.
51 J. Jovanović, 'Ogist Bop, (nekrolog)' [Auguste Boppe (Necrologue)], *Srpski književni glasnik*, nova, book III, 3, 01.07.1921, p. 240.
52 Sretenović, '*Srbija* Viktora Berara', pp. 574–575.
53 Lj. Dimić, 'Influences culturelle française dans le royaume de Yougoslavic', in *Francusko-srpski odnosi 1904–2004* [Franco-Serb International Relations 1904–2004], ed. M. Pavlovic and J. Novakovic. Beograd: Arhiv Srbije, 2005, pp. 57–72; M. Timotijević, 'A la France! Podizanje spomenika zahvalnosti Francuskoj na beogradskom Kalemegdanu' [A la France! Raising the Monument of Gratitude to France at Belgrade's Kalemegdan], in *Francusko-srpski odnosi 1904–2004* [Franco-Serb International Relations 1904–2004], ed. M. Pavlovic and J. Novakovic. Beograd: Arhiv Srbije, 2005, pp. 193–218; Sretenović, *Francuska i Kraljevina Srba Hrvata i Slovenaca*, pp. 243–304, 419–425, 461–463; V. Cvetković, 'La présence économique de la France en Yougoslavie 1918–1940', in *La Serbie et la France – une alliance atypique*, ed. D.T. Batakovic. Belgrade: Institute for Balkan Studies, SASA, 2010, pp. 557–574.
54 P. Lanux, *La Yougoslavie: la France et les Serbes*, Paris: Librairie Payot et Cie, 1916, pp. 228–233.
55 Ibid., 233.
56 NBS, Hartije Grgura Jakšića, P558/IX/617, G. Jakšić – M. Pašić, 28.10.1913.
57 NBS, Hartije Grgura Jakšića, P 558/ X/533, A. Male – G. Jakšić, 21.6.1915; Malet, *Dnevnik sa srpskog dvora*, pp. 53–54.
58 A. Magru [A. Magrou], 'Srbi i Srbija (uspomene od četiri godine provedene u Srbiji od 1889–1893. godine) [Serbs and Serbia (Memories of Four Years Spent in Serbia from 1889 to 1893], *Delo*, book 73 (1915), p. 122.
59 'Beleške' ['Notes'], *Srpski književni glasnik*, book XXIX, no. 11, 1.12.1912, p. 875.
60 Magru, 'Srbi i Srbija', p. 123.
61 Ibid.
62 Bérard, *La Serbie*, pp. 43–46.
63 M. Pavlović, *Francuzi o Srbima i Srbiji 1912–1918* [French on the Serbs and Serbia 1912–1918]. Beograd: Narodna knjiga, 1988, p. 351.

Bibliography

Primary sources

AJ/16/113, AJ/16/6019 (Dossier Haumant);
AJ/16/6074 (Dossier Mallet);
ANF (Archives nationales de France, Paris):
F/17/25832 (Dossier Leger).
F/17/26707 (Dossier Berard);
F/17/2987a (A. Mallet – *Mission en Macédoine études éthnographiques*, 1902);

Hartije Grgura Jakšića
NBS (Narodna biblioteka Srbije, Beograd)

Dokumenti o spoljnoj politici Kraljevine Srbije 1903-1914. 1986. t. V, v. 3, Beograd: SANU.
Slovenski jug. Beograd.
Srpski književni glasnik. 1901-1914. Beograd.

Secondary sources

Albert Kahn: photographies, films, jardins. Un monde aux portes de Paris. Paris: Musée Albert-Kahn, Conseil Général des Hauts de Seine, 2006.
Alber, Pjer, *Istorija štampe* [History of the Press] Beograd: Plato, 1998.
Barby, Henry, *Les Victoires serbes*. Paris: Grasset, 1913.
Barby, Henry, *Brégalnitza. La guerre serbo-bulgare*. Paris: Grasset, 1914.
Barby, Henry, *Avec l'armée serbe: de l'ultimatum autrichien à l'invasion de la Serbie*. Paris: Albin Michel, 1916.
Bataković, Dušan T., 'Francuski uticaji u Srbiji 1836-1914. Četiri generacije Parizlija' [French Influence in Serbia 1836-1914: Four Generations of Parisians], *Zbornik Matice srpske za istoriju*, 56 (1997), pp. 73-95.
Bérard, Victor, 'Questions extérieures. Entente Austro-Russe', *La Revue de Paris*, 15 March (1908), pp. 416-448.
Bérard, Victor, 'Indépendance Serbe', *La Revue de Paris*, 15 January (1909), pp. 436-448.
Bérard, Victor, *La Serbie*. Paris: Librairie Armand Colin, 1915.
Bjelica, Mihailo and Zoran Jevtović, *Istorija novinarstva* [History of Journalism]. Beograd: Megatrend, 1996.
Boppe, Auguste, *Za srpskom vladom od Niša do Krfa* [A la suite du Gouverment Serbe de Niš à Corfu]. Ženeva: Štamparija Ujedinjenja, 1918.
Brigs, Asa and Piter Berk, *Društvena istorija medija* [Social Media History]. Beograd: Clio, 2006.
Broc, Numa, *Regards sur la géographie française de la Renaissance à nos jours*. Paris: Presses Universitaires de Perpignan, 1995.
Chéradame, André, *Douz ans de propagande en faveur des peuples balkaniques*. Paris: Plon, 1913.
Cvetković, Vladimir, 'La présence économique de la France en Yougoslavie 1918-1940', in *La Serbie et la France – une alliance atypique*, ed. D.T. Batakovic. Belgrade: Institute for Balkan Studies, SASA, 2010, pp. 557-574.
Diga, Žak, *Kulturni život u Evropi na prelazu iz 19. u 20. vek* [Cultural Life in Europe at the Turn of the Nineteenth and Twentieth Centuries]. Beograd: Clio, 2007.
Dimić, Ljubodrag, 'Influences culturelle française dans le royaume de Yougoslavie', in *Francusko-srpski odnosi 1904-2004* [Franco-Serb International Relations 1904-2004], ed. M. Pavlovic and J. Novakovic. Beograd: Arhiv Srbije, 2005, pp. 57-72.
Denis, Ernest, *La grande Serbie*. Paris: Librairie Delagrave, 1915.
Denis, Ernest, *Du Vardar à Sotcha*. Paris: Bossard, 1923.
Djordjević, Vojin M. and Milan Stojadinović, *Sećanje na Bolije* [Memory of Beaulieu]. Beograd: Drag. Grefotića, 1930.
Eisenmann, Louis, 'André Chéradame et la question d'Autriche', *Revue historiorque*, LXXIX (1902), pp. 5-8.
Ekmečić, Milorad, *Ratni ciljevi Srbije 1914* [War Goals of 1914 Serbia]. Beograd: Politika, BMG, 1992.

Ekmečić, Milorad, 'Francuska nauka i Srbi 1914' [French Science and Serbs in 1914], *Letopis Matice srpske*, book 460, 5 (1997), pp. 665–674.

Haumant, Émile, *En Bosnie*. Paris: Impr. de P. Brodard, 1906.

Jovanović, J., 'Ogist Bop, (nekrolog)' [Auguste Boppe (Necrologue)], *Srpski književni glasnik*, nova, book III, 3, 01.07.1921, p. 240.

Kolaković, Aleksandra, 'L'Élite serbe et le modèle culturel français dans la revue "Delo" (L'Oevre) de 1894 à 1915', in *La Serbie et la France – une alliance atypique*, ed. D.T. Batakovic. Belgrade: Institute for Balkan Studies, SASA, 2010, pp. 205–216.

Kolaković, Aleksandra, 'French Intellectuals and the French Policy Change in the Balkans (1912–1913)', *Journal of Turkish World Studies*, XII, no. 2 (2012), pp. 199–212.

Kolaković, Aleksandra, 'Intelektualci, srpsko pitanje i velike sile (1894–1918)', in *Srbija i politika velikih sila 1914–2014*, ed. Djurić Živojin and Miloš Knežević. Beograd: Institut za političke studije, 2014, pp. 371–399.

Kolaković, Aleksandra, '– Road to Great War – Serbian Intellectuals and Austro-Hungarian Policy in the Balkans (1894–1914)', *Serbian Political Thought*, 1 (2014), pp. 67–89.

Kolaković, Aleksandra, *Francuski i srpski intelektualci: saradnja i uticaji (1894–1914)* [French and Serbian Intellectuals: Cooperation and Influences (1894–1914)], doctoral dissertation, Beograd, 2015.

Kolaković, Aleksandra, *U službi otadžbine: saradnja francuskih i srpskih intelektualaca 1894–1914* [For the Homeland: Cooperation of French and Serbian Intellectuals 1894–1914]. Beograd: Institut za političke studije, 2016.

Kolaković, Aleksandra, 'French Intellectuals on the Austro-Hungarian Interest in the Balkans 1894–1914', in *Balkan Entanglements – Peace of Bucharest*, ed. Matei Gheboianu and Cosmin Ionita. Bucharest: Universitatii din Bucuresti, 2016, pp. 13–29.

Kolaković, Aleksandra, 'War and Propaganda in 1915: French Intellectuals and Actualisation of Serbian Issues', in *The Great War in 1915*, ed. Denda Dalibor and Mario Christian Ortner. Belgrade: Heeresgeschichtliches Museum/Militärhistorisches Institut Strategic Research Institute Belgrade, 2017, pp. 330–352.

Ković, Miloš, *Zapadnoevropske ideje u Srpskom književnom glasniku 1901–1914* [The Western European Ideas in the *Serbian Literary Gazette* 1901–1914], master's thesis, Belgrade University, 2003.

Ković, Miloš, 'Civilizatorska misija Austrougarske na Balkanu: pogled iz Beograda (1901–1914)' [Civilizing Mission of Austria-Hungary in the Balkans: A View from Belgrade (1901–1914)], *Istraživanja*, 22 (2011), pp. 365–379.

Lanux, Pierre, *La Yougoslavie: la France et les Serbes*, Paris: Librairie Payot et Cie, 1916.

Loiseau, Charles, *Le Balkan slave et la crise autrichienne* [The Slavic Balkans and the Austrian Crisis]. Paris: Perrin, 1898.

Magru, A., 'Srbi i Srbija (uspomene od četiri godine provedene u Srbiji od 1889–1893. godine) [Serbs and Serbia (Memories of Four Years Spent in Serbia from 1889 to 1893)], *Delo*, book 73 (1915), p. 122

Malet, Alber, *Dnevnik sa srpskog dvora. – Journal de Serbie: 1892–1894*. Beograd: Clio, 1999.

Mayeur, Jean-Marie, *La vie politique sous la Troisième République 1870–1940*. Paris: Éditions du Seuil Points-Histoire, 1984.

Mazon, André and André Livondelle, 'Émile Haumant – Nécrologie', *Revue des études slaves*, 21, no. 21-1-4 (1944), pp. 174–179.

Mitrović, P., 'Dvije prijeke potrebe' [Two Pressing Needs], *Slovenski jug*, no. 27, 02.7.1911, p. 209

Mouzet, Alphonse, *Aux pays balkanique: Monténégro Serbie Bulgarie*. Paris, 1912.

Nora, Pierre, 'Lavisse, instituteur national', in *Les lieux de mémoire*, vol. 1, ed. C.-R. Ageon and P. Nora. Paris: Gallimard, 1997, pp. 239-275.

Okuefuna, David, *The Wonderful World of Albert Kahn: Colour Photographs from a Lost Age*. London: BBC Books, 2008.

Pavlović, Mihailo, *Jugoslovenske teme u francuskoj prozi* [Yugoslav Themes in French Prose]. Beograd: Institut za književnost i umetnost, 1982.

Pavlović, Mihailo, *Francuzi o Srbima i Srbiji 1912-1918* [French on the Serbs and Serbia 1912-1918]. Beograd: Narodna knjiga, 1988.

Pavlović, Mihailo, *Od Esklavonije do Jugoslavije* [From Esklavonia to Yugoslavia]. Sremski Karlovci, Novi Sad: Izdavacka knjižarnica Zorana Stojanovića, 1994.

Peri, Marvin, *Intelektualna istorija Evrope* [An Intellectual History of Modern Europe]. Beograd: Clio, 2000.

Popović, Bogdan, *Ogist Goven (1861-1931) i Viktor Berar (1864-1931)* [Auguste Gauvin (1861-1931) and Victor Bérard (1864-1931)]. Beograd: Narodna štamparija, 1931.

Radojević, Mira, 'Milenko Vesnić', in *Srpska enciklopedija* [Serbian Encyclopaedia], vol. 2. Novi Sad, Beograd: Matica srpska, Srpska akademija nauka i umetnosti, 2013.

Radojević Mira and Ljubodrag Dimić, *Srbija u Velikom ratu* [Serbia in the Great War]. Beograd: Srpska književna zadruga, 2014.

Renouvin, Pierre, *Evropska kriza i Prvi svjetski rat* [European Crisis and World War I]. Zagreb: Školska knjiga, 1965.

Roberts, Džon M., *Evropa 1880-1945* [Europe 1880-1945]. Beograd: Clio, 2002.

Scheikevitch, Antoine, *André Chéradame et son oevre*. Paris: Impr. du Réveil économique, 1928.

Spasić, Krunoslav, 'Srpska javnost o četvorici poznatih francuskih istoričara' [Serbian Public Opinion on the Four Famous French Historians"], in *Jugoslovensko-francuski odnosi* [Franco-Yugoslav Relations], ed. Slavneko Terzić. Beograd: Istorisjki institute, 1990, pp. 233-243.

Sretenović, Stanislav, *Francuska i Kraljevina Srba Hrvata i Slovenaca* [France and the Kingdom of Serbs, Croats and Slovenes]. Beograd: Institut za savremenu istoriju, 2008.

Sretenović, Stanislav, 'Srbija Viktora Berara: jedan pogled na doprimnos Srbije zajedničkim naporima saveznika 1915. godine' [Serbia by Viktor Berard: A View of the Contribution of the Joint Efforts of the Allies of Serbia in 1915], in *Prvi svetski rat balkanski čvor* [The First World War and Balkan Knot], ed. I. Pantelić, J. Milanović and M. Gatalović. Beograd: Institut za savremenu istoriju, 2014, pp. 574-575.

Tejlor, A. Dž. P., *Borba za prevlast u Evropi 1848-1918* [The Struggle for Mastery in Europe]. Sarajevo: Veselin Masleša, 1968.

Timotijević, Miroslav, 'A la France! Podizanje spomenika zahvalnosti Francuskoj na beogradskom Kalemegdanu' [A la France! Raising the Monument of Gratitude to France at Belgrade's Kalemegdan], in *Francusko-srpski odnosi 1904-2004* [Franco-Serb International Relations 1904-2004], ed. M. Pavlovic and J. Novakovic. Beograd: Arhiv Srbije, 2005, pp. 193-218.

Tissier, Jean-Luis, 'Brunhes (Jean)', in *Dictionnaire des intellectuels français*, dir. J. Julliard, M. Winock. Paris: Seuil, 1996, pp. 195-196.

Trgovčević, Ljubinka, *Naučnici Srbije i stvaranje Jugoslavije 1914-1920* [Scholars of Serbia and the Creation of Yugoslavia 1914-1920]. Beograd: Srpska književna zadruga, 1987.

Trgovčević, Ljubinka, *Planirana elita* [Scheduled Elite]. Beograd: JP Službeni glasnik, Istorijski institut, 2003.

Veyrenc, Jacques, 'Histoire de la slavistique française', *Beiträge zur Geschichte der Slawistik in nichtslawischen Länden*, 1985. Available at: http://www.etudes-slaves.paris-sorbonne. fr/IMG/pdf/J._Veyrenc_Histoire_de_la_slavistique_francaise_Wien_OAW_1985_.pdf (accessed 15 October 2014).

Vitanović, Slobodan and Gordana Vitanović, *Francuska civilizacija* [French Civilization]. Beograd: Geopolitika, 1996.

Vojvodić, Mihailo, *Putevi srpske diplomatije* [Paths of Serbian Diplomacy]. Beograd: Clio, 1999.

Vojvodić, Mihailo, *Izazovi srpske spoljne politike (1791–1918) ogledi i rasprave* [The Challenges of Serbian Foreign Policy (1791–1918): Essays and Studies]. Beograd: Istorijski institute, 2007.

Vojvodić, Mihailo, *Stojan Novaković u službi nacionalnih i državnih interesa* [Stojan Novakovic in the Service of National and State Interests]. Beograd: Srpska književna zadruga, 2012.

Winock, Michel, *La fièvre hexagonale. Les grandes crises politiques 1871–1968*. Paris: Éditions du Seuil, 1999.

Winock, Michel, *La France politique XIXe–XXe siècle*. Paris: Éditions du Seuil, 2003.

Živojinovic, D., *Nevoljni ratnici: Velike sile i Solunski front 1914–1918* [Unwilling Warriors: The Great Powers and the Salonika Front 1914–1918]. Beograd: Zavod za udžebnike, 2010.

Žujović, Jovan, 'Ernest Deni' ['Ernest Denis'], *Godišnjak SKA*, XXIX (1920), pp. 206–209.

11

The New Ottoman Conception of War, State and Society in the Prelude to the First World War[1]

Banu Turnaoğlu
University of Cambridge

The entry of the Ottoman Empire into the First World War has been widely discussed by diplomatic, military and political historians. Most historians generally characterized Ottoman leaders as driven by myopic selfish ambitions that pushed the Ottoman state blindly towards disaster. In Turkish historiography, this view was developed primarily by Yusuf Hikmet Bayur in his *Türk İnkılâbı Tarihi* (History of the Turkish Revolution), published between 1940 and 1967. He argued that the Ottoman Empire had been drawn into the war on the side of Germany and Austria-Hungary 'without compelling reason',[2] because the Ottoman leaders were of below average intelligence, simple-minded and unable to think and decide rationally.[3] His formulation, with its singular emphasis on the Ottoman leaders' incompetence as the main cause of the Empire's entry into the war, has widely influenced military historiography and the publications of the Turkish General Staff.[4] Recent Western scholarship also instructs us that the Ottomans' entry into the war was a consequence of 'unforeseen events'.[5] Most historians have neglected the ways in which public opinion and ideas that had been developed in the course of the Balkan Wars shaped the politics and diplomacy of the Ottoman decision-makers.[6]

This chapter stresses that a far more complex set of philosophical, political, psychological and military ideas developed in the course of the Balkan Wars lay behind Turkey's entry into the First World War. The world views of the Triumvirate and Ottoman military and nationalist thinkers at that time, influenced by German military theory and idealist philosophy as well as French social theory, played a pivotal role in framing their political ambitions. The Balkan defeats of 1912–1913 powerfully influenced Ottoman war aims and aspirations. To formulate a strong state ideology that could stand against their enemies, the Young Turk leaders defended a militant and transformative conception of national destiny in intense dialogue with public opinion in the prelude to the Great War. They and their intellectual allies glorified the state, and justified a new theory of offensive war, whilst public opinion itself had always assumed that offence conferred an advantage in warfare.

The Shift Towards Authoritarianism

The Second Constitutional Period (1908-1918), with its three decisive wars (in the Balkans and across the continent), had a huge impact on the ways in which Ottoman people thought about politics and on what they expected from it. It saw the birth of a new social, political, religious and military idealism, which overturned the universal commitments of the Young Turk Revolution of 1908. This shift was consolidated by the Triumvirate of Enver, Cemal and Talat Paşas, whose collective decisions dominated Ottoman politics from 1913 to 1918. They decisively adopted a blend of German militarist, nationalist and idealist elements, combining elitism and mass mobilization, positively valuing violence and normalizing war. The political rise of these three men and their consolidation of executive and military power, which left them unchallengeable and seemingly invincible, radically altered the orientation of Turkish politics.

The Young Turks believed that a state required a distinctive national and military ideology to face its enemies at home and abroad. Until the Balkan Wars, Ottomanism had served this purpose. But the Balkan Wars powerfully influenced Ottoman state ideology, war aims and aspirations. With the Empire reduced to Anatolia and the Arab provinces, having shed all its European territory except Thrace, the Young Turks recognized the inadequacy of this old ideal for holding Ottoman society together in an age of nationalism.[7] They sought to create fresh ideological resources to strengthen the state in its stand against its enemies.[8]

In the years before the First World War, there was widespread discussion in the press around the changing character of modern warfare and its implications for Ottoman policy. Defeat in the First Balkan War had been a traumatic shock, generating an entire new language of war, society, politics, and philosophy, along with a fresh set of aspirations. The defeat aroused shame and humiliation, and prompted hatred and a drive for revenge against the state's enemies, but it also offered a challenge, and the opportunity to learn from mistakes: to understand factors in the nation's defeat, analyse the actions of the belligerents, conceptualize the character of modern warfare and forestall future defeats. Unlike previous conflicts, driven mainly by *jihad* or the desire for economic expansion in trade and territory, modern warfare was seen as a complex blend of psychological, military, religious, political, idealistic and socio-national factors.

This new vision of warfare positioned that the state's survival could be assured only on the battlefield, and this required the strengthening of national spirit and morale. For the Ottomans, the Balkan Wars had validated the ideas expressed by Gustave Le Bon. Major Hafız Hakkı's (1878-1915) experiences had led him to focus carefully on the mass psychology of modern warfare. In *Bozgun* (Defeat), he attributed the mass disorientation and confusion that had occured on the battlefield to uncontrollable fear and irrationality.[9] Ottoman soldiers in the Balkan conflicts had proved lazy, unmotivated, unpatriotic and unwilling to sacrifice their lives for national goals.[10] Morale, Hakkı argued, was now the primary factor in military success: 'War is a question of spirit, more [important] than that of science.'[11] Following Le Bon's conception of the *psychologie des foules* (*ruh'ül cemaat*),[12] he insisted that mass groups require a 'myth', or 'race ideal', to organize themselves into a cohesive entity. To win future wars, the Ottoman elite must guide the masses and manipulate their shapeless, unconscious and unstable attitudes to create a stronger spirit.

This implied a Darwinian struggle between nations. In Filibeli Ahmed Hilmi's words: 'The struggle [in the Balkans] is over, but struggle itself will start again. Living means struggling. The absence of struggle can only be found in cemeteries. Only the dead are without struggle.'[13] He saw states as permanently at war, and considered that a state had absolute liberty to do what it judged most conducive to its advantage, and there was neither justice nor injustice between nations. In the absence of applicable international law, a state could resist, invade or exploit other states as needed.[14] The sole law that applied to humanity, for Ethem Necdet, an officer who joined the Tripoli and Balkan campaigns, was the Darwinian law: 'The right to live belongs to the strongest. The weak are condemned to die ... Life is an endless war.'[15] War was needed biologically to purify and renew humanity, and without it nations would become weak and effeminate.[16]

This Darwinian vision required the mobilization of all human and material resources for war under the absolute control of a military elite, and a state of permanent readiness, even in peacetime.[17] The martial virtues of the Turks and their proud independence needed to be joined both with the effective leadership that had long been lacking, and en exclusive focus on war throughout the nation.[18] The aim of warfare was to exhaust the enemies' armed forces, gain territory, and kill or permanently incapacitate them. An annihilative victory which brought peace was not considered a crime, but a natural right.

Such total war involved the wholesale, active participation of the civilian population. The phrase 'a nation in arms' (*millet-i müsellaha*) entered Ottoman military thought at the end of the nineteenth century through Colmar von der Goltz's famous work *Das Volk in Waffen*, translated into Ottoman Turkish in 1884 and used as a textbook at the *Mekteb-i Harbiye* (the Royal Military Academy) from 1886 onward.[19] Goltz was invited by Abdülhamid II in 1882 to modernize the army and improve military education, and remained in this post until 1895. His teachings at the *Harbiye* influenced the thinking of a new generation of Young Turk leaders,[20] military thinkers and future leaders of the Republic, amongst them Mustafa Kemal and Kazım Karabekir.[21]

The new vision of warfare did not preclude the earlier conception of justification by religious ideology. Tüccarzade İbrahim Hilmi conceived of parts of the Balkan conflict as total war, and the combined armies of the Balkan League (Bulgaria, Serbia, Greece and Montenegro) as a crusader force.[22] He imagined a future total war against the crusaders as an opportunity to take revenge on Christian civilizations (*Hristiyan medeniyeti*), a term which connoted evil, barbarism, cruelty, injustice and mercilessness, unlike its counterpart for European civilizations (*Avrupa medeniyeti*), which connoted science, progress, civilization, liberty, equality, rights and modernity.[23] As in the past, in the time of the Crusades, Christianity had attempted to annihilate Islam and threaten the whole of humanity (*insaniyet*), and the real enemy of the Ottoman Empire and Islam was Christianity, not Europe itself.[24] In time there would come a just war to purge Islam and humanity as a whole of all its religious enemies, to free Muslim nations from Western slavery, and create a Pan-Islamic unity.

Germany as the Ideal Social and Political Model for Renewal

The issue of the hour was whether a glorious and spiritually powerful nation could rise from the ashes of a humiliating defeat in the Balkans, and build a state fit to win wars. The model nation that answered both questions for Ottoman writers and politicians was the galvanizing example of Prussia. Its military success was seen as a result of an inspired German national consciousness which took up arms in defence of the fatherland under the guidance of its military leaders. Captain Osman Naci admired von Scharnhorst's vigorous system of national militia, and his use of conscription to transform the army into the school of the nation.[25] Colonel Pertev praised von Moltke for turning Germany into a nation-in-arms by infusing military education and discipline throughout society and its civil institutions: 'The military institution is a school, teaching them [the next generation] order, punctuality, cleanliness, obedience and fidelity.'[26]

Numerous works on Prussia's rebirth were translated into Ottoman Turkish, as[27] Ottoman interest in German idealism had already started to increase in nineteenth-century political thought. Beşir Fuat (1852–1887) praised Kant's contributions to philosophy, astronomy and metaphysics,[28] while the Tanzimat writer Münif Paşa (1828–1894) referred in his *Telhis-i Hikmet-i Hukuk* (*Philosophie du Droit;* Philosophy of Rights) to Kant and Fichte.[29] In *Schopenhauer'in Hikmet-i Cedidesi* (Schopenhauer's New Philosophy, 1887), Ahmet Mithat Efendi offered a Kantian interpretation of Schopenhauer's philosophy, and championed his characterization of Will (*irade*) in the world as an absolutely free, entirely self-determining and all-powerful force.[30] In 1911, Baha Tevfik (1881–1914), a formative influence on the political thinking of Ömer Seyfeddin and Ziya Gökalp, founded *Felsefe Mecmuası* (the Journal of Philosophy'). This aimed to introduce 'a philosophical language and way of living' capable of raising up a powerful nation like those in the contemporary West, and included extensive discussion of ethics, obligations, and Kantian philosophy.[31]

These translations, and the engagement with German though they fostered and reflected, did much to introduce new conceptions of the state and philosophical idealism to the Ottoman world. The role these ideas played became more prominent after the Balkan defeat, as Ottoman thinkers focused on how philosophy and literature had helped Germany to construct a new national idealism freeing the nation from the influence of French language, literature, and civilization, and endowing it with the national pride and sense of military might that defeated France in 1871.[32] Tekinalp praised Fichte for promoting a national ideal and consciousness (*vicdan-ı milli*) among Germans,[33] and Hafız Hakkı insisted that the Empire needed a 'Turkish Fichte, worshipping this [national] ideal'[34] to inspire his contemporaries through philosophy and popular writings.

If the Turkish state, too, was to rise and endure as a great and united nation, Ottoman intellectuals would need to draft a new idealist programme to mobilize the nation and counter the destructive plans of the West and Russia.[35] Gökalp believed that readiness for war required the formation of an entirely new spirit 'in the Age of Nations', stating that "The most powerful force over the mind of this age is national idealism."[36] Without 'a great national ideal' (*emel-i milli*), Sadri Maksudi (known by his pen-name, Can Bey) argued, 'a nation cannot live, and even if it lives, cannot progress. To revitalise the Turkish nation, the intellectual elite must uncover its soul and ideals, which would lead to an empowering 'national awakening' (*intibah*).[37] After the regeneration, there would be 'no discord, and not even the devil could disturb souls united in this blessed belief'.[38] In future, warfare would be a 'battle of national idealisms',[39] and its outcome determined by the power of ideas.

The Shift from Universalism to National Idealism

Two cities, Thessaloniki and Istanbul, played special roles in constructing the new doctrine. Administrative reforms in Thessaloniki, the largest Ottoman city in Rumelia, had since the late nineteenth century brought about a renaissance in social, economic, and intellectual life. The city expanded, its walls were torn down, and the first tram service began in 1888. With this modern face, Thessaloniki projected an openness and willingness to integrate fully into Europe. After the Young Turk Revolution, Thessaloniki became the symbolic city of 'freedom', and with the establishment of the Committee of Union and Progress (CUP) headquarters, its political significance increased dramatically, with many Ottoman intellectuals migrating there.[40]

Thessaloniki also emerged as a centre where the philosophy of Turkish nationalism was formulated. An official initiative for a new national programme was drafted by Kemal Bey, Secretary of the CUP branch in Istanbul, and Ziya Gökalp, a former delegate from the branch committee in Diyarbakır, appointed to chair the Central Committee as theorist of the nation in 1910. In 1911, Gökalp, Ömer Seyfeddin, and Ali Canip launched *Genç Kalemler* (Young Pens) to advance this programme and the national movement, promoting a new national language (*milli lisan*), consciousness (*milli vicdan*) and ideal (*yeni bir ülkü*) to fashion a new generation and build a better future.[41]

The centrality of language in nation-building was stressed in Seydeddin's articles 'Yeni Lisan' (New Language), insisting that a New Life (*Yeni Hayat*) required a New Language (*Yeni Lisan*).[42] Turkish was the pre-eminent vehicle of the national spirit and rooted in the native culture, but it had been invaded by foreign tongues, and rendered artificial, 'diseased' and 'cosmopolitan'. A new autonomous Turkish language purified of Arabic and Persian traces was a pre-requisite for a national awakening.[43] This ideal grew into a philosophical movement, *New Life, New Language* (*Yeni Hayat, Yeni Lisan*), with ambitious goals: 'We must be ourselves, that is, we must build up our intellectual life on our national traditions and cultivate our new talents. We must borrow from Europe method and technique only. Our whole literature, which is not Turkish in any respect, must be reformed and founded on a new basis, it must become purely national in character.[44] The figures who formed it drew their inspiration from Alfred Fouillée, Gustav Le Bon, Henri Bergson, Arthur de Gobineau and Friedrich Nietzsche, and particularly, in due course, from Émile Durkheim, whose presence was felt throughout the social and political thought of the late Ottoman Empire and early Turkish Republic.

The most pressing question for the champions of the new nationalism was how to complete the political revolution with a social revolution which would secure progress, and rouse a sleepy nation. They saw the Young Turk Revolution and the re-promulgation of the constitution as necessary steps in revitalizing the declining Empire, but blamed the ruling elite's failure to identify an effective vision of how to reconstruct and reorganize the new society. Only a social revolution *(içtimai inkılab)*, a slow and patient transformation in Ottoman society itself, led by the elite and working peacefully through intellectual means, could discover the values and ideals to carry Ottoman society steadily and reliably forward.

The new programme was advanced by Gökalp in his 'New Life and New Values'.[45] He saw values as social forces embedded in collective representations, 'ideals', and 'the real factors in the evolution of humanity'.[46] Ideals did not exist only in the imagination, nor were they Platonic standards of perfection. Instead, following Fouillée and his rendering of Kant, they were constructed by individuals within a society and had no existence independently of individual mind and consciousness. His idealism was neither metaphysical nor anti-realist, but grounded in deep social structures and the collective spirit of a nation. The Young Turk Revolution, for Gökalp, was not a genuine revolution, since it merely appealed 'the machinery of a constitutional regime to government'.[47] Declaring republican ideals, the *idées-forces* of liberty, equality and fraternity, meant nothing unless they were combined with the particular *sentiments-forces*, a further term borrowed from Fouillée, that are the products of social consciousness and cohesiveness, and sources for a genuine revolution.[48] This union would give Turks a new life of harmony and unity, bound collectively together as a stronger nation than ever before: 'The *Übermensch (fevkalbeşerler)*, envisaged by the German philosopher Nietzsche, are the Turks. They are the new people of every century. Therefore, the new life will be born from Turkism, the mother of all youth.'[49]

Alongside this new national vision, Pan-Turkism developed in Istanbul.[50] It was formulated originally by Crimean Tatars beyond the imperial boundaries, as a social and cultural programme of response to the pressures of Pan-Slavism and the prevailing Russification policy in Crimea.[51] The leading Tatar intellectual İsmail Gaprinsky (1851–1914), or Gaspıralı İsmail,[52] inspired the *Jadidist* movement among Muslim Tatars, a cultural initiative aimed at reforming education by implementing a secular 'new method' *(usul-i jadid)* and restoring the power, wealth and dignity of the Tatar Turks.[53] It aroused Pan-Turkist sentiments, disseminated mainly through Gaspıralı's journal *Tercüman* (Translator, 1883–1918) with its motto 'unity in language, thought and action' *(dilde, fikirde, işte birlik)* among all Turkic groups in Russia.[54] Hüseyinzâde Ali, Yusuf Akçura and Ahmet Ağaoğlu were all close and enthusiastic followers of this movement.

Yet, at the turn of the century, Pan-Turkism was not a dominant political current within the borders of the Ottoman Empire. Indeed, Ottoman intellectuals feared it would trigger separatism and threaten the Empire's multi-ethnic unity. In 1903, Ali Kemal's *Türk* was the first journal to bring a cultural and historical awareness of the Turkish race *(ırk)* to the forefront,[55] and Yusuf Akçura's articles of 1904, 'Üç Tarz-ı Siyaset' (Three Ways of Politics),[56] formed its first systematic manifesto.[57] Akçura rejected Ottomanism for its failure to respond to separatism and Western imperialism, and championed 'a political union of Turks based on race', or Pan-Turkism, as the best and the only reasonable choice for maintaining the social and religious unity of the Empire.[58]

After the Young Turk Revolution, the atmosphere of freedom encouraged prominent Tatar intellectuals like Akçura, Ağaoğlu and Gaspıralı to return to the Empire, bringing their ideas to the capital. Under Akçura's supervision, periodicals like *Türk Yurdu* (Turkish Homeland, 1911) and *Halka Doğru* (Towards People, 1913–1914) were launched and nationalist organizations such as *Türk Derneği* (Turkish Association, 1908)[59] and *Türk Bilgi Derneği* (Turkish Association of Knowledge) established, with *Türk Ocağı* (Turkish Hearth, 1912) and its periodical *Türk Yurdu* being the most influential.[60] These thinkers did much to shape a sense of national idealism by founding clubs and schools, organizing public lectures and literary and artistic meetings and publishing books and periodicals. Despite initial declarations from these publications and associations that they would stay outside politics and lead a strictly social movement, the Young Turks Party supported them financially and collaborated with them to give the state an ideological agenda.

With the loss of Thessaloniki from the Empire in 1912, the leading idealists of *Genç Kalemler* settled eventually in Istanbul, bringing the visions of Thessaloniki, Crimea, and Istanbul itself to the capital of the Empire. The new Turkish idealism that emerged as an outcome of colliding viewpoints was a synthesis of elements from three broader intellectual enterprises. From French sociology, it drew on the ineluctable place of religion in individual existence; from German idealism, the notions of national language, *education*, economy and *state*; and from Pan-Turkism, a revivalism and populism along with a drive for modernization.

Gökalp and his 'Üç Cereyan' (Three Currents of Thought)

The founding document of the new idealist programme was drafted by Gökalp, the official chief ideologue of the Young Turks. His 'Üç Cereyan' (Three Currents of Thought), serialized in *Türk Yurdu* from 20 March 1913 before the loss of Edirne, expressed a new social and national idealist programme. It was later reprinted as a book, *Türkleşmek, İslamlaşmak, Muasırlaşmak* (Turkism, Islamism, Modernism) in 1918, and republished in 1923 as *Türkçülüğün Esasları* (The Principles of Turkism).

Gökalp synthesized Turkism, Islamism and modernization (or Westernization) harmoniously, despite the apparent contradictions between them: 'We are of the Turkish nation (*millet*), of Islamic religious community (*ümmet*), and of Western civilization (*medeniyet*).'[61] Nationally, Turks belonged to a Turkish culture, while internationally they belonged to the Islamic *ümmet* and Western civilization. He claimed that 'Turkism means furthering the ascendancy of the Turkish nation',[62] through promoting indigenous Turkic customs, habits and virtues. Like his contemporary Turkists, Gökalp believed that the Turkish nation was a bearer of shared values and traditions, which would bind its members together and define the culture, but he did not attempt 'to re-institute the ancient Turkish civilization'[63] by reviving fossilized ancient Turkish words or dialects as Çağatay, Kazak, or Tatar had done. Rather, he aimed 'to discover national ideas peculiar only to the Turkish people'[64] by eliminating artificial values taken from other civilizations while concurrently discovering institutional similarities between different nations.[65]

Nevertheless, Gökalp did see social decay and disintegration, the obliteration of tradition and the alienation of the elite from the common people (*halk*) at the same time. The roots of this lay in the *Tanzimat* elites' uncritical admiration and imitation of Western civilization, their neglect of national culture and their failure to assimilate Western science, technology and knowledge into it.[66] To reverse this cultural decline, the Ottoman Empire needed to keep pace with the technology of the age, and emulate the civilization of the West.[67] Yet Gökalp, in contrast to Abdullah Cevdet, did not believe that Turkey should adopt Western values wholesale, but embrace theoretical, material and practical sciences and techniques from Europe without absorbing European moral and cultural elements.[68] The Turkish nation needed to be modernized enough to incorporate those aspects of European civilization compatible with its own culture and faith, while also developing its own alternative forms of modernity and science.

While Turkism became Turkey's cultural and national ideal – and westernization its international one, Islam remained its spiritual context, providing a collective discipline that imposed itself on society with the overpowering authority of habit. Since Gökalp believed that Turks were part of a conjoined Islamic civilization, he saw no contradiction between Turkism and Islamism:[69] 'Turkism is simultaneously Islamism'.[70] In its evolution over time, the Turkish nation had drawn cultural elements from Arabic and Persian traditions and institutions, gradually diluting the distinctively Turkish character of its religious practices. The primary task of Turco-Islamic scholars was to discover by scientific study the inherent beliefs, practices, local customs, habits, beliefs and practices of Islam, while eliminating intruding foreign elements. To disseminate this nationalization of Islam, Gökalp and Halim Sabit published *Islâm Mecmuası* (Islamic Journal, 1914–1918), stressing the need to unify the divided *ümmet* of Islam and prevent further division between Turks and Muslims in the face of religious antagonisms.[71] He did not envisage a greater Pan-Islamic community united as a single nation, as propounded by rival intellectuals in the Islamist journal *Sebilü'r-Reşad* edited by Eşref Edip Fergan and Mehmet Âkif, on the grounds of its vagueness and impracticality, but proposed a wider Turkic-Islamic alliance.[72]

For Gökalp, if Turks could realize that they belonged nationally to Turkish culture, and internationally both to the Islamic *ümmet* and to Western civilization, a successful nation and state could be created. By impressing this ideal upon the people would these philosophical viewpoints become practical and useful for everyone.

Conceptualizing the State

Executing this ideal required effective political organization. After the Young Turk Revolution and subsequent constitutional reforms, Ottoman thinking about state and society changed profoundly. In the age of Abdülhamid II's absolutism, the state's sole unity lay in the personality of the sultan. The Young Turk Revolution changed this conception of the state as embodied in a single person to a French-inspired model of the state as a provider of formal legal liberty and equality that embodied both justice and fraternity. In the debates of the second half of the Constitutional Period

(1913–1918), the concept underwent a further shift towards a German understanding of the state as a particular type of organization and a spiritual and social organism.[73]

Like the German 'organic state theorists' of the late nineteenth and early twentieth century,[74] Ottoman national idealists saw the state as the true embodiment of social power and national spirit, with an authority derived from the collective conscience of society and a personality that mirrored national identity.[75] Citing Hegel, Recai wrote that 'All power held by a nation will serve the exaltation of the state.'[76] Tekinalp particularly admired the German state:

> 'Deutschland, Deutschland über alles ...' Every German knows this song from his childhood, all through his life it rings in his ears and with those words on his lips he dies – 'Deutschland, Deutschland über alles', and in very truth every German longs with his whole soul and will to see his nation 'über alles'. In striving for this ideal, the Germans have become so great and powerful a nation that they are now able to defy a whole world of assailants ...[77]

To rise as the German state had done, the Turkish nation would also need to exalt the state above all, and to make that elevation its national ideal. Once again citing Hegel, Recai wrote: 'The state is an absolute state above the reality of mankind, it is a divine will on earth.'[78] This notion of an exalted state and absolute sovereignty seems to have held a strong attraction for Ottoman writers and politicians. It suggested that the sultan must stand below the state, holding a much less sovereign form of power than before, while the legislative power of the political elite or rulers, the Triumvirate, was to be elevated. Through the creation of this profoundly new Turkish state and nation, great successes in war, science and economics would be achieved, and the superiority of Turkishness would prevail. To maintain the domestic peace and order of the society and protect it from foreign influences, the state had to regulate all life through the nationalization of economy, education, and the militarily.

National economy

The state as the supreme administrator of human affairs had the right to compel its wards for their own welfare. Inspired by Friedrich List's economic thinking, the Young Turk leaders and intellectuals rejected British economic liberalism, advocated by the prominent economist Mehmet Cavit Bey, and promoted a state-controlled economy free from foreign imposition. Israel Lazarevich Helphand (1867–1924), a German socialist (known widely by his nickname, Alexander Parvus) who spent the years between 1909 and 1914 in Istanbul,[79] attributed the decline of the Ottoman Empire to its capitulations, as they made the state economically dependent on the West.[80] Unlike Marx, Parvus did not call for a socialist revolution to overthrow existing structures; instead, like List, he pressed for the creation of a strong national economy through rapid industrialization.[81] Parvus engaged with nationalist intellectuals and published articles, mainly on political economy in *Türk Yurdu*. His affinity with the Young Turk leaders shaped the latter's wartime economic policy. To nationalize the economy, Muhittin Birgen encouraged the creation of a new Muslim-Turkish bourgeoisie through the opening of banks, provision of financial support and protection of craftsmen from foreign competition,[82] principles put into practice by the Young Turk Party during the Great War.

National education

Since devout and earnest attachment to the state was necessary to strengthen the state sufficiently, as Germany had shown by cultivating spiritual union within the nation and state through university reforms, Turkish intellectuals were convinced that it must form its citizens actively through the provision of national education.[83] This would establish a dialectic between state and nation in which each would determine the other: the state would express the nation, and the nation form the social and spiritual basis for the state. On the model of the *Bildung zum Menschen*, Ottoman national idealists believed that education must promote the moral and material improvement of the nation, producing 'good Turks in place of useless Ottomans'.[84] Ağaoğlu maintained that, 'Education is for the common good of the nation if it serves the national aims. Nations trained without a national education will never be content.'[85]

Following Albert Sorel, Akçura criticized the universal history taught in Ottoman school books since the Young Turk Revolution,[86] for undermining the distinctive history of Turkish nations and alienating people from their shared past.[87] He considered it was necessary to introduce national history, so that students could explore the richness of the Turkish past, discover the features of the Turkish nation, and develop their patriotism by studying the lives of national heroes like Attila and Cengiz Khan. A further purpose of national education was to educate pupils in true religion.[88] In the face of the deficiencies of the *maktabs* and many *madrasas*, the nationalists advocated religious reform to free pupils' minds from Islamic fatalism, prompt social revolution (*içtimai inkılab*), and 'nurture a modern Turkish nation'.[89] Stressing Martin Luther's role in the Reformation, Hafız Hakkı stressed the need for an 'Islamic Luther, who would sacrifice life to purify Islam', and launch Islamic reform.[90] National education was to foster a sense of civic responsibility within the community and teach the new generation to subordinate selfish desires, cultivate a collective identity and unite the Turks in pursuit of a common interest. It would make stable, unfailing patriots, and complete and responsible citizens. The Young Turks Party opened new and modern elementary and secondary schools (some using Turkish exclusively as the language of instruction); passed the 1915 *Tedrisât-ı ibtidâiye Kanun-u Muvakkati* (Interim Primary School) law; and opened a number of *İttihat ve Terakki Mektepleri* (Schools of Union and Progress) with a secular and scientific curriculum.[91]

Militarism

The final component of this conception of the state, and the most obviously pertinent to its eventual entry into the First World War, was the doctrine of militarism. The state would realize its full existence only after destroying all internal and external threats to its unity. In this view, violence and war were not the sole means used by the state, but those most specific to state action. The purpose of the state was to provide security, and its duty was to militarize the nation through conscription in preparation to fight. Alongside Germany, Japan appeared as a second striking example of a modern militarist state and society. In *Rus-Japon Harbinden Alınan Maddi ve Manevi Dersler ve Japonların Esbab-ı Muzafferiyeti* (Material and Spiritual Lessons from the Russo-Japanese War and the Reasons for Japanese Victory), Colonel Pertev, a reporter on the Russo-Japanese War, argued that the Japanese victory had been secured by its military's unhesitating sacrifice of human life. He conceived this as the product of a national unity around a single goal, thanks to the state militarization of society: 'Like the Japanese, if we teach love of fatherland and martial spirit starting from primary school, and if we train the army as heroes who are ready to die for the sultan, the fatherland, and nation, then the Ottoman Army will fear no one in the world except Almighty God.'[92] Like the Japanese state, the Turkish state would have to modernize itself and its society and retain its commitment to tradition.

Ottoman State as a War Machine

Unflinchingly committed to a strong state, the Young Turks' ideological and moral considerations converged with the German conception of the constitution, laid down by Bismarck in 1871, which Enver Paşa deeply admired.[93] To ensure both the national unity of the Ottoman community and a continuing political order through dynastic stability, Cemal Paşa, also pressed for centralization, since decentralization could bring only the end of the Empire.[94] From advocates of a strong, centralized state came new understandings of sovereignty challenging revolutionary notions of liberal democracy and representation. For both Enver and Said Halim Paşas, the notion of the general will was too abstract to serve as the foundation for successful governance. 'How can a regime be called democratic', Said Halim Paşa contended, 'when it receives its support from only fifty percent plus one of all votes cast?'[95] For him, the source of sovereignty lay not in the people but in the sacred laws of the *Sharï'a*.[96] He discarded the liberal notion of the right to natural freedom because 'there is nothing more false and anti-liberal than advocating that man possesses natural laws (*droit naturels*) and natural rights. Rights are not given but created only after the accomplishment of duty.'[97] Enver Paşa did not fully reject parliamentarianism but adopted a limited and elitist view of representation, in which sovereign power rested in the will of the wisest and best-fitted to rule: the Triumvirate. Echoing the principle of 'the state above all', he wrote, 'the parliament is necessary for our control over the state, but a strong centralized state is more important [than a representative system]'.[98]

To secure its power and control over society, the state sought to mould public opinion through Young Turk societies, nationalist societies, publications and organizations across the Empire. The Party formed new branches of women, *ulema* and the army to increase mass support and strengthen its image as an all-absorbing mass party, with all other affiliations extraneous and eliminable. To regulate social life, the state enacted a series of laws and reforms. In 1913, it introduced a new law of inheritance, based on the German law, the same year it made primary education compulsory for girls. At first, it limited women's higher education to teacher training colleges, but from 1914 a number of courses at the University of Istanbul were opened to female students.[99] The 'nation in arms' project was implemented following Enver Paşa's self-promotion to the position of Minister of War in 1914. To rejuvenate the army, an imperial decree was passed enforcing compulsory retirements for senior officers, and replacing them with younger successors.[100] A German-led military mission, led by General Liman von Sanders, was created to reform the army and reorganize the offices of the Ministry of War, German commanders were appointed to head various departments, and military schools, hitherto subordinate to the General Inspectorate of Education and Instruction, were attached to a new General Directorate of Military Schools, and placed under state control. The new hierarchy placed Enver Paşa higher in the chain of command than the sultan himself.[101]

To raise a generation of fit and healthy young people, who were morally and physically ready to serve their nation and defend the fatherland as soldiers, the state organized sports and youth clubs. The Ottoman Strength Clubs (*Osmanlı Güç Dernekleri*) were founded in May 1914 on Enver Paşa's initiative.[102] During the First World War, in 1916, a further paramilitary organization, the Ottoman Youth Clubs (*Osmanlı Genç Dernekleri*), was created in Istanbul under the supervision of Colonel Von Hoff, a disciple of Goltz, to supply manpower for the army.[103] Associational networks were propagated in various cities of the Empire.

Politics was understood as an endless struggle between friends and enemies.[104] Conspiracy, corruption, fear and suspicion permeated the Young Turk political language and agenda. The state became a bulwark against conspiratorial elements in society. To discover and punish traitors and internal enemies, the volunteer officers (*fedais*) who had carried out confidential missions before 1908 were formally organized by Enver Paşa in 1914 as the Special Organization (*Teşkilât-ı Mahsusa*), a secret committee to carry out missions and 'unmask' traitors in Anatolia, the Arab peninsula and the Caucasus. In defence of public safety and in an effort to maintain peace, the use of violence and the elimination of all those hostile or apathetic towards the CUP rule were justified: 'For domestic peace, the government must be more severe than Nero. What Nero did for his amusement, the government must do if it is necessary to calm the country.'[105] The pace of violence accelerated during the First World War. The government struck out against perceived traitors and internal enemies, unleashing violence to frighten national enemies and prevent future traitors. Arab nationalists and leaders were executed in Beirut and Damascus in 1915–1916 on the orders of Cemal Paşa, and the Armenians were massacred in 1915.[106]

International politics, too, was seen as an arena of struggle. Cemal Paşa stressed that the Balkan Wars had shown the impossibility of maintaining peace without annihilating the enemy. In its wake, the Young Turks broke completely from their earlier pacifist foreign policy and adopted an entirely new, active, aggressive and determined militarism. They saw war as 'the only way to save Turkey from the complications which threatened on every side, building up her strength and giving her a true place among the nations.'[107] Enver Paşa, in particular, was a strong believer in the need for a war from which the Empire, with Germany's support, would emerge victorious, ending the Russian threat and restoring the honour and pride of the Turkish nation.[108] This view was widely shared in public opinion and among Unionists, and war became a 'national goal'.[109]

Conclusion

The Ottoman Empire joined the war as a result of a secret diplomatic agreement signed in August 1914 by three members of the Young Turk inner circle (Enver, Talat, and Said Halim Paşas) and Germany, shortly before the outbreak of the international crisis.[110] The events leading up to Turkey's entry into the war involved two German ships, the *Goeben* and *Breslau*, which had arrived in Istanbul that same month and were fictitiously purchased by the Ottoman government. The two ships, under the command of Admiral Wilhelm Souchon, attacked the Russian fleet in October, leading the Allied Powers to declare war on the Ottoman Empire, but the Empire remained neutral until making its official war declaration on the side of Germany and Austria in November 1914.

The war arrived at a time when the militaristic youth organizations were barely formed, the army had yet to recover fully from its Balkan defeats, and the economy was still weak. But, despite these disadvantages, neither the Young Turk leaders nor the public were unprepared in terms of readiness to fight. They fully expected it – intense literary and ideological work had prepared Ottoman minds and spirits for it. Complex theories and shifts in the conception of the state had done much to determine how the war was imagined, experienced and remembered. It was seen as the fulfilment of the new national and international ideal. As Enver Paşa proclaimed: 'Our participation in the World War represents the vindication of our national ideal. The ideal of our nation and our people leads us towards the destruction of our Muscovite enemy, in order to obtain thereby a natural frontier to our Empire, which should include and unite all branches of our race.'[111] From one perspective, the war was viewed within the Empire as an offensive, total war. From another, it was seen as an act of self-defence against an enemy intent on occupying the homeland of Muslim and Turkic nations. From both perspectives, it was confidently hoped that the war would solve the long-lasting Eastern Question, free the Ottoman Empire and the Muslim nations from Western oppression and slavery and bring peace to East and West. It was these ideas, and new conceptions of state, society and politics that motivated the Ottomans to fight, and served as propaganda tools in the First World War. Despite its prominence, the new theory of war brought the Empire not success but defeat. Nonetheless, the ideas produced prior to the First World War did not fully disappear; nationalism, political and financial independence, militarism and a strong centralized state became central to the ideology of the Republic of Turkey within the next decade.

Notes

1. A different version of the chapter was published in my book, *The Formation of Turkish Republicanism*. Princeton, NJ: Princeton University Press, 2017. I acknowledge the support of Leverhulme Trust Early Career Research Fellowship (ECF-2016–624) and Isaac Newton Trust (Ref: 1608 (ag)).
2. Y.H. Bayur, *Türk İnkılâp Tarihi*, vol. 3: *1914–1918 Genel Savaşı* [History of the Turkish Revolution, vol. 3: The Great War, 1914–1918]. Ankara: Türk Tarih Kurumu, 1982, pp. 267–269.

3   Y.H. Bayur, *Türk İnkılâbı Tarihi*, vol. 2: *Paylaşımlar* [History of the Turkish Revolution, vol. 2: Sharings]. Ankara: Türk Tarih Kurumu, 1983, pp. 2-5.
4   Chief of the General Staff of the Republic of Turkey, *Birinci Dünya Harbi'nde Türk Harbi, Osmanlı İmparatorluğu'nun Siyasi ve Askeri Hazırlıkları ve Harbe Girişi*, ed. Cemal Akbay, vol. 1. Ankara: Genelkurmay Basımevi, 1970, rev. 1991, pp.1-154, 201-20; K. Yetiş, 'İkinci Meşrutiyet Devrindeki Belli Başlı Fikir Akımlarının Askeri Hareketlere ve Cepheye Tesiri' [The Effect of Major Ideological Trends of the Second Constitutional Era on Military Movements and Fronts], in *Bildiriler: Dördüncü Askeri Tarih Semineri*. Ankara: Genelkurmay Basımevi, 1989, pp. 59-69; V. Yılmaz, *Birinci Dünya Harbi'nde Türk-Alman İttifakı ve Askeri Yardımlar* [Turkish-German Alliance and Military Aids in the First World War]. İstanbul: Cem, 1993, pp. 1-16, 73-94; D. Hacipoğlu, *29 Ekim 1914: Osmanlı İmparatorluğu'nun 1. Dünya Harbine Girişi* [29 October 1914: The Entry of the Ottoman Empire in the First World War]. İstanbul: Deniz İkmal Grup Komutanlığı, 2009, pp. 5-25, 103.
5   F. Ahmad, 'War and Society Under the Young Turks, 1908-18', in *From Empire to Republic*. İstanbul, Bilgi University Press, 2008, p. 242; Ahmad, 'Great Britain's Relations with the Young Turks, 1908-1914', *Middle Eastern Studies*, 2, no. 4 (1966), pp. 302-329.
6   For a comprehensive work on the significance of ideas and public opinion before the First World War, see M. Aksakal, *The Ottoman Road to War in 1914: The Ottoman Empire and the First World War*. New York: Cambridge University Press, 2008. See also, E. Boyar 'The impact of the Balkan Wars on Ottoman history writing: searching for a soul', in Special Issue: *The First World War in the Middle East, Middle East Critique*, ed. H Yavuz, 23/2 (2014), pp. 147-159.
7   E.J. Erikson, *Defeat in Detail: The Ottoman Army in the Balkans, 1912-1913*. Westport, CT: Preager Publishers, 2003, pp. 331-332. Edirne was recaptured in 1913.
8   Debates over war were embedded in larger discussions of how best to respond to changing world circumstances, and particularly to the economic and military rivalry and expansionism of the major European powers and the separatist nationalist movements in the Balkans. While some journals, like the Westernist *İçtihat*, were largely inclined towards a peaceful conduct of relations between the Great Powers, others like *Asker* (Soldier), *Başçavuş* (Sergeant-Major), *Silah* (Weapon), *Top* (Cannon), *Süngü* (Bayonet), *Kurşun* (Bullet), *Bıçak* (Knife) and *Bomba* (Bomb) frequently promoted the notion of readiness for the imminent danger of total war and invoked national hatred for enemies. These journals were financially supported by the CUP, and thus represented the voice of the government. For a comprehensive study of military thinking in the period from 1908 to 1914, see H. Nezir-Akmeşe, *The Birth of Modern Turkey: The Ottoman Military and the March to WWI*. London: I.B. Tauris, 2005.
9   Hafız Hakkı Paşa, *Bozgun* [Defeat]. İstanbul: Tercüman 1001 Temel Eser, [1913] 1973, pp. 50-51.
10 Ibid., p. 83.
11 Ibid., p. 115.
12 Gustave Le Bon's *Les Lois Psychologiques de l'Évolution des Peuples* [1894] and *Aphorismes du temps présent* [1913] were translated by Abdullah Cevdet into Ottoman Turkish in 1907 and 1913 respectively, which helped popularize his theories in Ottoman intellectual circles. See G. Le Bon, *Ruhü'l-akvam* [Psychological Laws], trans. Abdullah Cevdet. İstanbul: Matbaa-i İctihad, 1907; *Asrımızın Nusûs-ı Felsefiyesi* [Aphorisms of Present Times], trans. Abdullah Cevdet. İstanbul: Matbaa-i İctihad, 1913. See also, Abdullah Cevdet, 'Doktor Gustave Le Bon', *İçtihad*, June 1905, p. 120. For a detailed analysis of the political thought of Abdullah Cevdet, see M. Hanioğlu,

Doktor Abdullah Cevdet ve Dönemi [Dr. Abdullah Cevdet and His Age]. İstanbul: Üçdal Neşriyat, 1981.
13 Quoted in Aksakal, *The Ottoman Road to War in 1914*, p. 30. Şehbenderzade Filibeli Ahmed Hilmi, *Türk Ruhu Nasıl Yapılıyor? Her Vatanperverden Bu Eserciği Okumasını ve Anlatmasını Niyaz Ederiz*. Darülhilâfe: Hikmet matbaa-ı İslamiyesi, 1913, p. 4.
14 On the reception of Darwinism in the Ottoman Empire, see A. Doğan, *Osmanlı Aydınları ve Sosyal Darwinizm*. İstanbul: Küre Yayınları, 2012.
15 Ethem Necdet, *Tekâmül ve Kanunları* [Evolution and Its Laws]. İstanbul: Matbaa-yı İctihad, 1913, pp. 4–5.
16 Ibid.
17 Hafız Hakkı, *Bozgun*, p. 120.
18 Ibid., pp. 130–134.
19 M. Beşikçi, *The Ottoman Mobilization of Manpower in the First World War: Between Voluntarism and Resistance*. Leiden, Brill, 2012, p. 218. The work was published as Colmar von der Goltz, *Millet-i Müsellaha: Asrımızın Usûl ve Ahvâl-i Askeriyesi*, trans. Mehmed Tahir. İstanbul: Matbaa-i Ebüzziya, 1886.
20 After the Revolution, in military books and journals, particularly in *Asker*, translations of German military thinkers' works, notably those of Goltz, became widespread, preparing public opinion for a war and the defence of the fatherland. Other German instructors who had served the Ottoman army, like the infantry instructor Marshal Kamphövener Paşa and the artillery instructor Lieutenant-General İmhof Paşa, were also published in this journal. See Lieutenant-Colonel Osman Senai, 'Almanya'da Harbiye Nezareti' [Ministry of War in Germany], *Asker*, no.1 (3 September 1908), pp. 23–28; Senai, 'Alman Erkan-ı Harbiye Dairesi' [German General Staff Office], *Asker*, no. 2 (14 September 1908); Major Ali Vasfi, 'Almanya Ordusu' [German Army], *Asker*, no. 14 (14 April 1909), pp. 84–88.
21 M.Ş. Hanioğlu, *Atatürk: An Intellectual Biography*. Princeton, NJ: Princeton University Press, 2011, pp. 35–39.
22 Tüccarzade İbrahim Hilmi, *Türkiye Uyan* [Turkey Awake], Ankara: Alter Yayıncılık, [1912] 2013, p. 26.
23 Ibid., pp. 39–45.
24 Ibid., p. 42.
25 Osman Naci, 'Bölük Kumandanı' [Division's Commander], *Asker*, 28 December 1908, p. 355.
26 Colonel Pertev, *Rus-Japon Harbinden Alınan Maddi ve Manevi Dersler ve Japonların Esbab-ı Muzafferiyeti*, İstanbul [Material and Moral Lessons Drawn from the Russo-Japanese War and Reasons for Japanese Victory]. İstanbul: Kanaat Kitabhane ve Matbaası, 1913, p. 133.
27 An important work translated by Recai in 1913 was Antoine de Tarlé's *La préparation de la lutte économique par l'Allemagne* Recai, foreword to *Amanya Nasıl Dirildi? Harbe Nasıl Hazırlanıyor?* a translation of *La préparation de la lutte économique par l'Allemagne*, by Antoine de Tarlé, Dersaadet, Nefaset Matbaası, March 1913–March 1914.
28 O. Orhan Okay, *Beşir Fuad: İlk Türk Pozitivist ve Natüralisti* [Beşir Fuad: The First Positivist and Naturalist Turk]. İstanbul: Dergah Yayınları, 2008, pp. 131–132, 166.
29 Münif Paşa, *Telhis-i Hikmet-i Hukuk* [The Prudence of Law]. İstanbul: İdare-i Sirket-i Mürettibiye, 1895, p. 227.
30 Ahmet Mithat, *Schopenhauer'in Hikmet-i Cedidesi, Felsefe Metinleri* [Schopenhauer's New Philosophy, His Philosophical Texts]. Erzurum: Babil Yayınları, 2002, p. 39.

31 H. Anay, 'Ödev Ahlâkının Türk Düşüncesine Girişi ve Baha Tevfik'in Kant Hakkındaki Yazıları' [The Duty of Ethics: Introduction to Turkish Thought and Baha Tevfik's Articles about Kant], *Dini Araştırmalar*, 13, no. 36 (2010), p. 154.
32 Tekinalp, 'The Turkish and Pan-Turkish Ideal', p. 135.
33 M. Kohen [Tekinalp], 'Alman Müteallimlerinin Yaşayışı' [The Life of German Students], *Bilgi Mecmuası*, 1914, pp. 311-23.
34 Hafız Hakkı Paşa, *Bozgun*, p. 88.
35 Recai, *Amanya Nasıl Dirildi?*, pp. 9-11.
36 Ziya Gökalp, 'Mefkûre' [Ideal], *Türk Yurdu*, no. 32, 1913, reprinted 1918 in *Türkleşmek, İslâmlaşmak, Muasırlaşmak* [Turkification, Islamization, Modernization], in *Turkish Nationalism and Western Civilization: Selected Essays*, ed. N. Berkes. London: Allen & Unwin, 1959, p. 72.
37 Can Bey [Sadri Makdusi], 'Büyük Milli Emeller, 2' [Grand National Ideals], *Türk Yurdu*, 14 January 1911, p. 29. National awakening was a popular theme in poems, pamphlets, articles and books in the context of the Balkan Wars. See, especially, Tüccarzade İbrahim Hilmi, *Türkiye Uyan* [Turkey Awake], pp. 15-27.
38 Hafız Hakkı, *Bozgun*, pp. 82-83.
39 See Tüccarzâde İbrahim Hilmi, *Balkan Harbi'ni Neden Kaybettik?* [Why Did We Lose the Balkan Wars?]. İstanbul: İz Yayıncılık, [1913] 2012, p. 86.
40 Z. Toprak, *Türkiye'de Popülizm, 1908-1923* [Populism in Turkey, 1908-1923]. İstanbul: Doğan Kitap, 2013, p. 117. See also M. Mazower, Salonica, City of Ghosts: Christians, Muslims and Jews 1430-1950. London: Herper Perennial, 2004.
41 T. Alangu, *Ömer Seyfettin: Ülkücü Bir Yazarın Romanı* [Ömer Seyfettin: The Novel of a Nationalist Writer]. İstanbul: Yapı Kredi Yayınları, 2008, pp. 154-159.
42 Ömer Seydeddin, '"Yeni Lisan" [New Language], vol. 2, no. 3, 19 May 1911', in *Genç Kalemler Dergisi* [Young Pens Magazine], ed. İ. Parlatır and N. Çetin. Ankara: Türk Dil Kurumu Yayınları, 1999, p. 127.
43 Ibid., pp. 128-129.
44 Tekinalp, 'The Turkish and Pan-Turkish Ideal', p. 106.
45 Ziya Gökalp, '"Yeni Hayat ve Yeni Değerler" [New Life and New Values], *Genç Kalemler*, no. 8, 1911', in *Turkish Nationalism and Western Civilization: Selected Essays*, ed. Niyazi Berkes. London: Allen & Unwin, 1959 , p. 56.
46 Ibid., p. 57. To describe an ideal, he used the word *mefkûre*, derived from the Arabic word *fıkr* (idea), just as the European term *ideal* is derived from the Greek notion *idea*. See Gökalp, 'Mefkûre' [Ideal], p. 70.
47 Gökalp, 'Yeni Hayat ve Yeni Değerler', p. 55.
48 Ibid.
49 Ibid.
50 During the reign of Abdülhamid II, a scholarly interest in Turcology by historians such as Ahmet Vefik Paşa, aimed to identify the history, lands and language of the Turks, and fostered academic studies, translations from other languages and research into Turkish origins and heritage. Necip Asım (1861-1935) translated Léon Cahun's *Introduction Générale à l'histoire de l'Asie* [1896]. Şemsettin Sami (1850-1904) compiled a Turkish dictionary *Kâmûs-i Turkî*.
51 Jacob M. Landau, Pan-Turkism in Turkey: A study in Irredentism. London: C. Hurst, 1981, p. 8.
52 For the life and works of Gaspıralı İsmail, see, Y. Ekinci, *Gaspıralı İsmail*, Ankara, Ocak Yayınları, 1997.
53 John L. Esposito, 'Jadidism', in *The Oxford Dictionary of Islam*, Oxford, New York, Oxford University Press, 2003, pp. 153-54.

54 Landau, *Pan-Turkism in Turkey*, p. 10.
55 For the intellectual activities of *Türk*, see especially, M.Ş. Hanioğlu, 'Turkism and the Young Turks 1889–1938', in *Turkey Beyond Nationalism: Towards Post-Nationalist Identities*, ed. Hans-Lukas Kieser. London: I.B. Tauris, 2013, pp. 3–20.
56 Yusuf Akçura, 'Üç Tarz-ı Siyaset' [Three Ways of Politics], *Türk*, 14 April 1904, 28 April 1904, 5 May 1904.
57 F. Georgeon, *Türk Milliyetçiliğinin Kökenleri* [The Origins of Turkish Nationalism], trans. Alev Er. İstanbul: Yurt Yayınları, 1986, p. 37.
58 Akçura, 'Üç Tarz-ı Siyaset', p. 1. The publication of this article produced prolonged discussion within intellectual circles, and in general the idea of Turkism was not well received among the intellectual elite. Ahmet Ferid (1877–1971) refused to abandon Ottomanism despite its lack of promise for the future, since it still provided the best basis for protecting and assimilating all those subjects to Ottoman rule at the time. See Ahmet Ferit, 'Bir Mektup' [One Letter], in *Üç Tarz-ı Siyaset*. Ankara: Türk Tarih Kurumu Yayınları, 1991, pp. 60–63.
59 In 1908, with the support of Ottoman intellectuals Veled Çelebi (İzbudak) and Necib Asım (Yazıksız), Yusuf Akçura founded *Türk Derneği*, to explore the past and present activities of all ethnic groups of Turks and inform the public of the Turks' cultural richness. They explored Turkish history, language, literature, ethnography and ethnology, arranged public lectures, issued journals and pamphlets and opened branches throughout the Empire.
60 *Türk Ocağı* was open only to Muslim Turks. Its goal was 'to work for the national education of the Turkish people which forms the most important division of Islam; to work for the raising of her intellectual, social and economic standard and for the perfection of the Turkish language and race.' (Tekinalp, 'The Turkish and Pan-Turkish Ideal', p. 116.) The union spread quickly and reached 1,800 members in Istanbul alone, including 1,600 students and academics. It had established 16 branches throughout the Empire by 1914.
61 Ziya Gökalp, '"Üç Cereyan" [Three Currents of Thought], *Türk Yurdu*, vol. 3, no. 35, 1913', in *Turkish Nationalism and Western Civilization: Selected Essays*, ed. Niyazi Berkes. London: Allen & Unwin, 1959, p. 76.
62 Gökalp, '"Millet Nedir?" [What is a Nation?], *Küçük Mecmua*, no. 28, Diyarbakır, 1923', in *Turkish Nationalism and Western Civilization: Selected Essays*, ed. Niyazi Berkes. London: Allen & Unwin, 1959, p. 137.
63 Gökalp, '"Milli Terbiye" [National Education], *Muallim*, nos. 1–4, 1916', in *Turkish Nationalism and Western Civilization: Selected Essays*, ed. Niyazi Berkes. London: Allen & Unwin, 1959. , p. 237.
64 Gökalp, '"Türkçülük Nedir?" [What is Turkism?], *Yeni Mecmua*, no. 28, 1917', in *Turkish Nationalism and Western Civilization: Selected Essays*, ed. Niyazi Berkes. London: Allen & Unwin, 1959, p. 284.
65 Ibid., p. 287.
66 Ibid.
67 Ibid., p. 75.
68 Gökalp, 'Türkçülük Nedir?', p. 288.
69 Gökalp, 'Üç Cereyan', p. 75.
70 Gökalp, *Türkleşmek, İslâmlaşmak, Muasırlaşmak*. Ankara: Kültür Bakanlığı Yayını, 1976., p. 230.
71 Gökalp, '"Cemaat Medeniyeti, Cemiyet Medeniyeti" [The Civilization of Community and the Civilization of Society], *Türk Yurdu*, vol. 4, no. 47, 1913', in *Turkish*

> *Nationalism and Western Civilization: Selected Essays*, ed. Niyazi Berkes. London: Allen & Unwin, 1959, p. 101.
72 Gökalp, '"Üç Cereyan", p. 71.
73 Gökalp, '"Millet ve Vatan", *Türk Yurdu*, vol. 6, no. 66, 1914', in *Turkish Nationalism and Western Civilization: Selected Essays*, ed. Niyazi Berkes. London: Allen & Unwin, 1959, p.78.
74 See, especially, D. Kelly, *The State of the Political: Conceptions of Politics and the State in the Thought of Max Weber, Carl Schmitt, and Franz Neumann*. Oxford: Oxford University Press, 2003, pp. 79–81.
75 Gökalp, 'Millet ve Vatan', p. 78.
76 Recai, 'Mukaddime' [Foreword], p. 1. [*Millette hayy olan her kuvvet; devletin i'lâsına hizmet için müsabaka edecektir.*]
77 Tekinalp, 'The Turkish and Pan-Turkish Ideal', in Tekinalp, Turkish Patriot 1883–1961, ed. Jacob M. Landau. Leiden: Nederlands Historisch-Archaeologisch Instituut te Istanbul, [1916] 1984, p. 137. Tekinalp published this book in 1914 in Turkish, entitled Türkler bu muharebede ne kazanabilirler? Büyük Türklik: en meşhur Türkçülerin mütalaatı [What Can the Turks Gain in this Battle? Great Turkishness: The Most Famous Deliberation of the Turkists]. In 1915, it was enlarged and translated into German as Türkismus und Pantürkismus, which was later translated into English by E. Denison Ross.
78 *Devlet; hakikat-i beşeriyenin fevkinde bir devlet-i mutlakadır; yeryüzünde ilâhî bir kudrettir*, Recai, 'Mukaddime', p. 1.
79 A. Karaömerlioğlu, 'Helphand-Parvus and His Impact on Turkish Intellectual Life', *Middle Eastern Studies*, 40, no. 6 (2004), p. 145.
80 Parvus, 'Türkiye Avrupa'nın Maliye Boyunduruğu Altındadır 2' [Turkey is Under the Financial Oppression of Europe], *Türk Yurdu*, 1912; Parvus 'Türkiye'de Ziraatin İstikbali' [The Future of Agriculture in Turkey], *Türk Yurdu*, 1913.
81 Parvus, 'Esaret-i Maliyeden Kurtulmanın Yolu' [Guide to Emancipation from Financial Slavery], *Türk Yurdu*, 1912, p. 587.
82 Muhittin, 'İktisadî Hasbihâl: En Büyük Eksiğimiz' [Economic Dialogue: Our Biggest Deficiency], *Halka Doğru*, 26 May 1913, p. 48.
83 M. Kohen [Tekinalp], 'Alman Müteallimlerinin Yaşayışı', 1914.
84 Cami Baykut [Abdurrahman Cami Baykut], *Osmanlılığın Âtisi: Düşmanları ve Dostları* [The Ottoman Future: Its Enemies and Friends]. İstanbul, İfham Matbaası, 1913, pp. 10–11.
85 Ahmed Ağaoğlu, 'Terbiye-i Milliye' [National Training], *İçtihad*, 28 July 1911, p. 783.
86 Yusuf Akçura, 'Tarihî Görüşe Dâir' [A Historical Perspective], *Türk Yurdu*, 1912.
87 Akçura, 'Portekiz İhtilâli Münasebetiyle' [Marking the Portuguese Revolution], *Sırat-ı Müstakim*, 21 October 1910, p. 119.
88 Ahmed Ağaoğlu, 'Türk Medeniyeti Tarihi, Mukaddime' [History of Turkish Civilization], *Türk Yurdu*, 29 May 1913.
89 Nafi Atuf, 'Maarifimiz Hakkında' [About Our Education System], *Türk Yurdu*, 1 June 1916, p. 94.
90 Hafız Hakkı Paşa, *Bozgun*, pp. 88–89.
91 S. A., 'Maarif Yılı' [A Year of Education], *Türk Yurdu*, 23 March 1916, p. 24.
92 Cited in Nezir-Akmeşe, *The Birth of Modern Turkey*, p. 79.
93 Enver Paşa, *Kendi Mektuplarında Enver Paşa*, ed. M.Ş. Hanioğlu. İstanbul: Der Yayınevi, 1989, p. 175. This work contains Enver Paşa's personal letters in French and Turkish.

94 Cemal Paşa, *Hatıralar* [Memoirs]. İstanbul: İşbankası Kültür Yayınları, [1919] 2006, pp. 344–346.
95 Said Halim Pasha, *Les Institutions Politiques Dans La Société Musulmane*. Rome: Imprimerie Editrice Italia, 1921, p. 10.
96 Ibid.
97 Ibid.
98 Hanioğlu, *Kendi Mektuplarında Enver Paşa*, p. 175.
99 Zürcher, *Turkey: A Modern History*, pp. 121–122.
100 This retirement included two marshals, three generals, thirty lieutenant-generals, 95 major-generals and 184 colonels. See Cemal Paşa, *Hatıralar*, p. 100.
101 Nezir-Akmeşe, *The Birth of Modern Turkey*, pp. 161–163.
102 The Ottoman Strength Clubs absorbed the Ottoman Scout Committee (*Keşşaflık Cemiyeti İzci Ocağı*), established in Istanbul in 1914 under the supervision of Harold Parfitt at Enver Paşa's invitation. The Scouts were formed to raise brave, selfless and patriotic youth as part of the CUP's nation-building strategies imbued with solidarity and responsibility. Their activities were concentrated on the high schools in the capital and other big cities like Bursa, İzmit and Beirut. See, especially, Z. Toprak, 'II. Meşrutiyet Dönemi'nde Paramiliter Gençlik Örgütleri', in *Tanzimat'tan Cumhuriyet'e Türkiye Ansiklopedisi*, ed. Murat Belge and Fahri Ara. İstanbul: İletişim Yayınları, 1985; 'Meşrutiyet ve Mütareke Yıllarında Türkiye'de İzcilik', *Toplumsal Tarih*, 9, no. 52 (1998), pp. 13–21.
103 Goltz had formed a similar association in Germany in 1911, *der Jungdeutschlandbund*, to prepare young German boys for military service, where he met Von Hoff, a junior officer at that time. It was Goltz who recommended von Hoff for the supervision of the Ottoman Youth League. Beşikçi, *The Ottoman Mobilization of Manpower*, pp. 216–218.
104 Hanioğlu, *Kendi Mektuplarında Enver Paşa*, p. 175.
105 Ibid.
106 See, especially, R.G. Suny, F.M. Göçek and N.M. Robert (eds.), *A Question of Genocide: Armenians and Turks at the End of the Ottoman Empire*. Oxford, New York: Oxford University Press, 2011.
107 Cited in Nezir-Akmeşe, *The Birth of Modern Turkey*, p. 145.
108 Ş. Yılmaz, 'An Ottoman Warrior Abroad: Enver Paşa as an Expatriate', *Middle Eastern Studies*, 35, no. 4 (1999), pp. 44–46.
109 Ahmed Emin [Yalman], *Turkey in the World War*. New Haven, CT: Yale University Press, 1930, p. 68.
110 Y.T. Kurat, 'How Turkey Drifted into World War I', in *Studies in International History*, ed. K. Bourne and D. C. Watt. London: Longmans, 1967, pp. 291–315.
111 Cited in Nezir-Akmeşe, *The Birth of Modern Turkey*, p. 189.

Bibliography

Primary sources

Abdullah Cevdet, 'Doktor Gustave Le Bon', *İçtihad*, June 1905.
Ahmed Ağaoğlu, 'Terbiye-i Milliye' [National Training], *İçtihad*, 28 July 1911, pp. 782–786.
Ahmed Ağaoğlu, 'Türk Medeniyeti Tarihi, Mukaddime' [History of Turkish Civilization], *Türk Yurdu*, 29 May 1913.

Ahmed Emin [Yalman], *Turkey in the World War*. New Haven, CT: Yale University Press, 1930.
Ahmet Ferit, 'Bir Mektup' [One Letter], in *Üç Tarz-ı Siyaset*. Ankara: Türk Tarih Kurumu Yayınları, 1991.
Ahmet Mithat, *Schopenhauer'in Hikmet-i Cedidesi, Felsefe Metinleri* [Schopenhauer's New Philosophy, His Philosophical Texts]. Erzurum: Babil Yayınları, 2002.
Ali Vasfi, 'Almanya Ordusu' [German Army], *Asker*, no. 14 (14 April 1909), pp. 84–88.
Cami Baykut, *Osmanlılığın Âtisi: Düşmanları ve Dostları* [The Ottoman Future: Its Enemies and Friends]. İstanbul: İfham Matbaası, 1913.
Can Bey [Sadri Makdusi], 'Büyük Milli Emeller, 2' [Grand National Ideals], *Türk Yurdu*, 14 January 1911.
Cemal Paşa, *Hatıralar* [Memoirs]. İstanbul: İşbankası Kültür Yayınları, [1919] 2006.
Enver Paşa, *Kendi Mektuplarında Enver Paşa*, ed. M.Ş. Hanioğlu. İstanbul: Der Yayınevi, 1989.
Goltz, Colmar von der. *Millet-i Müsellaha: Asrımızın Usûl ve Ahvâl-i Askeriyesi*, trans. Mehmed Tahir. İstanbul: Matbaa-i Ebüzziya, 1886.
Hafız Hakkı Paşa, *Bozgun* [Defeat]. İstanbul: Tercüman 1001 Temel Eser, [1913] 1973.
Hey'et-i Merkeziye, 'Osmanlı Terakki ve İttihad Cemiyeti Hey'et-i Merkeziyesi'nin Teşkilât-ı Dahiliyesi', *Şura-yı Ümmet*, 1 October 1906.
Kendi Mektuplarında, *Enver Paşa*, ed. M. Şükrü Hanioğlu. İstanbul: Der Yayınevi, 1989.
Le Bon, G., *Ruhü'l-akvam* [Psychological Laws], trans. Abdullah Cevdet. İstanbul: Matbaa-i İctihad, 1907.
Le Bon, G., *Asrımızın Nusûs-ı Felsefiyesi* [Aphorisms of Present Times], trans. Abdullah Cevdet. İstanbul: Matbaa-i İctihad, 1913.
Muhittin, 'İktisadî Hasbihâl: En Büyük Eksiğimiz' [Economic Dialogue: Our Biggest Deficiency], *Halka Doğru*, 26 May 1913.
Münif Paşa, *Telhis-i Hikmet-i Hukuk* [The Prudence of Law]. İstanbul: İdare-i Sirket-i Mürettibiye, 1895.
Nafi Atuf, 'Maarifimiz Hakkında' [About Our Education System], *Türk Yurdu*, 1 June 1916.
Ömer Seydeddin, '"Yeni Lisan" [New Language], vol. 2, no. 3, 19 May 1911', in *Genç Kalemler Dergisi* [Young Pens Magazine], ed. İ. Parlatır and N. Çetin. Ankara: Türk Dil Kurumu Yayınları, 1999.
Osman Naci, 'Bölük Kumandanı' [Division Commander], *Asker*, 28 December 1908.
Osman Senai, 'Almanya'da Harbiye Nezareti' [Ministry of War in Germany], *Asker*, no.1 (3 September 1908), pp. 23–28.
Osman Senai, 'Alman Erkan-ı Harbiye Dairesi' [German General Staff Office], *Asker*, no. 2 (14 September 1908).
Parvus, 'Esaret-i Maliyeden Kurtulmanın Yolu' [Guide to Emancipation from Financial Slavery], *Türk Yurdu*, 1912.
Parvus, 'Türkiye Avrupa'nın Maliye Boyunduruğu Altındadır 2' [Turkey is Under the Financial Oppression of Europe], *Türk Yurdu*, 1912.
Parvus 'Türkiye'de Ziraatin İstikbali' [The Future of Agriculture in Turkey], *Türk Yurdu*, 1913, pp. 859–860.
Pertev Paşa, *Rus-Japon Harbinden Alınan Maddi ve Manevi Dersler ve Japonların Esbah-ı Muzafferiyeti*, İstanbul [Material and Moral Lessons Drawn from the Russo-Japanese War and Reasons for Japanese Victory]. İstanbul: Kanaat Kitabhane ve Matbaası, 1913.
Said Halim Paşa, *Les Institutions Politiques dans la Société Musulmane*. Rome: Imprimerie Editrice Italia, 1921.

Şehbenderzade Filibeli Ahmed Hilmi, *Türk Ruhu Nasıl Yapılıyor? Her Vatanperverden Bu Eserciği Okumasını ve Anlatmasını Niyaz Ederiz. [How to Make a Turkish Spirit? We request Every Patriot to Read and Explain this Booklet.]* Darülhilâfe: Hikmet matbaa-ı İslamiyesi, 1913.

Tekinalp, 'Alman Müteallimlerinin Yaşayışı' [The Life of German Students], *Bilgi Mecmuası*, 1914, pp. 311–323.

Tekinalp, 'The Turkish and Pan-Turkish Ideal', in *Tekinalp, Turkish Patriot 1883–1961*, ed. Jacob M. Landau. Leiden: Nederlands Historisch-Archaeologisch Instituut te Istanbul, [1916] 1984.

Tüccarzâde İbrahim Hilmi, *Balkan Harbi'ni Neden Kaybettik?* [Why Did We Lose the Balkan Wars?]. İstanbul: İz Yayıncılık, [1913] 2012.

Tüccarzade İbrahim Hilmi, *Türkiye Uyan* [Turkey Awake]. Ankara: Alter Yayıncılık, [1912] 2013.

Yusuf Akçura, 'Üç Tarz-ı Siyaset' [Three Ways of Politics], *Türk*, 14 April 1904.

Yusuf Akçura, 'Üç Tarz-ı Siyaset' [Three Ways of Politics], *Türk*, 28 April 1904.

Yusuf Akçura, 'Üç Tarz-ı Siyaset' [Three Ways of Politics], *Türk*, 5 May 1904.

Yusuf Akçura, 'Portekiz İhtilâli Münasebetiyle' [Marking the Portuguese Revolution], *Sırat-ı Müstakim*, 21 October 1910.

Yusuf Akçura, 'Tarihî Görüşe Dâir' [A Historical Perspective], *Türk Yurdu*, 1912.

Ziya Gökalp, 'Mefkûre' [Ideal], *Türk Yurdu*, no. 32, 1913, reprinted 1918 in *Türkleşmek, İslâmlaşmak, Muasırlaşmak* [Turkification, Islamization, Modernization], in *Turkish Nationalism and Western Civilization: Selected Essays*, ed. N. Berkes. London: Allen & Unwin, 1959.

Ziya Gökalp, '"Millet ve Vatan", *Türk Yurdu*, vol. 6, no. 66, 1914', in *Turkish Nationalism and Western Civilization: Selected Essays*, ed. Niyazi Berkes. London: Allen & Unwin, 1959.

Ziya Gökalp, '"Milli Terbiye" [National Education], *Muallim*, nos. 1–4, 1916', in *Turkish Nationalism and Western Civilization: Selected Essays*, ed. Niyazi Berkes. London: Allen & Unwin, 1959.

Ziya Gökalp, '"Milliyet Mefkûresi", reprinted in *Türkleşmek, İslâmlaşmak, Muasırlaşmak*', in *Turkish Nationalism and Western Civilization: Selected Essays*, ed. Niyazi Berkes. London: Allen & Unwin, 1959.

Ziya Gökalp, '"Türkçülük Nedir?" [What is Turkism?], *Yeni Mecmua*, no. 28, 1917', in *Turkish Nationalism and Western Civilization: Selected Essays*, ed. Niyazi Berkes. London: Allen & Unwin, 1959.

Ziya Gökalp, '"Üç Cereyan" [Three Currents of Thought], *Türk Yurdu*, vol. 3, no. 35, 1913', in *Turkish Nationalism and Western Civilization: Selected Essays*, ed. Niyazi Berkes. London: Allen & Unwin, 1959.

Ziya Gökalp, '"Cemaat Medeniyeti, Cemiyet Medeniyeti" [The Civilization of Community and the Civilization of Society], *Türk Yurdu*, vol. 4, no. 47, 1913', in *Turkish Nationalism and Western Civilization: Selected Essays*, ed. Niyazi Berkes. London: Allen & Unwin, 1959.

Ziya Gökalp, '"Yeni Hayat ve Yeni Değerler" [New Life and New Values], *Genç Kalemler*, no. 8, 1911', in *Turkish Nationalism and Western Civilization: Selected Essays*, ed. Niyazi Berkes. London: Allen & Unwin, 1959.

Ziya Gökalp, '"Millet Nedir?" [What is a Nation?], *Küçük Mecmua*, no. 28, Diyarbakır, 1923', in *Turkish Nationalism and Western Civilization: Selected Essays*, ed. Niyazi Berkes. London: Allen & Unwin, 1959.

Ziya Gökalp, *Türkleşmek, İslâmlaşmak, Muasırlaşmak*. Ankara: Kültür Bakanlığı Yayını, 1976.

Secondary sources

Ahmad, F., 'Great Britain's Relations with the Young Turks, 1908-1914', *Middle Eastern Studies*, 2, no. 4 (1966), pp. 302-329.

Ahmad, F., 'War and Society Under the Young Turks, 1908-18', in *From Empire to Republic*. İstanbul, Bilgi University Press, 2008.

Akçam, Taner, *A Shameful Act: The Armenian Genocide and the Question of Turkish Responsibility*. New York: Macmillan, 2006.

Aksakal, Mustafa, *The Ottoman Road to War in 1914: The Ottoman Empire and the First World War*. Cambridge: Cambridge University Press, 2008.

Alangu, Tahir, *Ömer Seyfettin: Ülkücü Bir Yazarın Romanı* [Ömer Seyfettin: The Novel of a Nationalist Writer]. İstanbul: Yapı Kredi Yayınları, 2008.

Anay, H., 'Ödev Ahlâkının Türk Düşüncesine Girişi ve Baha Tevfik'in Kant Hakkındaki Yazıları' [The Duty of Ethics: Introduction to Turkish Thought and Baha Tevfik's Articles about Kant], *Dini Araştırmalar*, 13, no. 36 (2010), p. 154.

Balcıoğlu, Mustafa, 'Osmanlı Genç Dernekleri'nden İnkılap Gençleri Dernekleri'ne' [From the Young Ottoman Associations to the Revolutionary Youth Societies], *Atatürk Araştırma Merkezi Dergisi*, 43 (1992), pp. 98-102.

Bayur, Yusuf Hikmet, *Türk İnkılâbı Tarihi*, vol. 2: *Paylaşımlar* [History of the Turkish Revolution: Sharings]. Ankara: Türk Tarih Kurumu, 1983.

Bayur, Yusuf Hikmet, *Türk İnkılâp Tarihi*, vol. 3: *1914-1918 Genel Savaşı* [History of the Turkish Revolution, vol. 3: The Great War, 1914-1918]. Ankara: Türk Tarih Kurumu, 1982.

Berkes, Niyazi, 'Ziya Gökalp: His Contribution to Turkish Nationalism', *Middle East Journal*, 8, no. 4 (1954), pp. 375-390.

Berkes, Niyazi, *The Development of Secularism in Turkey*. New York: Routledge, 1998.

Beşikçi, Mehmet, *The Ottoman Mobilization of Manpower in the First World War: Between Voluntarism and Resistance*. Leiden: Brill, 2012.

Chief of the General Staff of the Republic of Turkey, *Birinci Dünya Harbi'nde Türk Harbi, Osmanlı İmparatorluğu'nun Siyasi ve Askeri Hazırlıkları ve Harbe Girişi*, ed. Cemal Akbay, vol. 1. Ankara: Genelkurmay Basımevi, 1970, rev. 1991.

Doğan, A., *Osmanlı Aydınları ve Sosyal Darwinizm*. İstanbul: Küre Yayınları, 2012.

Erikson, Edward J., *Defeat in Detail: The Ottoman Army in the Balkans, 1912-1913*. Westport, CT: Praeger Publishers, 2003.

Georgeon, F., *Türk Milliyetçiliğinin Kökenleri* [The Origins of Turkish Nationalism], trans. Alev Er. İstanbul: Yurt Yayınları, 1986.

Hacipoğlu, D., *29 Ekim 1914: Osmanlı İmparatorluğu'nun 1. Dünya Harbine Girişi* [29 October 1914: The Entry of the Ottoman Empire in the First World War]. İstanbul: Deniz İkmal Grup Komutanlığı, 2009.

Hanioğlu, M. Şükrü, *Doktor Abdullah Cevdet ve Dönemi* [Dr. Abdullah Cevdet and His Age]. İstanbul: Üçdal Neşriyat, 1981.

Hanioğlu, M. Şükrü, *Atatürk: An Intellectual Biography*. Princeton, NJ: Princeton University Press, 2011.

Hanioğlu, M. Şükrü, 'Turkism and the Young Turks 1889-1938', in *Turkey Beyond Nationalism: Towards Post-Nationalist Identities*, ed. Hans-Lukas Kieser. London: I.B. Tauris, 2013.

Karaömerlioğlu, Asım, 'Helphand-Parvus and His Impact on Turkish Intellectual Life', *Middle Eastern Studies*, 40, no. 6 (2004), pp. 145-165.

Kelly, Duncan, *The State of the Political: Conceptions of Politics and the State in the Thought of Max Weber, Carl Schmitt, and Franz Neumann*. Oxford: Oxford University Press, 2003.

Kurat, Y.T., 'How Turkey Drifted into World War I', in *Studies in International History*, ed. K. Bourne and D. C. Watt. London: Longmans, 1967, pp. 291–315.
Landau, Jacob M., *Pan-Turkism in Turkey: A study in Irredentism*. London: C. Hurst, 1981.
Landau, Jacob M., *The Politics of Pan-Islam: Ideology and Organization*. Oxford: Clarendon Press, 1990.
Necdet, Ethem, *Tekâmül ve Kanunları* [Evolution and Its Laws]. İstanbul: Matbaa-yı İctihad, 1913.
Nezir-Akmeşe, Handan, *The Birth of Modern Turkey: The Ottoman Military and the March to WWI*. London: I.B. Tauris, 2005.
Okay, M. Orhan, *Beşir Fuad: İlk Türk Pozitivist ve Natüralisti*. [Beşir Fuad: The First Turk Positivist and Naturalist], 2nd ed. İstanbul: Dergâh Yayınları, 2008.
Rogan, Eugene, *The Fall of the Ottomans: The Great War in the Middle East, 1914–1920*. London: Allan Lane, 2015.
Suny, R.G., Göçek, F.M. and Robert, N.M. (eds.), *A Question of Genocide: Armenians and Turks at the End of the Ottoman Empire*. Oxford, New York: Oxford University Press, 2011.
Thomas, Lewis Victor, *A Study of Naima*. New York: New York University Press, 1972.
Toprak, Zafer, 'II. Meşrutiyet Dönemi'nde Paramiliter Gençlik Örgütleri', in *Tanzimat'tan Cumhuriyet'e Türkiye Ansiklopedisi*, ed. Murat Belge and Fahri Ara. İstanbul: İletişim Yayınları, 1985.
Toprak, Zafer, 'Meşrutiyet ve Mütareke Yıllarında Türkiye'de İzcilik', *Toplumsal Tarih*, 9, no. 52 (1998), pp. 13–21.
Toprak, Zafer, *Türkiye'de Popülizm, 1908–1923* [Populism in Turkey, 1908–1923]. Istanbul: Doğan Kitap, 2013.
Üstel, Füsun, *İmparatorluktan Ulus-Devlete Türk Milliyetçiliği Türk Ocakları (1912–1931)*. İstanbul: İletişim Yayınları, 1997.
Yetiş, K., 'İkinci Meşrutiyet Devrindeki Belli Başlı Fikir Akımlarının Askeri Hareketlere ve Cepheye Tesiri' [The Effect of Major Ideological Trends of the Second Constitutional Era on Military Movements and Fronts], in *Bildiriler: Dördüncü Askeri Tarih Semineri*. Ankara: Genelkurmay Basımevi, 1989.
Yılmaz, Şuhnaz, 'An Ottoman Warrior Abroad: Enver Paşa as an Expatriate', *Middle Eastern Studies*, 35, no. 4 (1999), pp. 40–69.
Yılmaz, V., *Birinci Dünya Harbi'nde Türk-Alman İttifakı ve Askeri Yardımlar* [Turkish-German Alliance and Military Aids in the First World War]. İstanbul: Cem, 1993.
Zürcher, Erik J., *Turkey: A Modern History*. London: I.B. Tauris, 2004.

12

War, Revolution and Diplomacy: The October Revolution of 1917 and the Turkish Anatolian Resistance Movement, 1919–1922

Nikos Christofis
Shaanxi Normal University

Introduction

The modern concept of 'revolution' was born in 1789 with the overthrow of Bourbon absolutism. The French Revolution marked 'a break in the continuity of history, a political and social upheaval and reorganization of social relations and a radical opening of the historical horizon'.[1] As Marx eloquently remarked, 'revolutions are the locomotives of history', and as such they are associated with both enlightenment and social progress.[2]

The Bolshevik Revolution of 1917, which put an end to the Romanov dynasty once and for all and is considered the most important revolution of the twentieth century, affected the entire world, including the Ottoman Empire. Not long after the fall of the Romanovs in Russia, another dynasty followed suit, that of the House of Osman. The Ottoman Empire breathed its last breath with the signing of the Armistice of Mudros on 18 October 1918 after it was defeated by the British in Palestine and Mesopotamia, to be followed in 1919 by the nationalist resistance movement in Anatolia – the Turkish 'revolution' as it is often called – which led to the establishment of the Turkish Republic in 1923.

Despite the obvious differences between the two empires and their constant rivalries throughout the nineteenth and early twentieth centuries, the similarities between them are also striking. To some extent, these resemblances actually outweigh the differences, especially with regard to imperialism and nationalism: 'Two nationalisms – or perhaps, more accurately, ideologies of empire – collided, and shaped the other.'[3] Within this context the present chapter seeks to explore the interaction between the two revolutionary processes in terms of how the October Revolution of 1917 impacted the Turkish National Resistance Movement (1919–1922) with the aim of examining the ways the latter was influenced by the former. Finally, the chapter explores how relations between the Turkish Nationalists and the Bolsheviks developed during the period and the motives that underpinned this interaction.

Revolutions Connected, Revolutions Affected

Starting with the French Revolution in 1789, nearly all subsequent revolutions have been marked by a common feature: the desire for constitutional reform. The revolutions that swept across the globe in a 'revolutionary wave', ranging from the Americas to Europe and Asia, demonstrate the global nature of the modern world and the urgent need to shift the focus beyond centre-oriented national histories.[4]

Scholars tend to describe what has been occurring in the world, both in the past and in the present, in terms of 'waves of protests', 'revolutionary waves' and even 'pro-democracy waves'. While 'there is no denying that [later] revolutions borrowed techniques of mobilization and even symbols from earlier ones, the use of the wave metaphor obscures the fact that the goals and styles of the revolutions have varied widely from country to country'.[5] In terms of the former, some protests have demanded reform while others have called for the overthrow of regimes. In terms of the latter, there have been times when protests were predominantly peaceful and other times when they took a violent turn.

This makes it of paramount importance to proceed with caution before drawing generalized conclusions and developing grand theories, as many factors bear on the emergence of revolutionary change. One of the most important of these is human agency: the individual decision to take part in revolution is a crucial, if often under-emphasized, factor in this context.[6] It has been noted that 'due to their vantage point within social contexts, [individuals] interpret global doctrines in a manner most advantageous to their own situation'. In addition, 'global ideologies collide and interact with indigenous notions and change as a result. Actors make sense of global doctrines by localizing, or indigenizing, them based on their own received categories'. And lastly, 'problems, grievances and injustices at the point of reception have their own way of indigenizing the global. In order to mobilize the public, the revolutionary elite is forced to address parochial concerns and, by doing so, assimilate local issues into its offered global solutions.'[7]

A revolution, regardless of its driving forces (ideological, social, cultural), can affect and transcend national borders and transmit the ideas that motivate it – and the practices and repertoires that characterize it – to other revolutions. Revolutionary waves are ideological events with clear ideational and cultural components, yet they are also transnational events with origins and dynamics that are exogenous to any single society. For example, if we turn our attention to the 'first' period of globalization in the latter half of the nineteenth century, which was followed by constitutional and republican revolutions in Russia in 1905, the Ottoman Empire in 1908, Mexico in 1910 and China in 1911,[8] we can readily identify interdependencies and the interconnectedness of political and social changes, as well as the acts of individuals, that have shaped the world.[9]

The revolutionary 'wave of constitutionalism' that started with the French Revolution of 1789 constituted a tremendous blow to monarchical absolutism, although it was not until the end of the First World War that the system was completely discredited and eliminated. Within this framework, the Young Turk Revolution of 1908, which was also characterized by, among other distinct features, its constitutional character, became part of this long-term constitutional tidal inflow that ended with the Russian Revolution of 1917.

Nevertheless, the French model of 'constitutional revolution' was replaced in 1917 with a new and powerful revolutionary archetype. The October Revolution marked a new era by initiating the socialist model of revolution: 'the French Revolution', Furet contends, 'ceased to be the model for a future that was possible, desirable, hoped for ... Instead, it became the mother of a real, dated and duly registered event: October 1917.' In other words, 'Russia [...] took the place of France as the nation in the vanguard of history'.[10] Revolutions after the Bolshevik example 'mobilized for a sudden overthrow from the very beginning without any prospect of a temporary ceasefire and diversion of struggles through a new legal framework'.[11]

The 'Revolutionary Tide' Before the Anatolian Resistance Movement

By the time of the Young Turk Revolution in July 1908, all the necessary conditions for the launch of a revolution were in place. Because of the technological, military and economic advances of Europe – themselves spurred by the changes of the Industrial Revolution – and the challenges the latter posed to the Ottoman Empire through the rising tide of capitalism, the empire had been weakened and decentralized and thereby left highly vulnerable to outside pressure.[12]

At the same time, while the French Revolution clearly affected the Ottoman Empire a great deal, its immediate ideological influence was not so clear.[13] The impact of the French Revolution would only become clear later, as evidenced in the intellectual movement in the 1860s embodied by the Young Ottomans (and the later Young Turk movement) who considered 1789 to be both the first constitutional revolution and the harbinger of progress in Europe. In other words, constitutionalism was more 'a doctrine of political, administrative and legal rationality, on which basis the Ottoman state was to rebuild strength, prevent disintegration and recover lost glory through greater centralization, economic progress and military advancement'.[14] The Young Ottomans advocated a combination of Western ideas and Islamic values in order to restrain the absolutist power of the Ottoman sultan and promote the idea of constitutional monarchy,[15] thus reflecting both Western influence and France's evolution towards a 'liberal empire'.[16] In many respects, using Lenin's metaphor, we can say that the 1860s movement was an Ottoman 'dress rehearsal' for the Young Turk Revolution of 1908.

Towards the end of the nineteenth century, the notion of modernity was further enhanced by the Meiji Restoration in 1868, the success of which rendered Japan a model Eastern nation exemplar of non-Western modernization. Japan's success gave Ottoman and Turkish statesmen a clear model of 'how to become modern by "Western" standards without losing one's "Eastern" essence'.[17] Meiji Japan combined a constitutional monarchy with technological modernization and socio-political reforms that the Ottomans imagined they could adapt to salvage their own empire from the challenge of European encroachment. In other words, Japan represented a powerful nation-state that had successfully managed to resist the European imperial advance, a crucial issue given the European powers had become so deeply embroiled in Ottoman domestic affairs.

Ottoman reality was shaped by the experience of other countries as well. The Russian Revolution of 1905 was prompted by the Russian liberal movement's mobilization of public opinion against the old order.[18] The Russian revolutionaries were highly praised by many Young Turk journals, a sign that the Ottomans were at least somewhat aware of the revolutionary ideas of the nineteenth century.[19] The anti-government uprising opened the way for a more popular based movement in the Ottoman Empire and the Russian example provided concrete suggestions for methods of protest.

Nevertheless, to describe the Eastern Anatolian revolts as exemplary of 'Leninism's role in the awakening of the Asian peoples' is far-fetched.[20] The Young Turk Revolution was a child of the times and failed to 'obtain international recognition' as there was no legal change in the status of the state,[21] marking a striking difference with other revolutions, especially after October 1917. The future leading Bolshevik figures expressed a certain degree of admiration for the Young Turk Revolution, which had occurred in July. For example, in October of the same year, both Lenin and Trotsky were assessing the Young Turk Revolution, and at the same time, they were using it to target the European powers.[22]

The Committee of Union and Progress (CUP) – as the Young Turks were officially known – managed to force the sultan to restore the constitution, whereupon it reconvened parliament in July 1908 and won a resounding victory in the autumn elections of the same year. The CUP's consolidation of power, brought about as the result of opposition forces and events such as the rebellion of 1909 and the army junta in 1912, coincided with the Balkan states' attacks on the Ottoman Empire in 1913.

Turkish-Russian Relations during the Anatolian Resistance Movement

The outbreak of the First World War after the assassination of Franz Ferdinand, the heir to the Habsburg throne, and his wife in Sarajevo in June 1914, plunged the whole of Europe into crisis. It didn't take long for the Russian and Ottoman Empires to be drawn into the war and for old rivalries to re-emerge.

Soon it became evident that the Ottomans were incapable of defending their frontiers from attack, especially considering the territorial sprawl of the empire. Poor weather conditions caused the death of tens of thousands of Ottoman soldiers on the Russian frontier before the Sarıkamış campaign in the spring of 1915. The Ottomans retreated on all fronts, including the Caucasus, Basra, Yemen, the Aegean and Cilicia. In 1916, the Arab revolt – spurred and emboldened by the British – ended with the loss of almost all the Ottoman Empire's Arab territories, bringing about the end of the empire.[23]

For Russia, the defeat at Gallipoli in 1915 marked a further weakening and thus indirectly helped the Bolsheviks launch their revolution.[24] In February 1917, a new regime replaced tsarism in Petrograd, but the empire itself began to dissolve soon after the authority of the provisional government declined precipitously due to the chaos in Russian cities and villages. The years that followed (up until 1921) can be usefully understood in terms of a series of overlapping revolutions. From early March until October 1917, there was a second (or 'liberal') revolution led by middle-class politicians and some of the intelligentsia attempted to create a constitutional order.[25] In October, the workers resumed their revolutionary activities and contributed to the establishment of Soviet power, but intellectuals and party activists 'governed in the name of the workers, gradually displacing the class they purported to represent'.[26] Simultaneously, a peasant revolution was taking place that succeeded in seizing land, expropriating the nobility and doing away with landholding practices in 1918.

The Bolshevik *coup d'état* was also the *coup de grâce* for the Ottoman Empire. The Bolshevik Party denounced the war as an imperialist project and sued for a negotiated peace 'without annexations and indemnities'. During the Second All-Russian Congress of Workers' and Soldiers' Soviet Deputies, which took place a day after the Revolution, a Decree of Peace was passed (unanimously) and a Decree of Land was instituted (one against and eight abstentions), both of which were written by Lenin.[27]

Esat Bey, the Ottoman chargé d'affaires in Stockholm, had delivered news of the revolution in early November 1917[28] and the prospect of peace was received favourably by the Ottomans.[29] The Bolshevik seizure of power could not have come at a better time for the Young Turk government, as the Ottoman army was by this time severely weakened. At the peace negotiations held in Brest-Litovsk (December–March 1918), the Russians agreed to remove their forces from eastern Anatolia, including the areas they had taken in 1878. On 18 December, Russian and Turkish commanders signed an armistice at Erzincan, a forerunner for the Brest-Litovsk agreement,[30] and Russian forces withdrew. While the Russians hoped to recover territory lost to Germany and Austria, only the Ottomans stood to gain from the Bolshevik pledge of peace. Not long after, and as both the Macedonian and Palestinian fronts could no longer be held and collapsed almost simultaneously, it was the Ottoman Empire's turn to sue for an armistice. The armistice forced on Turkey in Mudros on 30 October 1918 allowed the British fleet to sail unopposed through the Straits.

Around that time, Bolshevism began to appear attractive to other Muslim peoples. Lenin's address at the Second All-Russian Congress – where he averred that 'the socialist revolution will not be solely, or chiefly, a struggle of the revolutionary proletarians in each country against their bourgeoisie [...], it will be a struggle of all the imperialist-oppressed colonies and countries, of all dependent countries, against international imperialism'[31] – was followed by a call for Jihad against Western imperialism, pointing out the need to support Muslim movements with the same goals.[32]

The Young Turk leadership, which had found shelter in Germany after the Mudros Armistice, wished to take advantage of this conjuncture and began to form a strategy to cooperate with all Muslims working or studying in Germany at the time (alongside local socialists), against the common enemy: European imperialism. Their ultimate goal was to free the empire with Russian help through Muslim uprisings in India and in other colonies and to thereby regain power. This was not the first time that a call for Jihad was used to mobilize the Muslim population in the colonies. In November 1914, a Jihad was proclaimed and justified with the argument that 'the Islamic state (the

Ottoman Empire) and the Muslim community had come under unprovoked attack from Russia, France and Britain'. The Jihad was aimed at the Muslim subjects of France, Britain and Russia in their colonies, calling upon them to resist their oppressors.[33] Sometime later, Mustafa Kemal himself would make use of the same argument, presenting anti-imperialism as the ideological bridge between Islam and communism.[34]

The political vacuum that arose when the Young Turk leadership fled abroad left many groups competing for power. Members of the CUP, nevertheless, had already laid the ground both for armed resistance and for the mobilization of public opinion even before the war ended. The so-called Societies for the Defence of National Rights were established in many cities and notables such as Islamic legal advisors (*müftü*) and members of the local elite (*esraf*) were drafted onto the boards of those societies, which emphatically declared their non-partisan status.[35] These societies organized congresses from November 1918 to October 1920 where issues such as the threat of takeovers by Greece, Armenia and the Allies were discussed. The Western powers were seen as the enemies of the Turks, whereas the Bolsheviks and Muslims of Asia provided monetary and moral support. The leaders of *Karakol* (The Guard)[36]– the origins of which can be traced to the intelligence organization of the CUP, the *Teşkilat-ı Mahsusa* (Special Organization) – approached Mustafa Kemal.

For its part, Bolshevism had already begun to make an impression in the interior of the empire. Its influence was small but still palpable, as can be seen also by the CUP leadership. On 5 April 1917, the Grand Vizier (and member of the CUP), Talât Paşa, welcomed the fall of tsarism, and recalled that 'the new Turkey was also a child of a revolution'.[37] At the same time, he attempted to turn the fall of tsarism to the benefit of the Ottoman government and highlight the similarities between the revolutions. He shared propaganda leaflets celebrating the 'felicitous revolution' (*ihtilâl-i mesut*) emphasizing the common goal for 'civilizational progress' (*terakkiyat-ı medeniye*).[38] He did not neglect, though, to point out that the fall of tsarism opened the way to preserving the empire's territorial integrity, especially in the east.[39] Students from *Darülfünun* (Istanbul University) also hung a picture of Lenin at a university building[40] and suggested that he be given the Nobel Prize.[41] This influence increased after the Anatolian Resistance Movement provided support for the new Russian government, and the return of Turkish prisoners of war indoctrinated with communist ideas helped in the establishment of left-wing parties.[42]

Partly due to doctrinal reasons, but mainly because of the presence of Allied troops in the Crimea and Odessa to help the Russian White Army fight the Bolsheviks, Mustafa Kemal and the nationalist movement were received with enthusiasm by Russia. The movement was presented by the editor of *Izvestia* 'as the first Soviet Revolution in Asia'.[43] For the Bolsheviks, the Turkish nationalists were a key target for solidarity in the undermining of the Allies[44] and revolutionary Turkey was seen as the vanguard of the Bolshevik Revolution in the Muslim world. At the tenth congress of the Russian Communist Party in March 1921, Stalin declared Turkey to be 'the most politically developed country among the Muslim peoples [which had] raised the banner of revolt and rallied around itself the peoples of the East against imperialism'.[45]

Russian enthusiasm was consciously and purposefully exaggerated, since helping a Muslim country in its war against imperialism (i.e. the capitalist West) would create a positive image among the Muslim populations of Central Asia. In late 1919, Mustafa Kemal and his closest confidantes first met with the Bolsheviks, hinting that an independent Turkey friendly to communism might be possible in exchange for guarantees of support.[46] For the Bolsheviks, the nationalist movement offered a good opportunity to pin down Allied troops in Odessa and Crimea. General Budyonny, who was leading the Russian mission,[47] asked Mustafa Kemal what kind of regime he had in mind for Anatolia. Kemal responded: 'a Soviet regime just like in Russia', clarifying a moment later that he meant 'a [regime of] state socialism'.[48]

Nevertheless, Turkish-Russian rapprochement was based on necessity and common interests rather than a common ideological commitment to Bolshevism.[49] Certain indicators suggested that Mustafa Kemal's public musings about a potential socialist Turkish state were more calculated than sincere. In her memoirs, Halide Edip does not seem to share the above opinion, and she claimed that Mustafa Kemal was studying the Soviet system in preparation for all possible scenarios.[50] At the same time, Chicherin – the Soviet People's Commissar of Foreign Affairs – made a radio broadcast to the 'workers and peasants of Turkey' in mid-September 1919 in which he attacked the 'ill-fated' Ottoman Parliament as an assembly of 'exploiting Paşas' and called upon Turkish workers and peasants to join Russia in driving off 'the European robbers' and destroying irresolute political parties, while taking the affairs of their country into their own hands.[51]

Certainly it is true that Mustafa Kemal saw an alliance with the Bolsheviks in a positive light and he sent a commission to Moscow to establish connections with the Russian government. He insisted, however, that concrete promises should be made before any agreement was signed. Some people around him were opposed to striking a deal with the Bolsheviks and many nationalist commanders feared that the Russians would refuse military and economic assistance unless Anatolia was 'Bolshevized'. Hüşrev Bey, for example, expressed his concerns to Kâzım Karabekir – another leading member of the resistance movement, former CUP member, and close friend of Mustafa Kemal – that any assistance to the movement would bring about the 'Bolshevization' of the Caucasus and the creation of a 'state socialism' favourable to the Soviets.[52]

Mustafa Kemal summarized the situation in a letter to his generals on 5 February 1920,[53] stressing the importance of good relations with the Bolsheviks. He warned them that if the Western powers succeeded in isolating the movement from the Caucasus and the Bolshevik region, areas that were important to the viability of the movement, it would lead to the immediate occupation of Turkey. At the same time, his pragmatism is evident when he noted that the Allied powers wanted the Turkish resistance movement to turn against the Bolsheviks and meet Turkish demands by starting with a withdrawal from Turkish-occupied Arab land.

While the Turkish nationalist leadership was busy discussing and formalizing the possibilities and the prospects of a relationship with the Bolsheviks, another contact was established through a different channel under the initiative of the still influential once wartime leader, Enver Paşa, who aimed to establish an anti-Entente alliance between Turkey, the Soviet Union and Germany. Little is known of how Enver's discussions with the Soviet emissary, Karl Radek, ended but according to Soviet documents, 'Enver has already showed great sacrifice for the realization of the Turkish-

Soviet relations.'⁵⁴ Enver, as the leader of the exiled Young Turks, was inspired by the anti-imperialist stance of Moscow and he participated in the Congress of the Peoples of Anatolia in Baku in 1920. The ideology he developed consisted of a mixture of Islamism and socialism, with a strong dose of corporatism.⁵⁵

As Bolshevik-Turkish relations improved, creating a friendly and encouraging atmosphere, left-wing activities gained additional momentum, one of the most important of which, and with direct relation to our discussion, was the Turkish Communist Party (*Türkiye Komunist Partisi*/TKP), established by a Turkish émigré group under the leadership of Mustafa Suphi (1883-1921), a former Unionist himself, in Baku in June of 1920. The party was accepted in the Communist International and Suphi himself was appointed head of the propaganda bureau of the Third International in Turkistan. The group participated in the Baku Congress of September of 1920, promoting the TKP as a significant force in the anti-imperialist fight against colonialism and semi-colonialism. The importance of support for national liberation movements like the one led by Mustafa Kemal was stated repeatedly and the party showed its willingness to support the Turkish struggle for independence against the Allied forces. The party came to a tragic end, however, in 1921 when the founder and many of its members were drowned on their way to Ankara to join the Turkish national liberation movement. This calamity, however, had no serious repercussions for Turkish-Russian relations, a point we shall return to below.⁵⁶

If the Greek landing of 1919 created the nationalist movement in Turkey, the Allied occupation of Istanbul converted the movement into an effective separate government.⁵⁷ After mid-1920, the national resistance movement became an organized entity and party that assumed complete control of the resistance. Its official demands were contained in the so-called National Pact (*Mısak-ı Milli*), which closely matched the provisions that had been discussed at nationalist congresses held in Erzurum and Sivas.

In an attempt to reverse the situation and reclaim its authority, the Ottoman government rejected these moves and even claimed that its leaders, including Mustafa Kemal, were men without any stake in the country as they had no connection of blood. As late as 1922, Sultan Vahdeddin was propagandizing in Istanbul, still under occupation by the Allied forces, that 'the National leaders are not a Government, but a collection of rebels and revolutionaries, [...] a reincarnation of the Committee of Union and Progress. [...] In policy and conviction they are nothing else but Bolsheviks. They are only Bolsheviks (*Bunlar sadece Bolşevikler*)!'⁵⁸

Soon after declaring the movement the only legitimate representative of the people, Mustafa Kemal appealed to Soviet Russia for recognition, assistance and mutual operations as a means of expelling the 'imperialist' powers occupying Turkish territories. He also requested that the Caucasus route be opened.⁵⁹ Chicherin's reply reveals that Turkey was of critical importance to the Bolsheviks:

> In order to bring about amicable relations and enduring friendship between Turkey and Russia, the Soviet Government proposes the immediate establishment of diplomatic and consular representations... The Soviet Government is following with the greatest interest the heroic struggle which the Turkish people are waging for their independence and in the present difficult days of Turkey it is happy to

establish a firm foundation for the friendship which is to unite the peoples of Turkey and Russia.⁶⁰

Chicherin also proposed Soviet mediation regarding the settlement of Turkish-Armenian and Turkish-Iranian border issues, a recommendation that Mustafa Kemal appears to have accepted in a reply he sent on 20 June.⁶¹ Based on the correspondence of the two leading figures, it seems that both of them considered an alliance to be in their best interests. Mustafa Kemal could not refrain from complaining to Chicherin, however, about the killings of Muslims by Armenians, and he asked for his help to put an end to the massacres.

In the years after 1920, and especially after the Baku Congress in September the same year, the Bolsheviks tried to strengthen relations by advocating a united front against Western imperialism between communists and Eastern nationalists. The Soviet strategy here was multi-faceted, consisting of concurrent alternative policies, and combined 'peaceful coexistence' with, and 'fraternal aid' to, communist parties and movements with collaboration and assistance to reactionary nationalist governments that were suppressing those same parties and movements.⁶² Thus, the Soviet Union could infiltrate and target countries to further its 'cause' and influence. What mattered for the Soviet Union was not necessarily the success of a particular communist party, but rather its potential to advance the foreign policy goals of the Soviet Union. World Communism remained the publicly stated, long-range goal, but that was always secondary to the immediate goal of promoting Soviet state interests.⁶³ It is no surprise then that the Soviet policy of friendship with Mustafa Kemal's Turkey was unaffected by the fact that the government murdered the leader of the Turkish Communist Party, and this applied to the Communist International as well. At the Third Comintern Congress, Süleyman Nuri declared that though he condemned the Black Sea incident he thought Mustafa Kemal should still be supported 'to the extent that he fought against imperialism'.⁶⁴

Soviet influence was evident not just in the socialist parties and organizations that were being formed at the time, but in the workings of the Grand National Assembly as well. The very first decision made by the newly formed National Assembly was to send an official delegation to Moscow with Foreign Minister Bekir Sami. By 24 August, Sami had made enough headway in Moscow to launch a draft treaty, but the formal signing was delayed for seven months due to considerable friction in the Transcaucasia region, where both Russia and Turkey were trying to increase their influence. Russia had signed an agreement with Armenia which recognized Armenian control over territory which the Turks considered their own, an area including the land route from Turkey to Russia. Chicherin demanded that the Turks cede territory to Armenia, which put a halt to Bekir Sami's negotiations.⁶⁵ The stalemate was proving to be detrimental to both parties, however, so talks were renewed after Chicherin sent a more formal mission to Ankara in October. Eventually, the situation culminated in the Sovietization of Armenia, and for the first time in many decades the Russians and Turks again had a common frontier.

The Treaty of Sevres, signed on 10 August 1920, led the Kemalist government to turn once again to Soviet Russia. The humiliating terms of the Treaty were rejected by the Nationalists. Mustafa Kemal's proclamation to the people of Anatolia in protest to the Treaty showed that desperate times call for desperate measures, and those included the Communists:

> Brethren in Islam, Communist Comrades! A horrible injustice is about to occur. The Great Powers are strangling the new Muslim victim, which is on the brink of destruction. But we will die with weapons in our hands, defending the territory of our fatherland, for which we made bold to claim rights. Our peasants will defend their land, their hearts and their villages against the ravishers, and they can die assured that the day is near when all Islam, having united with communism, will avenge them.[66]

The appeal to religious sentiment in Mustafa Kemal's discourse sought to mobilize the force of Islam in a struggle against the Allies and the non-Muslim Ottoman groups they supported. A different discourse would have perhaps endangered the vital support of portions of the Turkish population, and the Soviet leaders, who viewed pan-Turkism as a major threat to the Bolshevization of Central Asia and the Caucasus.[67] He used both 'an extreme Islamist and pan-Islamist rhetoric and augmented his nationalist opposition to imperialism with a purely rhetorical socialism'. 'Our nation', Mustafa Kemal wrote in a letter to Chicherin, 'has become a vicious target of European imperialists due to its defense of Muslim countries ... I strongly believe that [...] when the enslaved peoples of Asia and Africa comprehend that international capital exploits them for their masters' maximum profit and their own enslavement [...] the power of the bourgeoisie will come to an end.'

Kemal expressed similar ideas during a speech in the Grand National Assembly when he said, 'Bolshevism includes the most exalted principles and rules of Islam.'[68] In other words, he gave the impression, at least in this period, of being a Muslim communist. In this way it seems that Mustafa Kemal spoke one way with the Turkish masses about the retention of the caliphate, while he wrote to Chicherin and other Soviet leaders as if he were a comrade in the revolution. Lenin was well aware that Mustafa Kemal was not a communist, but he recognized that the Turkish leader was 'a good organizer ... [and] he understood the importance of our [Bolshevik] socialist revolution well'.[69]

As might be expected, Turkish-Soviet relations foundered whenever one of them looked to its own interests at the expense of the other and when the Allied powers moved successfully to freeze relations between the two countries. On 23 February 1921, the Entente powers decided to reach a settlement in the Near East, summoning Greek and Turkish leaders to attend as well. The fact that both Turkish governments were present shows that the Anatolian Resistance Movement amounted to de facto recognition. Turkey's pragmatism also became apparent at the London Conference when Bekir Sami said that he was open to accepting better terms by pledging that Turkey would join the anti-Soviet front. Nevertheless, the conference ended in a stalemate.

After negotiations resumed, a Turkish delegation, this time headed by Yusuf Kemal Bey, arrived in Moscow in February 1921. In the spirit of reviving good relations,

Chicherin opened the Moscow conference on 26 February by referring to the Soviet role in the Turkish struggle against foreign intervention:

> If for the past six months the Turkish situation has changed radically, along with the heroism evinced by the Turkish workers and peasants against the foreign invaders, a considerable part of the credit should be given to the friendly relations existing between Russia and Turkey, which strengthened the position of the latter. These friendly ties must be reinforced by a formal treaty.[70]

Under the direct supervision of Lenin and Stalin, the negotiations progressed successfully, and on 16 March they led to a Treaty of Friendship, the first diplomatic treaty concluded by the nationalists. In the agreement, the Turks agreed to cede Nachicevan and Batum and to give the Bolsheviks a say in the future status of the Straits.[71] Despite their criticism of the Kemalist government, the Soviet leaders realized that the treaty strengthened the Soviet government's international position. From the Soviet point of view, this treaty – together with similar agreements concluded with Iran and Afghanistan in the same year – weakened the position of the Allied camp. From the Turkish point of view, the accord was equally beneficial for Turkey. It was a decisive factor in strengthening the international position of the Kemalist movement both *vis-à-vis* Greece and the Entente powers and a means of getting additional Soviet aid. In that year, the political situation changed crucially in favour of the Turkish nationalists.

It became clear that the French and the Italians had begun to have strong reservations about Greek expansionism under the leadership of Eleftherios Venizelos, who had lost in the elections of December 1920 to King Constantine. Once the monarchists came to power, it became apparent that they intended to continue the irredentist campaign in Asia Minor. They had miscalculated, however, the strength of the Turkish nationalist movement and the shift in the power balance in favour of Turkey. With the successful Turkish offensive at the Sakarya River, the political situation changed fundamentally in favour of the Turkish nationalists. Mustafa Kemal ordered a final Turkish offensive on 26 August 1922 and four days later the battle was won after the retreat of the Greek army to the coast. On 9 September Turkish troops entered Izmir, marking total Greek defeat.

Turkish relations with the Soviets soured at the end of 1922 when persecutions of communists started anew under the Kemalist regime and Soviet aid was no longer needed.[72] Mustafa Kemal wanted to show to the capitalist world that Bolshevik interference in the domestic affairs of Turkey would no longer be tolerated. In the following year, the signing of the Treaty of Lausanne brought about recognition of the Turkish Republic and put an end to the First World War in the Middle East.

Conclusion

The twentieth century changed dramatically after the Bolshevik Revolution, as global ideologies influenced and interacted with the indigenous notions tied up with other national revolutionary movements. As a result, they changed as they collided with these other revolutionary movements and local actors made sense of global doctrines by localizing or indigenizing them based on their own perceived categories. Once recognized, national claims for independence, grievances, injustices and revolution have their own way of indigenizing the global. At the same time, the revolutionary elite is forced to address parochial concerns to mobilize the public, and, in doing so, assimilate local issues into the global solutions it offers.

Mustafa Kemal's blend of Islamist and socialist rhetoric is a clear case in point. The ideas that he constantly formulated and reformulated, even later during the republican era, and the times in which he seemed to temporarily take on a communist worldview, do not present enough ground to argue that the movement he led was affected to such a point that the two revolutionary movements shared the same worldview.

His rhetoric and ambiguous messages are down to the indigenous ideological contradictions of the time, but the two revolutionary movements did not share the same ideological worldview.[73] For example, while Mustafa Kemal emphasized in the newly established Grand National Assembly on 14 July 1920 that the principles and laws of Islam can be found in Bolshevism and congratulated the Bolsheviks for beating a common enemy, this 'Islamic Bolshevism' was soon replaced with a different rhetoric. The following year, Mustafa Kemal asserted that communism could provide a solution to the political issues of Turkey, and was something foreign to Turkey's reality:

> Gentlemen, there might be two kinds of precautions. The first: To crush those who talk about Communism immediately, to utilize fierce, destructive measures such as not allowing any man coming from Russia to step on the land if he is coming by ship or expelling him directly if he is coming by road. We have recognized such precautions as useless in two respects: Firstly, the Russian Republic which we deem good political relations as a necessity is entirely communist. If we have taken such radical measures, under no circumstances we should have any relation with and had any interest in the Russians. [...] Therefore, we considered the most effective remedy as explaining our people, as enlightening the public opinion of the nation that Communism is unacceptable for our country in view of our religious requirements.[74]

Similar characteristics should not be overdrawn in the analysis. It is true that both the Bolsheviks and the Turkish Republican People's Party (CHP) – an all-inclusive 'political party' formed in mid-1920 and in power until 1950 – did share the mass support of the peasants and the army. They also held anti-imperialism in common. But these similarities were more a result of the given historical juncture than any real shared commitments. Mustafa Kemal himself stated that communism would never have been a suitable solution for the issues existing in Turkey. His policies after 1923 underscore that statement. Despite the direct impact of the revolution in the Ottoman Empire and the formation of several socialist parties, communism played a negligible role in the leadership of the resistance movement. Rather, it would be more correct to see Bolshevik-Turkish relations and interaction during the period from 1919 to 1922 as fundamentally pragmatic. They were mutually beneficial relations, promoting the interests of the two countries in the region, while at the same time resisting the imperialist policies of the Allied powers – a 'marriage of convenience'.

Pragmatism, not shared ideological commitment, was thus the key element that brought the two countries closer together, while anti-imperialism provided the missing link to achieve the movement's goals (i.e. mobilization of the people towards independence and national self-identification). In that respect, Russia's introduction of the reorganization of imperialism, its programme of peace and the denunciation of conflict as an expression of the expansionist brutality of imperialism was pivotal. It was also out of a sense of genuine pragmatism and *Realpolitik* that both governments decided to ignore each other's faults and sacrifice their pawns to win the battle. The Russians ignored the drowning of the leading members of the Turkish Communist Party, while Ankara cemented Bolshevik relations with Enver, relations launched in mid-1919 that were of immense significance in bringing the countries together. Additionally, the saying 'the enemy of my enemy is my friend' seems to apply in the case of the two countries, at least to a point. Ankara's help in leading Azerbaijan to Soviet control in 1920 was meant to prevent its capture by Britain and thus minimize the influence of the latter in the region.

From the very beginning of Turkey's nationalist resistance, there was mutual cooperation and understanding but also mistrust between Mustafa Kemal and the Soviet leadership. The cooperation they established was based on the necessities of the times and the difficult post-war situation in which the Ottoman Empire and Soviet Russia found themselves. Instrumental for both countries was the pressure applied by the Allied powers, mainly the British and the Greeks, and the claims they made on the territories of the Empire. Overall, what was common to both governments, and in particular in the rhetoric of the leading figures of the two countries, was their staunch anti-imperialism. If we needed to find common elements in the discourse of both countries, this would be first and foremost the notion of anti-imperialism. Nevertheless, it makes little sense to get carried away by the common use of the word as the content of the concept (and most importantly its end-goal) differed in time and depended on the national context of each country. Thus, even as we notice how Bolshevik prompting in the form of the anti-imperialist declarations of the Russian Revolution that sought to influence all oppressed peoples, Turkish anti-imperialism – so closely linked with Ziya Gökalp's ideas on nationalism – was strictly confined within the country's national borders, making class struggle pointless.

Notes

1   Stefan Rinke and Michael Wildt, 'Revolutions and Counter Revolutions: An Introduction', in *Revolutions and Counter-Revolutions: 1917 and its Aftermath from a Global Perspective*, ed. Stefan Rinke and Michael Wildt. Frankfurt: Campus, 2017, p. 9.
2   Karl Marx, 'The Class Struggles in France, 1848 to 1850', in Karl Marx and Friedrich Engels, *Collected Works*, vol. 10. London: Lawrence & Wishart, 2010, p. 122.
3   Norman Stone, Sergei Podbolotov and Murat Yaşar, 'The Russians and the Turks: Imperialism and Nationalism in the Era of Empires', in *Imperial Rule*, ed. Alexei Miller and Alfred J. Rieber. Budapest: CEU, 2004, p. 28.
4   Christopher Bayly, *The Birth of the Modern World 1780–1914: Global Connections and Comparisons*. Oxford: Blackwell, 2004.

5   James L. Gelvin, *The Arab Uprisings: What Everyone Needs to Know*. Oxford: Oxford University Press, 2015, p. 36.
6   Ibid.
7   Nader Sohrabi, 'Revolutions as Pathways to Modernity', in *Remaking Modernity: Politics, History and Sociology*, ed. Julia Adams, Elisabeth S. Clemens and Ann Shola Orloff. Durham, NC: Duke University Press, 2005, p. 305.
8   Colin J. Beck, 'Ideological Roots of Waves of Revolution', PhD thesis, Stanford University, 2009, p. 78; for the Ottoman case, see François Georgeon (ed.), *'L'ivresse de la liberté'. La Révolution de 1908 dans L'Empire Ottomane*. Leuven: Peeters, 2012.
9   Pankaj Mishra, *From the Ruins of Empire: The Revolt Against the West and the Remaking of Asia*. London: Penguin, 2013.
10 François Furet, *Interpreting the French Revolution*. Cambridge: Cambridge University Press, 1997, pp. 5-6; Nader Sohrabi, *Revolution and Constitutionalism in the Ottoman Empire and Iran*. Cambridge: Cambridge University Press, 2011, p. 5.
11 Sohrabi, 'Revolutions as Pathways to Modernity', p. 304.
12 Reşat Kasaba, *The Ottoman Empire and the World Economy: The Nineteenth Century*. New York: State University of New York Press, 1987.
13 Erik J. Zürcher, *Turkey. A Modern History*. London: I.B. Tauris, 2004, pp. 25-27.
14 Nader Sohrabi, 'Global Waves, Local Actors: What the Young Turks Knew about Other Revolutions and Why It Mattered', *Comparative Studies in Society and History*, 44, no. 1 (2002), p. 50.
15 İsmail Kara, 'İslam Düşüncesinde Paradigma Değişimi. Hem Batılılaşalım hem de Müslüman Kalalım', in *Modern Türkiye'de Siyasi Düşünce*, vol. 1: *Tanzimat ve Meşrutiyetin Birikimi*, ed. Mehmet Ö. Alkan. Istanbul: İletişim, 2001, pp. 234-364.
16 Şerif Mardin, *The Genesis of Young Ottoman Thought*. Princeton, NJ: Princeton University Press, 1962.
17 Renée Worringer, *Ottomans Imagining Japan: East, Middle East, and Non-Western Modernity at the Turn of the Twentieth Century*. Basingstoke: Palgrave, 2014, p. 1.
18 For a comparative account, see Klas-Göran Karlsson, 'The Young Turks in Power: A Comparative and Critical Perspective', in *Religion, Ethnicity and Contested Nationhood in the Former Ottoman Space*, ed. Jørgen S. Nielsen. Leiden: Brill, 2012, pp. 11-28. The idea of constitutionalism was so great that Chinese news articles referring to the war of 1904-1905 attributed the Japanese victory to the fact that Japan had a constitution and the Russian defeat to its lack thereof. Ivar Spector, *The Soviet Union and the Muslim World, 1917-1958*. Seattle, WA: University of Washington Press, 1959, p. 23.
19 Uygur Kocabaşoğlu and Metin Berge, *Bolşevik İhtilâli ve Osmanlılar*. Istanbul: İletişim, 2006, pp. 23-31; Helene Carrere d'Encausse and Stuart R. Schram, *Marxism and Asia*. London: Allen Lane, 1969, p. 21.
20 Şükrü Hanioğlu, *Preparation for a Revolution: The Young Turks, 1902-1908*. Oxford: Oxford University Press, 2001, p. 122.
21 Şükrü Hanioğlu, 'The Second Constitutional Period, 1908-1918', in *The Cambridge History of Modern Turkey*, vol. 4, ed. Reşat Kasaba. Cambridge: Cambridge University Press, 2008, p. 67.
22 V.I. Lenin, 'Events in the Balkans and in Persia', in *Lenin Collected Works*, vol. 15. Moscow: Progress Publishers, 1973, pp. 220-230; Leon Trotsky, 'The Young Turks', *Kievskaya Mysl*, 3 January 1909, in www.marxists.org/archive/trotsky/1909/01/1909-turks.htm [accessed in 6. December 2016].

23 For a recent account of the Ottoman Empire during the First World War, see Eugene Rogan, *The Fall of the Ottomans: The Great War in the Middle East*. New York: Basic Books, 2015.
24 Şükrü Hanioğlu, *Atatürk: An Intellectual Biography*. Princeton, NJ: Princeton University Press, 2011, p. 77.
25 Ronald G. Suny, 'The Russian Empire', in *After Empire. Multiethnic Societies and Nation-Building: The Soviet Union and the Russian, Ottoman, and Habsburg Empires*, ed. Karen Barkey and Mark von Hagen. Boulder, CO: Westview Press, 1997, p. 144.
26 Ibid.
27 A.M. Kulegin, 'All-Russian Congress of Workers' and Soldiers' Soviet Deputies, Second', Encyclopaedia of St. Petersburg, http://www.encspb.ru/object/2804022647?lc=en
28 Kocabaşoğlu and Berge, *Bolşevik İhtilâli ve Osmanlılar*, pp. 103–104.
29 Bülent Gökay, *A Clash of Empires: Turkey between Russian Bolshevism and British Imperialism, 1918–1923*. London: I.B. Tauris, 1997, pp. 17–18.
30 Stefanos Yerasimos, *Kurtuluş Savaşı'nda Türk-Sovyet İlişkileri 1917–1923*. Istanbul: Gözlem, 1979, pp. 44–48.
31 https://www.marxists.org/archive/lenin/works/1919/nov/22.htm
32 Ben Fowkes and Bülent Gökay, 'Unholy Alliance: Muslims and Communists – An Introduction', *Journal of Communist Studies and Transition Politics*, 25, no. 1 (2009), p. 31.
33 The fatwa also defined joining the fight against the Islamic (Ottoman) state as a grave sin that would carry the severest penalty in the hereafter for any Muslim who did so. Erik J. Zürcher, 'Introduction: The Ottoman Jihad, the German Jihad and the Sacralization of War', in *Jihad and Islam in World War I*, ed. Erik J. Zürcher. Leiden: Leiden University Press, 2016, p. 14.
34 Alp Yenen, 'The Young Turk Zeitgeist', in *War and Collapse: World War I and the Ottoman State*, ed. Hakan M. Yavuz. Salt Lake City, UT: University of Utah Press, 2016, p. 1201.
35 Erik J. Zürcher, 'Young Turks, Ottoman Muslims and Turkish Nationalists: Identity Politics, 1908–1938', in *The Young Turk Legacy and Nation Building: From the Ottoman Empire to Ataturk's Turkey*. London: I.B. Tauris, 2010, p. 221.
36 Erik J. Zürcher, *The Unionist Factor: The Role of the Committee of Union and Progress in the Turkish National Movement 1905–1926*. Leiden: Brill, 1984, pp. 80–87; Nur Bilge Criss, *Istanbul Under Allied Occupation, 1918–1923*. Leiden: Brill, 1999, pp. 94–114; Emel Akal, *Mustafa Kemal, İttihat Teraki ve Bolşevizm*. Istanbul: İletişim, 2012, pp. 185–191.
37 Kocabaşoğlu and Berge, *Bolşevik İhtilâli ve Osmanlılar*, p. 63.
38 Michael A. Reynolds, *Shattering Empires: The Clash and Collapse of the Ottoman and Russian Empires, 1908–1918*. Cambridge: Cambridge University Press, 2011, p. 168.
39 Gökay, *A Clash of Empires*, p. 17.
40 Kocabaşoğlu and Berge, *Bolşevik İhtilâli ve Osmanlılar*, p. 130, fn. 100.
41 Ibid.; Dimitir Şişmanov, *Türkiye İşçi ve Sosyalist Hareketi: Kısa Tarihi (1908–1965)*. Istanbul: Belge Yayınları, 1978, pp. 60–61.
42 Some of the parties that emerged during that time were the *Sosyal Demokrat Fırkası*, founded by a former CUP member, Dr. Hasan Riza, in December 1918; the *Türkiye Sosyalist Fırkası – Halk İştirakiyun Fırkası*, founded by Hüseyin 'İştirakçi' Hilmi on 20 February 1919; and the *Türkiye İşçi ve Çiftçi Fırkası*, founded in May 1919 by a group of young workers who had gone to Germany. They were all socialist parties that were directly influenced by the October Revolution. During 1918–1923, especially

after the occupation of the Triple Alliance, Ottoman workers and their labour organizations were on very good terms with the socialist movements. Yavuz Selim Karakışla, 'The Emergence of the Ottoman Working Class, 1839–1923', in *Workers and the Working Class in the Ottoman Empire and the Turkish Republic, 1839–1950*, ed. Donald Quataert and Erik J. Zürcher. London: I.B. Tauris, 1995, p. 28.
43 Spector, *The Soviet Union and the Muslim World*, p. 64.
44 Nur Bilge Criss, 'Images of the Early Turkish National Movement (1919–1921)', in *Historical Image of the Turk in Europe: 15th Century to the Present*, ed. Mustafa Soykut. Istanbul: Isis Press, 2003, pp. 269–270.
45 https://www.marxists.org/reference/archive/stalin/works/1921/03/08.htm
46 Ayşe Zarakol, *After Defeat: How the East Learned to Live with the West*. Cambridge: Cambridge University Press, 2010, passim.
47 Yerasimos, *Kurtuluş Savaşı'nda Türk-Sovyet İlişkileri 1917–1923*, p. 108.
48 Rasih Nuri İleri, *Atatürk ve Komünizm*. Istanbul: İleri Yayınları, 2005, p. 38. See also, Abdulhamit Kırmızı, 'After Empire, Before Nation: Competing Ideologies and the Bolshevik Moment of the Anatolian Revolution', in *Revolutions and Counter-Revolutions: 1917 and its Aftermath from a Global Perspective*, ed. Stefan Rinke and Michael Wildt. Frankfurt: Campus, 2017, pp. 119–139.
49 On the Russian ideological influence, see also Nikos Christofis, 'The Ottoman Empire in the Aftermath of the October Revolution: Ideological Identification or Realism?', *TA ΙΣΤΟΡΙΚΑ*, 67 (2017), pp. 145–164 [in Greek].
50 Halide Edip, *The Turkish Ordeal: Being the Further Memoirs of Halide Edib*. New York: Century, 1928, p. 175.
51 Yerasimos, p. 124–126.
52 Paul Dumont, 'L'Axe Moscou-Ankara: Les Relations Turco-Soviétiques de 1919 a 1922', in *Du Socialisme Ottoman A L'Internationalisme Anatolien*, Istanbul: The ISIS Press, 1997, p. 147.
53 Yerasimos, *Kurtuluş Savaşı'nda Türk-Sovyet İlişkileri 1917–1923*, pp. 134–137.
54 Gökay, *A Clash of Empires*, pp. 67–68.
55 Alp Yenen, 'The Other Jihad: Enver Paşa, Bolsheviks, and Politics of Anticolonial Muslim Nationalism during the Baku Congress 1920', in *The First World War and its Aftermath: The Shaping of the Middle East*, ed. T.G. Fraser. London: Gingko Library, 2015, pp. 273–294.
56 Silvio Pons, *The Global Revolution: A History of International Communism, 1917–1991*, trans. Allan Cameron. Oxford: Oxford University Press, 2014, p. 55.
57 Roderic Davison, 'Diplomacy from Moudros to Lausanne', in *Essays in Ottoman and Turkish History, 1774–1923: The Impact of the West*. Austin, TX: University of Texas Press, 1990, pp. 206–242, p. 212.
58 Gotthard Jaeschke, *Kurtuluş Savaşı ile İlgili İngiliz Belgeleri*, vol. II. Istanbul: Cumhuriyet, 2001, p. 100 as quoted in Abdulhamit Kırmızı. Translation by A.K.
59 Yerasimos, *Kurtuluş Savaşı'nda Türk-Sovyet İlişkileri 1917–1923*, p. 223.
60 Ibid., pp. 228–229.
61 Ibid., pp. 230–231.
62 Fowkes and Gökay, 'Unholy Alliance: Muslims and Communists – An Introduction', p. 8.
63 Ibid., p. 9.
64 John Riddell (ed.), *To the Masses: Proceedings of the Third Congress of the Communist International, 1921*. Leiden: Brill, 2015, pp. 838–839.
65 Davison, 'Diplomacy from Moudros to Lausanne', p. 215.

66 Spector, p. 71-72.
67 Hanioğlu, *Atatürk*, p. 105.
68 All quotations from Ibid, p. 105-106.
69 Semyon İvanoviç Aralov, *Bir Sovyet Diplomatinin Türkiye Anıları*. Istanbul: İş Bankası Kültür Yayınları, 2014, p. 39.
70 Spector, *The Soviet Union and the Muslim World*, p. 75.
71 Zürcher, *Turkey: A Modern History*, p. 153.
72 Dumont, 'L'Axe Moscou-Ankara', p. 171.
73 Mete Tunçay, 'Mustafa Suphi Öldürülmeseydi Muhtemelen Bakan Olurdu', in *Sol Kemalizme Bakıyor*, ed. Levent Cinemre and Ruşen Çakır. Istanbul: Metis Yayınları, 1991, pp. 13–24.
74 As quoted in Rasih Nuri İleri, *Atatürk ve Komünizm*, p. 280.

Bibliography

Akal, Emel, *Mustafa Kemal, İttihat Terraki ve Bolşevizm*. Istanbul: İletişim, 2012.
Aralov, Semyon İvanoviç, *Bir Sovyet Diplomatinin Türkiye Anıları*. Istanbul: İş Bankası Kültür Yayınları, 2014.
Bayly, Christopher, *The Birth of the Modern World 1780-1914: Global Connections and Comparisons*. Oxford: Blackwell, 2004.
Beck, Colin J., 'Ideological Roots of Waves of Revolution', PhD thesis, Stanford University, 2009.
Christofis, Nikos, 'The Ottoman Empire in the Aftermath of the October Revolution: Ideological Identification or Realism?', *ITA ΙΣΤΟΡΙΚΑ*, 67 (2017), pp. 145–164 [in Greek].
Criss, Nur Bilge, *Istanbul Under Allied Occupation, 1918–1923*. Leiden: Brill, 1999.
Criss, Nur Bilge, 'Images of the Early Turkish National Movement (1919–1921)', in *Historical Image of the Turk in Europe: 15th Century to the Present*, ed. Mustafa Soykut. Istanbul: Isis Press, 2003, pp. 259–286.
Davison, Roderic, 'Diplomacy from Moudros to Lausanne', in *Essays in Ottoman and Turkish History, 1774–1923: The Impact of the West*. Austin, TX: University of Texas Press, 1990, pp. 206–242.
d'Encausse, Helene Carrere and Stuart R. Schram, *Marxism and Asia*. London: Allen Lane, 1969.
Dumont, Paul, 'L'Axe Moscou-Ankara: Les Relations Turco-Soviétiques de 1919 a 1922', in *Du Socialisme Ottoman A L'Internationalisme Anatolien*. Istanbul: Isis Press, 1997.
Edip, Halide, *The Turkish Ordeal: Being the Further Memoirs of Halide Edib*. New York: Century, 1928.
Fowkes, Ben and Bülent Gökay, 'Unholy Alliance: Muslims and Communists – An Introduction', *Journal of Communist Studies and Transition Politics*, 25, no. 1 (2009), pp. 1–31.
Furet, François, *Interpreting the French Revolution*. Cambridge: Cambridge University Press, 1997.
Gelvin, James L., *The Arab Uprisings: What Everyone Needs to Know*. Oxford: Oxford University Press, 2015.
Georgeon, François (ed.), *'L'ivresse de la liberté'. La Révolution de 1908 dans L'Empire Ottomane*. Leuven: Peeters, 2012.

Gökay, Bülent, *A Clash of Empires: Turkey between Russian Bolshevism and British Imperialism, 1918–1923*. London: I.B. Tauris, 1997.
Hanioğlu, Şükrü, *Preparation for a Revolution: The Young Turks, 1902–1908*. Oxford: Oxford University Press, 2001.
Hanioğlu, Şükrü, 'The Second Constitutional Period, 1908–1918', in *The Cambridge History of Modern Turkey*, vol. 4, ed. Reşat Kasaba. Cambridge: Cambridge University Press, 2008, pp. 62–111.
Hanioğlu, Şükrü, *Atatürk: An Intellectual Biography*. Princeton, NJ: Princeton University Press, 2011.
İleri, Rasih Nuri, *Atatürk ve Komünizm*. Istanbul: İleri Yayınları, 2005.
Jaeschke, Gotthard, *Kurtuluş Savaşı ile İlgili İngiliz Belgeleri*, vol. II. Istanbul: Cumhuriyet, 2001.
Kara, İsmail, 'İslam Düşüncesinde Paradigma Değişimi. Hem Batılılaşalım hem de Müslüman Kalalım', in *Modern Türkiye'de Siyasi Düşünce*, vol. 1: *Tanzimat ve Meşrutiyetin Birikimi*, ed. Mehmet Ö. Alkan. Istanbul: İletişim, 2001, pp. 234–364.
Karakışla, Yavuz Selim, 'The Emergence of the Ottoman Working Class, 1839–1923', in *Workers and the Working Class in the Ottoman Empire and the Turkish Republic, 1839–1950*, ed. Donald Quataert and Erik J. Zürcher. London: I.B. Tauris, 1995, pp. 19–34.
Karlsson, Klas-Göran, 'The Young Turks in Power: A Comparative and Critical Perspective', in *Religion, Ethnicity and Contested Nationhood in the Former Ottoman Space*, ed. Jørgen S. Nielsen. Leiden: Brill, 2012, pp. 11–28.
Kasaba, Reşat, *The Ottoman Empire and the World Economy: The Nineteenth Century*. New York: State University of New York Press, 1987.
Kırmızı, Abdulhamit, 'After Empire, Before Nation: Competing Ideologies and the Bolshevik Moment of the Anatolian Revolution', in *Revolutions and Counter-Revolutions: 1917 and its Aftermath from a Global Perspective*, ed. Stefan Rinke and Michael Wildt. Frankfurt: Campus, 2017, pp. 119–139.
Kocabaşoğlu, Uygur and Metin Berge, *Bolşevik İhtilâli ve Osmanlılar*. Istanbul: İletişim, 2006.
Lenin, V.I., 'Events in the Balkans and in Persia', in *Lenin Collected Works*, vol. 15. Moscow: Progress Publishers, 1973, pp. 220–230.
Mardin, Şerif, *The Genesis of Young Ottoman Thought*. Princeton, NJ: Princeton University Press, 1962.
Marx, Karl, 'The Class Struggles in France, 1848 to 1850', in Karl Marx and Friedrich Engels, *Collected Works*, vol. 10. London: Lawrence & Wishart, 2010, pp. 45–146.
Mishra, Pankaj, *From the Ruins of Empire: The Revolt Against the West and the Remaking of Asia*. London: Penguin, 2013.
Pons, Silvio, *The Global Revolution: A History of International Communism, 1917–1991*, trans. Allan Cameron. Oxford: Oxford University Press, 2014.
Reynolds, Michael A., *Shattering Empires: The Clash and Collapse of the Ottoman and Russian Empires, 1908–1918*. Cambridge: Cambridge University Press, 2011.
Riddell, John (ed.), *To the Masses: Proceedings of the Third Congress of the Communist International, 1921*. Leiden: Brill, 2015.
Rinke, Stefan and Michael Wildt, 'Revolutions and Counter Revolutions: An Introduction', in *Revolutions and Counter-Revolutions: 1917 and its Aftermath from a Global Perspective*, ed. Stefan Rinke and Michael Wildt. Frankfurt: Campus, 2017, pp. 9–30.
Rogan, Eugene, *The Fall of the Ottomans: The Great War in the Middle East*. New York: Basic Books, 2015.
Şişmanov, Dimitir, *Türkiye İşçi ve Sosyalist Hareketi: Kısa Tarihi (1908–1965)*. Istanbul: Belge Yayınları, 1978.

Sohrabi, Nader, 'Global Waves, Local Actors: What the Young Turks Knew about Other Revolutions and Why It Mattered', *Comparative Studies in Society and History*, 44, no. 1 (2002), pp. 45–79.
Sohrabi, Nader, 'Revolutions as Pathways to Modernity', in *Remaking Modernity: Politics, History and Sociology*, ed. Julia Adams, Elisabeth S. Clemens and Ann Shola Orloff. Durham, NC: Duke University Press, 2005, pp. 300–332.
Sohrabi, Nader, *Revolution and Constitutionalism in the Ottoman Empire and Iran*. Cambridge: Cambridge University Press, 2011.
Spector, Ivar, *The Soviet Union and the Muslim World, 1917–1958*. Seattle, WA: University of Washington Press, 1959.
Stone, Norman, Sergei Podbolotov and Murat Yaşar, 'The Russians and the Turks: Imperialism and Nationalism in the Era of Empires', in *Imperial Rule*, ed. Alexei Miller and Alfred J. Rieber. Budapest: CEU, 2004, pp. 27–46.
Suny, Ronald G., 'The Russian Empire', in *After Empire. Multiethnic Societies and Nation-Building: The Soviet Union and the Russian, Ottoman, and Habsburg Empires*, ed. Karen Barkey and Mark von Hagen. Boulder, CO: Westview Press, 1997, pp. 142–154.
Tunçay, Mete, 'Mustafa Suphi Öldürülmeseydi Muhtemelen Bakan Olurdu', in *Sol Kemalizme Bakıyor*, ed. Levent Cinemre and Ruşen Çakır. Istanbul: Metis Yayınları, 1991, pp. 13–24.
Worringer, Renée, *Ottomans Imagining Japan: East, Middle East, and Non-Western Modernity at the Turn of the Twentieth Century*. Basingstoke: Palgrave, 2014.
Yenen, Alp, 'The Other Jihad: Enver Paşa, Bolsheviks, and Politics of Anticolonial Muslim Nationalism during the Baku Congress 1920', in *The First World War and its Aftermath: The Shaping of the Middle East*, ed. T.G. Fraser. London: Gingko Library, 2015, pp. 273–294.
Yenen, Alp, 'The Young Turk Zeitgeist', in *War and Collapse: World War I and the Ottoman State*, ed. Hakan M. Yavuz. Salt Lake City, UT: University of Utah Press, 2016, pp. 1181–1216.
Yerasimos, Stefanos, *Kurtuluş Savaşı'nda Türk-Sovyet İlişkileri 1917–1923*. Istanbul: Gözlem, 1979.
Zarakol, Ayşe, *After Defeat: How the East Learned to Live with the West*. Cambridge: Cambridge University Press, 2010.
Zürcher, Erik J., *The Unionist Factor: The Role of the Committee of Union and Progress in the Turkish National Movement 1905–1926*. Leiden: Brill, 1984.
Zürcher, Erik J., *Turkey: A Modern History*. London: I.B. Tauris, 2004.
Zürcher, Erik J., 'Young Turks, Ottoman Muslims and Turkish Nationalists: Identity Politics, 1908–1938', in *The Young Turk Legacy and Nation Building: From the Ottoman Empire to Ataturk's Turkey*. London: I.B. Tauris, 2010, pp. 213–235.
Zürcher, Erik J., 'Introduction: The Ottoman Jihad, the German Jihad and the Sacralization of War', in *Jihad and Islam in World War I*, ed. Erik J. Zürcher. Leiden: Leiden University Press, 2016, pp. 13–28.

Internet sources

Kulegin, A.M., 'All-Russian Congress of Workers' and Soldiers' Soviet Deputies, Second', Encyclopaedia of St. Petersburg, http://www.encspb.ru/object/2804022647?lc=en
Trotsky, Leon, 'The Young Turks', *Kievskaya Mysl*, 3 January 1909, in www.marxists.org/archive/trotsky/1909/01/1909-turks.htm https://www.marxists.org/archive/lenin/works/1919/nov/22.htm
https://www.marxists.org/reference/archive/stalin/works/1921/03/08.htm

Index

1848 Revolution 3–6, 15n11

À la suite du Gouvernement Serbe de Niš à Corfu (Boppe) 205
Abdul Hamid I, Sultan 78
Abdülhamid II 226, 234n50
Abdulkadir Bey 83
Adrianople, siege of 159
Adrianople, Treaty of 5, 115, 117
"Advice to the Youth" (Katartzis) 51–2
Aeon (newspaper) 4–5
Ağaoğlu, Ahmed 228
Ahmed III, Sultan 23, 24
Akçura, Yusuf 224, 225, 228
Akropolis (newspaper) 8–9
Alexander I, Emperor 75
Alexandria, Battle of 84
Ali Tepedelenli of Janina 70, 74
Apology (Moisiodax) 42, 44, 45, 46
Aristotle 51, 52
armatoles 141–2
Armenian massacre 151–2
army reform. *See* military reform
artisans 20–1, 25
Aubert-Dubayet, Jean-Baptiste Annibal. *See* Dubayet, Jean-Baptiste Annibal Aubert
Austria 1, 4, 5, 104, 201–2, 231
  Eastern Crisis 1875–1878 6–7
  occupation of Bosnia and Herzegovina 12, 183–95
  Serbian revolts 96
Austro-Hungarian Compromise 184
Austro-Turkish Wars 2
authoritarianism 220–1
Ayan Revolt 94, 95–6

Baker, George Philip 122–3
Balkan Wars 156–63, 202, 204, 220, 230
Balta Limanı, Treaty of 94, 100
banditry

haiduk activities 139–46
  theoretical background 139–42
Bandits (Hobsbawm) 139–40
Bandits and Bureaucrats (Barkey) 141
Banja Luka 190–3
Barby, Henry 200, 202, 205–6
Barkey, Karen 141
Battle of Alexandria 84
Bayur, Yusuf Hikmet 219
Bérard, Victor 200, 202, 204, 205, 208
Berlin Congress (1878) 102
Birgin, Muhittin 227
Blok, Anton 140
Bolsheviks 3, 247, 248
Bonneval, Alexander, Comte de 20
Boppe, Auguste 200, 205, 206
Bosnia and Herzegovina 102
  Austria-Hungarian occupation 183–95
"Brigands and State-Building in Modern Egypt" (Brown) 141
Brown, Nathan 141
Brunhes, Jean 204
Bulgaria 103
Bulgarian illustrated press 149–74
  Balkan Wars 156–63
  Great War 163–71
  turn of the century 150–6
Bulgarian military history
  haiduk activities 139–46
  theoretical background 139–42
Bulgarian Uprising 102
Bulgarianness 142, 143–4, 147n16
Burke, Peter 149

Callimachi, Alexander 73
Campo-Formio, Treaty of 74
Canip, Ali 223
Canning, Stanford 122, 129n29
Cantemir, Dimitrie 25
Cara-Saint-Cyr, Claude 74
cartography 120–1. *See also* map-making

Cavit Bey, Mehmet 227
celali 141
Cemal Paŀsa 13–14, 220, 229, 230
Central Union 167
Chalŭkov family 98–9
Chéradame, André 200, 202
Chicherin, Georgy 249, 250–1, 252, 253
Choiseul-Goffier, Marie-Gabriel-Florent-Auguste de 66, 70, 78, 79, 82
Christian alliance 67
Christianity 5, 51, 221
Christians 16n17, 16n18, 98, 99
  Bosnia 187, 188
  Ottoman army 73
  Ottoman-Greek border 114, 123
  Romioi 90
Committee of Union and Progress (CUP) 223, 246, 248
communitarianism 48–53
Constantinople Conferences 116–21
constitutionalism 244–5
Couderc, Anne 112
Crete uprising 102
Crimean Tatars 224, 225
Crimean War 93, 100–2
Croatia 185–6
  Ante Starčević 187–8
  Eugen Kumičić 188–95
  Josip Strossmayer 186–7
  Party of Rights 189, 190
Croatian lands 184, 195n2
Croatian Question 184, 186

Dapontes, Kaisarios 39–40
Darwinian law 221
Davud Pasha, Kara 25
de Juchereau de St. Denys, Antoine 69
Denis, Ernest 200, 202, 205
Descorche-Ste-Croix, Marie 71, 75
Divine Providence 40–1
Dochoğlu, Ivan 102
Dubayet, Jean-Baptiste Annibal Aubert 67–8, 71–3, 80
Dumat, Dushan 81–2
Dutch Republic 46

Eastern Crisis 1875–1878 6–7
economy 227–8
Edip, Halide 249

education 42, 68–9, 100–1, 200–1, 205, 206, 228, 229–30
Egypt
  banditry 141
  France / Napoleon 1, 67, 68, 72, 74–5, 84, 200
  Ottoman Empire 94, 99
Eldem, Edhem 153
English-Transvaal War 155
enlightened absolutism 20
entrepreneurs 94–104
  Crimean War 100–2
  Greek War of Independence 98–9
  Kircali and Ayan Revolts 95–6
  Russo-Ottoman War 1806–1812 97–8
  Russo-Ottoman War 1828–1829 99
  Serbian revolts 96–7
  tumultuous years of 1875–1878 102–3
Enver Paŀsa 13, 220, 229, 230, 231, 249–50, 255
Esat Bey 247
Europe 45, 49, 52

February Revolution 3–6, 15n11
Felsefe Mecmuasi (Tevfik) 222
Fergo, Pierre 67, 81
Ferry, Jules 200
Fichte, Johann Gottlieb 222
Filibeli Ahmed Hilmi 221
First World War. *See* Great War
folk songs 208
Fouillée, Alfred 223, 224
Foundations of Government in Various Orders (Müteferrika) 19–28
  Book 1 26–8
  mechanical arts and Russian precedent 24–6
  merchants and artisans 20–1
  military reform 20, 21–2
  new order of 1732 23–4
  rebellion of 1730 22–3
France
  February Revolution 3–6
  Jihad 248
  Ottoman-Greek border 112, 114
  public opinion towards Serbia 203–4
Franco-Ottoman War 83
Franco-Prussian War 201

French intellectuals 199–209
    and the Balkans 200–2
    cooperation between France and Serbia 202–3
    and French public opinion towards Serbia 203–4
    support for Serbs in the Great War 204–9
French-Ottoman relations 65–85
    French military experts and the Nizam-i Cedid 78–80
    French military experts in the Ottoman army 66–9, 81–5
    as part of the international political systems 69–77
French press 199, 202
French Revolution 243, 244, 245
Friendship, Treaty of 253
Fuat, Belsir 222

Ganchev, Dobre 102
Gaprinsky, İsmail 224
Garibaldi, Guiseppe 143, 145
Gauvain, Auguste 200, 204–5
Gavriilidis, Vlassis 8–9
Georgiev brothers 103
German nationalism 201
German thought 222–3, 227
Gianitzou 123
Gökalp, Ziya 222, 223, 224, 225–6
Goltz, Colmar von der 221
Goudie coup 1909 7–9
Graditzas 123, 124
Great Britain 72, 75–7, 80, 83, 84
    Cyprus 7
    Jihad 248
    Ottoman-Greek border 112, 113, 114, 117, 118, 119
Great Eastern Crisis 1875–1878 6–7
Great War 2–3, 219, 231
    intellectuals 199, 200, 204–9
    visual representations 163–71
Greco-Turkish War 154–5
Greece 4, 5, 6, 253. *See also* Orlov Revolt
    banditry 141–2
    Eastern Crisis 1875–1878 7
    French propaganda 73–4, 75
    Goudie coup 1909 7–8
    land redistribution 103

Greek political thought 39–42
    Dimitros Katartzis 38, 48–53, 54–5
    Iosipos Moisiodax 38, 42–8, 48–9, 54–5, 57n35
Greek Revolution 111–26
    border demarcation 122–6, 146n13
    Constantinople Conferences 116–21
    Greek boundary problem 112–16
    Ottoman terminology 121–2
Greek War of Independence 94, 98–9
Grigorios Alexandros Ghikas III, Prince of Moldavia 42
Groignard, Antoine 67, 81
Guilleminot, Charles 121

haiduks
    haiduk activities 139–46
    theoretical background 139–42
Hakki, Hafız 220–1, 222, 228
Hapsburg, House of 4
Haumant, Emile 200, 202
Hellenes 43, 45, 49, 50
Helphand, Israel Lazarevich 227
Hindenburg, Paul von 169, 179n86
historical continuity 49–50
Hobsbawm, Eric 139–40
Hölderlin, Friedrich 37
humanitarian aid 204–5
Hungarian Revolution 184
Hüseyin Bey 119, 120, 123
Hyperion oder Der Eremit in Griechenland (Hölderlin) 37

Illustration Light (*Ilyustratsiya Svetlina*) 150–74
    Balkan Wars 156–63
    Great War 163–71
    turn of the century 150–6
imperial nationalism 6–9
In Praise of the Philosopher (Katartzis) 53
intellectuals 199–209
    cooperation between France and Serbia 202–3
    French intellectuals and the Balkans 200–2
    and French public opinion towards Serbia 203–4
    support for Serbs in the Great War 204–9

Ishak Bey 81
Islam 5, 21, 113–14, 221, 228, 247–8.
    See also Muslims
Islamism 225–6, 250, 252, 254
Italy 143, 145

Jadidist movement 224
Jakšić, Grgur 202, 205
Japan 229, 245
Jihad 247–8
Jovanović, Jovan 206

Kahn, Albert 204
Kalpazanov, Ivan 102
Kapodistrias, Ioannis 115, 117, 121
Karadjorgje 96
Karastoyanov, Dimitri A. 157, 159, 173, 178n54
Karitsa river 125
Karlowitz, Treaty of 113–14
Kaser, Karl 156
Katartzis, Dimitros 38, 48–53, 54–5
Kemal, Ali 224
Kemal, Mustafa (Atatürk) 3, 248, 249, 250, 251, 252, 253, 254
Kemal Bey, Ali 223
Khadzhitoshev, Dimitraki 97
Kırcalı Revolt 94, 95–6
Kiriakov, Peter 142–3. See also Petko Voivoda
klephts 141–2
Koffer, Francois 82
Koliopoulos, John 141–2
Kosciuszko, Tadeusz 71
Kosovo 208
Küçük Kaynarca, Treaty of 38, 39–42
Kumičić, Eugen 188–95

La Serbie (Bérard) 205
Labbé, Paul 203, 205
Lamartine, Alphonse de 15n11
Lanaux, Pierre 200
land redistribution 103
language 47–8, 49, 50–2, 94, 223
Lanux, Pierre 207
Lavisse, Ernest 201
Le Brun, Jacques-Balthazard 68–9, 83–4
Lenin, Vladimir 247

Lesseps, Jean-Baptiste Barthélemy de 67, 71, 81
liberal sensibilities 42–8, 57n35
Loiseau, Charles 200, 201–2
London, Treaty of 115, 119
Louis XVI, King 66, 67, 70, 78

Macedonian uprising 152–4
Mackensen, August von 168, 179n85
Magrou, Alphonse-Désiré 208
Mahmud I, Sultan 19, 20, 23
Mahmud II, Sultan 114, 116
Maksudi, Sadri 222–3
Malet, Albert 200, 207
map-making 25, 120–1
Maritsa (newspaper) 144
Marx, Karl 243
mass psychology 220–1
Mavroyanni, Jean 119–20
mechanical arts 20, 24–6
mechanicism, thick 19–20
Meiji Restoration 245
merchants 20–1, 94
merchants and artisans 25
Milićević-Lunjevica, Nikola 96
militarism 228–9
military reform 20, 21–2, 26
    French military experts and the Nizam-i Cedid 78–80
    French military experts in the Ottoman army 66–9, 81–5
Mirkovich, Ruscho 103
Mitchell, Thomas 144
Mithat Efendi, Ahmet 222
modern warfare 220–1
Moisiodax, Iosipos 38, 42–8, 48–9, 54–5, 57n35
Moldavia 73, 76, 82
Moldavia-Wallachia 4, 5, 6
Moral Philosophy (Ludovico, trans. Moisiodax) 42, 44
morale 220–1
Mount Veluchi 123, 124
Mousouros, Constantinos 125–6
Mttev, Plamen 73–4
Münif Paŀsa 222
Muradgeo d'Osson, Ignatius 79
Muslims 27, 67, 247–8, 248–9. See also Islam
    Bolsheviks 247–9

Bosnia and Herzegovina 185, 191, 193
business collaborations 104
emigration 103
Ottoman army 73
Ottoman-Greek border 113–14, 119, 123
Mustafa III, Sultan 78
Müteferrika, İbrahim
  Foundations of Government in Various Orders 19–28

Nabi Efendi 119
Napoleon Bonaparte 68, 73, 75–6, 84
Napoleonic expansion 94
Napoleonic Wars 1
national economy 227–8
national education 228
nationalism 223–5. *See also* German nationalism; imperial nationalism
nationalist movements 1, 3
nationhood 52
natural frontier argument 114, 118
Necdet, Ethem 221
Necip Efendi 116
"Negroes" 169
Nelson, Horatio 83
"New Life and New Values" (Gökalp) 224
New Life, New Language 223
New Order (Nizam-i Cedid), Sultan Selim III 78–80, 82
New Order of 1732 23–4
Nietzsche, Friedrich 223, 224
Nizam i-Cedid 78–80, 82
Novaković, Stojan 202, 211n21

Obrenović, Miloš 96, 97
October Revolution 243, 247
Olga and Lina (Kumičić) 190
Orlov moment 38, 42, 48, 53–4
Orlov Revolt 37–8, 39, 40, 41, 52
Osman Pałsa, Topal 20
Ottoman Empire
  First World War 2–3, 219, 231
  impact of German thought 222–3, 227
  military clashes seventeenth – twentieth century 1–2
  modern warfare 220–1
  nationalism 223–5
  sovereignty 229–30
  state conceptualization 226–9

Ottoman-Greek border 111–26
  border demarcation 122–6, 146n13
  Constantinople Conferences 116–21
  Greek boundary problem 112–16
  Ottoman terminology 121–2
Ottoman-Prussian Union 69–70

paintings 150–1
Palairet, Michael 103
pamphlets 25
Pan-Turkism 224
Paraphrase to Nicocles (Moisiodax) 43–4, 45
Party of Rights 189, 190
Parvus, Alexander 227
patriotism 51, 207–8
Pavel I, Emperor 73, 74, 75
Pazvantoglu of Vidin, Osman 70, 74, 75, 96
"Peasant and the Brigand, The" (Blok) 140
Pertev Efendi 114, 115
Peter the Great 20, 23–4, 25
Petko Voivoda 144–5
Petmezas, Socrates 99
Petrine Russia 19–20, 24–6
philosophy 222, 223
photography 152–3, 156, 157–9, 160–2, 165–71, 172, 173–4, 204
Pitrowski, Antoni 150–1
poetry 208
Poland 70–1
political plurality 23–4
popular sovereignty 44
Poros conference 114
portfolio capitalists 94
press. *See* Bulgarian illustrated press; French press; printing press
pre-Tanzimat Period 94–9, 104
Prigkos, Ioannis 40–1
primitive rebels 139
printing press 25, 26
property transfers 103
psychology 220–1

Rachkov, Khristo 95, 98
rebellion of 1730 22–3, 25
Recai 227
Reis Efendi 114, 115, 124
Rełsit Pałsa, Mustafa 119
republicanism 46

Revolution of 1848 3–6, 15n11
revolutions 1–9, 243, 244–5
Romania 5
Romioi 38, 39–41, 49–53
Rudolf II, Holy Roman Emperor 47
Ruffin, Pierre 74
Rum (Roman, Greek Orthodox) 121–2
Rumistan (Hellas) 121
Russia
    Black Sea 66
    Bosnia and Herzegovina 185, 186
    Eastern Crisis 1875–1878 6–7
    February Revolution 4, 5
    First World War 2–3
    French-Russian relations 74, 75–7
    Greek borders 113, 114, 117
    October Revolution 245
    Petrine project 19–20, 24–6
    Poland 70–1
    Turkish Anatolian Resistance Movement 246–55
Russian Revolution 1905 154, 246
Russian-Ottoman Iasi peace agreement 70
Russo-Japanese War 155
Russo-Ottoman War 1768–1774 38, 39–42, 53, 54
Russo-Ottoman War 1806–1812 94, 97–8
Russo-Ottoman War 1828–1829 94, 99
Russo-Ottoman War 1877–1878 102, 150
Russo-Swedish War 69
Russo-Turkish Wars 2, 114, 143, 146

Said Halim Palsa 229, 231
Saint-Croix, Marie-Louis 70
Sami, Bekir 251
Schopenhauer, Arthur 222
Sebastiani de la Porta, Horace François Bastien 75, 76, 77
Selim III, Sultan
    French military experts and the Nizam-i Cedid 78–80, 82
    French military experts in the Ottoman army 66, 67, 68, 83–4
    international political systems 69–77
Semonvil, Charles-Louis de Huge 70
Serbia 3, 185
    French intellectuals' perception of 199–209
Serbian folk poetry 208

Serbian revolts 94, 96–7
Serbo-Bulgarian War 150–1
Sevres, Treaty of 251–2
Seyfeddin, Ömer 222, 223
Shari'a 229
Sloboda (newspaper) 189
social bandits 139–40
Societies for the Defence of National Rights 248
socio-economic transformations 94–104
    Crimean War 100–2
    Greek War of Independence 98–9
    Kircali and Ayan Revolts 95–6
    Russo-Ottoman War 1806–1812 97–8
    Russo-Ottoman War 1828–1829 99
    Serbian revolts 96–7
    tumultuous years of 1875–1878 102–3
South Slavism 186
sovereignty 229
Soviet Union 247–55
Spanish-American War 155
Stalin, Joseph 248
Starčević, Ante 187–8, 189
state conceptualization 226–9
Strossmayer, Josip Juraj 185, 186–7
Sugar, Peter 95
Sutsu, Michael 71
Swiss Republic 46

Talleyrand-Périgord, Charles Maurice de 76
Tanzimat reforms 4, 99–100
Tatars 224, 225
tax farming 95, 101
Tekinalp 222, 227
Tepedelenli, Ali. *See* Ali Tepedelenli of Janina
Tevfik, Baha 222
Theory of Geography (Moisiodax) 42, 46–7
Thessaloniki 223, 225
thick mechanicism 19–20
thuggee 140
Tilsit, Treaty of 77
Todorov, Nikolai 98
Toshev, Dimitraki 97
Tott, François de 66, 78
Treaty of Adrianople 5, 115, 117
Treaty of Balta Limanı 94, 100
Treaty of Campo-Formio 74

Treaty of Friendship 253
Treaty of Karlowitz 113–14
Treaty of Küçük Kaynarca 38, 39–42
Treaty of London 115, 119
Treaty of Sevres 251–2
Treaty of Tilsit 77
Tüccarzade İbrahim Hilmi 221
Tŭpchileshtov, Khristo 100, 101
Turkish Anatolian Resistance Movement 243, 246–55
Turkish Communist Party (TKP) 250
Turkish Republican People's Party (CHP) 254
Turkish-Italian War 156
Turkism 225–6
Tyufekchiev, Naum 168

"Üç Cereyan" (Gökalp) 225–6
Under a Gun (Kumičić) 189, 190–5
Uzundzhovo fair 100

Veluchi (mountain) 123, 124
Venizelos, Eleftherios 253
Vergennes, Charles Gravier de 78
Verninac Saint-Maur, Raymond de 71
visual representations 149–74
    Balkan Wars 156–63
    Great War 163–71
    turn of the century 150–6

Voulgaris, Eugenios 39, 47, 48
Vouvala island 125

Wagner, Kim A. 140
Wallachian massacres 170, 172
war
    as revolution 1–2
    revolution as 2–3
warfare 220–1
world order 24
World War I. *See* Great War
writing 47–8

Xanthos, Emmanuel 38

Young Turk Revolution 2, 7, 8–9, 154, 224, 226, 245, 246
Young Turks 220, 221, 227, 247
Yugoslavia: France and the Serbs (Lanux) 207
Yugoslavism 186
Yunan (Hellen, Greek) 121–2

Zeitoun district 119–20
Živković, Stevan 96
Živojinović, Dragoljub 205
Zrinski-Franopan Conspiracy (Kumičić) 190
Žujović, Jovan 205

www.ingramcontent.com/pod-product-compliance
Lightning Source LLC
Chambersburg PA
CBHW072130290426
44111CB00012B/1845